Piffle

Simon Weakley & Shirley Mclean

ACKNOWLEDGEMENTS

We have benefitted from the help of many people whilst writing this book.

Firstly, we want to thank our good friends John Goodeve, Peter Godfrey, and Eldora Brown who have read the manuscript as it has been written and given us invaluable feedback, suggestions and support to help make the book better than it otherwise would have been. In particular, their belief in us pushed us forward to eventual completion.

A special thanks to the author (now deceased) Tom Sharpe, who is our hero and inspiration for the brand of humour hopefully found in this book. The traditional British farce is a form of humour that is not practised much these days, but Tom Sharpe, in his day, was the master of it with bestselling books throughout his writing career.

Finally, a thank you to my publishing editor, copy writer and fellow author for believing in us and allowing this book to find a wider audience.

CHAPTER 1

Sydney Dresden Piffle lumbered across the number two car park at Alicante International Airport and looked around furtively for signs of the English paparazzi before climbing into the back seat of his Rolls Royce Silver Spur. His chauffeur, Paeleo closed the heavy door with a resounding clunk and they sped off along the A1 towards Benidorm where Piffle owned a luxury villa that more than matched his status as a successful businessman.

As the Rolls sped down the A1 towards Benidorm overtaking lesser cars, Piffle reflected, in air-conditioned luxury, on just how far he had come in his life. The son of a railway signalman, Henry Herbert Piffle, a staunch trade unionist and a leading light in the Hull Branch of the Wheel Tappers and Boiler Makers Union, Piffle junior emanated from an impeccable working-class background.

Piffle's father Henry, it is fair to say, had a difficult war, having been on hundreds of bombing raids across Germany in Halifax heavy bombers. The city of Dresden had been pulverized by Piffle and his comrades in bomber command, and in recognition of that indisputable fact, Henry had awarded his only son the middle name of Dresden. In

1

fact, it is almost certain that Sydney Dresden Piffle was conceived on the night of Victory in Europe (VE) day, as Henry celebrated on the 25th May 1945 as a final vindication of the last five years of total war.

As a result Piffle was born into the austere world of Hull in 1946, and brought up on a diet of extreme left wing trade unionism, that subscribed to the fact that the working man was totally exploited by the bosses and ruling classes and only a true labour revolution could right the wrongs and give the working man his dues – earned or otherwise. In Henry's world the only thing standing in the way of this glorious revolution and the just and fair society waiting to be grasped, was the hated Tories. In fact, Henry was very fond of saying that the only good Tory was a dead Tory, and Dresden Piffle's formative years were completely immersed in this diatribe of class hatred and blame, directed at a group that Piffle only knew by name and not association.

Whilst other boys on the Gipsyville estate were playing football and having a carefree existence, Piffle was attending trade union and Labour Party meetings and being indoctrinated with grievances real or imagined. Most of the people Piffle came across dreamed of a world of utopian collective endeavour, five-year plans, equality, diversity, tolerance and restrictive practises based on strict rules and regulations. There was no room for doubt in Piffle's world, only the unshakable certainty of a better future and a chip on his shoulder so large that the only solution was to try and emulate the material successes of the rich and powerful.

In short, Piffle was an enigma. On the one hand he believed in equality of outcome and on the other he wanted a better life for himself, one that elevated him far above his starting point in life, and the comrades he so cherished.

'Eh up Paeleo, how long before we get to villa?'

'Ah señor, about twenty minutes if the traffic remains good, yes.'

'Well I'm on a bit of tight schedule lad, as I've got to get changed and get to Black Chicken for 7.30 p.m. for a business meeting, and I bloody well hope Honolulu is at villa to unpack me bags. So, I need you back at villa at 7.00 p.m. sharp Paeleo to take me into town, it's an important meeting is this, with leader of Benidorm Municipality.'

Despite his less than sophisticated demeanour, no one could accuse Piffle of not having an eye for a business opportunity. Native cunning would be the best way to describe his approach to business. It was fair to say that Piffle was now a millionaire, largely due to one very fortuitous opportunity that presented itself at the fag-end of Tony Blair's Government in 2007. To be more precise, Piffle's business was based solely on a piece of EU legislation, passed into law and then rigorously applied by councils in a way far beyond that envisaged by the EU Commission that dreamed up the idea.

That piece of legislation was called 'The Diversity and Equality Act, 2009', which basically stated that all employers had to employ staff in such a way that did not discriminate on the grounds of race, gender, disability, sexual orientation, religion or any other identifiable difference that a person could cite as reasonable grounds for going against the spirit of the act. This harmless and, in many ways, laudable ideal was then interpreted by individual councils and their ever-cautious legal teams in varying degrees of lunacy, much to the benefit of Sydney Dresden Piffle. Despite being a Councillor at the time for Hull City Council, he heard that Grimewold Council, Grimewold being 20 miles from Hull was putting out to tender a five-year contract to enforce their interpretation of the Diversity and Equality Act, 2009. Like many PFI contracts at the time, this one was heavily weighted in favour of the private company that won the bid. As it turned out, Piffle's newly created company was the only bidder.

After a lengthy council meeting the Ways and Means Committee decided that all businesses in the Grimewold post code district had to employ people in a strict percentage of diversity of the population of the Council area, to take into account the groups identified in the act. For example: 52% of Grimewold's residents were male and 48% women, therefore each company had to employ 52% males and 48% females within the workforce; likewise, disabled people (6%), transgender (1%), ethnic minorities (22%), and religious groups according to the percentage of the population practising, including atheists. This act of lunacy would be hard enough for a large company

4

to adhere to but impossible for a small business with only a handful of employees. Firms failing to comply would be fined up to £2000 per identified breach of the quota system, per year or face a court summons.

In short, Piffle's new company, which was called The Diversity Action Partnership Limited, had won a license to print money and, shrewdly, Piffle had negotiated the contract on the basis that the Council would receive 35% of the fines and his company would receive 65%, and cover the cost of administering the scheme. The more Piffle's company sent out fines to other companies, the more money he would make. And so it proved, after five years Piffle was a millionaire.

Another fortuitous piece of luck which came Piffle's way when he was setting up his company, was in the form of the ghastly Grimewold Central Library building. The Ways and Means Committee chaired by the redoubtable leader of the Council, Ms Penelope Sykes, decided to close the building down as a cost-cutting purge due to central government cuts.

The building had been conceived in 1963 as a modest affair, but took on a new significance, after the new Prime Minister visited the town soon after his election win, and bizarrely praised the town's spirit as an example of the 'white heat of technology' that was his slogan at the time. The chairman of the biggest steel mill in the town, McGreggor's Steel, decided to donate a good proportion of his estate to the creation of a 'state-of-the-art' library, in the mistaken belief that the workers of the town would lift themselves up and aspire to better things. Not to mention his visceral hatred of his wastrel family and his belief that his transgender son, Ronald, sometimes called Rowena, in particular, was not to see a penny of his hard work.

So it came to pass that the most avant-garde architect was employed to build a huge monument to the ego of Josiah McGreggor, the great-grandson of the founder of largest independent steel rolling mill in the country.

The building constructed was a vast edifice of steel and concrete, double-fronted with a double height atrium as a centre piece to the entrance. Huge ugly concrete columns all around the building supported the large plate-glass structure. In short, the building was like a botanical greenhouse and sadly had many of the characteristics. Boiling hot in summer and freezing cold in winter. The architect, though undoubtedly talented, had no concept of thermodynamics.

The heating system, a huge oil-fired boiler in the underground basement, failed miserably to keep the building warm in the winter months. The vast glass panels produced so much condensation that many of the books became damp and, as it got colder, the pages froze together when it was particularly cold outside.

In the summer it was the opposite. The glass panels acted as a giant solar collector of heat, and roasted the poor inhabitants, making it impossible to stay in the building for long. The council became so distressed by this unfortunate turn of events that it installed a sophisticated air-conditioning system for the summer months. This hugely expensive state of affairs continued for many years, indeed decades until two things happened to finally persuade the Council leaders to close the building and sell it off.

Firstly, a market research firm was employed to analyse the dwindling usage of the building and it's services. It was found, much to the horror of the Directorate of Culture, Media and Sport, that the two top book withdrawals were *The Lemon Bumper Book of Jokes*, and the sequel to *Fifty Shades of Grey*, with precious few of the extensive book collection being read at all.

Secondly, a very unfortunate incident tainted the library forever. The constant warming and cooling of the vast structure with the boiler and the air-conditioning unit resulted in one of the large pieces of glass in the top of the atrium shattering and crashing down onto the hapless chief librarian, who was in the process of masturbating in his office at the top of the atrium whilst reading *Big Ones* magazine.

Miss Metcalf had the unfortunate experience of finding the severed body of the chief librarian, still sat at his desk, his trousers round his ankles with his pants pulled down, and the obvious evidence of what he had been up to before his untimely demise. Miss Metcalf, a timid, mouse-like lady, never recovered and is still off on long-term sick to this day. The Ways and Means Committee took no time in deciding that the central library would close forever and it would be put up for sale or lease to the highest bidder.

After six months of the dreadful building sitting empty, Piffle made his move and negotiated a long-term lease of ten years at the unbelievably generous sum of £10,000 a year. It was not long before Piffle was able to sublet the top half of the building to another PFI funded company who had been awarded the contract to run the 'Humberwold Speed Camera Action! Limited', headed up by a shrewd ex-copper called Mike Morrell, and he was willing to pay £10,000 a year, thus ensuring that Piffle paid nothing.

Piffle had wisely decided that given the unfortunate experience of the ex-chief librarian, and the renaming of his office unofficially as 'dead man's folly', he was going nowhere near the top half of the building, and Mike Morrell was welcome to it.

CHAPTER 2

Piffle's Rolls Royce soon arrived at Villa Almeria in the Andalucía Mountains overlooking Benidorm, and not far from the upmarket resort of Althea. The villa was a grand mock-colonial affair with an in/out gravel drive set in beautiful gardens with lemon and orange groves.

Paeleo rushed round to the back of the car and opened the door to allow Piffle to exit. Getting on in years and weighing all of twenty-five stone with a 52" waist, it was no easy task, even though the long wheelbase Silver Spur afforded ample leg room. Paeleo then got the suitcases from the boot and, as expected, Honolulu, the house-keeper, was there to meet her master at the double-sized front door.

Home from home, thought Piffle. Even in early spring the weather was warm and sunny, not like the cold damp and overwhelmingly depressing town of Grimewold, the source of his extensive income.

Piffle was in the enviable position of visiting his offices infrequently since he'd had the bright idea of putting in charge an extremely capable, indeed zealous, Diversity Manager called Zara Bindle. This was a double-edged sword for Piffle because over the months of her tenure he had grown to increasingly despise the bitch, whilst acknowledging her undoubted success in growing the business and increasing profits by nearly 100%. In fact, he was going to have to phone her before 6.00 p.m. as he did every week, to find out if there were any problems and more importantly how much the 'fine' income had been for the week. But first he had to get inside, freshen up and have a cup of tea or maybe something stronger before ringing Bindle.

'I'll see you at seven sharp Paeleo, lad, and don't be late.'

'No problem Señor, I will be at your service.'

Meanwhile, Honolulu had waddled out and was bending over to pick up Piffle's suitcases, whereupon Piffle slapped her huge posterior, as was a rather unfortunate habit of his. Half Italian and half Spanish, Honolulu had not really benefitted from the Mediterranean diet, and too much pasta and rich Italian sauces over the years had taken their toll. Piffle liked very large women, and Honolulu certainly fitted the bill, unlike his skinny Clothes Horse of a wife, Pauline Piffle, who was back in Hull at his other extensive home, called Maxwell House.

'Eh up Honolulu, its grand to see you again lass, let's get inside and have a nice cuppa and then you can help me with my accoutrements.' It was fair to say Honolulu had become somewhat more than just the live-in housekeeper.

'Oh that is good yes, Dresden, to see you again. I have missed you so much stuck here at the villa on my own.'

'Oh well Honolulu, you can't have everything, and I can't be here all the time. There are matters to attend to in Grimewold and I have to see me lady wife Pauline.'

They were only just through the door when Piffle embraced Honolulu. Immediately his greedy hands were clasped tightly round her soft buttocks, and her ample bosom was pressed hard against his massive chest.

It was fair to say that their relationship was purely a physical one, and in no time they were naked in the hallway and more than ready to take things further in the master bedroom, even at the expense of Piffle's important business meeting.

It was 6.45 and Piffle was in lather.

'Bloody hell Honolulu, where in God's name have you put me dress suit and waistcoat? Paeleo will be here in a few minutes and I've got to get to Black Chicken for 7.30. Can't be late.'

'It is in your dressing room Dresden, do you not have eyes to see?'

'Of course I've got bloody eyes woman, but there's so many bloody clothes in here I can't see the wood for the bloody trees.'

Finally, Dresden located the clothes he was looking for. No jeans and T- shirts for him. He had been brought up to believe that a man was judged on his appearance, and he wanted to look the part for this important, albeit informal, meeting.

'Get in here Honolulu and give us hand with this bloody frilly shirt, never have been able to do cufflinks or me belt for that matter.'

The Rolls had already sped up the driveway and Paeleo was waiting impatiently for his boss to appear.

'Why he says 7.00 sharp,' Paeleo muttered under his breath, 'when he 10 minutes late already?'

Piffle rushed out of the front door, immediately tripped, fell down the steps and landed in giant heap on the gravel drive, his battered briefcase cushioning the blow. Getting up was another thing entirely however.

'Bloody hell,' he shouted, 'give us a bloody hand here why don't you?'

Honolulu rushed down the steps and Paeleo came from the other side round the back of the Rolls to assist their hapless boss who looked like a beached whale in a vast multi-coloured waistcoat and shiny black dress suit. To make matters worse, a macron crow decided to fly over-head and shat on the front of Dresden's jacket just as he was trying to get up. The white, acrid, gooey fluid added to Piffle's woes.

'Now look what's bloody happened. Can you bloody useless buggers give me a hand up or what?'

It was easier said than done. Once down, twenty-five stone was not easy to shift and get upright again. It took another five precious minutes of heaving and yanking, by both Paeleo and the less than useful, Honolulu, to get Piffle on the vertical again. Both were panting heavily by that stage and Piffle didn't look too well either.

'Get inside will you Honolulu and get me a bloody wet sponge and be quick about it, I'm already late for this meeting.'

'I be very quick Dresden.' In a flap, Honolulu ran as fast as she could back into the house and fetched a sponge as requested.

Piffle's misfortunes were not quite over; when he tried to move, he realized that as he had cockled over he had sprained his ankle, and now he was unable to walk without assistance.

'Hey up Paeleo, give us a hand into back of Rolls, I'm in bloody agony here.'

By this time, Honolulu had returned with a sponge and was frantically dabbing at his black jacket while Paeleo manoeuvred Piffle into the back seat of the car. It was now 7.20 and Piffle was going to be nearly thirty minutes late for his important business meeting with the head of Benidorm Municipality.

In no time, the Rolls was speeding out of the gravel drive with Piffle in the back barking orders at Paeleo, and now clearly in a foul mood.

'Put your bloody foot down lad and don't spare the horses.'

The Rolls lurched forward at speed and just as Piffle was finally settling down, the car phone rang with more bad news. In the mayhem he had forgotten to phone Zara Bindle at 6.00, and she was now phoning him. He hated speaking with the bitch the best of times and he really wasn't in the mood for one of her feminist diatribes, which he knew would be coming his way.

CHAPTER 3

'Dresden? Dresden is that you?'

'Of course it's bloody me, who do you think it is when you ring me number, the Queen of bloody Sheba?'

'There is no need to be facetious Dresden. As you well know, you are supposed to ring me at 6.00 every week for an update given your long absences from the office, and I have to say I was not at all happy that you didn't do so. What's more, I have had to cut short my Pilates class to ring you now, and I haven't got home yet to have a meal, and Hugo will not be impressed that we are not eating together after the effort he will have put into it. So, can I have an undertaking from you that this, simply unacceptable, behaviour won't happen again?'

'Won't happen again, I bloody well hope it won't happen again,' boomed Piffle down the phone.

'Have you any idea what I've been through, bloody awful flight into Alicante, Paeleo late as bloody usual, then unexpectedly delayed, a domestic incident with Honolulu, and then to cap it all, I fell down steps, got shat on by a malicious fucking macron crow, and then sprained my bloody ankle. So I'm in absolute bloody agony and forty minutes late for meeting with leader of Benidorm Municipality at the Black Chicken'

'Your rather unsavoury domestic arrangements are no concern of mine Dresden. I am far more concerned with my domestic arrangements and giving you an update on the business.'

'Well let's crack on then love, I haven't got all bloody night.'

'I've told you before Dresden, do not under any circumstances call me love. I am vice chair of the Women's League of Feminist Action, and we are trying to move men like you into the 21st century, if indeed that is at all possible.'

'Possible or not, can we please get on to matter at hand? Otherwise I'm going to be at Black Chicken before I know what figures are.'

'Well Dresden, there is good news and bad news.'

'Well come on then, spit it out.'

'The good news, as you know Dresden, is that fine income is up 26.3% on the same period last year, and the new mandatory courses on Safeguarding Diversity are generating an additional £4000 a week in consultancy income.'

'And the bad news?'

'Due to my efficiency and expediency in following the letter of the law and sending out fines promptly, I'm afraid that the Grimewold Chamber of Commerce are organising a protest movement and some hefty employers are considering relocating to other council districts. Sheffield and Rotherham have been extremely active in that regard.'

Zara did not want to also relay the indisputable fact that over two hundred small and medium sized enterprises had closed for good, or relocated, in the last six months alone. In short, the golden goose was attempting to fly the nest. Even the Council's Economic Development Unit was starting to get worried, not to mention the growing phone calls and irate protests at the highly lucrative business networking club they ran.

'We can't do much about that, can we lass? The law is the law, and is not to be mocked. If a few fat cat capitalists are starting to squeak, then we know we are doing our jobs properly.'

'Well of course Dresden, on that point I entirely agree with you, and as you know I am especially keen to demonstrate to the wider world that Grimewold will be the first council in the country, if not the world, where men and women are employed in equal numbers based upon the diversity of the population, not to mention the other disadvantaged groups in society. The suffragettes didn't succeed by giving in at the first sign of resistance, and resistance, Dresden, is what we are beginning to see. Let the glorious revolution continue.'

'Well anyway, just remind me what the fee income was for the week and what the consultancy income was and then the net figure after wages and expenses have been covered?'

'The total income was £206,826 and the costs were £26,025, making a net taxable profit of £180,801, but as I've said to you before if you let me introduce a new computer system we could cut costs by making at least 50% of the predominantly male staff redundant and replace those that are left with females.'

'Well we can look at that another time, but I've told you before I'm not sacking me mates that rely on me for a job. Some of them ex-miners and steel workers are in their 50s and 60s and will never work again if I get rid. Anyway, I'm nearly at Black Chicken so I'll ring you next week.'

'But I wanted to talk to you about new female diversity workshops,' but the line had gone dead.

CHAPTER 4

Sydney Dresden Piffle arrived at the Black Chicken Restaurant and Karaoke Bar forty-three minutes late.

As a result, the bar was already filling up with middle-aged and elderly British tourists, and the karaoke had already started. 'Delilah' was blaring from a very fat, and out of tune, man called Dennis sporting a Hawaiian shirt and Adidas leggings.

When he was at the villa, Piffle was a very good customer of the Black Chicken. When he wasn't having sexual trysts with Honolulu, he could usually be found in the Black Chicken from around 9.00 p.m. through to closure at 1.30 am with the hapless Paeleo having to wait nearby in the Rolls for the duration.

The owner of the Black Chicken rushed out to greet Piffle, bowing and fussing over one of his most lucrative clients.

'Ah Mr Dresden, it is so good to see you again, come, come this way, your favourite table is ready, and Mr Alfonse is already waiting for you, come, come.'

'Thanks very much Marco, good to see you too lad, get a bottle of champagne on table, think we're going to have something to celebrate.'

Marco ushered Piffle in through the entrance as quickly as possible.

'This way Señor this way, please, please.'

Piffle's beady eyes were scanning the table for the leader of Benidorm Municipality, his next lucrative business venture in the offing. He spotted Alfonse sitting at his table smoking a cigar and looking decidedly peeved off. He was over in a shot, or as long as his limping leg would take him.

'Eh up Alfonse, hope you haven't been waiting too long?'

'Well Mr Piffle, I have to say I have been waiting in this godforsaken place for quite some time, and it doesn't really agree with my, how you say, constitution.'

'Sorry I'm late Alfonse, but I've had a swine of a day and it's all gone tits up to be honest, but I'm here now and I think it's going to be a worthwhile meeting.'

'I sincerely hope so Mr Piffle, my time is very valuable, and I hope you have not brought me here on what you English call a wild goose chase.'

At that point Marco brought over the bottle of champagne and Dresden started to feel better about the evening and the chances of the deal succeeding that he had been planning for quite some time. He started to relax for the first time.

'So Mr Piffle, you said you had a lucrative business opportunity that you wanted to speak to me about, am I not correct?'

'Listen Alfonse, call me Dresden, we are going to become mates and I am sure you will be very interested in what I have got to say lad. But let's have glass of champers first and listen to a bit of karaoke and have a bit of nosh, eh?'

'Well Dresden, I am happy to, as you say, have a bit of nosh and a glass of champagne, but as for the singing, I have to say that my ears do not function like yours,' Alfonse said smiling for the first time.

'That's the spirit lad, always say business comes after a bit of lubrication and a good meal eh?'

So that is what they did. The champagne flowed, Marco brought a huge paella over to them and they both relaxed into the evening. The dreadful karaoke was ever present in the background as everyone around them got more and more drunk and raucous. Piffle and Alfonse were not immune to the atmosphere of the Black Chicken, and before long they were also very merry, and in danger of becoming drunk before they had discussed the business offer that Piffle had devised.

'Right lad, I think it's time I got round to telling you what this is all about Alfonse, don't you think?'

'That will be good, I need to get home soon as I have an important council meeting in the morning, and I need to be fresh as the daisy as you say in England.'

'Well Alfonse, it comes down to this. You know that big piece of derelict land out on outskirts of Benidorm near where IKEA have their store, set in pine forest with a few old rotting caravans?'

'Ah you mean the Playa de Sol caravan park established many years ago but now derelict with a few gipsies and vagrants living there?'

'That sounds like the one lad. Well, I've got option to buy it from owner and the money to develop it into a bloody great luxury park full of log cabins. I reckon, five hundred log cabins can fit on that site with a swimming pool, club house and restaurant. That's what I want to do Alfonse.'

'Log cabins, what do you mean log cabins?'

'You know Alfonse, Scandinavian style luxury lodges complete with decking and hot tubs, go down a storm selling them to Brits. Bit of luxury, set in the pine forest with added benefit of year round sun. Here, I've got a few pictures to show you. These are made by my me mate's company in Hull. Idea is Wack will make five hundred luxury log cabins and ship them out on site, and we use local builders to put in concrete pans and services for water and electricity.'

'Wack, who is this Wack?'

'Oh, sorry lad, I mean Gary Wacker, me best mate from days at fish docks, owns a company called GDW Log Cabins, called Wack 'cause of his name, and he used to whack people in playground if they got in his way. Not much has changed to be honest.'

'Ah I see, so where do I fit into your grand plan Mr Dresden?'

'Simple Alfonse, need you to oil the wheels to get planning permission and building permits and recommend a decent builder who can put in concrete pads, roads and services, and I need it in double quick time.'

'Well Mr Dresden, it will not be easy, that land has no longer got planning permission and has been re-zoned as a retail area on the outskirts of Benidorm, it would be very difficult. I am afraid I can't see a way to help you.'

'Let's cut to chase Alfonse, €100,000 of baksheesh says I have planning by end of year.'

'Impossible Mr Dresden, it cannot be done, but maybe, just maybe, €200,000 could persuade the right people and I make a small commission for myself.'

'€150,000.'

'I think we can have a deal Mr Dresden.'

'Shake on it lad.' And that they did.

CHAPTER 5

Soon after Alfonse left the Black Chicken. It was already midnight, but Piffle wanted to stay until the place closed at 1.30 a.m. to celebrate his business achievement.

He was already working out the figures on a napkin left after the meal. Buy the land for €1,000,000, pay Alfonse €150,000 for planning permission, develop the site for €850,000 and buy in luxury log cabins from Wack for €50,000 each delivered and erected. Total cost of project, €27,000,000 Euros. Sell log cabins for €100,000 each, generating €50,000,000. Profit to Piffle, €23,000,000, or about 20 million quid, his biggest business coup yet.

The problem was, Piffle, although rich, didn't have €27 million. At a pinch, he had about 2 million quid. So he would have to sell the log cabins off-plan as he went along using touts in Benidorm to lure the happy tourists. A snide grin came over his face. €23 million profit. He could sell the business in Grimewold, ditch the Clothes Horse and retire to the villa with Honolulu, in luxury, with the lifestyle he had always dreamed of.

With that happy thought he staggered outside and found Paeleo waiting with the Rolls to whisk him back to the Villa Almería. All in all, a very profitable night indeed. Before he got home he needed to phone Wack with the good news. Five hundred luxury log cabins were not to be sniffed at.

'Eh up Wack, it's me Dresden. The deal is in the bag with Benidorm Municipality, so we can plan getting log cabins delivered next year and up for sale asap, off plan.'

'Bloody hell Dresden, never thought you'd pull it off, bloody well done. This means a lot for the people of Hull and me in particular. I'll bid you goodnight otherwise Tracy is going to be pissed off with me talking business at nearly two in the morning, she's asleep beside me here in bed. Anyway, be in touch,' said Gary Wacker delighted at the unexpected news.

It had been a long hard road, but finally Piffle thought he had made it and the sunny uplands were within his grasp. Paeleo dropped him off and he went to bed that night with a feeling that everything in the world was going his way. Little did he know what the future held.

CHAPTER 6

Zara Bindle hailed from impeccable ultra-left-wing feminist stock. Her grandmother, Philomena Bindle, had left Islington in 1936 and travelled with her then, live in, boyfriend, Pedro Constantine, to fight General Franco's fascist troops in the Spanish Civil War. You could hardly call Pedro battle hardened, his only experience being as a junior clerk at Islington Council. He was soon captured, never to be seen again. Philomena fought on valiantly, was captured by a division of Franco's troops near Madrid, gang raped in a chicken coop and finally managed to escape in the back of a Migual beer wagon, reaching Islington in the summer of 1937, pregnant to a fascist solder, name unknown. The product of this brief and unfortunate encounter was born in February 1938 and christened Daphne.

In the local Islington Labour Club, Philomena was a hero, and word of her heroic exploits soon spread in the wider labour movement. What impressed most, was the fact that Philomena had taken the fight to the fascists, rather than just talk about it.

Philomena was also a rare example of feminist ideology in 1938; she was a single mother in a world where illegitimacy was positively taboo, and thrived on the notoriety of her position, helped financially by her father Ernest, a Harley Street doctor. Her visceral hatred of men, fired up by her experiences in war-torn Spain, were seamlessly passed onto Daphne throughout her formative years, as were her extreme left wing feminist views. As a result, Daphne was sent to an all girls grammar school in Islington, and had next to no contact with boys or indeed any males, apart from her Grandfather Ernest, a distant and cautious man of few words, and even fewer deeds.

As a result, Daphne threw herself headlong into her studies and career, gaining a first from Cambridge in Women's Studies. She then carried on working at Cambridge as a senior lecturer in the same department having gained a research scholarship. Highly paid and highly respected, Daphne continued her career in isolation of anyone other than her feminist friends in the groups she was involved in, her students and visits to her mother in Islington. Men were always a distant enigma to Daphne, and relationships were non-existent. That enabled her to develop her views on men and feminist ideology in isolation of reality.

All was to change in 1979 during the Winter of Discontent. The labour movement was in turmoil, with the hard left militants trying to gain control of the party and James Callaghan fighting on to a general election he was doomed to lose. Daphne had become ever more involved in her feminist causes and as a representative of Feminist Action, which campaigned for the rights of women to undertake jobs in predominantly male roles, she attended the Durham Miner's Gala. Only

to end up following the Bindle tradition of getting pregnant to a 6' 2",
20 stone Miner called Jake. Who, due to her drunkenness, she was
unable to identify and never saw again. It was one of the few times in
her life she got drunk and one of the even fewer that she had any
contact with the male of the species, even if it was the briefest of
liaisons but with significant results. Another female Bindle was born into
the world of Mrs Thatcher in January 1980, this time named Zara.

It was a very different world from 1938, and Daphne was not at
all unique in being a single mother. What was more unique was her
insistence on taking baby Zara into the lecture rooms and theatres all
the time due to the 'inadequate childcare' at Cambridge. Breast feeding
in front of the students, male and female alike, raised more than a few
eyebrows in academic circles.

Due to her highly paid job and a not unsubstantial inheritance
from her grandfather Ernest, which had been left in trust, Daphne was
able to pay for Zara to attend the best all girls schools the country had
to offer, attend finishing school in Switzerland and follow the Bindle
tradition of going to Cambridge University to read Modern History.

Because of this rarefied upbringing and her exposure to the
highest in society, Zara, although still exhibiting the extreme left wing
and feminist views of her mother and grandmother, had an altogether
more limited view of the realities of everyday life for the normal
working man and women that she claimed to identify with. Like her
mother though, she had a burning passion to take forward the feminist
cause. It was always going to be hard to live up to the romantic exploits

of her now deceased grandmother, Philomena, but she was going to try and leave her mark. She also had a romantic vision of the north of England where she assumed 'real' working class people lived and where the most prejudice amongst women could be found. So, when she saw the job advertised in Grimewold, a steel town of some notoriety, in the Guardian weekly jobs supplement she jumped at the chance of applying.

Operations Diversity Manager, working for Diversity Action Partnership Limited the advert said, and it caught Zara's eye immediately. The basic salary of £20,000 was far less appealing, but performance related pay was offered and the advert claimed it could double the salary. But the main draw for Zara was the job itself; ensuring women, and other disadvantaged groups, would be employed in the exact proportion to their percentage number in society. This was music to her ears, especially the opportunity to ensure that women gained their rightful position in the workplace and the diversity workshops that encouraged employers to promote women and other disadvantaged groups at the expense of the one group that had dominated for centuries, namely white privileged males.

In any event, and something Piffle hadn't expected, Zara Bindle was so good at her job that the performance related pay element ended up being £130,000 a year, not the £20,000 envisaged. It was a constant source of friction.

In short, Piffle was as tight as a gnat's arse where money was concerned and did not want to pay his Operations Diversity Manager

£150,000 a year even though she was earning him many times more than that. The problem was, she had negotiated a five year contract and his lawyers said he couldn't get out of it. Not to mention the reputation the Bindle's had in the Labour party, which could cause him real trouble. So, he was stuck with Bindle, her extreme feminist views and her gigantic, and in Piffle's opinion undeserved, salary.

If Piffle's Operations Diversity Manager was reaping the rewards bestowed upon her by Diversity Action Partnership Limited, the other staff were much less well rewarded. However, because Piffle had a complete ignorance of computer systems, and had invested next to nothing in new technology, the company relied on a huge army of clerks and enforcers to obtain the fine monies – over 100 members of staff to be exact.

The systems employed were out of the ark. In the huge open-plan area that used to be the central library first floor, fifty cheap desks could be found, laid out in rows for the clerks to sit at. Piffle had bought ex-local authority school desks from a secondary school that had been put into special measures and then closed down, and used them. At the far end of the office space were a huge wall of metal filling cabinets containing a file for each company registered in the Grimewold post code areas. This had taken a lot of man hours to put in place, but Piffle had a file for each company, a last contact sheet and visit report and a summary of fines imposed and fines outstanding. There was one central PC that contained all of the fine invoices which were printed off and sent out.

The other part of the operation consisted of enforcement. Piffle had purposely employed ex-miners and ex-steel workers of a particularly nasty and ignorant disposition to visit companies, issue writs and collect fines from those companies that had not paid within a month of receipt of the original fine. This was the most lucrative part of the operation as additional charges could take the £2000 fine up to nearly £4000 for a transgressor that had not paid. Threats, intimidation and eventual seizure of assets backed up Piffle's empire and ensured that fine income was usually recovered in the end. Piffle had over twenty enforcement vans circling the district of Grimewold, like vultures seeking out their prey. The efficiency of Zara Bindle's enforcement division and the prompt issuing of fines ensured that fine income had grown substantially. None of these rewards were passed onto the workers, mostly male and in their fifties and sixties, they were grateful for the zero hours contracts and minimum wages Piffle paid. He had even established a lucrative company canteen – where prices were high and service poor – that served the whole building, including Mike Morrel's Speed Camera Action team, over 250 staff in total.

The following morning after speaking to Piffle, Zara Bindle had driven the short commute from the exclusive gated estate called The Heights, to her office at the old Central Library building in Grimewold town centre. She had left Hugo, her live-in house husband, mopping the oak floors using a special cleaner containing carnauba wax. Hugo was ill suited to the world of work, but had an uncanny knack for cleaning, ironing, cooking and conducting other domestic chores that Zara's feminist instincts considered beneath her. The demeaning role reversal suited her views perfectly, and Hugo, being a weak man, knew best not to challenge them. The harsh truth was that Hugo was as ill suited to work as he was well suited to domestic chores, and the chances of him getting a professional job, or indeed any job in a place like Grimewold, was remote. In short, the arrangement worked amicably for both parties.

She parked the black VW Golf GTi in her private parking place and walked the short distance to the front entrance and into the atrium. The huge open plan workspace was laid out before her and already it was a hive of activity. The wooden school desks were laid out in rows, the central computer sat to the right with a large printer and the huge array of metal filling cabinets stood at the far end. Immediately the office supervisor came shuffling up to her, an obsequious, grovelling little man by the name of Jennings. Standing there in his tank top and ill-fitting trousers, he looked every bit the throwback he was. Bindle looked at him with utter contempt.

'Morning Ms Bindle, so nice to see you, have you had a good journey in today?'

'I have not Jennings, it's clearly unlikely that I have had a nice journey given the Council have dug up half the ring road and it has taken me thirty-five minutes to get here, thus making me late.'

'Sorry to hear that Ms Bindle, would you like a nice cup of tea?'

'Yes, you can make me a pot of tea Jennings, bring it to my office along with today's visit report, I need to see that the outreach teams are hitting their targets.'

'Yes Ms Bindle, right away Ms Bindle.' Jennings retreated head bowed in obvious deference to his boss. As Bindle moved through the open plan area she reflected on the horribly white, male and middle-aged composition of her workforce, and secretly vowed to change things despite Piffle's opposition.

Bindle ensconced herself in her spacious office as soon as possible and closed the door. The daily visit report was already on her desk and she wanted to review progress on outstanding fines' collections from the many businesses that were starting to resist the new regime. There was a hardcore of very difficult client firms that were refusing to pay, plus a great many soft targets that would pay up with a little bit of pressure applied.

Bindle called it the 80/20 rule. 80% would pay up without much difficulty and 20% would put every obstacle in the way to fight paying the fines due. Bindle had asked her twenty outreach teams to go after the soft targets since they would generate the most revenue.

In fact, the outreach teams were gearing up to leave. Twenty Ford Transit vans awaited them with the slogan 'building a fairer society' emblazoned on the side of the vans in large red lettering. Three men to each van, two enforcers and an apprentice enforcer all in their high-vis jackets and the full force of the equality and diversity act behind them.

The first visit of the day at 8.30 a.m. sharp was Benton's the

Butchers, a small company with four butcher's shops across the area and a total of twenty staff. The firm had been open since 1906 but had failed to comply with the equality and diversity act having failed to employ enough Muslims, transgender, or Bangladeshi staff according to a detailed analysis by Piffle's enforcement team. Outstanding fines totalled £6,000 for three serious transgressions and a refusal by Roy Benton to pay up.

Bindle had no sympathy for the likes of Roy Benton, it was his sort that was holding back the glorious feminist revolution. He was a man not willing to move with the times and accept that Britain was now a multi-cultural diverse society, and that needed to be reflected at all levels in order to create 'fairness' of opportunity, whatever that may mean. Benton needed to sack many of his white male employees of longstanding service and replace them with a suitably diverse workforce – then he wouldn't be fined. It was all so simple as far as Bindle was concerned. Her world view and that of the equality and diversity act must prevail either by persuasion or force, it was that simple.

CHAPTER 7

On the other side of town in an oak panelled office there was a particularly unpleasant man of great influence plotting the demise of Sydney Dresden Piffle and his obnoxious Diversity Action Partnership Limited.

His name was Josiah Archibald McGreggor III. McGreggor was the current owner and indeed inheritor of the largest steel rolling mill in Europe, and the main employer in Grimewold, employing some 5500 men full time. He employed a further 5000 men as casual contractors on zero hours contracts through a particularly vicious and uncaring agency called happy-worker.com. A company based in Bulgaria for tax domicile reasons and simply because the owner had connections to the Bulgarian Mafia.

Josiah Archibald McGreggor III also ran the Yorkshire branch of the Institute of Directors, with a direct link to the Secretary of State for Trade and Industry. He did not take kindly to a 'communist' upstart like Sydney Dresden Piffle fining his company many thousands of pounds a year. The bastard had to be stopped and pronto. Archibald, as he liked to be called, had the means and the will to do so.

Now in his late seventies, Archibald, after a stroke that had rendered his left arm useless plus a constitution that made him prone to extremely painful episodes of gout in his right foot, now had even less empathy with people than the very limited reserves he'd had in his younger days. The term 'he doesn't suffer fools gladly' was as a true as it could be for a man who had to put up with many fools working within his organisation. In short, he was an extremely nasty piece of work with a sharp mind, a very quick temper, a chip on his shoulder every bit as large as Sydney Dresden Piffle's and a hatred for his long-suffering family and his poor secretary of thirty-two years standing, June.

This Friday morning it was June who was taking the full force of his venom and anger against his new adversary. Piffle's company had issued yet another series of fines and was in the process of taking McGreggor's Steel to the High Court for non-payment of fines from last year and the year before.

'How dare that fucking communist, upstart bastard of a Hull fish filleter's prostitute think he can fine me 56,000 fucking English pounds and get away with it? I swear I am going to make sure he is six feet under a concrete pylon when I've finished with him!'

'Now calm down Archibald we don't want to have another stroke, do we?' June said in a particularly condescending voice that angered Archibald even more.

'We don't want to have another stroke? I don't ever remember you ever having a fucking stroke, and I don't give a flying fig whether you want me to calm down or not. Now get me some fresh hot coffee, not that weak piss that you seem to serve me up these days. I need to think and plan how I am going to sort that creature out once and for all.'

June casually lumbered off to do her masters bidding, which angered Archibald further.

'If I could just have that fucking coffee before one of us dies!' he shouted.

Archibald had a particularly nasty lopsided snarl on his face most of the time and cold steel blue eyes, but an occasional glint appeared when he had thought up some especially nasty act to annoy his family or his employees. He especially liked his long-standing run ins with the Iron and Steel Makers Union run by an extremely mild-mannered and reasonable trade unionist by the name of Frank Barraclough. In fact, he found Barraclough too tame for his liking and too willing to give in to his unreasonable demands and employment practises.

McGreggor's had signed a joint venture partnership with an Indian Steel concern called PING Steel Worldwide, which could produce rolled steel products for 40% less than McGreggor's could in Grimewold. Archibald could think of nothing better than to provoke a strike so that he could sack half the workforce without redundancy compensation.; an unofficial wildcat strike being best in this regard to meet his objectives.

Piffle in truth was only a small problem and did not dent his huge wealth financially but he had never been beaten and liked the thought of destroying an undoubtedly dangerous communist, which would serve him well and send a clear message to the wider business community that Archibald McGreggor III was the most formidable businessman in Britain today and worthy of that peerage that he so richly reserved.

The coffee duly arrived on a silver serving platter and June poured a generous cup of coffee into the overtly large Wedgewood bone china mug that Archibald insisted upon.

'There you are Sir, a nice cup of coffee to calm you down.'

'About bloody time, and as you know well, I won't be calm until I've thought of a way of stopping that bloody Piffle dead in his tracks. Anyway, when I've finished this piss water you've served me, get me my sticks and get the Bentley round to the front. I need to get to the golf club this afternoon and see someone.'

Sadly, Archibald needed two sturdy willow sticks capped with solid brass ends to hobble around after his stroke. Under no circumstances was he going to have one of those bloody four wheeled death machines and give into the weaknesses of the modern world. He had seen the old biddies in Grimewold, shooting around the town at speed on mobility scooters. He'd even seen some younger women who were clearly the size of semi-detached houses and had never, in Archibald's opinion, done a day's work in their lives, save for popping out unwanted off spring at the long suffering tax payer's expense. He would never give in to such stupidity, so the sticks it was and the 1962 Bentley S2 was more than adequate for getting him around. The doors opened outwards for starters, enabling a man of his importance unrivalled access to the back seat of the car. He had a permanent chauffeur on standby who had been in the employ of the McGreggor family right back to when the Bentley was new in 1962, and his father bought the car. He needed Wilfred now.

'I said get me Wilfred, woman, damn you. Why do you never do as I ask?'

'Well maybe if you recognised the many years of faithful service I have given to you Archibald, instead of bawling and shouting obscenities at me all the time, we might get a bit more cooperation mightn't we?'

'Well maybe we would, but I employ you, so If some lunatic communist upstart creature has ruined my fucking day, then I have every right to take it out on the person nearest to me, and that person is you.'

June had nothing further to say and was so used to his outbursts that it went clean over her head. She went to her phone in the outside office, dialled 926 and asked Wilfred to bring the Bentley S2 round to main reception and wait for his master to appear.

It took Archibald some time to get himself to the door of the Bentley. Out of his palatial office, along a very long corridor where Archibald had had a moving airport-style walkway installed at great expense, to the Otis lift that had been installed by his Grandfather in 1936, down three floors to main reception, across the Italian marble floor, through the swing doors and finally to the waiting car.

Wilfred manoeuvred the old man into the rear seat of the S2, not that he was much help since he was pushing 90 himself, and finally off they went to the golf club. Hessle View Golf and Country Club, located a safe distance from Grimewold itself, overlooked the Humber estuary and was set in a magnificent pine forest that had been planted by the Duke of Norfolk. The Duke had a country house and estate nearby and had originally sold the farm land for a huge profit in 1965 in order to pay death duties under the odious and ruinous taxation policy of the then Labour Government of Harold Wilson.

Although more than capable of high speed the Bentley S2 glided along at no more than 28 miles per hour, not helped by the fact that Wilfred had extremely poor eyesight. Along the A1072 they trundled through the pretty village of Appleton where a selection of particularly nasty and vindictive pensioners in high-vis jackets were being taught the art of using a speed camera by one of Mike Morrell's team from Humberwold Speed Camera Action Partnership Limited, in the hope of gaining yet more revenue from the hard pressed workers and taxpayers of Humberwold County.

The added benefit of not having to pay the pensioners and yet receiving the fines was even more appealing to Morrell and his team. 'Pure profit groups' was how he described them in team building meetings, and he wanted many more hundreds of such groups, not just the few that so far existed.

The small group of eight pensioners and the Speed Camera Safety Officer all scowled at the Bentley as it glided past because they knew from bitter experience that Wilfred would not be exceeding the speed limit and revenue would not be forthcoming. As luck would have it, a heavy deluge the night before had left the road in a sea of water, where the road surface had deteriorated due to decades of local government mismanagement and cuts in the road maintenance budget and the Bentley, with a little help from Wilfred, managed to spray the group with a shower of filthy brown rain water which had collected in the road next to them.

Through his rear-view mirror, Wilfred could see the group shaking their fists and flicking the V sign at him and the car, but at 92 nothing was really going to faze him any longer. The blighters got what they deserved and that was a fact.

Archibald saw none of this activity since he was avidly reading the Financial Times in the back. His company's share price was up 20% due to the rumours of the tie up with PING Steel Worldwide; the city traders were salivating at the potential cost saving advantages of moving most production to India. There was the little problem of the £382 million pension deficit the company had built up over the years due to all the pension holidays it had taken to boost profits and, in Archibald's opinion, the over generosity of his grandfather in granting lavish final salary pensions to his ungrateful workers in the first place. But he was sure of finding a way to either eliminate the deficit or his legal obligations to pay it!

Finally, after nearly an hour the Bentley glided into the Hessle View Golf Club, drove up the shaded tree lined drive and parked in the members area with a space specially reserved for the Bentley. Archibald was the Life-President of the club, such niceties were his due as the most successful businessman in the area.

CHAPTER 8

Archibald was meeting his old friend Winton J Cuncliffe-Owen, vice chair of the 1922 committee and Member of Parliament for the East Riding of Beverley and Horncastle, a true blue Tory heartland, unlike Grimewold, which had had the same dour Labour MP for the last 28 years. They had both been to Westminster School together and then Eton.

Archibald had little time for the latest incumbents of the Conservative Party. They were little more than blue rinse Communists as far as he was concerned. Infected with Blairite socialism, spending vast sums of taxpayer's money, not to mention Corporation Tax and Business Rates on feckless useless druggies and layabouts who had no intention of doing a hard days toil, whilst neglecting the armed services, roads, hospitals and support for manufacturing industry.

However, sometimes one needed 'friends at court' and Archibald needed to call in a favour or two in his pursuit of exterminating Piffle for good and driving him out of town, preferably in a pine box.

After about 15 minutes, with the help of his sticks, Archibald reached the member's lounge and spotted his quarry in one of the green leather winged chairs by the fireplace, the one to the right was vacant. A large gin and tonic had already been ordered and was waiting for him on the coffee table between the two chairs.

'Ah Winton, old fellow, how nice to see you. Must be all of six months,' said Archibald laying on his limited charm with all he could muster.

'Well, I must say the pleasure is all mine Archibald, splendid, splendid and you are looking so well. I took the liberty of ordering you a drink, your favourite double gin and tonic.'

'So kind Winton. How is it going in the corridors of power down at Westminster?'

'Bloody terrible old boy, like trying to herd sheep with a gun dog. Lots of casualties and very little damned progress. It's all political correctness these days, can't even talk to a filly without being accused of being a sexist pervert. Ask a gal out and you might as well throw in the towel. Better to be a shirt lifter these days, they leave those blighters alone.'

'I dare say Winton. We don't tolerate that sort of nonsense at McGreggor's. A woman is a woman, a man a man, and everyone knows their place. Always has been like that and always will as far as I'm concerned.'

'Anyway Archibald, I'm sure you've not brought me here to discuss the dire state of the Conservative Party, if we can even call it that anymore. How can I be of help?'

'Well Winton, I'm calling in a favour, a little local difficulty. I'm having a spot of bother with a lunatic communist upstart who runs a company called The Diversity Action Partnership Limited, who keeps sending me outrageous fines for non-compliance with some god-forsaken EU directive that Grimewold Council has took it upon itself to interpret in the most stringent way possible. Name of Piffle. Currently I'm fighting the blighter in the courts for outstanding fines of £56,000.'

'I see, I think I've heard of him, used to be a pain on the arse in Hull stirring up trouble, and fermenting strike action. What's he doing with this Diversity Action, what did you say?'

'Diversity Action Partnership Limited, the blighters send out never ending fines for non-compliance to a fucking EU directive that it's next to impossible to adhere to. Bloody liberty and a licence to print money. That piss poor upstart is worth a few million quid now off the backs of hard-working businessmen like me. Even we're struggling to pay the fines, and if that Piffle thinks that I'm going to sack workers of long-standing, pay exorbitant redundancy packages and then employ a bunch of unsuitable women, ethnic minorities, transvestites, gays and god know what other creatures he deems suitable, he can fucking well think again.'

'Well old boy, I see your problem, but I can't see how I can be of assistance. If what you say is true, then this Piffle fellow has got the might of the law on his side. What might you have in mind?'

'I tell you what I have in mind Winton, what I have in mind is a 'disrupter'. Get someone into the organisation who can suss it out. Work out its weaknesses and in particular the nefarious activities of Piffle and his key lieutenants. Then strike with horrible precision. Get the dirt on the blighters and feed them what they want, preferably illegal activity that can be taped, videoed and distributed to all the main news channels around the world. That way Piffle goes the way of the Romans, out the door with his tail between his legs.'

'Well Archibald, it won't be easy to find such a person. What you're looking for comes straight out of a Le Carré novel. What you really need is someone who can get a job in Piffle's organisation and disrupt it from within, someone who shares our belief that what Piffle is doing goes against natural justice. Someone with an ideological hatred of his communist, trendy, lefty beliefs.'

Winton's mind was going into overdrive now and he was warming to the challenge as Archibald surely knew he would.

'I might know someone,' Winton exclaimed. 'A filly who used to work for MI5, got expelled for being even more of a lunatic liability then most of them there, very right wing. Looks like a man, about 5'8" tall, built like a brick privy, arse the size of a block of flats, face like she has been chewing spanners, ended up working in Central Office. So incompetent she wrecked the computer system and we ended up sending key target voters reasons not to bother voting when we should have been sending the letters out to key labour voters. Absolute bloody disaster area, nearly lost us the last election, not to mention a bloody great fine from the electoral commission. Yes, she might do, a bloody walking disaster area, goes by the name of Tandori.'

'Tandori?' exclaimed Archibald.

'Sounds like a bloody Indian curry, but you might be onto something Winton. If she's as abominable as you say she is, and capable of wreaking havoc on Piffle's empire whilst at the same time having an ideological motive for doing so, we might have found the right person, a disrupter par excellence. How do we make contact with this Tandori?'

'Leave that to me,' said Winton.

'I have friends at court. I will sound her out and set up a meeting in London. The next time you hear from me will be to come down and meet this Tandori. It won't be cheap mind, you'll have to put her on your pay roll at McGreggor's, and it might take time for her to get a job at Piffle's outfit.'

So, the seed had been sown, and both men could leave the meeting with a clear understanding of what had been agreed. For the first time in a long time, Archibald had that dangerous glint in his eye. He liked nothing better than having an adversary, finding a strategy to destroy them and succeeding. It wasn't about the money, it was the challenge he liked.

At McGreggor's there was little real excitement, just a bunch of suited buffoon's to deal with and June berating him all the time and treating him like a child. Even the trade unions were reasonable and oh so politically correct. He longed for an Arthur Scargill-like character to pit himself against and relive the glory days of the miner's strike when there was a clear enemy and you could fight fire with fire. A straight forward gladiatorial fight to the bitter end with one winner and a clear, indisputable loser. That's what he wanted, a fight to the death. Himself, Josiah Archibald McGreggor, the clear winner and Sydney Dresden Piffle the loser; him the hero of capitalism with a vindication of his world view.

With that happy thought he left the cosy confines of the Hessle View Golf and Country Club and made his way back to his office, with a new challenge and a new determination.

CHAPTER 9

In London, Tandori Birkett-Morris wasn't having a good day. She had got wasted the night before and had woken up late and hung over; her room-mate, Beth, had already left for work. Tandori had an interview at Job Centre Plus to determine why, after six fruitless months of searching for a job, she was still unemployed. She was not looking forward to the interview at all. In her mind she saw no point in engaging with a bunch of tick box jobsworth morons who – if they had ever had a brain it had long since departed – had not a clue, nor indeed a desire, to help her back into the sort of job she so richly deserved.

Having been to Richmond Grammar School, gained a first in English Literature at Oxford, been recruited by MI5 as one of the first female intake and then, after a few unfortunate episodes, let go to work at Tory Central Office and finally summarily dismissed for the unfortunate computer episode, she was in no mood to listen to some half-wit tell her there was a zero hours contract going at the local chicken packing factory.

Today she was to be encouraged again to go on the course 'How to Write a CV'. How to write a CV! Bunch of complete fuckwit knob-heads. Writing the CV wasn't the problem, it was the dire content of her experiences at her last two jobs and the lack of suitable references that was forcing her down the chicken-factory-packing route. A route so unthinkable that she may as well go and jump off Vauxhall Bridge and end her miserable fucking existence.

But first to the bathroom to have a shower, get over the hangover and try and get to the job centre for 11.00.

She went off into the lounge to find the interview letter on the coffee table. It had come in Saturday's post, inviting her to see a Ms Roz Dwyer. She glanced at the letter, *'you are requested to report to section C of Wandsworth Job Centre Plus at 10.00 a.m.'*

'Shit, shit ,shit! 10.00 a.m., it was fucking 8.45 now! What the fuck!'

Tandori launched herself into overdrive, not an easy task given the size of her in all directions. Her mother called her 'unfortunate', and compared to her elder sister Tamara she certainly was. She had a long plain face with a pointed thin nose, her sparkling green eyes were her best feature. She was tall in body and leg, too tall in her opinion, but it was below the waist where things went horribly wrong as far as she was concerned. She had huge tree trunk legs and an arse that stuck out nearly a foot behind her back. Her extreme pear shape making clothes shopping all but impossible. Big thick arms and a male like upper physique completed the picture, with only moderate sized breasts which added to her male like appearance from the waist up. Short, cropped hair completed the picture of a girl without feminine grace or appearance. Her appearance was the least of her worries as she dived towards the bathroom and turned the shower on full blast.

As she stepped into the shower, which was over the bath, way too quickly she failed to notice that Beth had dropped a bar of Imperial Leather soap in the bath and as Tandori got one huge leg into the bath she slipped on the soap. Momentarily off balance, she grabbed at the only thing immediately to hand, which was the shower attachment. With the full force of her, not insubstantial, body the shower attachment didn't stand a chance. It yanked itself off the electric shower module which in turn detached itself from the main water pipe leading into the shower module itself.

High-pressure mains water was now gushing out of the exposed pipe and Tandori had no way of turning the fucking thing off, apart from finding the stop cock, and as they had only moved in recently she hadn't a clue where that was. She frantically tried to bung flannels down the exposed water pipe but they kept shooting out. Meanwhile, the old enamel bath was filling up fast.

Old Mrs Grayson in the flat below could hear the commotion and got her walking stick and started jabbing at the ceiling yelling for whoever it was to shut up and give her some peace and quiet.

Naked and dripping with soap and water, Tandori rushed out of the bathroom through the lounge to the kitchen and looked for the stop cock under the sink. It was not there.

She now rushed back, still soaking wet and naked, and saw the airing cupboard next to the bath, it must be in there. Meanwhile the heavy enamel bath was overflowing, and huge quantities of water were sloshing around the floor and seeping through the old Victorian joists and ceiling lathes. Water was pouring though the ceiling into Mrs Grayson's living room. She had a lot more to worry about now than a localized commotion, she now had gallons of water depositing itself on her expensive Wilton lounge carpet. Frantically Mrs Grayson jabbed at the ceiling screaming at the top of her voice. It was to no avail.

The combined weight of the enamel bath filled to the brim with water and overflowing, Tandori's not inconsiderable weight standing next to the bath trying to find the stop cock combined with the weakened ceiling joists after years of neglect and considerable hidden wood worm meant the ceiling could stand the weight no more.

Finding the stop cock became an irrelevance, as the main ceiling joists gave way. As the ceiling started to collapse Tandori, was thrown off balance and landed with a heavy thud in the bath. The continued effects of gravity and the thud finally ensured that the poor ceiling joists failed in their last stubborn resistance and gave way altogether. The inevitable happened, the entire enamel bath crashed through the ceiling, with Tandori scrabbling to save herself from certain death, and landed squarely in the middle of Mrs Grayson's lounge, together with the vast quantities of water that were still cascading through the gaping hole. Old Mrs Grayson hadn't had such a shock since her parents' house was totally obliterated by the Nazis in the summer of 1942, and duly had a heart attack and died in her armchair before she could survey the damage to her lovely flat.

Tandori hadn't died but she had knocked her head and passed out, still in the bath. Her arse was wedged in so tightly that when the fire brigade found her unconscious and naked some 30 minutes later it took three of them to dislodge her.

Sadly, water damage wasn't the end of the matter. The water had got into the main electricity supply to the flats and triggered an electrical fire in the fuse box which soon spread through part of the building. The billowing smoke out of the flat below Mrs Grayson's further convinced the authorities they were dealing with a serious ISIS inspired terrorist incident.

The chief fire officer had seen some sights in his time but he wouldn't forget the sight of a twenty stone, completely naked, Tandori wedged into a Victorian bath any time soon. As he said later to one of his colleagues, it was the stuff of fucking nightmares.

Both flats were severely damaged and at first the police, who had also been called, were convinced that an ISIS cell was trying to blow up a Victorian block of flats and duly cordoned off the whole area, enacted operation *Tiger's Claw* and sent in an armed terrorist response team. All the other emergency services were also present including the ambulance service, the air ambulance, special branch and MI5. Someone had tipped off Sky News, Russia Today and Al Jazeera and within thirty minutes a gaggle of press were present as well as ITN and the BBC News. Sky had their own helicopter bringing live coverage of the suspected terrorist incident.

Needless to say, Tandori didn't make her 10.00 a.m. Job Centre Plus appointment. Instead she was arrested as a suspected terrorist and taken to Parsons Green Police Station in the back of a BMW 4X4 vehicle with blacked out windows, handcuffed and considered very dangerous.

CHAPTER 10

Tandori found herself in a holding cell at Parsons Green Police Station, now a suspected ISIS terrorist and sympathiser. If she thought her day couldn't get any worse, she hadn't bargained for Inspector Fleece who was already convinced of her undoubted guilt and determined to use this particularly nasty terrorist incident to further his flagging career.

He looked through the two-way glass observation hatch and turned to his colleague, Constable Brahmes. 'Let the bitch stew, Brahmes. Let's give her another hour. In my experience when they haven't had a drink, anything to eat or human contact they're more likely to give us what we want. She can't have been acting alone, causing that much fucking damage. I want names and then we can close down the terrorist cell operating in the heart of my city.'

'Whatever you say Sir, but what about her human rights. I thought...'

'Don't fucking think Brahmes, that will get you into all sorts of trouble. Better you shuffle off pet and get me a nice cup of Nescafe.'

Brahmes didn't want to argue with thirty years of bitter police experience lodged in Inspector Fleece's brain and decided to drop it and comply with his wishes. A cup of coffee might just improve his mood, though she somewhat doubted it.

Tandori's mood certainly needed improving. Once she had fully woken up and discovered she was in some kind of holding cell instead of at Job Centre Plus on a Thursday morning, she started frantically banging on the heavy door shouting for attention. Not that anyone could hear her through the 6-inch heavy metal reinforced door with two-way safety glass through the observation hatch.

It was now past 12.00 and Ms Roz Dwyer was not in a good mood. Yet another feckless useless claimant in the form of Tandori Birkett-Morris had let her down and not turned up for her job search interview. She went into her file, which was now fully integrated with housing benefit and other benefits through Universal Credit, and took great delight in pressing the 'suspend' button. That meant all benefits were immediately suspended pending a case review which could take up to three months.

She had no idea that Tandori Birkett-Morris had been involved in a suspected terrorist incident, arrested and was currently in police custody. Not that the system made allowances for such inconsistencies of behaviour and circumstance. Not that housing benefit would make much difference to Tandori as her flat, along with several others, was completely obliterated and no longer inhabitable. The £71 Job Seeker's

Allowance was of more use to Tandori, but that little bit of support was now to be denied her.

At the Constabulary's pleasure she would be fed, watered and given accommodation of sorts and in any case Inspector Fleece had no intention of releasing her anytime soon. The Terrorism Act 2010 ensured that suspected terrorists could be kept for up to eight weeks for interrogation before charges were brought. In the meantime Tandori did not need to worry about board and lodgings.

Her friend Beth was not so lucky and had to move back with her mother and father in Milton Keynes, thus ensuring a long commute to London each day. She was not best pleased to find that her best friend Tandori was a suspected terrorist running a terrorist cell out of their tiny flat, and in truth, thought it was bollocks despite Tandori's MI5 connections and past employment.

CHAPTER 11

Tandori was brought through to the interview room. It had been hard to find her any clothes that fitted, but a particularly large duty-sergeant by the name of Linda, had kindly donated a pair of leggings and a t-shirt large enough to cover Tandori's modesty.

Tandori was already furious, having been denied any food, drink or legal representation for five hours- it was mid-afternoon.

Fleece entered the interview room with Constable Brahmes and sat down opposite Tandori.

'What the fuck do you think you're doing arresting me and keeping me here in a god awful cell with no facilities for five fucking hours. No food, drink or human contact. I want a drink at the very least.'

Fleece eyed the creature with loathing. 'Brahmes get the terrorist suspect a glass of water from the dispenser please.'

'What the fuck do you mean, "terrorist suspect"? The last thing I remember is slipping on a bar of Imperial Leather and pulling the shower off the fucking wall.'

Fleece had his own private thoughts, but given the fire and water damage, the complete destruction of a Victorian block of flats and Tandori's former MI5 connections and summary dismissal, there was no way on God's earth a simple bar of soap was responsible for such an unbelievable turn of events. Sky news, the BBC, Al Jazeera and Russia Today couldn't all be wrong.

' We will come to your offences in due course Miss. Turn on the tape recorder, Constable Brahmes.'

'I am arresting you for offenses under the Terrorism Act 2010. You do not have to say anything but anything you do say can be taken down and used in evidence against you. Do you understand?'

'This is fucking preposterous!'

'Do you understand?'

'Of course I fucking understand.'

'For the record, can you state your name, address and occupation.'

'You already know my fucking name, address and occupation.'

'The prisoner is being uncooperative and refuses to state her name, address and occupation.'

'All right, all right. My name is Tandori Birkett-Morris of Flat 6 Providence Flats, Western Avenue, Wandsworth. Occupation, unemployed and seeking employment through Job Centre Plus.'

'Let's start at the beginning shall we. When did you start taking an interest in extremist Islamic terrorist activity?'

'Look, I don't know what this is about Inspector, but all I did was get up for a shower to go to Job Centre Plus and pull the shower off the wall by mistake when I slipped on a bar of soap in the bath.'

'Listen Miss, I have been in this game for thirty-four years and I can smell a lying, conniving criminal at 100 yards. You don't honestly expect me to believe that the total destruction of a beautiful Victorian listed block of flats was the work of a careless incident with a bar of fucking soap do you?'

'Well if you are not going to listen to reason Inspector, I want legal representation before I answer any more of your stupid questions.'

'For the record, please state that the terrorist suspect is being uncooperative.'

'Let's get one thing perfectly clear Miss Birkett-Morris, I ask the fucking questions and I expect answers and when I don't get them I get very angry. Now me and Constable Brahmes here have got all fucking day, and night and the next day, and so on until you start telling us what we want to know. Do you understand? As for legal representation, as a terrorist suspect under the 2010 Terrorism Act you don't qualify for legal representation or legal aid until seven days are up, do you understand?'

'No comment.'

'And what are the names of the Islamist accomplices that have helped you plan and execute this terrorist act?'

'No comment.'

For the next three hours Fleece tried his hardest to get some information out of the bitch, but to no avail. She just kept saying 'no comment'. Too many episodes of her favourite *Midsomer Murders* had taught her how to deal with a police interrogation. Fleece could scarcely believe it. In all his thirty-four years he had never come across a criminal with such a cool disposition. As cool as a cucumber she was, and Fleece got more and more frustrated. It never occurred to him that Tandori Birkett-Morris was telling the truth and didn't have the slightest idea what he was talking about.

By 6.30 p.m. Fleece had had enough for one day. 'Brahmes, take her back to her cell and let her stew overnight. Perhaps she will have seen sense after spending a night in a piss-stained holding cell with a single thread-bare blanket and a concrete bed to lie on. We'll have another go at the bitch in the morning.'

Fleece buggered off to the Whippet Inn for a well-deserved pint, and to relieve the stress of dealing with a fucking maniac like Birkett-Morris. If only he had followed his father's advice and become an electrician, then none of this crap would have ever happened to him

Chapter 12

Back in his Parliamentary office Winton J Cuncliff-Owen had spent the morning fruitlessly trying to ascertain the whereabouts of Tandori Birkett-Morris. He had obtained her mobile number and last landline number from Central Office records but she was answering neither. He might have to go round to her last stated address and see if he could find her in. Failing that, he had contacts in the Met who might be able to trace her or at extremis, MI5 could track her down as a former employee.

Just as he was mulling over his options, his PPS (Private Personal Secretary) barged into his office. He did so dislike Geraldine doing that.

'If I've told you once, I've told you a thousand times Geraldine, please knock before you enter my private office. I could be doing anything.'

'Sorry Mr Owen, I keep forgetting, silly me.'

'What do you want anyway Geraldine?' Cuncliff-Owen said with some irritation.

'Got some news for you Mr Owen.'

'And stop calling me Mr Owen, you know full well my name is the Rt Hon Cuncliff-Owen, show some respect damn you.'

'Sorry Mr Owen, sorry I mean, Mr Rt Hon Mr Cuncliff-Owen, sorry.'

'What news have you got anyway, spit it out women.'

'It's about Tandori Birkett-Morris, you know the women you are looking for.'

'What about Tandori Birkett-Morris?'

'Been arrested.'

'What are you blathering about women, been arrested?'

'That's right, you know that incident yesterday about that block of flats in Wandsworth? It's her, Birkett- Morris, been arrested by Scotland Yard as a suspected ISIS terrorist. Being held at Parsons Green Police Station.'

'How on God's earth do you know that Geraldine?'

'Me friend Linda's the duty Sergeant at Parsons Green Police Station. She told me all about it over a glass of prosecco last night.'

'Well thank you for letting me know Geraldine, that will be all for now.'

Damn thought Winton. That's all he needed, Scotland Yard arresting the very women he needed to carry out his little scheme. He couldn't believe for one minute that Tandori Birkett-Morris was an ISIS terrorist running a cell in London. The stupid bitch was a walking disaster area, utterly incompetent, yes, but a terrorist, definitely not. However, getting Scotland Yard to see that they had made a mistake was tricky, he might have to pull a few strings to get her released.

He picked up the phone. Time to pull a few strings at MI5.

'Is that you Hazelhurst? It's Winton here from the 1922 Committee. Got a spot of bother that needs sorting out and pronto.'

'Fire away Winton, you always know that I am here to help, especially after you saved my bacon over the Bosnian incident, I still owe you one.'

'Thing is Hazelhurst, need the services of one of your ex-employees, goes by the name of Tandori Birkett-Morris. Thing is, a bit tricky this one, but she has been arrested for the Wandsworth incident as a suspected ISIS terrorist. God knows why the blithering idiots at Scotland Yard think Birkett-Morris could ever be a terrorist, couldn't find her fanny in a Rugby club shower room let alone mastermind a terrorist incident. So, what I need Hazelhurst is for you to pull a few strings. Tell Scotland Yard that she is still on a special undercover mission for MI5 and get her released on license. It only need be for a few months. I have a little project in mind for her. After that they can re-arrest her if they like and throw away the key.'

'Not easy old boy, but I think I can do it. Give me 24 hours and I'll come up with the necessary paperwork to get her released. Terrorist suspect eh? Hate to think what she did to get herself in that little spot of bother.'

The plot was hatched, and actually it suited Winton even better to have Birkett-Morris beholden to him. She was more likely to do as he said and at minimal cost if she thought the alternative was twenty years in prison for a crime she clearly hadn't committed. Splendid he thought, the day was getting better and better.

Chapter 13

The following day certainly wasn't getting any better for poor Inspector Fleece. By lunchtime, after six full hours of interrogation, he still hadn't got anything out of Tandori Birkett-fucking-Morris, other than, 'no comment'. He was beginning to regret taking on this case and, to add to his woes, forensics hadn't come up with a shred of evidence to implicate her in a terrorist plot. There had been no witnesses to her meeting gentlemen of Middle Eastern descriptions, or indeed anybody whatsoever, except for her flatmate Bethany.

He also hadn't bargained for the full force of Mrs Birkett-Morris's fury at discovering that her second daughter had been arrested and was being held on trumped up terrorism charges at Parsons Green Police Station. She had duly driven down in the Range Rover at high speed to get the immediate release for her beloved daughter. After parking illegally right outside the Police station entrance she stormed into the foyer and strode straight up to the front desk ignoring other members of the public waiting for attention.

'Now listen here my good man, I am not leaving this police station until I have seen my daughter and discussed her case with whichever imbecile of a detective is handling the situation. I want and expect her to be released immediately, you clearly have no evidence against the poor girl.'

The duty sergeant eyed her wearily having been on a twelve-hour shift with just one 15 minute break.

'And you are?'

'I am Mrs Clementine Birkett-Morris, the mother of Tandori Birkett-Morris and The Sun newspaper has kindly informed me that you are holding her on terrorism charges. I have never heard of anything so preposterous in all my born days.'

'Sadly madam we are not allowed to discuss individual cases, it's all down to the EU directive on privacy I'm afraid.'

'Afraid or not, I have it on good authority that you are holding my beloved daughter in custody and I want to speak to the inspector who is responsible for such an outrage.'

'I think you are looking for Inspector Fleece,' said the duty sergeant momentarily forgetting his oath of secrecy.

Just at that moment Fleece came round the corner and shouted to Constable Brahmes, 'Get me a Nescafe pet.

'Yes, Inspector Fleece,' she duly replied.

'Ah, so you're the creature I'm looking for – Inspector Fleece.'

'You what? And who may I ask are you?'

Bearing down on Fleece, Clementine Birkett-Morris extended her body to its full height of 6' and cast him a withering look.

'I am Tandori's mother, Mrs Birkett-Morris and I demand an immediate meeting with you, Inspector Fleece, to discuss when you intend to release my poor daughter with no charges brought and enact a full and unequivocal apology for the distress caused to her and myself.'

'You can demand what you like pet, but that isn't going to happen. Miss Birkett-Morris is still helping us with our enquiries and she will not be released, or seen by you or anyone else, until I have finished interrogating her, which could take many more days.'

'Firstly, Inspector Fleece, I am not your 'pet', and secondly, do you have any idea who you are talking to? My husband owns the largest private prison in the country and has direct contact with the Home Secretary every day, and I can assure you that this disgraceful state of affairs will not stand.'

'Well love, it will stand until I say so. Unless I get a message from the Chief Constable, which isn't going to happen, I don't care if your husband has links with the President of the United States. Come on Constable Brahmes, we have work to do.' With that, Fleece side-stepped Mrs Birkett-Morris and was off down the corridor towards the interview rooms.'

Mrs Birkett-Morris was shaking with rage and turned to the duty sergeant. 'Well, I have never been so insulted in all my life as by that ghastly little man. You have not heard the end of this!' And she was off, back towards the car park to get her Range Rover and phone her long-suffering husband.

As it happened, events overtook Mrs Birkett-Morris's plans, later that day the Chief Constable received a phone call from MI5 ordering the immediate release of Tandori Birkett-Morris on license for four months.

Inspector Fleece did not take the phone call well. 'What the fuck does he mean, Tandori Birkett-Morris is to be released on license?'

'I'm just passing on a message from the Chief Constable,' said Constable Brahmes. 'Don't take it out on me.'

'But I haven't finished interrogating her yet,' spluttered Inspector Fleece

'As far as I'm concerned, she is a dangerous terrorist suspect. I'm not releasing her until I've spoken to the Chief Constable myself and heard it from the horse's mouth.' With that he stormed off to get a Nescafe and find the Chief Constable's secretary.

Fleece stormed into the Chief Constable's outer office only to be confronted by an extremely efficient and implacable secretary, whose sole purpose was to make sure the Chief Constable was not disturbed by unnecessary intruders who did not have an appointment.

'I need to see the Chief Constable urgently, and I need to see him now.' stormed Inspector Fleece.

'Do you have an appointment?'

'Of course I don't have an appointment that's why I am here talking to a half-wit like you.'

'Unfortunately, you have to make an appointment and the Chief Constable is extremely busy,' said the secretary, ignoring completely the insult she had just received.

'Well, when is his next appointment, pet?' said Fleece his voice dripping with undisguised contempt.

'I'll just bring up his e-diary on the computer screen. Ah yes, next Wednesday at 3.30 p.m.' she said triumphantly.

'That's no bloody good to me, I have a dangerous terrorist being let out on licence and I bloody well went to know why, or if it's some ghastly mistake.'

'Ah, you mean Ms Tandori Birkett-Morris. I dealt with it myself. The order came direct from MI5, and we have specific instructions to let her go on an important mission. You can re-arrest her in four months if you have sufficient evidence by then. The email makes the situation perfectly clear, so I suggest you stop wasting everybody's time. What did you say your name was?'

'Fleece, Inspector Fleece.'

'Well Fleece, that's the situation so I suggest you be on your way to carry out some traffic duties or whatever else you get up to.'

Fleece had to withdraw with his tail between his legs, humiliated and seething. If it was the last bloody thing he was going to do, he was going to arrest Birkett-Morris and get the bitch put behind bars, but that would have to wait for at least four months now. It was lunchtime and he made the decision to retreat to the Whippet Inn for his usual pie and chips and a pint of smooth, and lick his wounds.

Chapter 14

Sydney Dresden Piffle was still in Benidorm at the Villa Almeria and had no idea of the goings on back in Blighty that were determining his fate.

After the night in the Black Chicken where he had stayed up till 1.00 a.m. celebrating his deal to build five hundred log cabins, he had gone home seriously drunk. He'd had a fumble with Honolulu and fallen asleep on the king size bed with his socks and underpants still on, and his dress shirt because he had been unable to undo the cufflinks.

He eventually woke with a stinking hangover at 11.00 o clock on Friday morning. He was disturbed by his phone bleeping loudly by his bed. It was a message from Wack saying Tracy and himself were getting a flight over Saturday morning and could Paeleo meet them in the Rolls? He wanted a good blow out to celebrate, and let the fox see the rabbit with regards the plot of land that Piffle had secured an option on. The flight was due in at 11.00 a.m. on Saturday, so he needed to remember to send Paleo to terminal 2 to wait in the usual spot for VIPs which

Piffle's Rolls secured.

'Mr Dresden, Mr Dresden, your breakfast is ready, if you come down there might be some extras!' shouted Honolulu.

Although normally Piffle would be more than happy to accept 'extras', this morning he was so hung over and knackered after last night at the Black Chicken, that extras were the last thing on his mind. He just wanted a good hearty breakfast of bacon, eggs, sausages and fried bread to mop up the excess alcohol and prepare himself for the busy day ahead. He had to be delicate though, because if he overtly spurned Honolulu's advances he was likely to get a violent reaction and he wasn't in the mood for that either.

'Eh up Honolulu, I'm on me way down, but I must warn you I'm feeling under weather,' he shouted hoping that it might put her off any hanky-panky.

'OK Mr Dresden, I have cooked you your favourite bacon, sausages, hash browns, eggy bread and beans just as you like it. Extras can wait until you are feeling less under the weather.'

Piffle arrived at the breakfast table grateful for the feast that awaited him. Honolulu certainly knew how to cook him his favourite fry-up. He was also more than pleased to see that she was wearing her naughty see-through nightie, which left nothing to the imagination. Maybe he should find the energy from somewhere to have extras after all. The old stirrings in his nether regions had already started to manifest themselves.

'You like Mr Dresden?' asked Honolulu, bending over provocatively on purpose exposing her massive posterior for his attention. She knew exactly what buttons to press.

'I bloody well do like,' exclaimed Piffle and, after tucking into his breakfast, he could not resist tucking into Honolulu again. The woman was just too much for him to resist. Yet again he was late for his afternoon meeting where he was to sign the papers purchasing the Playa de Sol caravan park.

As usual, Paeleo was waiting outside in the Rolls Royce Silver Spur, engine running to keep the air conditioning on, burning fuel at a gallon every 15 minutes.

'Why I have to wait here in the heat while Piffle gets his leg over?' muttered Paeleo under his breath. 'He could have said 1.30 instead of 1.00. No consideration, why he can't sort out Honolulu at night when it is cool like everyone else, not natural in the heat of the day, what they say? Mad Englishman go out in the midday sun, he should be having a siesta,' thought Paeleo. Never mind he was being paid €15 an hour, so what did he care?

Piffle rushed out to the car late as usual.

'Come on lad, let's get Rolls motoring, need to be at Playa de Sol in 30 minutes. Cheque to hand over to owner. This is the big one Paeleo' said Piffle grinning like a Cheshire cat.

Off they sped from the Villa Almeria, down the mountain road into Benidorm. Piffle was in the back with the burr walnut table in the down position, a shot of single malt scotch resting on the table in cut glass luxury. He was celebrating already, salivating at the deal he was about to sign. Piffle was soon on his second, and then third, double scotch and was getting more and more merry, especially as he had yet to recover from the night before. He started to sing loudly and out of tune, much to Paeleo's disquiet.

'Bring me sunshine, all the while, bring me sunshine with a smile, in this world that we live there can be more happiness, bring me sunshine bring me laughter bring me joy.'

He had got all the words wrong to the famous Morecambe and Wise theme tune, but the song put Piffle in a better and better mood, even if he couldn't get it quite right. On and on he sang, getting louder and louder. If anyone could have heard him other than Paeleo, they would have thought he was stark staring mad.

In no time they were turning into the Playa de Sol Caravan park. It didn't look like a million euros at the moment, but Piffle had a dream in his mind, five hundred luxury log cabins set in a pine wood. He could see it now, he just needed to write the cheque and hand it over to Cormac, the mad Irishman who owned the site. There he was, sitting in a top-of-the-range Lexus by one of the rotting caravans at the front of the site, a few stray dogs barking near the car.

'Eh up Cormac,' shouted Piffle as he got out of the Rolls, slurring his words and clearly already half pissed. 'I've got the boodle lad just ready to sign cheque and we can be away.'

'Ah be Jesus that sounds good to me young Piffle.'

Cormac was in a fine mood as well. He couldn't wait to get rid of the derelict piece of land he had won from a gambling bet many years ago which had gone to rack and ruin. He had no planning permission for development and couldn't really understand why this mad northern Englishman wanted to give him a million euros. He could only think that Piffle was building a supermarket, or maybe a factory or warehouse once he had cleared the site, which would be no mean feat given all the pine trees to remove.

'Come on my good friend lets go inside the caravan and sign the deeds over and you write me a cheque. I need it making out to Mallin Haulage Limited, helps me with the Irish tax authorities, save old Cormac a packet, they are registered in the British Virgin Islands'

'I don't bloody mind who I make cheque out to lad, as long as I get deeds signed over. That's the top and bottom of it and your dealings with the tax authorities are up to you'

They went into the grimy caravan that hadn't seen use in at least twenty years and sat down at the small table. Piffle got his company cheque book out and wrote out a cheque for €1 million. Cormac's eyes sparkled and he signed the document, prepared by the lawyers, signing over the deeds. It was that simple. Cormac shook Piffle's chubby hand and was off like a shot, back to the Lexus. Piffle couldn't believe the speed old Cormac moved, 'can't you stay for a quick celebratory drink' he shouted, but Cormac had other ideas.

'See you around young Piffle. I hope the good Lord brings you luck and happiness. I'm off back to the emerald isle to celebrate with the lads this weekend,' and he was gone out of Piffle's life forever.

Piffle just sat there in the caravan looking at the title deeds. Bloody hell, he thought. This is bloody it. €1 million in cash paid out, €27 million coming his way in the not too distant future. Then retirement to Spain and a life of womanizing, sun and sangria.

He started humming and then laughing and then singing loudly in the empty caravan.

'Bring me sunshine, all the while, bring me sunshine with a smile, in this world that we live there can be more happiness, bring me sunshine bring me laughter bring me fucking joy!'

Paeleo wondered what on earth his boss was doing. Crazy Englishman sitting in an empty caravan singing loudly. They are all mad as hatters thought Paeleo. Eventually Piffle emerged with a big silly grin on his face, which was most unusual, and staggered over to the Rolls.

'Come on Paeleo, me old mucker, get me to Black Chicken, I've got a lot to celebrate. You can have rest of day off and I'll text you when I want picking up tonight later on when I've had a skin full.'

Off they sped in the Rolls into town, with Piffle still singing loudly in the back.

'Who wants to be a fucking millionaire? I do! Who wants to drive a fancy car? I do! Who wants to go to a fancy hotel? A fancy hotel?

Yes, a fancy hotel. Who wants to go to St Tropez? I do...!' On and on until, within ten minutes, they were outside the Black Chicken.

'See you later Paeleo and remember lad, I'll text you when I'm ready, but it will be about midnight lad.'

With that, he staggered up the steps and disappeared through the double swing doors into the murky world of the Black Chicken and found his favourite table. It was only 3.30 p.m. but Piffle was determined to celebrate in style and enjoy the rest of the day. He would be busy entertaining Wack and Tracy over the weekend and discussing the log cabins in more detail, so it was time to let his hair down.

Marco, the owner of the Black Chicken, wasn't there at this time of day to meet and greet him. The bar was mostly deserted, save for a few English and Irish holidaymakers who had started early, or were playing cards or dominos. However, the staff at the Black Chicken knew that Piffle was one of their best customers and it didn't take long for a barman by the name of Christian to come over to his table and take the order.

'Eh up lad about bloody time. Get us a bottle of your best champers, I've got a lot of bloody celebrating to do.'

'Of course Mr Piffle, consider it done, the best champagne coming to your table in a jiffy.'

Piffle didn't mind drinking alone, and in any case as the evening progressed there would soon be someone he could talk to and so it proved. By about 8.00, Piffle was truly hammered and ready to boast to anyone who would listen. Three bottles of best champagne later and Piffle was singing like a canary.

He had latched onto a family from Dagenham. Although Frank Drake and his wife and daughter didn't really want to listen to a drunken Piffle extol the virtues of making money and buying a site to build five hundred log cabins, that was what they were destined to endure.

'Well the thing is Frank me old mucker, I can call you Frank can't I? Seeing as we are friends an all.'

'Whatever you say Dresden.'

'Well the thing is, it's like this. Money has to work for you lad. It's no use sitting there, five million quid of it earning you bugger all interest while some bastard of a bank lends it out at 18% to some other poor sod. Or even more if its them payday loans at hundreds of percent.'

'Waiter get us another bottle of champers, and whatever these good people want. What you having Frank, bottle of Becks, white wine for his missus and pear cider for young Emily there. As I was saying, thing is no point having five million quid earning you one bloody percent from a bunch of capitalist leeches, who lend your five million quid out ten times over at a huge profit for doing bugger all. That's why I joined Labour Party at 16, to right the injustices of the capitalist system and help working class reach their potential. So, bought me a huge plot of land on outskirts of Benidorm and going to build five hundred luxury log cabins and flog 'em to rich Brits wanting a bit of luxury, sun and sangria. What do you think Frank?'

'Sounds like a plan Dresden,' said Frank diplomatically. In truth, he was not the least bit interested in Piffle's dream of a log cabin empire, but quite interested in the free booze Piffle was providing him and his family.

On the next table Piffle's boasting of five million quid did not go unnoticed. Two mature, extremely fat, single ladies were on the look out for a bit of action from the local Spanish talent. They were not having much luck due to their extremely course behaviour, the deficiencies in the looks department and the fact that they were both challenged by extreme size. Tracy and Mandy were both well past their prime but not adverse to some lurid sexual activity and as much booze as they could get down their necks.

'Eh up Tracy, listen to him at next table. Sounds like he's got a bit of money to splash about, and we're skint now that week is nearly up,' said Mandy.

'Do you think he might be up for a bit. I certainly am, haven't had any

all week and I'm gagging for it.'

'Thought you wanted a young Spanish stud to do you doggie style in shower cubicle? That one is old and fat, not really what I was looking for' said Tracy dubiously.

'Listen Tracy, you don't look a gift horse in the gob do you. Maybe he is old, ugly and fat, but you heard him mention five million quid, and look how he's dressed. Full suit and tie. You don't get that in Black Chicken normally.'

'Eh up mate, do you fancy getting two sexy ladies a drink. I'm gagging for it here.'

Piffle looked round in a drunken stupor. He hadn't noticed the girls before now, but when he did, he realized that his night was going to get a whole lot better. In his drunken haze he saw two beautiful, sexy ladies, just the sort he liked and they were coming onto him. He couldn't believe his luck. The drink had taken its devastating toll and blinded Piffle to the consequences of his actions. His beer goggle eyes determined that Tracy and Mandy were goddesses and I couldn't resist their unlikely charms! It was a decision he was going to live to regret.

Chapter 15

Back in England, Gary Wacker and his wife Tracy were busy packing their suitcases to get the early morning flight from Robin Hood Airport to Alicante.

Over at Maxwell House, Church Lane, Beverley, Pauline Piffle was doing the same. Being friends with Tracy, she had phoned her only to discover that they were flying out on the 7.00 a.m. flight to Alicante and Paeleo was meeting them at 9.30 a.m. to take them to the Villa Almeria. On the spur of the moment she had decided to join them and surprise Dresden. She hadn't seen him all week and by all accounts they had something to celebrate as it appeared Dresden had finally got the planning permission for five hundred luxury log cabins on the Playa de Sol Caravan Park on the outskirts of Benidorm.

Pauline was a very proud women and not prone to travelling lightly, even for a short stay, although she planned to stay the week. She already had two extremely large suitcases filled to the brim and hand luggage as well. Piffle called her a Clothes Horse but in truth she just liked to look her best and liked nice things – even if she carried way too many of them. The telephone rang. It was Tracy Wacker.

'Hello love, it's Tracy. Just seeing if you're packed and alright for the morning? Gary and me will be round at 4.00 a.m. to pick so up so we can get to the airport for 5.00. Is that alright love?'

'Yes, that's fine Tracy. I'm all packed. Just got to drop the key off with next door so old Mr Stewart can come round and feed the cats. He loves my cats and it gives him something to do at his age. I'll be ready. I can't wait to see Dresden's face when I appear at the Villa without him expecting me. It's the first time I've ever done that.'

'That's nice love. I'm glad someone is looking after your pussy cats and yes, Dresden will be so surprised to see you. Though you know him, he'll be straight into talking business with Gary. He is made up you know about the order for five hundred log cabins. It's his biggest ever order and great for his firm and the staff in Hull who work for him. I'll see you in the morning then, 4.00 a.m. sharp.'

'Don't worry Tracy, I'll be up and ready. I always like to be early and look my best.'

Pauline went downstairs to make herself some tea, she needed to be in bed by 9.00 if she was getting up at 3.00. But first she did as she said she would, and took the key around to old Mr Stewart.

'Hello Mr Stewart. Here are the keys to the back door. Now you will look after my pussies won't you. They miss me terrible when I am away.'

'Don't you worry Pauline my dear, I love looking after them, gives me something to do at my age, and they are no trouble, popping in and out of their cat flap and eat their food they do.'

'I should be away about a week this time Mr Stewart. I'll ring you from Benidorm and let you know when I'll be back. Thanks again for stepping in at short notice.'

'No trouble my dear, I'll look forward to hearing from you.'

Lovely woman, thought Mr Stewart as Pauline walked back to her house. Too good for that ignorant Piffle. Never could abide the man, he mused.

Chapter 16

Aga-doo-doo-doo, push pineapple, shake the tree. Aga-doo-doo-doo, push pineapple, grind coffee...

The girls were up dancing with Piffle at the Black Chicken and everything was wobbling.

To the left, to the right, jump up and down to the knees...

Piffle couldn't take his eyes off Mandy's chest as is bounced up and down to the song.

'Eh up Mandy, I think the randy old goat wants to give you a good seeing to,' shouted Tracy above the music.

'Give over Tracy. Maybe if I get me knockers out, he might go for it.'

'Eh up mate, catch an eyeful of these big knockers,' and with that Mandy pulled her top down and out they popped, swinging in all directions.

Piffle's eyes nearly popped out of his head as well.

'Bloody hell lass, I haven't seen a pair as big as them since the Durham Miners Gala in 1982.'

Then the Black Lace song started and off they all went at speed.

Do-do-do. Come on and do the conga. Do-do-do. It's conga night for sure.

It's conga, its conga night so join the party everyone. The night has just begun and we're all having fun tonight. Dance the conga till you drop. We're never gonna stop. You better hang on tight.

So everybody...

Do-do-do. Come on and do the conga. Choo-choo-choo that train across the floor. You-you-you. Come on and join the conga. Do-do-do it's conga night for sure.

Round and round they went, until Piffle's head was spinning even more, from the mixture of drink and fun.

'Come on ladies. Let's get back to my villa and let the party continue,' shouted Piffle above the music. 'I'll get the Rolls and Paeleo can take us back.'

'Whatever you say big boy,' shouted Mandy.

'Come on Tracy, we're in here. Never done it with a millionaire before.'

Out they staggered to the long suffering Paeleo. It was past 1.00 a.m. and they all got into the back of the Rolls somehow, laughing raucously, landing on top of each other in a jumble of chaos.

'Home James, and don't spare the horses,' shouted Piffle now steaming drunk.

'Ooh bugger me Tracy, this is posh in here ain't it.'

'Get his pants off and we'll give him a blow job.'

'Bloody hell girls you don't hang about,' squeaked Piffle as his manhood received the Tracy and Mandy treatment.

Mandy started trying to suck as hard as she could, while Tracy grabbed poor Piffle's bits.

'Bloody hell Tracy he's shot his bolt and we've only been doing him for a minute. How am I going to get some manhood tonight now?'

'We'll have to give it time to recover,' Tracy said with a course laugh. Although in truth, given poor Piffle's state, that was highly unlikely.

Finally, they reached the Villa Almeria and poured themselves out of the car laughing hysterically. Fortunately, Honolulu was in the housekeeper's lodge that adjoined the property and didn't hear them come back. Piffle still had his trousers round his ankles and struggled to get to the front door, hopping along hopelessly.

Paeleo left them to it and he sped off in the Rolls so he could get some sleep in his own bed before the early morning pickup. He could see disaster looming if Mrs Pauline found out what had been going on, luckily it was just Gary and Tracy Wacker that he was due to meet at Alicante International Airport, or so he thought.

Up the stairs they staggered.

'Bet you've never had a three way for a while have you Dresden?' laughed Mandy.

As it turned out, Piffle was in no fit state to carry through the sexual antics the girls hoped for. In truth, however much they tried he couldn't get anything up again and they all fell asleep on the king sized bed. sandwiching Piffle in the middle with Mandy next to him and Tracy's legs resting against his face the other side as she had got into bed facing the wrong way, topping and tailing poor Piffle.

That was the best it got for Piffle – the next morning all hell was about to break out.

Chapter 17

It started with Honolulu coming into the main house in the morning to make Piffle his usual cooked breakfast. She could smell the cheap perfume, but it was the king-sized bras and pants she found strewn on the stairs that made her realize that Piffle was not alone. He had brought back a couple of tarts for the night, judging by the number of garments.

She was absolutely furious, and jealous. It was one thing that he was married. Quite another that she had to share her Dresden with a couple of tartlets, and large tartlets at that. How could he? Didn't she, Honolulu, provide him with all he needed in that department?

She started stomping around the kitchen muttering to herself in Spanish, but still preparing the breakfast. Bang clatter thump.

Not that Piffle heard a thing, he was still gone to the world as were Mandy and Tracy, and in any case they were all naked and their clothes were not immediately to hand. Honolulu bundled all the clothes up and put them in a black bin bag. If Gary and Tracy Wacker were coming this morning, she didn't want to embarrass them by leaving bras and knickers strewn on the staircase.

It was just before 10.00 a.m. when the Rolls Royce Silver Spur came up the gravel drive. Paeleo came round and opened the back doors for the guests and opened the boot to get the suitcases out. It was the first time Gary and Tracy Wacker had been to the Villa Almeria and they were very impressed. Paeleo had been very surprised to find that Mrs Piffle was with the party and secretly amused at the potential situation his master, Dresden Piffle, was about to find himself in.

'Bloody hell Tracy, my love this is a bit of alright. Not quite the Gipsyville estate is it?' said Gary in awe.

'It's beautiful Gary. Wish we could afford something like this.' Said Tracy eyeing the mock colonial property with obvious envy

'We will my pet, once we have delivered five hundred log cabins in two years' time.'

Gary wasn't joking. He would make a million quid out of this deal. More than enough to get a villa every bit as nice as the Villa Almeria.

Honolulu was at the double fronted solid mahogany door, scowling at the guests with her arms folded, even though they had no hand in Piffle's dubious actions of the night before.

'Hello, you must be Mr and Mrs Wacker and of course I have met you Mrs Dresden before, but I did not think you were coming?'

'Well Honolulu, I decided to surprise you both,' Pauline said with a flourish. She was fairly sure that Honolulu was more than just a housekeeper to Piffle, more like a friend with benefits.

In they went to the hallway.

'Where is Dresden?' asked Pauline, peering into the kitchen expecting him to be eating a full English breakfast by now.

'Not up yet, he got tipsy last night and I make breakfast. You want eggs and bacon?'

'That would be lovely,' said Gary.

'I'm going up to wake Dresden. It's after 10.00 and he should have been up to greet his guests. Unforgivable. I'm really sorry Gary.'

'Don't worry love, I am sure he had a celebration last night. The lad deserves that after signing the log cabin deal,' said Gary

She quickly climbed the stairs ready to surprise Dresden. As it turned out they were both in for a surprise, in fact a serious shock!

'Dresden, Dresden, it's me your Pauline,' she shouted as she climbed the stairs.

In his bed Piffle was stirring. He was sure he had heard his wife's voice, but he must be dreaming as the 'Clothes Horse' was back in Hull, where she belonged. It was obviously some terrible dream he was still having

'Dresden, Dresden are you up? I've come to surprise you.'

Suddenly, Piffle was awake.

There could be no mistaking. Pauline Piffle was in the bloody villa. Oh my god. He looked to his left to see a huge snoring Mandy and to his right, the tree trunk legs of Tracy. Both he and them were completely stark bollock naked.

It was too late. Pauline opened the bedroom door to be greeted by a site so disgusting that she could scarcely take it in. Piffle was so disorientated he didn't know who was in bed with him or why, and more to the point what, his wife was doing peering in at him. He must be still dreaming, but no, that avenue of hope was soon brutally taken away by Pauline's shrill voice.

Chapter 18

'You bastard!' screamed Pauline.

'Oh bloody hell Pauline, it's not what it seems.'

'Not what it seems Sydney Dresden Piffle, I'll give you it's not what it seems!' shrieked Pauline.

She spotted a baseball bat that Piffle kept by the bed in case of intruders and grabbed it. By this time the two drunken ladies, Mandy and Tracy, were both wide awake and had sized up the situation perfectly. Unfortunately, they were stark bollock naked and worse still ,didn't know where their clothes were. What they did know was that this crazy women had a baseball bat and was about to attack them and beat them to a pulp, or worse.

'Come on Tracy, let's make a run for it.'

For two extremely large ladies they were able to move at a remarkable pace and were soon flying out the door. Pauline was not interested in stopping them, her attentions were firmly focused on the hapless Piffle.

Mandy and Tracy flew down the stairs their bossoms bouncing in all directions and Honolulu was waiting for them with the black bin bag in the hallway.

'Here you are ladies, I have your knickers and bras here. I speak to Paeleo the chauffeur and he run you back into town. Otherwise I think Mrs Dresden will be after you soon enough.'

Mandy and Tracy didn't need convincing, they had seen the hatred in Pauline Piffle's eyes and the baseball bat, which had a deadly intent of its own. They managed to get their knickers on but at this stage just grabbed their bras and flew out to the car.

Paeleo had the engine running and the door open, they got in the back, closed the door and Paeleo sped off up the drive with gravel spraying in all directions. Paeleo's erratic driving completely out of keeping for a car of the Rolls Royce's stature.

'Bloody hell Tracy, I thought that mad bitch was going to beat us to death, and we didn't even get a good seeing to. Sod that for a game of soldiers.'

'Yeah, I know Mandy, we do get into some scrapes don't we? Have to see what Spanish talent we can pick up on our last night. I've come here for a good few sex sessions and still haven't had any takers. That Dresden was all mouth and no action. I've never sucked so hard and he still didn't get it up. I'd have bought your vibrating dildo along if I thought it was going to be that unresponsive.'

By the time they got to the Hotel Continental they had at least got their bras and knickers on, but walking to reception and getting their room key was an ordeal even they didn't want to repeat in a hurry.

Chapter 19

Sydney Dresden Piffle didn't want to repeat any aspect of the ordeal he was now facing. Pauline Piffle was repeatedly whacking him with the baseball bat and he was cowering by the bed. It was only the fact that he was extremely fat that she wasn't damaging vital organs, but she certainly was inflicting significant bruising. It was certainly the last time in a long time that he was going to let his penis rule his head.

'Leave it off woman, how was I to know you were coming to Villa to surprise me?'

'Oh yes, I certainly surprised you didn't I, Sydney Dresden Piffle? Well, let me tell you, if I ever catch you again in bed with another woman, and I use the term loosely in terms of the two ugly fat slags I have just witnessed, I will make sure your vital organ never works again, do I make myself clear? Anyway, I'm taking myself off into Benidorm and meeting my friend Marjorie as soon as Paeleo gets back, which will be shortly, and I will be going on a shopping spree the likes of which you have never seen, using your gold card. Do you understand?'

'Yes,' was all Piffle managed whimpering by the bed.

'Oh, and another thing, you've embarrassed our guests, so I suggest you get yourself showered and washed and into some decent clothes and then come down and entertain them whilst I'm gone. They have not come all this way to sit in our kitchen on their own, have they?'

And with that she flounced out of the room leaving Piffle to recover what little dignity he had left. She went downstairs and apologised to Gary and Tracy Wacker.

Soon, Paeleo returned and she got into the Rolls and was off into Benidorm town for the day.

'Bloody hell, I've never seen Dresden get into such a scrape before,' said Gary Wacker.

'No, well, from what I can see, he's had it too easy for too long. Too much rope and the bugger has gone and hanged himself. Poor Pauline. I didn't know where to put myself.'

'You're not wrong there lass. Anyway, let's see if we can get some breaky off Honolulu before the old bugger surfaces. I'm sure he is going to want to show us the log cabin development site. That's if he is up to it. Eh up Honolulu, any chance of some nosh, me and Tracy are bloody starving, what with all that excitement an all, you don't get anything on those cheap budget airlines anymore.'

'Ah Mr Wacker, I will get you a proper English fry up in a jiffy.

You just see if I don't, but I too have a few bones, as you English say, to pick with Dresden,'

Piffle might have been bashed black and blue by his wife, but he wasn't yet ready to concede defeat. It was still a bloody amazing day. The start of his plan to be extremely wealthy and the first step towards getting rid of the bloody 'Clothes Horse missus' that has held him back all those years.

Down the stairs he came, putting on a brave face and a beaming smile which was genuinely meant for his longstanding friend Gary Wacker.

'Eh up Gary, and nice to see you Trace, I hope the beautiful Honolulu is looking after you both. I see she has done you an English fry up.'

'Well it's great to see you too Dresden, sorry you've had a spot of bother lad with the missus like.'

'Don't you worry Gary, water under a duck's back, a little local misunderstanding. Once she's used the gold card with Marjorie she'll be right as rain, you mark me words.'

'Little local misunderstanding was it? And what about those two ladies of the night as you say that were in your bed?'

Honolulu had made an appearance and was not in the mood to be as conciliatory as Dresden's two guests.

'Now listen here Honolulu.'

'Don't you listen me, Sydney Dresden Piffle. I thought I was the special one, I thought it was me you wanted, and now I find that any old slapper will do. You can make your own breakfast Dresden, I am, as you say, otherwise dispossessed.'

'Disposed, woman, disposed, and I don't like you airing your dirty washing in public Honolulu. You're embarrassing me guests, now run along and make poor Dresden a fry up. You know it makes sense.'

'There is only one person with dirty linen and that is you. There is some spare breakfast in the frying pan, I suggest you get it yourself, as helping yourself seems to be, as you say, your speciality.'

With that, Honolulu waddled off to attend to more important matters.

'Take no notice of that stupid woman, she doesn't know what she is talking about. Seems she has got some kind of crush on me for Christ's sake.'

'Don't worry Dresden, we won't say anything.' said Tracy.

'What do you mean, won't say anything? There's bloody nothing to say. Look, let's just finish breakfast and get Paeleo to take us to log cabin site, you need to get a handle on what needs to be done.'

'OK Dresden, whatever you say. Can't wait,' said Gary, deciding wisely to change the conversation to more mundane things.

In due course the Rolls was summoned and off they went to the log cabin site to get down to business.

Chapter 20

Monday morning, 9.00 a.m. sharp, the team meeting was taking place at Humberwold Speed Camera Action! Limited. All the staff were present, standing in neat regimented rows, chanting the company's slogans.

'Mike is Great, Mike is Great, the greatest boss there ever was!'

'Mike is Great, Mike is Great, he's the best a boss can be, be sure to spread the word!'

Mike Morrell the boss of the Humberwold Speed Camera Action! Partnership Limited had been on one of those annoying team building courses and come away with the impression that his staff had to chant slogans of dubious authenticity to get the messages into their subconscious minds and thus improve performance or more accurately improve profits for Mike Morrell. As a result, the team building sessions took place every Monday morning for thirty long minutes.

'Death on the roads is due to speeding, death on the roads is due to speeding, death on the roads is due to speeding, ee-i-ee-i-o.'

'One mile an hour is all it takes, all it takes, all it takes, one mile an hour is all it takes to end a kiddies life.'

On and on the chanting went for the mandatory thirty minutes, with Mike Morrell standing at the front like a conductor of an important orchestra.

'Right people, back to work, speeders to be caught, criminal scum to be prosecuted, no exceptions and no mercy. I want all the major routes into Grimewold covered and I want as many villages patrolled by the Pure Profit Groups. Get to it and no bloody excuses.' That was his favourite saying, no excuses, together with bring me a solution not a problem!

Mike strode off purposely to the board room to have the morning targets meeting with his senior team.

'Janice, coffee and cream cakes for six of us this morning, it's going to be a long one.'

'Right you are Mr Morrell. I'll bring coffee and cream cakes immediately.'

Mike Morrell's senior management team were waiting in the board room expectantly. All six looked round as Mike entered the room.

'Right team, I'm not happy, do you all understand? I set targets three months ago and Janice has given me the figures and they bloody well don't stack up and I want fucking answers. Do you all understand?'

'Yes Mr Morrell,' they said in unison.

'I told you all that we needed one hundred pure profit teams recruited to cover every fucking village in North Humberwold, didn't I? And how many have we got Paul?' Paul began to stammer an answer but was interrupted by Mike Morrell again. 'I'll fucking tell you how many pure profit teams we've got Paul, two. Two fucking pure profit teams. That's a shortfall of 98 by my reckoning, so what have you got to say? What have you got to fucking say?'

Paul Purvis was in charge of business development and had the unenviable task of trying to implement the completely unrealistic edicts of Mike Morrell. One hundred pure profit teams in three months was not just challenging, it was impossible.

'The problem is Mike, it's impossible to recruit a hundred pure profit teams in the timescale you've given me. They don't get paid and it's bloody hard to recruit them.'

'What I want to know Paul, what I bloody well want to know is, what do I bloody pay you for? Remind me what you're on, that's right, fifty bloody grand, plus a work place pension, plus a Jag as a company car. You told me, or should I say, bullshitted me that you were a top bleeding Business Development Manager, and what I actually find is, you couldn't bloody organise a piss up in a brewery.'

'I think your being a bit unfair there, Mike,' Paul ventured. It was a mistake.

'A bit bloody unfair do you? Well I'll tell you what's a bit bloody unfair. I pay you fifty grand, plus perks, for not bringing in any extra fucking revenue. That's what's bloody unfair. Each of those old biddies you're going to recruit should be bringing in a thousand a week minimum. That's a hundred thousand quid a week extra for no additional outlay. That's why they are called pure profit teams. We get 65% of that revenue, so you, Paul, are costing me at least sixty five grand a week due to your utter bleeding incompetence. Do you all understand? I sincerely bloody hope so.'

Mike Morrell was now banging the table and his skin colour had turned decidedly puce. He was, in a word, livid and in no mood for compromise. The six managers round the table looked decidedly unwell themselves. They were used to Mike Morrell's unique management style and intense outbursts of frustration, but it still didn't make it any easier working with the man.

Emily Sanders, his Finance Manager, tried to calm the situation. A timid, but determined young lady, Emily had stood up to Morrell in the past and as he quite fancied getting in her knickers, she got away with things that the others would not be able to.

'Mike, if I may just say,'

'What now? What the hell have you got to say Miss Prissy Knickers?'

'Mike, what I've got to say is, look at the bigger picture. Revenue is up 38% in the last month that figures are available and costs are falling. We're making over a million pounds a month after paying the police their 35% share of revenue, and that makes us the second most profitable business in Grimewold after Mc Greggor Steel who've been around for over 150 years. You must admit that's an impressive achievement by the team, and we have overtaken Dresden Piffle by a country mile.'

Emily calculated that reminding Mike that he was far more successful than his arch-rival, Dresden Piffle, would calm the situation and lift his spirits. Thus is proved to be the case.

'Well alright Emily. I've got to admit you have a point there, a million a month eh?'

'That's right and when we've recruited the hundred pure profit teams that profit will rise by another two million a year. That will be £15 million a year and you will be making six times what Piffle is. And it's all down to your superior management Mike.'

Mike's chest puffed out, and for the first time in the meeting a wide smile came over his face. Emily had shrewdly calculated that massaging Morrell's huge ego was the way to smooth the meeting. Just to make sure, she leant forward showing him a glimpse of her cleavage and the promise of things to come, or not to come as Emily hoped.

'Well alright team, I suppose young Emily here has a good point, but I want those hundred teams in place pronto, and I want all of you to help Paul achieve it. Do I make myself clear? Better tuck into the cream cakes and coffee then.'

The meeting was swiftly brought to a close but as everyone was leaving, Mike asked for John Harper to stay back. John was his right-hand man, his fixer who had been there from the start.

'John just a quick word may I?' said Morrell in a conciliatory tone.

'What do you want Mike?'

'Listen, just between you and me. I want us to win the contract off Piffle. I know the council aren't happy. He's upsetting a lot of people and we can benefit from that. I've always hated him and I want the bugger sunk so bleeding deep that the body will never be found. Can you start making a few enquiries, you know putting the feelers out. I'm sure we can win that contract.'

'Consider it done Mike. I think we can achieve that.'

And with that, the morning meeting drew to a close and Mike Morrell went back to his office in the atrium a relatively happy man. He reflected on the Senior Management meeting and basked in the thought that he was very much in charge and they were all too scared to stand up to him, just how he liked it. He also gave some thought to young Emily, much promise there he thought in more ways than one!

Chapter 21

Piffle was equally happy as he took Gary and Tracy Wacker to the Playa de Sol Caravan Park which he had just brought and showed Gary the lie of the land.

'As you can see Gary, it's a flat site with lovely conifer trees. Just needs clearing and the hard standing, drains and roadways putting in and then you can work your magic with the log cabins. If we get a couple erected, then we can sell off plan and take deposits and then final payment once the log cabins have been built and fitted out. Should be a piece of piss. As we go on, the profits from one set of log cabins will pay for the next set. Just do them in sets of ten, that's me idea.'

Paeleo was overhearing his master's thoughts on the log cabin sight and saw an opportunity to enhance his meagre salary and make some back shish, as Piffle called it.

'I say Mr Dresden, I might be able to help you with the hard standing, the roads and the drains. I know very good man with a building company who can do all of it for a very good price and bring in workers from Indian subcontinent and put them in dormitories. Very good price, you just trust me.'

At hearing the words 'very cheap price' Dresden's ears pricked up and he was immediately interested. If he could save a few bob then the profits would be that much greater.

'Eh up lad, did I hear you say you might know someone who could do ground works for good price? If you can put him in touch with me there might be a little something in it for you young Paeleo.'

Paeleo was thinking along similar lines, but had something a little more substantial in mind. He was thinking of an introductory fee of around 10% and as he estimated that the ground works would cost around €2 million for five hundred log cabins, including landscaping, then he could be in for 250 thousand euros, enough to retire from being Piffle's dogsbody. Yes, Paeleo deserved the finer things in life.

'Ah yes Mr Piffle, I can get you very good price. My friend knows the main contractor who did the Benidorm bypass. His name is Miguel Andretti. My friend gets you special, what you English say, mates rates. He brings in labour from Indian state of Kerala and that saves many thousands of euros which he will gladly pass onto you Mr Piffle. He is a very generous man.'

'Well young Paeleo, sounds bloody ideal. What do you think Gary? Must be a good contractor if he's done Benidorm bypass.'

'Well Dresden, you'll have to check him out and make sure he's kosher. Can't be too careful if you are spending millions of euros putting in ground works. Can't erect the log cabins until all that work is done. I'd be very careful Dresden. If I were you, I'd bring in an English contractor with proper English labour. Pay you in the long run, less hassle and they'll have all the public liability in place and a proper contract with payment for over runs.'

'Have to see Gary. It's alright you telling me that I've got to have this and that protection and use top drawer tradesmen, but you're not stumping up the bloody bills, are you? Money doesn't grow on trees. I hear what you're saying, but I think young Paeleo might be onto something.'

'I'm just saying Dresden, be careful. You know what Spanish builders are like.'

'I know what bloody British builders are like an all Gary, and it's not a pretty sight.'

'I thought you was Labour party through and through, up the workers and all that?' Gary quipped.

'Don't take the piss out of me, Gary. Money is money and graft is graft and that is that. I'll say no more.'

'I've said my piece and that's all on the matter. When the ground works are in, I can deliver the log cabins and erect them ten at a time, no problem, but I'll need to be paid the full price on delivery and erection. I can't carry the cost of ten log cabins or more on my books. Is that ok with you Dresden?'

'No problem Gary, I'll already have the deposits from the punters, and they've got to pay the full price as soon as the log cabins are handed over to them. Cash flow won't be a problem and that's a fact.'

So they shook on the deal there and then, Gary was over the moon having his biggest ever contract that would keep his Hull firm going for two years and Piffle could see huge profits coming in once he had got the deposits coming in, a win win as Piffle liked to say.

'Think we need a little celebration don't we Gary, so they got back into the Rolls and Piffle instructed Paeleo to take them all to the Black Chicken, they would be there by lunch time and he could carry on avoiding the clothes horse and Honolulu until things had calmed down!

Chapter 22

Despite being arrested as a suspected ISIS terrorist, Tandori Birkett-Morris found herself released on license and was now a free women. Constable Brahmes escorted her from the cell and into a waiting room where her mother was waiting for her.

'Oh my darling Tandori, I never thought I was ever going to get you out and away from that horrible Inspector Fleece, this is marvellous, just marvellous.'

'Oh mummy, it's been fucking horrendous. All I did was slip on a bar of Imperial Leather soap and look what's happened to me. I am seriously thinking of suing Proctor and Gamble for making their soap so fucking slippery.'

'Never mind about that Tandori, I'm just glad to have you back. Now let's get to the Range Rover and get you home to your bedroom. You must be exhausted poor dear, and away from these horrible policemen.'

Within no time they were out of Parsons Green Police Station and soon on their way to the little village of Brampton on Stow in an exclusive part of the Cotswolds, not far from Broadway. There were clear advantages to owning the largest male high security prison in the country, and Mr Birkett-Morris was one to take full advantage of his extensive wealth.

However, if Tandori Birkett-Morris thought she was going to be staying in the lap of luxury for long in her bedroom, well away from the realities of life, she was very much mistaken. Others, who she was unaware of, were already plotting her future. Unfortunately for her, it involved the town of Grimewold and a certain Sydney Dresden Piffle, a man she knew nothing about but would soon come to dominate her every waking hour. In the meantime Birkett-Morris could enjoy her freedom and the loving company of her close family.

Winton J Cuncliff-Owen had gone to all the trouble to have Tandori Birkett-Morris freed on licence by MI5 and now it was time to reel her in; it was payback time for Miss Birkett-Morris.

He needed her recruited into Dresden Piffle's business as soon as possible, preferably in a position of authority where she could be given explicit instructions to wreak havoc on Piffle's empire. Not that he believed for one moment she would need much encouragement. If that poor grade two listed Victorian block of flats was anything to go by, Piffle didn't stand a chance. She had utterly destroyed the place and he hoped she would do the same to the Diversity Action Partnership Limited. Given her track record of incompetence at MI5 and the Tory

Central Office, he was in no doubt that she was the right 'man' for the job, so to speak.

He had already had a preliminary meeting with Hazelhurst at MI5 headquarters. Hazelhurst had been diligently doing background checks on Piffle's little empire and had dug up some very interesting information about how it was run and who was really in charge.

It transpired that Zara Biddle was the power behind the throne and she was already a 'person of interest' as far as MI5 was concerned. An extremely dangerous ultra-left-wing feminist, with views so extreme they threatened the whole established order of how things were done in Great Britain, and she was the de facto boss of the Diversity Action Partnership Limited. Sydney Dresden Piffle was never there and not in day to day charge, spending most of his time at his luxury villa in Spain. If anyone was going to offer Tandori Birkett-Morris a job it was this Zara Bindle.

Hazelhurst had also found out that Zara Bindle had progressed from ultra-feminist views onto her new hobby horse which was that of transgender politics and transgender identity. This concept relied on the fact that a woman could 'self-identify' as a man, or vice versa, and thus assume, with the help of drugs, the new gender identity they had selected. This was a whole new area of discrimination and unfairness as far as Bindle was concerned. Hazelhurst shrewdly calculated that if he could get Ms Tandori Birckett-Morris to self-identify as a man and get Zara Bindle to believe that she had been discriminated against because of it, despite her fantastic qualifications she was bound to take pity on

Birkett-Morris and offer her a job. Especially as she was unemployed and shunned by society. Yes, that could work very well. So the plot was set and so was Birkett-Morris's immediate future.

Chapter 23

Tandori was allowed one last supper with her beloved family. In the morning she was going to receive some very unwelcome news, an assignment that kept her out of jail and away from Inspector Fleece, but a dangerous and unpleasant experience never the less.

But for now, Tandori was relaxing at home in her bedroom listening to music and reading her beloved heroic fantasy novels of the mills and boon variety.

'Tandori, Tandori, your father's home and your sister, Tamara. Come down dear and have a nice pot of tea.'

Oh shit why can't I stay up here and relax after that fucking horrendous cell thought Tandori.

'Be down in a minute mum, can't wait.'

She lied, didn't much like her bullying father and loathed her sister who was so far up her own arse it was surprising she could still draw breath. Bitch with a capital B.

'Hello Tandori, Constantine tells me you've been in a spot of bother, yet again,' said her father.

'Well that's a bit of a fucking understatement father.'

'Tandori, language in front of your father,' Constantine admonished.

'Oh he's used to it, owns a bloody prison with the worst inmates in the country, doesn't he?'

'Yes Tandori, but you don't think for one minute he has ever met any of them? Or those ghastly guards from the Prison Officers Union he's forced to employ at extortionist wages? No, your father only deals with the Home Office, his management team and, of course, the Home Secretary herself.'

'I see Tandori hasn't improved any after her spell in the nick, and she's still as fat as a pig with an arse the size of a block of flats.'

'That's enough Tamara, we can't all have a size eight figure like you. You're a very lucky girl, and you should be more understanding of your sister. It's not her fault she has an unfortunate figure, and looks to match.'

'I'd rather be the way I am than look like a high-class hooker on steroids with so much make up that coco the fucking clown can't fucking get any.'

'And I'd rather be the way I am with a boyfriend who drives a BMW, rather than have an arse so big you could rest a pint of special brew on it when you're down the working men's club, which incidentally, is the best place for you since you look like a fucking man from the waist up!'

'That's enough girls. We're supposed to be celebrating Tandori's release. It's so lovely to have her back in the Cotswolds.'

'It's a shame the Cotswolds doesn't feel the same way.'

'That's enough Tamara,' said her father, 'or you'll be off to your room with no supper, despite being twenty-six years of age.'

Tamara knew when to shut up and her father was not one to be trifled with. In any case, she was hoping he would buy her a convertible Mini and she needed daddy on side.

The afternoon tea and then supper didn't really go all that well and after long periods of silence they broke up and went their separate ways. Tandori to her room, Tamara out to the pub with her boyfriend in his BMW, Constantine to the TV room and soaps, and Tandori's father to his man cave in the garden with his beloved Hornby train set.

Chapter 24

The next day the Birkett-Morris household received an unexpected call from Hazelhurst at MI5.

'I'd like to speak with Tandori Birkett-Morris, it's MI5 here.'

'Just a minute I'll get her, who should I say is calling?' asked Constantine.

'Just say it's her old boss Hazelhurst, that should make her day.'

'Tandori, phone call dear.'

'Who the fuck is it?'

'It's a nice Mr Hazelhurst from MI5.'

'I'm not fucking in.'

'I've already told him you are dear, so you'll have to come to the phone, he sounds very nice.'

'He's only fucking nice if you like rattlesnakes as friends,' said Tandori. Reluctantly she took the phone from her mother, 'Hello,

Tandori here.'

'Ah Tandori, so nice to speak to you again,' said Hazelhurst, trying his hardest to be pleasant to the bitch whom he loathed with a passion.

'Well it's certainly not nice to speak to you Stephen, after what you did to me.'

'Come, come my dear, let bygones be bygones. It's due to me that you're home with your loving family in the Cotswolds. It was me that got you released from custody. You should be grateful. I've always had your best interests at heart you know.'

'The fuck you have. Now tell me what you want. You always want something.'

'Well my dear, for once you are entirely right. I do want something, but it's a little delicate and we need to meet in person. Shall we say your local pub, the Fox Inn, at 1.00 p.m. today?'

'Can't you just tell me now Stephen. Why the cloak and dagger stuff? Anyway, I'm going shopping today with Mummy and Tamara, so it's not possible.'

'Now you listen here Birkett-Morris, and you listen good. I've been nice, but now I'm telling you. You're released under licence for four months, but on my word you can be back in that holding cell with Inspector Fleece breathing down your pretty little neck in no time, so I suggest you change your plans with mummy and Tamara, and do the right thing and meet your old boss Hazelhurst. Do I make myself clear?'

'Yes perfectly. I see underneath you haven't changed one bit. I'll see you at the Fox Inn at 1.00 then, but don't expect any fucking favours off me.'

'It's not favours I want Tandori, just a little cooperation. It'll be just like the old days. The old team back together, eh. You know it makes sense.'

Chapter 25

'Sorry mummy, I can't go shopping with you and Tamara today. I've got to meet my old boss from MI5, you know the one that called this morning.'

'Oh what a pity dear, we were so looking forward to having you back and spoiling you at John Lewis in Birmingham. Anyway, it does sound so exciting. Maybe they have seen the error of their ways and want you back. Maybe they've got a mission for you. How terribly exciting.'

'I doubt if it's as exciting as you think mummy, and as for having me back, don't build your hopes up. According to Hazelhurst I fucked up too many times. No second chances I'm afraid, although it was mostly circumstance and others that weren't ever blamed like I was.'

'Never mind Tandori, I'm sure once they see how good you are they'll take you back on. You were only suspended after all, technically speaking.'

'Anyway, I'm meeting him at the Fox at 1.00, so you might as well still go shopping with Tamara. She was looking forward to spending on your credit cards anyway ,and she's bound to get more out of it than I would. No, you go and enjoy yourselves. I can see you at teatime.'

'That's very sweet of you Tandori, you always were such a nice girl, heart of gold.'

It soon came round to 1.00 p.m. and Tandori had walked the short distance to the Fox Inn from her parents' house and made sure she was 15 minutes early. It didn't take long for Hazelhurst to appear.

'Ah there you are Tandori, what's your favourite tipple, still those ghastly Desperados? Lime flavour I seem to remember. Mind you, good choice as far as your concerned, Desperados eh, a bit like art imitating real life.'

'Yes Stephen, a lime flavoured Desperados will be fine, with plenty of ice. I need something to cope with this unpleasant meeting, as I am sure it will be.'

'Come, come Tandori I'm sure it's nowhere near as bad as you think. Just a little favour we need, which will soon be over and well in the scope of your limited capabilities. Hazelhurst always looks after you whilst you're on my team. Just a little cooperation and I promise I will do my best to have the terrorism charges dropped and Inspector Fleece off your back for good.'

'I doubt very much it is within your powers, Stephen, to have the terrorism charges dropped. In any case, I haven't been charged yet and Fleece hasn't got a shred of evidence that I have been involved with ISIS or any other terrorist group. All I did was slip on a bar of Imperial Leather soap.'

'That's as maybe, but Fleece doesn't see it that way and you know as well as I do that the Met has a history of fitting people up and putting you away would do Fleece's flagging career the power of good. Anyway, you haven't heard what we want you to do yet, have you?'

'Well come on then Stephen, I'm all ears to hear what you have in mind. You don't get me sprung from jail for nothing do you?'

'Well my dear, no I don't. It's a simple operation really. Have you ever heard of the businessman Sydney Dresden Piffle?'

'No, should I have done.'

'Well no my dear, but to fill you in, he's a hypocritical communist subversive of the worst kind. He has a history of being a professional agitator going back to the 1960s, friends and comrades with the likes of Arthur Scargill, John Prescott and other left-wing trade unionists. He's been a person of interest for years as far as MI5 is concerned. Has always wanted to over throw capitalism and bring in a red revolution of complete state ownership and seizure of private assets including an Englishman's home, which as we know is his castle my dear. Can't let that happen can we?'

'But all that was a long time ago Stephen, what possible threat does this Piffle pose today?'

'As you know dear, when Tony Blair's Government came in, they continued Mrs T's revolution of privatization of state assets and more importantly, PFI contracts. Piffle was lucky enough to win a contract to run a company that administers the equality and diversity act for North Grimewold Council. Problem is, the council and Piffle's company interprets the act in such a way that it's a license to print money. He has made many millions of pounds in just five years and forced many small businesses to close. More importantly, he's upset some very powerful people, including the Chairman of McGreggor's Steel, who runs the biggest steel rolling mill in Europe and employs 10,000 people in the town of Grimewold. Let's say he's contacted us to put a spanner in the works of Piffle's little empire.'

'So it's one of our sting operations, get some dirt on Piffle and find a way of closing him down or getting him in the slammer. A bit like we did with that American automotive magnet in Northern Ireland, when we did the cocaine sting on him after he cost the government seventy million quid.'

'That's right my dear, you're on the right lines. We thought of you my dear. We want you to get a job at the Diversity Action Partnership Limited at a fairly senior level and infiltrate the operation. Piffle is old school with almost no computer capability, so it shouldn't be hard for you to make sure all the fines being sent out get mixed up and sent to the wrong companies. That should cause a furore, and counter claims in court that will close the blighter down for good. For good measure, you can get close to Piffle. Every man has his little weaknesses, sexual or otherwise, and you might be able to get some dirt on him, which would be the icing on the cake. Nothing beyond your capabilities Birkett-Morris.'

'That all sounds fine Stephen, but how do you propose I get a job at this Diversity Action Partnership?'

'Well that should be easy my dear. Luckily for us, Piffle employs a left-wing ultra-feminist called Zara Bindle who has years of being involved with ultra-feminist politics and has recently become a leading proponent of transgender politics, which she sees as the next big thing. We're going to get you an extremely convincing story whereby you are a transsexual who has self-identified as a man and been sacked from Tory Central office as a result of their sexist and racist instincts. For good measure we are arranging a letter from North Grimewold Council pointing out that 92% of the staff at the Diversity Action Partnership are men and the council wants this reduced to 48% in line with the population of North Grimewold as per the act's provisions. You applying on spec for a job at the same time will be sure to get Bindle's interest and she'll employ you on the spot. Especially if you express interest in transgender politics and equality of opportunity for women and trannies. You should only need about four months to carry out the operation, and if you are very good, who knows, I might be able to encourage the powers that be at MI5 to reinstate you and drop the ridiculous charges that Inspector Fleece is dreaming up.'

'So you're wanting me to self-identify as a fucking man?'

'Well my dear, just think of it as acting a part in a play. We just need to reel that lunatic Bindle in and make sure she employs you so you can carry out the mission. She's started to go to transgender meetings and has joined a few radical groups so it's an ideal cover for you, and let's be honest my dear, you do look a bit butch, well from the waist up anyway.'

'Well I'm not convinced that she's going to buy the fact that I've self-identified as a man, and surely being a feminist she would prefer a man self-identifying as a women?'

'That's where you're wrong my dear, there is a huge debate raging amongst radical feminists which rejects men self-identifying as a women because they feel that transgenders are not real women and are taking the piss out of their feminist ideals. No, it'll work far better with you identifying as a man, and she will have sympathy for your plight, especially being sacked by Tory central office which is indeed true and she can check that one out. The bitch will be outraged and sure to offer you a job as a way of putting right a wrong and helping her meet her quota of women and transgenders working for the Diversity Action Partnership.'

'Well I'll have to take your word for it Stephen,' said Tandori doubtfully.

'I've taken the liberty of writing a letter from you, if you'll just sign it, we can post it with your fake CV to Zara Bindle and set the trap. You go home my dear and I'm sure that she'll make contact with you within the next week and then you can make arrangements to infiltrate the organisation.'

Tandori dutifully signed the letter and Hazelhurst sealed the envelope with the CV contained. The trap was set, it just needed posting which Hazelhurst intended to do in the little village after his meeting ended. It had been easier than he thought recruiting Tandori, and he was sure she would soon wreak havoc on Piffle's organisation. The poor fucker wouldn't know what had hit him that's for sure.

'Another Desperados Tandori? I know when you've had one you can't resist two or more.'

'Go on then Stephen I'll have another one, especially if the agency is paying.'

'No Tandori, this one is on me. It's a, shall we say, private mission, sanctioned by a very important client who saved my life in Afghanistan.'

Hazelhurst spent the next two hours getting Tandori well and truly sozzled, and two Desperados turned into ten. She never could resist alcohol, one of her little weaknesses, thought Hazelhurst. He drove her home as she clearly wasn't capable of getting there under her own steam.

'Fucking hell Hazelhurst, you know how to get a lady to do what you want don't you?' said Tandori slurring her words.

'I haven't been this pissed since Tarquin proposed to me and I went out with Beth on a bender in Milton Keynes back in 2008. Why do you fucking hate me so much Hazelhurst? Got me sacked, put all the blame on me, not fair,'

'Life's not fair my dear, had to blame someone and it just happened to be you. Tossed a coin actually between you and Smedley, and you lost. Tough titty eh, last in first out, rule of the service I'm afraid.'

'Fuck, fuck fuck, do you mean my whole fucking life and its spiral into oblivion was decided on the flip of a fucking coin?'

'That's right Birkett-Morris, but unlike most, you're being given a second chance of redemption. The universe is helping you Tandori, don't look a gift horse in the mouth as they say.'

And with that Tandori was dropped off at her parents' house and Hazelhurst sped away in the jet-black Rover 75, supplied by the department as his company car.

Tandori staggered up the gravel drive and into the house. It was deathly quiet as no one was in. Her mother and sister were still buying up Birmingham at John Lewis, and her father was at the Golf Club or in some useless meeting with the Home Office, she couldn't remember which. What she could remember was how she had been stitched up on the throw of a fucking dice and her life had taken a turn for the worst as a result. She no longer felt in control of her destiny. Others were determining it, and she didn't like it but was too drunk to think clearly. She collapsed on the lounge sofa and immediately fell asleep, snoring loudly. Soon Gizmo the cat came and lay across her and that was where they both stayed for the afternoon.

Chapter 26

The very next day two letters arrived in Zara Bindle's in-tray. One from North Grimewold Council's HR department and the other from an unknown person by the name of Tandori Birkett-Morris. Both were interesting in their own way.

The letter from the council was typically threatening and overbearing, pointing out in no uncertain terms the Council's displeasure that their flagship PFI contracted company responsible for diversity policy was itself in breach of the regulations, and they wanted immediate action to rectify the potential PR disaster should the tabloid press get hold of the story. In short, they wanted Zara Bindle to sack some of the male employees and replace them with a more diverse workforce of women, transgender and ethnic workers preferably of Muslim and/or African backgrounds. Words such as, 'positive discrimination' and 'female only quotas' and 'short lists' were banded about for good measure. This of course was music to the ears of Zara Bindle. She now had the ammunition she needed to force Piffle to adopt her way of thinking and sack all those ghastly coarse ex-miners and steel workers who the idiot had employed, and introduce a proper functioning computer system. She could already think of the first useless wastrel she was going to sack, but at least the buffoon could make her a nice cup of tea.

'Jennings,' she barked.

'Make me a nice pot of tea will you, and be a dear and bring some of those nice chocolate wafers, you know the expensive Scottish ones.'

'Yes Ms Bindle, right away Ms Bindle.'

Jennings might be the office senior administrator, but he was no better than an obedient tea boy. Yes, Jennings would be the first casualty she mused, and I might just have found a replacement.

The tea was brought in by a bowing and scraping Jennings who retreated as if in the presence of the Queen herself.

Zara Bindle picked up the letter and CV from a Miss Tandori Birkett-Morris. Obviously a very intelligent young women, and attendance at a prestigious ladies' college and then university where she gained a first. But what really caught her attention, listed under hobbies and interests, was 'Transgender Politics' and the fact that the lady was in the process of self-identifying as a man. A real transgender employee, now that would be truly amazing and so topical. She could see a number of research papers, speeches and a huge boost to her career, and hopefully a return to London or at least Manchester. The covering letter was even more interesting. Sacked from Tory Central

Office for her views on transgender politics and her self-identification as a man, and unemployed for six months with no chance of a job or a decent reference. Outrageous! Zara could feel her blood start to boil. How dare those fascist Tory scum discriminate against a poor helpless woman on the grounds that she wanted to self-identify as a man.

She decided there and then, interview or not, Tandori Birkett-Morris was going to replace Jennings as chief office administrator and be the first transgender employee in the Diversity Action Partnership Limited and she, Zara Bindle, was going to reap the rich rewards of her enlightened approach to gender politics. She would tell Dresden immediately.

Chapter 27

Bindle picked up the phone and rang Piffle. He was, as he often was, ensconced in the back of the Silver Spur driving back from the Playa de Sol to his luxury villa when the phone rang.

'Piffle here, who's speaking?' boomed Piffle down the receiver of the car phone

'It's me Dresden, Zara Bindle, I need to speak with you urgently, we have a problem at this end.'

'What, I say, who is that? I can't bloody hear you.'

'It's me Dresden, Zara, I need to speak to you urgently.'

'I can't bloody hear you properly. Paeleo, Paeleo, bloody slow down on this concrete bloody motorway will you, I can't hear myself think.'

'It is not possible Señor, I have large arctic truck up you say my backside.'

'Hello, hello, can you hear me Dresden?'

'No, I bloody can't woman, I'll be at villa in twenty minutes I'll call you back then.'

'Did you say you'll call me back Dresden?'

'Yes, I bloody well did.' and with that he put the phone down.

Zara Bindle now had twenty minutes to kill and she wasn't going to waste another minute. She picked up Tandori Birkett-Morris's CV and dialled the contact number.

'Hello, it's Tamara here.'

'I'd like to speak to Tandori Birkett-Morris if I may?'

'I think she's in her room, that's if she is not pissed like she was yesterday.'

'I beg your pardon?' said Zara confused, 'who am I speaking with?'

'I'm Tandori's sister, Tamara, the pretty one. I'll just try and get her. Tandori, Tandori, phone for you, some nutter actually wants to talk to you.'

'I'm upstairs, I'll pick up the phone in the study,' shouted back Tandori.

'Hello, Tandori speaking.'

'Ah finally Tandori. My name is Zara Bindle and I'm calling from the Diversity Action Partnership. I have your CV in front of me and I would like to invite you for an interview to head up our administration department. You have a very impressive CV if I may say so young lady, or should I say young man.'

'I am still a women, but on a journey to becoming a man. That's great news, when would you want to interview me?'

'Well it's Thursday today, shall we say tomorrow at 10.00 here in Grimewold? I'll get my secretary to e-mail you the details'.

'Well that's great, I can't believe it. What do you want me to bring?'

'Just yourself, I am sure we are going to get on very well indeed, I will see you at my office tomorrow. Bye for now.'

'Bye,' stammered Tandori. The trap was set and Bindle had responded immediately, just as Hazelhurst had predicted she would.

Chapter 28

Piffle finally arrived back at the Villa Almeria, after staying at the Black Chicken far longer than he should have done. Fortunately, his friends Gary and Tracy Wacker and his wife 'the Clothes Horse' had already caught a flight home. He was alone in the villa, save for Honolulu cooking his tea a bit later. He went to the office where he dialled the number to phone Zara Bindle back in peace. Why that dreadful women always seemed to have bad news for him he couldn't fathom. At least the money was still rolling in, more than ever if he was being honest. It was Thursday however, so maybe she was just going to give him the weekly figures.

'Hello, Bindle here.'

'It's me Dresden, now what's this all about love?'

'I'll ignore the love, the thing is Dresden we've had a letter from the HR Department of North Grimewold Council.'

'What the bloody hell do they want with us?'

'They are very unhappy Dresden that the Diversity Action

Partnership predominantly employs white older men, 92% male employees against 48% in the population of Grimewold generally. They want us to employ a more diverse group of people.'

'Bloody hell, do you mean they want me to sack me mates? Well, I won't bloody do it, some of them lads have been with me from the beginning.'

'I'm sorry to say Dresden, they are giving us no alternative, and as I am in charge and technically responsible, I have to insist we abide by their edicts, starting with Jennings. I'm afraid he has to go and I've already taken the liberty of lining up a very able replacement who I am interviewing tomorrow.'

'You bloody well can't get rid of Jennings. He's been in me Labour branch at Gipsyville for best part of forty years, proper mate he is,' spluttered Piffle.

'I'm not debating with you Dresden, I'm simply informing you of my decision, and as I am in charge of the day to day running of the Diversity Action Partnership, you have no choice but to accept my decision. I also have to say that Jennings is highly unsuitable as an employee and as a human being. He is purely a glorified tea boy, which seems to be the limit of his capabilities, such as they are.'

'Well, who is this woman you have in mind?'

'Her name is Tandori Birkett-Morris and she is a very capable young lady who used to work for the Conservative Central Office. She was sacked due to their overt racism and sexism and from our point of view she is ideal. She is a transgender woman who is self-identifying as a man, so meets our transgender quota.'

'Self-identifying as a bloody man. What in God's name does that mean? Do you mean to tell me we're sacking poor Jennings because he is a man only to employ a women who thinks she's a man? Or in your words, is self-identifying as one? I'm swapping one man for another bloody man. What's the point in that?'

'Tandori is transgender which means she meets our quota. She is clearly a women who simply is self-identifying as a man.'

'Well I don't bloody understand. If she is self-identifying as a man does that mean she has a dick or does she attach a plastic one to her, well, her women's bits?'

'Don't be so disgusting Dresden, of course she doesn't attach a plastic penis to her nether regions. She simply takes hormones to make her feel masculine.'

'Well where I bloody come from men have dicks and women have fannys, it's as simple as that. At least Jennings knows what he is and who he is.'

'All this is getting us nowhere Dresden. It's irrelevant whether Tandori has a penis or intends to have one attached in some way. What matters is that she is transgender and thus meets our quota for having one, which Dresden, keeps the council off our backs for now until I can replace some more of your useless white male staff with a diverse workforce.'

'Well I'm not happy. For starters this Tandori has worked for the Tories which means she has Tory sympathies, and it's over my dead body that I would employ a bloody Tory toff. It goes against everything I stand for.'

'I'm sure after being sacked by them for simply being different she hates them as much as you do. I'm going ahead and calling in Jennings tomorrow to tell him the bad news, assuming Tandori is a suitable replacement which I am sure she is.'

'Bloody hell, you can't just sack Jennings like that, he's me mate, I've know the lad years and he'll be devastated. Listen, hold off sacking him till Monday and I'll see if we can employ him on a self-employed basis. I need a driver and gardner back in England. Anyway, lass I think I need to come back next week as shit is obviously hitting the fan.'

'I'll hold off till Monday Dresden, but I am going ahead with this and I'm interviewing Tandori Birket-Morris tomorrow, and if she is as good as her CV claims, then I'm moving ahead with the appointment.'

The phone went dead and Piffle was left alone in his study pondering the turn of events. There was something about this Tandori Birkett-Morris that didn't feel right. It might just be the Tory Party connection that was bothering him and colouring his thinking. Maybe he was getting too old for this game and didn't like change. He didn't understand all this transgender politics and couldn't understand the concept of a women self-identifying as a man.

For once he felt a little depressed. The world was moving on and Sydney Dresden Piffle was no longer keeping up. He liked the Labour Party of the 1960s. The party of miners, steel workers, dockers and ship builders and car workers. Real men doing real men's work, with the women at home looking after the kids and keeping house. It had all changed with women like Zara Bindle. Yes, it was time to leave England, make his stash from the log cabin deal and see out his days in Benidorm at the Villa Almeria with Honolulu – minus the Clothes Horse.

Chapter 29

Tandori got off the train at Grimewold station. It had been a challenging journey. Tamara had had to drive her to Milton Keynes, then a train to Doncaster and then a change to another track to get her into Grimewold – three hours in total. Luckily the man she was going to replace was waiting in the station car park.

Jennings was standing at the entrance with board saying 'Tandori Birkett-Morris'. He was in one of his signature tank-tops and nylon trousers from BHS.

Tandori's cropped hair with mauve streaks and a denim boiler suit affair couldn't be missed. Transgender she certainly looked.

'Is that you, er, Ms Birkett-Morris? I'm here to deliver you to your meeting with Ms Bindle at the Diversity Action Partnership, I'm Jennings.'

'Hello Jennings, pleased to meet you.'

'This way, this way.' Jennings ushered her towards the car park and into his ancient Austin Maestro, in that horrible hearing aid beige so popular in the 1980s, a time Jennings was still firmly stuck in.

'Sorry about the mess in the car, I live alone and don't often take passengers, just move those old newspapers into the back. I must clean her out sometime,' fussed Jennings, clearly embarrassed over the state of the interior of his car.

'Don't worry about it, my sister's car is far worse.'

Off they went in the Maestro, with Jennings peering over the steering wheel, rarely getting above twenty miles an hour with horns blaring from other irate drivers being held up. Eventually they drove into the car park of the old library building, the home that was the Diversity Action Partnership Limited.

Tandori was intrigued by the grand scale of the building with its huge concrete columns and plate glass infused with green algae, making it look like a giant botanical greenhouse.

Once Tandori had signed the visitors' book she was left in reception whilst Jennings scuttled off to tell Zara Bindle that her guest had arrived. Tandori was not offered a coffee and was still waiting twenty minutes later when an extremely overbearing and officious women appeared.

'Hello, you must be Tandori, I'm Zara Bindle, we meet at last. Would you like to come this way please. Would you like tea Ms Birkett-Morris? I'll ask Jennings to make us a pot.'

'That would be great, but please call me Tandori.'

Soon they were alone in Bindle's office and the tea duly arrived. Jennings was dispatched with a cursory dismissive wave of the hand by Zara.

'Tell me Tandori, why do you want to come and work for the Diversity Action Partnership?'

'Well Ms Bindle, being transgender and subject to the most unspeakable prejudice, especially by Tory Central Office, I want to work for an organisation that's moving minority rights forward so this country is a leader, not a follower. Until recently no one has shown interest in transgender people like me, especially ones that are self-identifying as a man. Even radical feminists are against us, but mostly men self-identifying as a woman which clearly I am not.'

'Well, I'm a radical feminist and I certainly am not against transgender persons. I can well believe the Tories being completely prejudiced against people different from themselves. I'm amazed you ever agreed to work with such horrendous people, living in a racist, sexist Britain of a bygone age that people like me are changing. Action today, as Churchill said. What exactly did the Tories do and why were you sacked?'

'They started to exclude me from meetings and decisions. They gave me tasks that I couldn't complete, using terms like a square peg in a round hole, and telling me to improve my time management skills when I didn't hit impossible deadlines. Every excuse to build a case to get rid of me. I should never have worked there, but my mother is a Conservative and said it would look good on my CV. Instead, I am now basically unemployable, despite having a good degree, because they won't give me a reference.'

'Well Tandori, none of this surprises me at all. I've already made up my mind that we can offer you a senior position here to right the wrongs of the past and inject a bit of verve into our organisation. I can see that we will get on and you will report to me every day. I am thinking of a salary of thirty-five thousand to attract a person of you quality, what do you say?'

'Ms Bindle, I am totally shocked and delighted. I have no hesitation in accepting your kind offer. When can I start?'

'Well I need to reorganise the office as you will be the new Administrative Manager. Shall we say two weeks on Monday? That gives you time to find accommodation here in Grimewold. We will of course pay you relocation expenses up to a total of two thousand pounds, as long as receipts are provided. Have you any further questions?'

'What's the number one thing you want me to do?'

'I want you to computerise our records system and issuing of fines so clients can pay us more easily – by direct debit, or instalments, for example. I'm afraid our owner, Dresden Piffle, is living in the 1960s and we need to drive efficiency, cut costs and employ people of diversity, like yourself.'

'Won't this Mr Piffle be upset with your changes?'

'You leave Piffle to me, he has no choice as the council want the changes we will be implementing. I'm afraid white, male, middle-aged men, 'too pale and too stale as they say' will be the casualties of this purge – a purge that is long overdue in my opinion. Anyway, I have a lot to do, so we'll conclude the interview, and I will see you at 8.30 a.m. in two weeks' time, ready for your new challenge. Well done Tandori.'

So that was that, Tandori had reached her first objective of her mission to disrupt and destroy the Diversity Action Partnership. She would contact Hazelhurst later that day and tell him the good news. Jennings was summoned to take her back to Grimewold train station a mere 2 hours after she had last been there. Little did she know that poor bloke she waved to as he drove away in his oh so beige Maestro was the man she was going to replace in a brutal cull masterminded by her new boss. And little did the Diversity Action Partnership know what was about to engulf it once Tandori Birkett-Morris started her campaign of total destruction!

Chapter 30

It was Monday morning, 8.30 a.m.

'Jennings, may I have a word please?'

'Yes Ms Bindle, at your service Ms Bindle,' said Jennings bowing slightly.

'There is no easy way to say this Jennings, so I'm just going to be straight with you. We have had a letter from the Council expressing concerns about our own diversity policy. That means, Jennings, that we have to employ a more diverse workforce, so unfortunately you are going to be a casualty of that. I'm afraid despite your obvious loyalty I am going to have to let you go. However, I understand that Dresden is in need of a gardener at his house in Hull and you are welcome to ask him about that position.'

'What do you mean Ms Bindle, let me go? Let me go where?'

'I'm sorry Jennings, I'm afraid you're being made redundant. I will not require you to work your notice and I am putting you on gardening leave for the rest of the month until you have, er, well possibly, become a gardener for Mr Piffle. As you know you are on a zero hours self-employed contract so there is no requirement to pay you redundancy. Have you any questions Jennings?'

'But, but, this is all I've known for the last five years. I haven't done anything wrong,' whined Jennings, tears starting to stream down his face.

'I have nothing more to add Jennings, my decision is final.'

Jennings shot from the room openly howling now with tears streaming down his face making for the men's toilets.

'What on earth is wrong?' said one of the clerks as Jennings shot past, but he was far too upset to speak. He simply disappeared into one of the men's cubicles and stayed there for the rest of the morning.

Zara Bindle wasn't too concerned. She didn't like Jennings and, in any case,, the Council was right, how could the Diversity Action Partnership Limited impose diversity quotas on other companies whilst failing to adhere to the Council's policy itself whilst making millions of pounds in fines? Jennings was just a minor casualty of a glorious policy of diversity. There would be many more people in Jennings' position in the future, he was just an early casualty, and a deserved one at that. The incompetent buffoon would never have been employed if he had not been a personal friend of Sidney Dresden Piffle and apparently went to school with his wife Pauline Piffle.

The deed was done and it sent out a clear message to others. Hopefully there would be resignations from some of the white males employed when they saw the writing on the wall and looked for alternative opportunities. What those opportunities were, Zara Bindle did not know and cared even less. What mattered to her was the policy of diversity and equality, something she had believed all her life with every sinew of her body.

Out in the main office, mutterings were starting and rumours spreading. People knew something bad had happened to Jennings but so far, they didn't know what. A few of the older ex-miners were idly talking about strike action. They'd had enough of zero hours contracts, low pay and disinterest from management, and most of them loathed Zara Bindle, a posh southerner with no regard for their feelings or circumstance. The Diversity Action Partnership was certainly not a happy ship. Not that Bindle noticed, like nearly all modern management her concern for staff welfare was purely synthetic, her interest in them amounted to zero and her hostility and dislike palpable for people she considered to be her intellectual and social inferiors. In fact in truth everything Bindle supposedly stood for was a veiled attempt to boost her own huge ego, fit in perfectly with the modern orthodoxy of transgender politics with a view to furthering her own career, standing in the community and wealth through her slavish adherence to the latest fashionable ideology. In summary Bindle like so many others was a total fraud, but a dangerous one willing to put into practise her chosen political direction, however she would soon find that course of action was going to have severe consequences for both her and the Diversity Action Partnership.

Chapter 31

Piffle had had one last weekend with Honolulu and wouldn't be back at the Villa Almeria for a few weeks. Back to that dreadful steel town of Grimewold. Paeleo drove him to the airport and dropped him off by the entrance, people staring at the Rolls Royce Silver Spur as if he was royalty. He was not going to let a little local difficulty upset his plans for the Playa de Sol log cabin site. That was his future with Honolulu and his chance to escape from England and the dreary 'Clothes Horse'.

'Eh up Paeleo, you take care lad and remember there is a drink in it for you if you arrange building contractor as you said you would. Look after the Rolls while I'm away and make sure that garden is sorted at villa lad.'

'I will do that Señor, you have my word as a Spanish man. Your interests are safe with me.'

'Eh lad well you make sure they are,' and with that Piffle was off into the terminal building to catch the Monday lunchtime flight to Doncaster Robin Hood Airport.

He had taken the precaution of booking two seats next to each other as first class was not an option with Easy Jet flight who he booked with, and his wide girth made travel extremely uncomfortable in what he dubbed 'cattle class'. It was worth paying double the £69.99 cost. No one could ever accuse Sydney Dresden Piffle of being a skinflint, or so he liked to tell himself. Others might have a very different view, especially his long-suffering staff.

Just as he was waiting in the queue for check-in his mobile phone rang.

'Piffle here, who's that?' he answered.

'It's me Zara, Zara Bindle.'

'What in God's name do you want? I'm just catching flight back to England.'

'I'm just phoning to inform you that I have employed Tandori Birkett-Morris and had to let Jennings go. He's on gardening leave until the end of the month, so you can interview him for the job of gardener at your Hull residence.'

'Bloody hell women, you've done what? I thought I told you to hold off until Monday when I return, and we could discuss it then? You had no right—'

'Dresden, now you listen to me. Am I not the Director in charge of the Diversity Action Partnership Limited and responsible for staff appointments and dismissals? If you remember, I told you that I would wait until Monday which I have done. Jennings was called in at 8.30 and given the news and he is currently in the gentleman's washroom and has been all morning. If you wish to employ the buffoon as your gardener then that is your clear choice, but I am now making the changes that should have been made a long time ago. Jennings is just the first of many horribly white middle-aged males of dubious capability that you have employed because they are your "mates" as you put it. That will now change. We will have a diverse workforce of females, transgenders, Africans, Muslims, and disabled people to replace most of the current workforce. Although in truth a new computer system could render 50% of them redundant in any case and they simply will not need to be replaced. Do I make myself crystal clear Dresden?'

Dresden knew when to fight and when to back off, and in this instance, he knew that Zara Bindle had the law on her side and the bulletproof contract her lawyers had drawn up, which he had stupidly signed without getting his own legal advice, just to save a few quid. He also knew from working for a Council for many years there was no point fighting them. They would spend unlimited amounts of taxpayers' money proving they were in the right.

'Alright lass, I take on board what you're saying, but in future I want to be consulted more on the decisions you are taking about me staff and I want Jennings handled sympathetically – Pauline and I have known the lad for years and I, for one, consider him a friend. Anyway, I'll be at office by 3.00 and we can discuss things then and I can see Jennings if he's still around.'

We can discuss that when you arrive. I've got a lot of very important matters to attend to so I'll say goodbye.'

And Zara was gone, just in time for Piffle to get on his Easy Jet flight with his two adjacent seats reserved.

Zara had no one to make her a pot of tea now Jennings had gone AWOL. She thought about making a pot herself, but that would mean going into the main office and she sensed that she would not get a warm reception. Despite her haughty manner, she was actually a natural coward who did not like to be challenged especially by groups of disgruntled ex-miners, steel workers and dockers. She called one of the juniors, Jade, and asked her to bring in a pot of English breakfast tea and a plate of Thurrock's Scottish chocolate wafers.

Chapter 32

Jennings emerged from the gents' washroom about two hours later still sniffling. He got his jacket and made his escape. Everyone was staring at him, but no one wanted to ask why he had been dismissed, and he clearly did not want to speak about it.

He walked briskly out to the car park and got into his Austin Maestro. He didn't look back but drove off at a higher speed than he had done in years. Back to his small flat on the notorious Cromwell Estate. He had the unfortunate luck to own a small two-bedroom flat above the dilapidated row of shops that had long since closed. Apart from the bookies and the Oliver Cromwell pub across the way where a few drunkards and drug dealers congregated during the day, and prostitutes plied their trade at night for a fix of coke or the new drug sweeping the estate, Spice.

Jennings had made the mistake of buying the flat when his mother died since he got a 70% discount from Mrs Thatcher's Government. He had only paid £9,000 for the flat in 1988 at the height of Thatcherism, but now, 30 years on, the flat might have a theoretical value of £60,000 but he knew there would be no takers. Save for webuyanyhouse.com that had already offered him just £20,000 and then he would have limited money and nowhere to live. Yes, the future looked decidedly bleak for Anthony Jennings.

However, there was a glimmer of hope for Jennings which he knew nothing about. In the world of Dresden and Pauline Piffle, friendship, indeed comradeship, ran deep, and despite his often disregard for humanity in his quest to better himself, Piffle did have a heart, and in her way, his wife did too.

Many years ago behind the bike sheds at Gipsyville Secondary Modern, Pauline had had more than a teenage grope with Anthony Jennings, in fact she had had a full on sex session aged 14, in fact the first of many suiters who 'had' Pauline before she settled on Sydney Dresden Piffle as the most promising and ambitious lad on the estate.

Anthony Jennings was totally different back then, confident, good looking, cocky and, in his view, a great future ahead. Of course coming from the Gipsyville estate with no qualifications or academic achievements to his name, his promise and ambition were crushed like so many others, and he found himself working as a labourer on the docks with most of his friends and contemporaries. Slowly over the years he let his early ambition and promise drift away and he settled for a life of mediocrity, eventually looking after his aged mother. He did have a sister, a very attractive one in her youth, but she had realized that the Gipsyville estate was not going to bring her the riches she craved and she went to London working in one of the new casino's springing up in the 60s where she met a succession of rich Arabs and travelled the world. She was Jennings' only surviving relative, but he hadn't seen her in years and believed that she was residing in the Canary Islands somewhere, living off the proceeds of the Arab sugar daddies who had kept her financially secure.

So it was a great surprise to Jennings when, after making himself a cup of tea, the phone rang and it was Pauline Piffle. He hadn't spoke to her in years.

'Anthony my dear, it's me Pauline.'

'Sorry, who am I speaking to?' said Jennings, confused by a female caller.

'It's me, Pauline Piffle, Dresden's wife. Don't you remember me? And to think what we used to mean to each other, did our sexual trysts not mean anything to you? I still think about them to this day,' said Pauline with mock humour and her clumsy attempt to lift Jennings spirits.

'Oh, sorry Pauline,' stammered Jennings.

'It's been so long and after the day I've had I didn't expect to hear from anybody, least of all you. In fact, I was going to go across the road to the Oliver Cromwell and have a good drink. I've never felt so low in a long time. I've been sacked you know, and to think all I've done for the Diversity Action Partnership.'

'I know my dear, that's why I'm calling. Dresden phoned me

from the airport. He's flying back specially to sort things out. That bitch Bindle had no right to sack you without consulting Sydney and if you had to go then a man of your loyalty should have been given clear notice and options for the future. I hope they've organised a leaving party for you?'

'No, she shouldn't have sacked me, and no one even said goodbye or mentioned any leaving party, not even a card. I just left, too distraught to handle it.'

'Well that is disgraceful Anthony. I will be making arrangements myself to organise a party for you. I shall organise a suite at the Grimewold auditorium which has just been refurbished and everyone, including the Gipsyville Labour members, will be invited. I am sure Sydney is going to speak to you about a job offer at our house. We would never see you on the streets Anthony, you know that don't you?'

'Well that's very kind Pauline, I'm feeling a little bit better already.'

The call ended and Pauline Piffle started work straight away on organising Jennings' leaving do for the following week. In the meantime, Piffle had landed and was in a taxi from Robin Hood Airport to Grimewold so he could get back to his company headquarters and take charge of the deepening crisis. He was getting too old for this.

Chapter 33

Thirty minutes later he was dropped off at the Diversity Action Partnership entrance and swept into the building at speed, or at least the quickest speed his legs would take him.

'Eh up people, I'm back,' he boomed. 'I'm off to see Zara,' and with that he made for her office for yet another showdown. He didn't bother to knock but strode straight in.

Zara Bindle looked up from her desk as he entered unannounced.

'What on earth is the meaning of this Dresden? You barging into my office like this, I could have been doing anything.'

'No secrets at Diversity Action Partnership Zara, you know that. We need to talk about Jennings and other matters that have been going on behind me back.'

'May I remind you Sydney that I am in charge and I don't take kindly to you barging into my private office, and as to things going on behind your back, I have been completely transparent with regards to

Jennings, the hiring of Tandori Birkett-Morris and the compliance regulations that Grimewold Council are imposing upon us. Namely that you, yes you, have employed a bunch of elderly white male halfwits into this organisation so that there is no diversity at all when we need to be the shining beacon of diversity within the community.'

'Now listen here woman, those elderly white male halfwits, as you call 'em, are me mates and we go back to before a slip of a lass like you was born. Most of them have helped create Labour Party in this area and fight Tory scum for years to create a more equal society that you bang on about. I will not have 'em spoken about like that. Jennings went to school with wife, Pauline, and I can tell you, she is spitting feathers that poor lad has been sacked and replaced by a closet Tory transgender woman who is self-identifying as a bloody man, for God's sake.'

'Look Sydney, this bickering is getting us nowhere. Let's stick to the hard facts and take the emotion out of the situation. North Grimewold Council quite rightly are concerned that their flagship Diversity Action agenda is being run by a company that itself does not meet the requirements of the 2010 Diversity and Equality act as laid down by parliament as a response to primary European Legislation. That much we know. We have to get our own house in order, and that means letting go some of the white male employees and replacing them with a more diverse workforce. Employing Tandori Birkett-Morris, a female transgender person and replacing Jennings sends a clear signal to the Council of our intent and is just the first of many such examples that we will be undertaking to meet to Council's policy and retain may I say the very lucrative PFI contract that they have awarded to us. I am just trying to look after the best interests of the company and, in particular, yourself Sydney. Do I make myself clear?'

'Well, if you put it like that, I suppose I can see where you are coming from, but I still want consultation and I want staff treated fairly and given plenty of notice to sort 'em selves out. Do I make myself clear? Loyalty is big thing for me lass and it cuts both ways.'

Bindle smiled to herself, despite all his bluster Piffle had backed down. Faced with the prospect of losing the very lucrative PFI contract when it came up for renewal was not a prospect that he could contemplate. She would just have to tread more carefully to achieve her objectives.

'Well Sydney, I too can concede that I could and should have handled the Jennings situation with more tact and sympathy. I will make sure that I put in place a policy which does that in the future. However, I think it is the right decision and you will be highly impressed with Tandori Birkett-Morris and what she can achieve for us.'

The meeting ended and after a walk around the office glad handing his loyal staff, Piffle was off to see Pauline and stay at the family home in Hull. Little did either Piffle or Bindle know that Tandori's appointment would be the start of fundamental changes at the Diversity Action Partnership, none of them for the better as far as the company was concerned. Tandori was about to unleash a terrible tsunami of catastrophe, just as she had been instructed to do, that would have far-reaching consequences for all of them.

Chapter 34

Josiah Archibald McGreggor III was, for once, in an excellent mood. He had just come off the phone after a very fruitful conversation with Winton J Cuncliff-Owen, his partner in crime. The trap was set and Tandori Birkett-Morris had been appointed by the Diversity Action Partnership Limited as their Chief Administrator no less. It was all going exactly to plan and soon that communist upstart wouldn't know what had hit him.

'June, splendid news. Soon we will be free of Dresden Piffle and his infernal Diversity Action Partnership and the disgraceful fines that go with it. Get Wilfred to bring round the Bentley, I'm off to the golf club to celebrate our good fortune and have some lunch.'

'I think Wilfred is busy cleaning the Bentley, so I'll have to see when he can fit you in,' said June being intentionally provocative.

'Can you never just do as I say woman? There always has to be a bloody problem, or reason why my explicit instructions can't be followed. Now get Wilfred to bring the car round washed or otherwise, do I make myself clear?'

'If you say so Sir.'

Archibald had another important reason to be cheerful that day. Ping Steel had been in contact and were willing to sign an exclusive agreement to provide rolled steel at 40% below McGreggor's production cost, thus boosting profits by 100% and enabling half the McGreggor workforce to be sacked. Given that half of the blighters were contract staff on zero hours contracts employed through the Bulgarian recruitment agency, Happy.Worker.com, costs could be reduced without redundancy payoffs. A strike would be even better since some of the older, less productive, staff on enhanced employment contracts could be dismissed for breaching the terms of their employment. He would speak to his lawyers today about signing by the end of the week.

Meanwhile, back in the Cotswolds, Tandori was making preparations for her move to Grimewold. She was due to travel up Monday morning and then arrive at the Diversity Action Partnership for an important 1.00 meeting to discuss the implementation of the new strategy of computerising the company, reducing the workforce by 50% and replacing the rest with a diverse workforce to reflect the community the company serves.

'Mummy, mummy. Where have you put my dungarees? I need them for next week if I have any chance of looking like a transgender person.'

'I think they're in the wash room dear,' her mother shouted up.

'I'll get Eunice to dig them out and iron them for you. You must look smart dear for your first day. How exciting.'

Eunice was the particularly lazy, and in Tandori's view, retarded housekeeper that mummy insisted upon keeping on, despite her woeful work attendance and record of utter incompetence.

'I'll get them myself and iron them. I wouldn't trust that Eunice not to fuck them up somehow just before my important first day, and I've got to look the part. Zara has given me the name of someone called Jennings, who I think gave me a lift last time, who's renting his flat out in Grimewold. Remind me to ring him up today, I don't want to be in a Holiday Inn all week if I can help it, although Zara said they would pay.'

Monday morning came round quicker than expected. An important day at the Diversity Action Partnership. It was rather insensitive of Zara Bindle to employ Tandori Birkett-Morris on the very same day that Jennings was to leave the employ of the Diversity Action Partnership.

To be fair to her, Pauline Piffle had arranged the actual details and chosen the day, and Zara was keen to get Tandori in the post as soon as possible. Getting Jennings to meet Tandori on the grounds that he knew what she looked like was, to say the least, hurtful and crass. Jennings leaving do was to be held at the Grimewold Auditorium later on in the day. It was to be announced that Jennings was going to be reemployed by Dresden and Pauline Piffle as their personal chauffer and gardener, and live in at their grand home in Hull. As he no longer needed, or wanted, to live in his flat on the Cromwell estate, Zara had

had the brainwave of arranging it to be sublet to Tandori, and the rent paid for as part of the employment package being offered. All in all a fortuitous arrangement.

After being dropped off by mummy in the Range Rover at Milton Keynes central railway station, Tandori got a fast train direct to Doncaster where she had an hour and a half to kill before the connecting train to Grimewold. Tandori could not be missed. Following Hazelhurst's instructions she'd had her hair cropped even shorter, dyed it mauve, put on the baggy boiler suit, and worn doc martin boots to complete the ensemble. She had a large pink suitcase with essentials for the week, and a rucksack with some sandwiches and a drink.

Once at Doncaster, she put her pink suitcase in a locker and decided to kill some time by going to a Wilkinson's she spotted across the way from the railway station. Being of a practical nature, she soon spotted a couple of items she knew mummy wanted for the garden. Because it was late in the season, 1 litre liquid Miracle Grow bottles had 75% off so she bought several together with some electric mouse traps for daddy's man cave – mice were a constant problem.

These eclectic purchases were to be yet another fatal mistake in the life of Tandori Birkett-Morris, as subsequent events would prove. She popped them in the rucksack and thought nothing more about them. Checking her watch, she realized that her connecting train was due, and feeling rather pleased with herself, she collected her pink suitcase and boarded the cross-country sprinter to Grimewold. She looked out of the train window aimlessly thinking to herself what a flat desolate landscape she had entered into not helped by the grey overcast sky and general air of despondency. Yes she thought I hope this mission is over soon and I can be back in the Cotswolds, compared to this dump it was sheer paradise.

Chapter 35

Pauline Piffle was also going to find that Monday 2nd September was to be a seminal day in her life. After years of being ignored and derided by Dresden, who openly referred to her as the 'Clothes Horse', she was about to receive the male attention she deserved and craved.

It happened in the most unlikely venue of the reception area of the Diversity Action Partnership, where she made an impromptu visit to see Dresden and make final arrangements for Jennings' leaving do later in the day.

To be fair, she had glammed up for the event wearing a sequined evening dress in shocking pink. Her hair, complexion and nails looked immaculate as she wanted to look her best for Jennings. Not because she fancied him, but because she owed him for how he had been treated, and the poor hand life had dealt him over the years. All that promise in his youth and now look at him.

As she was waiting in the reception nursing the coffee Laura had made her, who should stride in but Mike Morrell with his entourage of sycophants. Recently divorced, he was missing female company and all that it entailed. He immediately clocked Pauline, who, despite his visceral hatred of Piffle and their close working proximity, had never had the pleasure of meeting his wife. If he had given it a second thought, which he had not, he would have imagined that Piffle would be married to an ugly, fat, course slapper from the Gipsyville estate with all the grace and style of a Russian female shot putter. So when he saw Pauline, he didn't imagine for an instant that she was Piffle's wife. He couldn't help smiling broadly and saying good morning to the gorgeous, classy women sat in reception. In short, he was smitten.

After he was out of earshot and through the double doors towards the stairs to the upper floor where his offices were, he turned to his secretary, 'Who in God's name is that gorgeous women in reception? Do you know her?'

'I'd have thought you would have known Mike, that's Dresden Piffle's wife, Pauline.'

'Bloody hell! Do you mean to tell me that beautiful classy women is married to that fat, uncouth, motor-mouthed arsehole? I just can't believe it. What in God's name is she doing married to that?'

'I'm not sure Mike, I think she married him when she was very young.'

'Young? She would have had to have been an embryo to be attracted to Piffle. What's the situation now?'

'All I know is that Piffle spends most of his time in Benidorm and

Pauline rarely accompanies him. I think their marriage is one of convenience.'

'Well I tell you what Gloria, I'm going to bed that women, make no mistake and give her the life she so richly deserves. I'm going to marry that women, just you wait and see.'

Tandori's life was also about to be turned upside down yet again that day.

The cross-country train arrived at Grimewold station, and Tandori made a simple mistake which was going to unleash a chain reaction that was to, yet again, land her in deep trouble. She had been reading *Hello!* magazine and nearly missed her stop. If she had not got off at Grimewold the train would have carried onto Cleethorpes, some 30 miles further east and made her very late for her afternoon meeting with Zara, not a good start. So she moved with uncharacteristic speed, grabbed the pink suitcase and headed for the exit.

She yanked the pink suitcase out of the carriage in front of her and then realized that she had left the rucksack on her seat. Never very good at making decisions, Tandori froze between the door and the platform and that momentary delay meant that the doors closed on her trapping her baggy dungarees in the hydraulic powered doors. Being a brand-new carriage built by Hitachi, a Japanese company famed for its precision engineering the doors were not about to release their victim. Fearing being dragged along the platform to her death, Tandoori tried her hardest to break free, and applied maximum forward velocity. The doors were not about to give up their quarry, but the realisation there was an obstruction, set off an ear-splitting alarm, which alerted the driver not to move forward. In fact, the sophisticated Hitachi Train disabled itself and would not work until the obstruction was no longer detected.

It was now a battle of wills and Tandori only broke free by pulling so hard that the dungarees eventually gave way and left a large tear in her not insubstantial rear. In her panic, and the fact that she feared arrest by British Transport Police, she moved at speed through the concourse, her pink and black spotted knickers on display and headed outside, immediately seeing Jennings' beige Austin Maestro and dived in.

'Drive, drive Jennings, as fast as you can.'

'What's wrong, why?'

'Just bloody drive Jennings, and keep your foot down hard.'

Jennings did as he was told and soon they were out of the station car park and off at speed towards the town centre and the Diversity Action Partnership offices. It was only then that Tandori remembered that she had still left her rucksack on the seat. Never mind, she would phone Northern Rail later and get it recovered from lost property. There couldn't be many rucksacks left on a train carriage with Miracle Grow and electric mouse traps in them.

As usual in Tandori's life, things were not that simple. It took a while for British Transport Police to arrive and assess the situation. They had been dealing with a particularly unpleasant incident up the line with a group of youths and a down's syndrome victim that they were torturing with paint stripper and gaffer tape. Inspector Plow was not in a good mood.

The train was still stationary. The doors were still jammed, which meant the train could not move. It was now 20 minutes behind schedule to Cleethorpes and the whole network was grounded. It wasn't just a simple case of opening the hydraulic doors and removing the offending denim remnants of Tandori's dungarees. A Miss Tibbles had reported the offending rucksack and added to the confusion by stating that a very dangerous looking terrorist had left the carriage at speed and ran along the concourse. She couldn't tell whether it was a man or a women, but they looked very shifty.

Plow wasn't about to take any chances. The sniffer dogs were bought in and once the door was opened by the over-ride system, they entered and went mental once they sniffed the Miracle Grow, a fertilizer based liquid in Tandori's rucksack. That was enough for Plow. He soon had a robot infra-red sniffer approach the carriage and inspect the offending rucksack. The Miracle Grow combined with unknown electrical appliances in the form of the electric mouse traps which the robot discovered were enough to convince Inspector Plow that he was dealing with a particularly nasty terrorist incident the likes of which Grimewold Station had never seen.

The Bomb Squad were duly called from the nearest military establishment and by late lunchtime a controlled explosion was enacted, which resulted in the brand new £2 million Hitachi carriage being reduced to smouldering ash and twisted metal after the rest of the train had been detached and moved a safe distance away. The whole of the North East rail franchise was grounded for the rest of the week and Northern Rail Group lost at least £12 million in earnings, plus compensation to the ever inconvenienced traveling public.

The man, or women, hunt was now on. Inspector Plow had a major terrorist on the loose somewhere in Grimewold. In his opinion ISIS, or possibly North Korea, had come to Grimewold. Nothing could be further from the truth, but for the second time in a month, Tandori was going to face possible terrorist charges. She just didn't know it yet.

Chapter 36

'I want the whole area locked down, no one enters or leaves Grimewold railway station, do I make myself clear?'

Plow was determined that the British Transport Police, North Lincolnshire and East Riding Division, were going to solve this crime and arrest the perp. He did not want interference from the Met who were nationally responsible for terrorist crimes, the local Humberwold Police force or indeed MI5.

He soon assembled a small team of colleagues to help him in his quest for glory. Hives, Maxine Collins, and Robottom were the principal players.

Meanwhile Tandori had reached the Diversity Action Partnership Limited, blissfully unaware of the absolute chaos she had left behind at Grimewold Railway Station. She was more concerned that she had reached her new employer in time for the 2.00 meeting arranged with Zara and her team. Jennings dropped her off and headed for his flat on the Cromwell estate so he could shower and get ready for his leaving do at the Auditorium arranged by Pauline Piffle.

Pauline, meanwhile, was still in reception nursing a coffee and waiting for her husband to come and get her and discuss final arrangements for Jennings leaving do. Much to her surprise, it was not Piffle who entered reception, but Mike Morrell.

He could wait no longer after reaching his office, having a sniffy of scotch from his hip flask he made up his mind. He was not going to let Pauline Piffle slip through his hands, it was love at first sight. Like most things in Morrell's life, he engaged action before thought or consequences. Sometimes things worked in his favour and sometimes they did not, but no one could accuse Morrell of procrastination, he was a man of action make no mistake.

'Excuse me love, I understand your name is Pauline, Pauline Piffle?'

Pauline looked up quizzically. 'That's right can I help you?'

'Help me, you bet you can help me love. I think you're the most beautiful women I've ever set eyes on Pauline.' By this time Morrell was bended on one knee and took Pauline's limp and reluctant hand.

'I want to spend the rest of my life with you Pauline. No, I'll go further, I'm going to marry you Pauline Piffle. You're the woman of me dreams.'

'But, but you'ave never met me, and who are you?'

'Sorry my love in my haste I didn't introduce myself. My name is Mike Morrell, Managing Director of the Humberwold Speed, Action

Partnership Limited, I share these offices with Piffle, I mean Dresden Piffle.'

'My husband.'

'Yes. I can't believe that such a beautiful, sophisticated, erudite, gorgeous women is married to a fat, loud-mouthed, uncouth, unsophisticated, motormouthed prat like Sydney Dresden Piffle. The man is an afront to humanity. Well, all will change now Pauline Piffle. It's me that loves you and together we will face the world together and build an amazing future, together. Picture it Pauline, you and me against the world.'

At that moment Tandori entered the reception with her mauve cropped hair, torn dungarees, and spotted pink and black knickers showing from the huge tear down her not insubstantial behind. The moment was lost as Morrell, and Pauline looked on in amazement at the spectacle before them.

Tandori approached reception.

'This is a bit embarrassing. I'm here to see Zara Bindle, but I've had an accident with my dungarees and need to use your ladies' room to change. I've ripped them and I can't walk around like this. I've got spare clothes in my suitcase here.'

'Well dear, we can't have you looking like that for your important meeting. Come this way and I will help you get changed. Zara is expecting you dear.'

Mike Morrell and Pauline Piffle looked on, mesmerized by the black and pink knickers and Tandori's enormous arse clearly on display for the world to see.

'Well that's buggered the moment hasn't it Pauline?' said Mike Morrell, chuckling for once.

'Tell you what love, I'm going to give you my business card. Call me any time, day or night when you're ready and I promise you, you won't regret it. I always mean what I say, and I mean it Pauline, you are the one.'

With that, he was up and off through the double doors leaving Pauline with a mix of emotions, bewilderment being the dominant one, closely followed by anxiety.

Chapter 37

Back at Grimewold Railway Station things were moving apace. Inspector Plow had got Maxine Collins going through the CCTV footage at the front of the station. Sadly, one of the key cameras had recently been vandalized and the one that was working didn't have the right angle to capture which direction the perp went in. She would have to look at every car that left the station within a twenty-minute time frame and hope that the terrorist didn't leave the station on foot, which Collins thought unlikely. She was particularly interested in cars that had sped away from the scene. All of this would take valuable time.

Meanwhile, Inspector Plow had got Hives interviewing passengers on the concourse and in the carriage which had been detained in the waiting room on the concourse. In many cases, people were not happy with the inconvenience, but Plow was determined that his team were to get the maximum information they could before people dissipated and vital information was lost.

The star witness, Miss Tibbles, was of particular interest as she shared a carriage with Tandori and had the best description of the terrorist.

Sadly, Inspector Plow's attempts to keep the investigation within British Transport Police were in vain. His boss had decided that the Met had to be informed and once Tandori had been identified as the perp, it would not be long before Inspector Fleece was back in charge and on his way up to Grimewold to take over the investigation.

'Now look here Maxwold, it was me who was first on the scene and can I remind you that the crime took place within British Transport Police jurisdiction. There is no need to get the Met involved at this stage, if at all.'

'I appreciate what you are saying Inspector, but this is obviously a terrorist incident and nationally the Met and MI5 are responsible for terrorist acts of this magnitude. A £2 million brand new Hitachi carriage has been blown up and the whole northern line rail franchise brought to a standstill. I have to inform the Met and MI5, and I am doing that now. I am sure they will take over the investigation immediately. In the meantime, I suggest you keep your colleagues on the scene carrying out the investigation until they are asked to stand down.'

With that, Maxwell Brant, Chief Inspector of the British Transport Police North Lincolnshire and East Riding Division, made the call to the Metropolitan Police Terrorist hotline, and was immediately put through to the Chief Inspector who already had knowledge of the incident in Grimewold from BBC News 24 that was constantly playing on his flat screen Television at the far end of his substantial office. After being brought up to speed by Maxwell Brant, he did indeed instruct that a crack team of officers from the Met should be dispatched immediately to Grimewold to take over the investigation.

'Joyce, get hold of Inspector Fleece and Constable Brahmes, I need them to go up to Grimewold pronto to head up this latest terrorist investigation.'

The chief constable's secretary remembered Fleece from her last unpleasant encounter.

'Are you sure that's wise Sir, Fleece I mean?'

'Yes Joyce, it gets him out of our hair and gives him something to get his teeth into after the issues surrounding the Birkett-Morris case.'

'Will do Sir, I will make sure they leave for Grimewold today.'

Chapter 38

'And what exactly did this woman look like?'

'Not sure it was a woman,' said Miss Tibbles.

'Looked like a terrorist to me, very shifty beady little eyes, shining bright.'

'Can you be a bit more specific Madam?' asked Hives. The British Transport Police officer being given the dubious honour of interviewing the prime witness.

'Well officer, it sat opposite me in the carriage, wore blue denim dungarees, had short cropped pink hair, very fat, the lower part anyway, and as I said shifty bright beady little eyes. It was reading *Hello!* magazine to cover its face, an obvious cover, left the ruck sack on purpose and moved with speed to the exit. Then the alarm went off and it ran along the concourse and disappeared.'

'And you're not sure if it was a man or a woman?'

'Hard to tell, could have been one of those, you know, Lesley types.'

'Lesley types? what do you mean Miss?'

'You know, queer, goes with other women.'

'Oh, you mean Lesbian women.'

'That's right, a Lesley.'

'Well, from your description I dare say we are looking for a women, I'll update the description and check the CCTV.'

Hives relayed the dubious description back to Inspector Plow and it wasn't long before Tandori was spotted on CCTV, by Maxine Collins, getting into the beige Austin Maestro, and driving off at a speed, uncharacteristic of the cars age and driver.

'Bingo sir, there she is, look getting into that car.'

Maxine Collins was elated, she had found the Terrorist suspect.

'Has to be her,' said Inspector Plow, 'well done, very well done. Can we get a registration on that Maestro, there can't be many of them about now.'

'No Sir, only one of the CCTV cameras is working and we can only get a side view of the car as she gets in.'

'Damn, let's see if there's any CCTV up the street and we might be able to get a registration off that.'

Inspector Plow was in luck, the council soon tracked down the Maestro registration number heading along Cromwell Road towards the town centre. F293 TOJ, an original Coventry registered vehicle Plow noted, the vehicle keeper being a one Anthony David Jennings with an address on the notorious Cromwell Estate.

Plow immediately requested that his team stake out the flat until someone returned so that an arrest could be made. This one was in the bag, and he, Inspector Plow, was going to get the credit for apprehending a terrorist and making an arrest before the Met or MI5 turned up sticking their noses in where they were not wanted. Plow was still smarting over being overruled by his superior officer. He wanted the glory for himself and arresting Anthony David Jennings was a sure way to get it. He might even get interviewed on News at Ten.

Chapter 39

'Come on pet, I'll just have a Nescafe and we can be on our way. I hope you've requisitioned a fast car.'

'Yes sir, a BMW M5 high pursuit vehicle sir, good for 155 mph.'

'Excellent Brahmes, you can drive, I've some paperwork to attend to. I'll book us into a Premier Inn on the way, I think we'll be up there for quite some time.'

Soon Inspector Fleece and Constable Brahmes were on their way up north, flying up the M1 at 90 mph, blue lights flashing whenever a lesser vehicle got in their way.

'We'll settle in at the Premier Inn overnight and make a start in the morning. I wonder if there's a good curry house in Grimewold? Don't like to start a new case on an empty stomach,' said Inspector Fleece.

It didn't take long for Fleece to want a pee break and to stretch his legs.

'Bloody hell Brahmes, I could kill for a Nescafe. Look, Leicester Forest East is coming up, pull in there so I can stretch my legs and grab a coffee.'

So the high speed journey was broken and Inspector Fleece had his customary 30 minute coffee break, much to the annoyance of Constable Brahmes who failed to see why they needed to travel at 90 mph in a fast pursuit BMW if only to waste 30 minutes at a very sub-standard motorway service area.

Meanwhile, at the Diversity Action Partnership, after getting changed, Tandori had made her 2.00 p.m. meeting with Zara Bindle. All her earlier troubles seemed to be behind her.

'So good of you to be able to start at short notice Ms Birkett-Morris,' purred Zara. She was in a splendid mood. Finally, a like-minded transgender person who could come into the organisation and transform it into a highly profitable, diverse and modern organisation. An example of what gay people, transgenders and ethnic minorities could achieve without the dead weight of white, conservative middle-aged men.

'Please, call me Tandori, all my friends and colleagues do.'

'Well Tandori, there is a lot to do as you can see. We are, I'm afraid, stuck in the dark ages up here, more like 1959 than 2022. Dresden Piffle, who owns the company, is somewhat set in his ways I'm afraid, and sadly his ways are more akin to Fred Kite, 1959. What we need is to introduce computer technology to track the invoices and send out the fines from a dedicated CSI database, streamline the staff and replace the old guard with new female, transgender, gay and ethnic minority blood. Did you know, there are even some Afghan and Syrian refugees in the town? We might be able to bag a couple of those.'

'Well Ms Bindle I would like to help you in any way I can. My specialism is CSI computer database systems. I set one up for Conservative Central Office, very successful,' Tandori lied. It had been an unmitigated disaster with Conservative voters told not to vote and Labour voters targeted to vote Labour by mistake. Nearly cost the Tories the last General Election, and now they had a wafer thin majority, in no small part due to the bloody CSI system Tandori had managed.

'That sounds splendid Tandori, and like-wise you must call me Zara, us girls have got to stick together. It has been so tedious here having no one on my wave length to talk to.'

On the meeting went, with Zara keen to demonstrate to Tandori how the existing paper-based filing system worked. Each company had a file, in alphabetical order. Within each file there was a summary sheet of fines issued and fines paid, usually by cheque. There was also a visit report detailing all the visits made by the enforcement team and finally any details of court action taken, completed or outstanding. A case worker was assigned to each company, so although the system generated large amounts of revenue, it was also very time consuming and costly.

'The thing is Tandori, if we set up a CSI database linked directly to a client account and an automatic fine system paid by BACS, then the amount of visits can be reduced by the enforcement teams and they can concentrate their firepower on the difficult clients who simply won't pay without court proceedings. I estimate also that at least half of the hundred admin staff can be let go once the system is automated.'

Just at that time, Piffle barged into Zara's office without knocking as was his usual habit. He had just arrived by taxi from his Hull residence in order to make final arrangements for Jennings' leaving do that evening. He did not want Zara Bindle to attend given the delicate situation with regards to Jennings' dismissal. The bitch could have her way for now but wasn't going to rub salt into the wound.

As he opened the door to Zara's office, he was greeted with the site of an enormous arse protruding either side of a far-too-small wooden chair which had come from the school that had closed down.

Tandori had had to wear the only thing that came to hand, which was a pair of black leggings that showed every bump and curve. Piffle could not believe his eyes, immediately there were uncontrolled stirrings in his nether regions. In short, Piffle had the most enormous erection at the site of Tandori's magnificent arse and, for once, didn't know where to put himself.

'Blood and sand!' he exclaimed.

They both looked round, not sure what he meant. And Tandori's case, not knowing who this larger than life character was.

'I see your manners still haven't improved Dresden. Tandori, this is your ultimate boss and Chairman of the Diversity Action Partnership

Limited, Sydney Dresden Piffle.'

'Very pleased to meet you Mr Piffle,' gushed Tandori in awe of the man before her.

'And bloody pleased to meet you an all. Welcome to the good ship Diversity Action Partnership,' boomed Piffle with a lustful look he could hardly contain.

'This is Tandori Birkett Morris, our new transgender recruit who is self-identifying as a man,' Bindle said as if by way of clarifying the situation.

'Well she certainly doesn't look like any man I've ever clapped eyes upon – man my arse. Excuse me my dear, I speak as I find and I can be rather blunt at times.'

'That's the understatement of the year,' butted in Bindle.

'That's all right Mr Piffle, I'm sure you're a very nice man.'

Zara was keen to bring this awkward three-way conversation to an end, and ended the meeting with Tandori as swiftly as possible.

'What do you want Dresden?'

'Just to tell you that all the preparations are made for Jennings' leaving do at Auditorium and I think it best, given the situation, that you don't attend. Me and Pauline have it all in hand, leaving speech and presents etc, and after all, he is staying on in a different capacity. Offered him the gatehouse at me house in Hull, you know the one,

Maxwell House near Beverley.'

'That's fine with me Dresden, Hugo and myself are hosting a diner party tonight so that fits in perfectly. I hope you have a good time, if that is all...'

'Just one more thing,' said Piffle turning to Tandori. 'What are you doing tonight love? First night an all, must be lonely, why don't you come to the do? Chance to meet some of the staff and mingle.'

'Well Mr Piffle,—'

'Call me Dresden.'

'Well Mr Dresden, I'm only staying at the Premier Inn this week, so I am at a bit of a loose end. I could come I suppose, but I haven't got an evening dress.'

'You come in what you like love, I'm sure you'll look a picture. There's a minibus laid on from here at 7.00 p.m. so why not pop back and get on that? Take you straight to Auditorium.'

'That's very kind Mr Dresden, I will do just that.' beamed Tandori.

Piffle of course had ulterior motives for inviting Tandori, very much linked to his lustful desires for his new found employee that he was determined to take advantage of in any way he could, starting at poor Jennings leaving do.

Chapter 40

Inspector Fleece and Constable Brahmes arrived at the Grimewold Premier Inn just in time for a buffet dinner. Constable Brahmes had a light chicken salad, whereas Inspector Fleece's culinary tastes were more carnivorous and substantial. In short, Fleece filled a substantial plate with three burgers, hot chicken wings, a gammon steak with fried egg, thick cut chips and fried onion rings, plus a side order of salad. Not forgetting a desert of chocolate cheesecake with white cream custard. While they were both tucking into their food an important text came through from the Met with an attached grainy photo of the terrorist at Grimewold station getting into an Austin Maestro car. There could be no mistaking who it was in Fleece's mind.

'I knew it Brahmes. They've just sent through a picture of the terrorist, and guess who we're looking for? Don't answer that Brahmes, its quite obviously that bitch, Tandori Birkett-Morris, who MI5 forced me to release back into the community. I told them Brahmes, I told them we were dealing with a particularly nasty ISIS terrorist, but would they believe me? No! And now look what's happened, she's done it again and blown up a bloody expensive train carriage and then escaped our grasp. Well this time we will track her down Brahmes, and this time we will keep her behind lock and bloody key until her trial.'

'You're so clever Inspector Fleece, she can't have got far and when you make the arrest you will be a national hero.'

Fleece puffed his chest out at this compliment 'It's not about me Brahmes, I'm just the catalyst. It's about justice and keeping this wonderful country safe from misguided scum like Birkett-Morris who are trying to destroy our way of life.'

Fleece had a dreamy, far-away look as he fantasised about a Great Britain that had long since ceased to be: warm beer, cricket on a Sunday afternoon, neighbours looking out for one another and borrowing bowls of sugar, their doors left open all day, mothers pushing their offspring in Silver Cross prams while father went to work in a factory proud of the manufacture of products stamped, *Made in Great Britain.*

'Are you all right Sir? You look a bit queasy,' said Brahmes, a worried look on her face.

'I'm fine Brahmes, just remembering a time long since passed.'

'Anyway, I suggest we go and get freshened up and meet down here around 7.30. Then we can get a taxi to a curry house in town, we can start hunting down Birkett-Morris in the morning. My instinct tells me, Brahmes, that the bitch is close at hand, and it won't be long before we have her behind bars again.'

Little did Inspector Fleece know just how close Birkett-Morris was, in fact she was lodging in the very same Premier Inn that they were, and Fleece's plans for another huge 'all you can eat' buffet were to be put on hold.

It was pure coincidence that Tandori was spotted at all. She got back to the Premier Inn at 5.00 p.m., checked in and went to freshen up, shower and change into the most glamorous dress she had bought with her, ready to go to Jennings' leaving do at the Grimewold Auditorium later that evening.

Tandori came down to order a taxi back to the Diversity Action Partnership offices to get the minibus to the auditorium, it was 6.30 p.m. Unlucky for Tandori, Constable Brahmes had also come down to reception to get some extra Nescafe pouches for Inspector Fleece, knowing he would need some later. As Tandori was going out of the double doors to the waiting taxi, Brahmes caught sight of her and realized from their last encounter that she was looking at the 'terrorist'. Brahmes rushed out, but not in time to stop Tandori. The taxi was speeding away, but she did manage to get the taxi company's name, *Kate's Cabs*.

Brahmes rushed back inside and reached Fleece's room in no time, banging vigorously on his door.

'Wait a minute pet, I'm just coming, have you got my Nescafe?'

'Sir, sir, I've seen her sir. Speeding off in a taxi.'

'Seen who?'

'The terrorist sir, you know, Birkett-Morris, staying here at this very hotel she is. I've got the name of the taxi firm sir, *Kate's Taxis*.'

'Right, very well done Brahmes. Game on. Go to reception and see if they booked that cab and if they know where it's going, and get the phone number of the cab company. We're close to tracking the bitch down.'

'Right away sir.'

Constable Brahmes rushed down to reception and found that they had booked the cab to take Tandori to a company address called the Diversity Action Partnership. The receptionist was pretty sure the company was based at the old Central Library Building in the centre of town. Brahmes also managed to get the taxi cab number, 666999. After a quick Nescafe, Inspector Fleece was down in reception.

'What have you got for me Brahmes?'

'Sir, she's on her way to a company called the Diversity Action Partnership Limited, already been dropped off in the car park apparently. The cab company is ringing me back in a couple of minutes after speaking to the driver.'

The phone rang almost straight away.

'Hello, Constable Brahmes speaking. Yes, yes, good, fantastic. Thank you so much.'

'Well, what did they say?'

'Sir, the driver said that Tandori was boarding a minibus and apparently going to a leaving do for one of the staff of the Diversity Action Partnership at Grimewold Auditorium. She has booked a cab back with them for 11.00 p.m., so she'll be in the auditorium for quite some time.'

'Excellent work Brahmes. That gives us ample time to organise an armed response unit and conduct a raid. We're close to getting the bitch Brahmes, so close. Excuse me a minute, I just want to make a quick phone call.'

At the far end of the lobby away from Constable Brahmes, Fleece made his call.

'Is that you Phinella, Phinella Phuton?'

'It is, who am I speaking to?

'It's me, Inspector Fleece of the Metropolitan Police. Listen pet, I have the scoop of the decade for you.'

'I'm listening Inspector.'

'You know that terrorist incident a few weeks ago? That block of flats being blown up by a suspected ISIS terrorist?'

'Yes of course I do, I covered it on News at Ten.'

'Well yesterday, a train carriage was blown to smithereens up north at a place called Grimewold, same terrorist, and we know she is attending the Grimewold Auditorium tonight. If I take in an armed response unit and arrest her around 10.15 p.m. you could be there filming live for the ITN News. You get the scoop of the decade, and I get the accolades for arresting the most dangerous terrorist in Great Britain. What do you say?'

'Excellent Inspector, you have a deal. I'll get the ITN helicopter and a camera crew, and we'll fly up to, where did you say, Grimewold?' We can be in the Auditorium reception when you make the arrest and bring the terrorist out, live on air. We'll get Martin Buckley to announce a major terrorist incident is taking place and go live to the scene at 10.15. It will indeed be the scoop of the decade, and time for the pictures to be syndicated for the morning papers. I'll make sure that my tame photographer is there and we can share in the proceeds of the sale of photos to the world's press. This is going to be as good as the Iranian Embassy siege, which made Kate Aidie's career. Happy days Inspector, I can't believe our luck!'

Fleece came off the phone with a nasty self-congratulatory sneer. Not only was he, Inspector Fleece, going to be the hero of the hour, he was going to be paid handsomely for the photos sold to the world's press. Might make him fifty grand, enough to retire maybe with what he had already got stashed away. He hadn't been in the drugs squad for nothing in a previous role.

'Right Brahmes, you get onto Humberwold Police HQ and organise an armed response team. I want ten men heavily armed, plus tear gas, smoke canisters and an armed response Land Rover. We're going to burst in at 10.00 p.m. sharp whilst the party is in full swing. It's only 7.00 p.m., I think we still have time for a quick curry, Brahmes, before the action commences. We'll meet the Humberwold armed response team and their commanding officer at 9.00 in the auditorium car park ready for action.

'Yes sir, right away sir'

So the stage was set, Birkett Morris was going to be arrested live on national television and Inspector Fleece was going to be a national hero, and many thousands of pounds richer for the photo's. Sometimes the universe just aligns to create the perfect scenario, and for Fleece that moment had come!

Chapter 41

Inspector Plow was having an altogether less satisfactory evening staking out the run-down flat belonging to Anthony Jennings on the Cromwell Estate. No one had turned up in two hours and the whole block was eerily quiet.

He was sitting in the back of a transit van, with external lenses fed to a tv monitor in a confined sweaty hell hole with his motley crew consisting of Hives, Maxine Collins and Robottom. Around the corner, underneath the notorious high rise, renamed Hugo Chavez court by the hapless Labour Council, sat an unmarked Police BMW as backup.

As nothing was kicking off, the two officers had nipped across to the only shop still open on the estate, a Paddy Power bookies, to place a five way bet on the Premier league for the coming Saturday. Which, in the unlikely event of all five matches going their way, would net them £106,000 for a £20 bet. Like Fleece, they too had dreams of escaping Grimewold to a retirement villa in Florida.

More immediately, what the officers didn't realise, was that their new BMW 5 Series Touring Estate, valued at more than £40,000, was about to suffer an ignominious fate.

Local yobs had a particularly dangerous game that they undertook every Monday evening which involved the 'throwing of the fridge' competition. This involved collecting as many heavy white goods as possible such as fridges, washing machines, fridge freezers and tumble dryers, taking them in the lift up to the twelfth floor flat, owned by one of the gang, and throwing them off the balcony at passing pensioners in the hope of getting a direct hit and killing one of them. Too many violent video games had sanitized the yobs to this 'harmless' crime and no one had even challenged them. The local Romanian Gypsy Gang came and took the scrap metal away in the morning, no one except the terrified residents were any the wiser, and up until now nothing had been damaged and no one hurt. Just a bit of fun as far as the yobs were concerned.

As usual a 7.5kg drum Samsung washing machine was thrown off the balcony and landed a direct hit on the roof of the unmarked BMW high pursuit vehicle. There was the most almighty crash. like a bomb going off. The vehicle was a write off. Even the yobs realized they had made a terrible mistake despite being coked up and not able to analyse what they had done in any detail.

Sergeant Didcott and Constable Leach ran out of the Paddy Power Bookies and looked in disbelief at the remains of their pride and joy. The BMW had only come into active service at the weekend and now it was a write off, and more importantly, they had not been on guard when the crime occurred when they should have been. Privately they thought they were bloody lucky not to be dead as they almost surely would have.

Inspector Plow and his team heard the crash but could not see what was happening. Fearful of attack they leapt into action

'Go go go!' shouted Inspector Plow and the four of them exited the Transit van at speed and headed for the direction of the noise. Round the corner they saw the BMW, or what was left of it, and the two hapless police officers standing by it wondering what to do next. Someone had phoned the fire brigade and the distant wail of sirens could be heard approaching in the background.

Once the fire engine arrived a huge number of local kids emerged from the shadows throwing stones and rocks at it, and one of the young yobs climbed into the cab and tried to get the engine started so they could steal it. Other police cars arrived and the area was cornered off for public safety. All in all, a complete bloody fiasco, and one that wasn't going to do Plow's career any good at all.

Chapter 42

Jennings' leaving do was just getting going. Guests arriving from far and wide. Dresden and Pauline had done Jennings proud. There were many members of the local Gipsyville local Labour group in attendance, some from way back arrived in a 53 seat Plaxton's coach. Many of the staff from the Diversity Action Partnership, some of Jennings school friends from Gipsyville Secondary Modern had been tracked down, including some from his form group 4B. In all, nearly 150 guests had turned up to hear Dresden give a leaving speech, drink lots of beer and have a dance on the dance floor with a disco laid on.

Dresden stood outside greeting guests like a glorified doorman, and Pauline mingled inside in a black sequined dress and matching black stiletto shoes. Then, out of the blue, a very unwelcome guest arrived, at least as far as Piffle was concerned - his wayward son, Bradley who he wasn't on speaking terms with.

Bradley Normal Piffle, aged 52, had been driven up from London in his Maybach limousine, with his gay black husband, Lemar, and his hapless personal assistant, Tiggy, in tow.

It had never occurred to anyone in Piffle's household that

having the initials BNP in, probably the most left-wing Marxist seat in the country, might prove a handicap at school. Bradley Norman Piffle was bullied mercilessly from a young age and it wasn't long before Pauline Piffle decided to send the young Piffle to a private school called King Alfred the Great's College in North Yorkshire to escape the torment. It was in such an environment of male-only dorms, with no female contact at all, that young Piffle identified himself as gay. Dresden Piffle was not impressed, especially when Bradley started coming home dressed like Boy George, complete with mascara and lip stick. Explosive rows ensued and Bradley escaped to London and got involved in the 80's music scene aged just 17.

Various auditions, bit parts and many years later, and he was cast in a new risqué Friday night programme for Channel 7even called *Purple Haze*, which involved minor celebrity guests and wannabe celebrities getting coked off their heads before coming onto the panel show to be mercilessly ridiculed by Bradley who had assumed the stage name of Bradley Plumb, and dressed head to toe in purple velvet pants and jacket. As was the dire state of comedy in the new millennium, Bradley adopted the abhorrent catch phrase of 'how long are your turds?' and his career sky rocketed challenging the viewing figures of established entertainers such as the Jonathan Ross Show.

Now, much to Piffle's disgust and embarrassment, his son was a household institution and very highly paid. He earned well over £2 million a year for hosting what Piffle could only describe as utter filth and garbage that was neither funny nor entertaining.

Tiggy exited the Maybach first and from a large satin bag started dropping purple rose petals on the ground as Braders, as he liked to be called, emerged with his lover Lemar, who was dressed in tight black jeans and a gold string vest with a massive gold chain round his neck and gold studded hand cuffs. A London photographer had obviously been tipped off and was taking photos to be syndicated to the gutter press and *Hello!* magazine. The two of them strutted towards the entrance, with Tiggy throwing purple rose petals on the floor, before reaching a furious Sydney Dresden Piffle who barred their entrance to the Auditorium.

'What the bloody hell are you doing here Bradley?'

'His friends call him Braders,' chipped in Lemar.

'Well I'm his bloody father and I call him Bradley, alright son?' said Piffle giving Lemar a withering look of contempt.

'I think, father, It's fairly obvious what I'm doing here. Ma-ma has invited me because Anthony is my godfather and has been a close friend and mentor over the years. I'm here to show support for the contemptible way your company has treated him after years of loyal service, father.'

'Well you can bloody well turn round, with your crushed velvet clothes and nancy-boy purple petals, and get back into the bloody great German monstrosity of a car and head back down to your Tory friends in the south. Do you realize your grandfather, Henry Herbert, would be spinning in his bloody grave if he knew that a Piffle was driving a

German car after what he went through?'

'I will not turn round, the national press is here Father and I suggest you don't make a scene. As for being a Piffle, with a nasty bigoted father like you, I am a Plumb, do you hear me? I am Bradley Plumb, and in any case, Channel 7even supply that limousine not me, so you are wrong again father.'

With that, he pushed past with Lemar and Tiggy in tow, scurrying behind and entered the Auditorium, leaving Piffle fuming. Soon after, Tandori turned up in a Taxi just as Piffle was about to go into the Auditorium.

'You made it then love,' grinned Piffle eyeing Tandori approvingly.

'Well I do feel a bit embarrassed Mr Piffle. I don't know anyone and I am replacing Mr Jennings, but you did invite me so here I am.'

'You do right love, and don't you worry, I'll look after you all night. If anyone so much as passes a comment about you taking Jennings' job, they'll have me to answer to.'

'Oh Mr Piffle you are so kind, it's nice to know a big strong man is looking out for me.'

'No worries love, shall we go inside?' and with that, Piffle opened the swing doors to the Auditorium and in they went together.

One more unwanted guest arrived in the car park a few moments later - Mike Morrell. He knew Jennings of course, but his real quarry that night was Pauline Piffle and the unfinished business they had started.

Chapter 43

As the party was getting started in the Atlee Suite of Grimewold Auditorium, an altogether different party was assembling their fire power.

Inspector Fleece was in his element. He could smell victory that night, and success. He dreamed of an SAS raid on the Auditorium just like the Iranian Embassy siege with a crack team of highly professional soldiers entering the auditorium via helicopters, with tear gas and machine guns and taking out the terrorists inside. The reality was, at short notice, that he had had to make do with the firearms team of Humberwold Police, plus himself and Constable Brahmes to make the arrests. Even so, it was going to be a spectacular finale to the night, all filmed live by ITN News at Ten, with Phinellla Phutton broadcasting live from inside the auditorium foyer.

'Right Brahmes, we're assembling at Grimewold Police Headquarters at 8.00 p.m. sharp. Then we will be liaising with Deputy Assistant Mallard and briefing the team of firearms officers. The plan is to enter the Auditorium at 9.55 p.m. sharp with tear gas, secure the

Atlee Suite, get everyone on the deck and then make the arrests. The terrorist, Birkett-Morris, and her assistant, who we now know is Anthony Jennings, whose leaving do it is at the Auditorium. We will then exit via the foyer with the terrorists and be filmed for the Ten O'clock ITN News with a live feedback to Broadcasting House, with the lead anchor, Phinella Phutton, doing the commentary. I tell you Constable Brahmes, this will be the making of both our careers.'

'Can't wait sir. It looks like you've got all the bases covered. I am so honoured to be working for such a successful police officer, sir.'

'Just the luck of the.draw Brahmes. It was only you spotting Birkett-Morris tonight that has got us this far. Sometimes a dose of luck is all you need in life Brahmes.'

One person not having any luck that night was Inspector Plow of British Transport Police. A fruitless stakeout at Anthony Jennings' flat, and the destruction of an expensive BMW would need some explaining to his superiors. The crushed BMW was just being loaded onto a recovery truck and their work on the Cromwell Estate was done for the night.

'Come on team, nothing else to be doing here. Let's go and have a swift pint at the pub before we clock off for the night.'

So off they went in the transit van, Hives, Maxine Colins, Robottom and Inspector Plow, to a small secluded public house called the Honest Accountant in the business district of the town on Humber Road.

'Don't worry team. We're doing background checks on Jennings and it won't be long before we make an arrest, either at his place of work or his home. He's a local man, so he won't get far and then he should lead us to the terrorist Tandori Birkett-Morris.'

The ITN Helicopter sped north with a full camera crew and Phinella Phutton making notes of what she was going to say. The Home Secretary had been briefed and was due to give a live statement at the end of News at Ten should the terrorists be successfully arrested. After all the stabbings and criminality of late, not to mention the asylum seekers, the Home Secretary desperately needed a good PR story and a boost to the Government's appalling popularity ratings.

As they sped past Daventry, heading North, Phinella mused on how beautiful the country looked at night with all the twinkling lights. she could see to her right the M1 snaking north with all the red rear car lights present, a truly awesome sight but as she knew, far from the reality of life on the streets below.

Chapter 44

Fuelled by cheap alcohol, Jennings' leaving party was really getting started. The Atlee Suite was ideal for a party, there was a stage at the back, a dance area in front, tables and chairs for one hundred seated guests, plus a substantial bar area. Pauline had employed a professional disco outfit who had installed laser lights in various colours. Apart from the bar area, the normal lights were heavily dimmed to create the right atmosphere, and dance music from the '80s and '90s was playing.

Older men were propped up at the bar and family members were seated at the tables. A few clusters of men and women were standing around, drinks in hand, making conversation. A few brave souls were already on the dance floor getting things going.

Bradley Plumb and his entourage had found the only comfortable lounge style sofas and had bagged them, Tiggy bringing drinks to the table on request.

Piffle was doing the rounds glad-handing his old mates, pressing the flesh, whilst Pauline was talking to some of the wives she hadn't seen in ages.

The person who the night was about, Jennings, was seated at one of the tables, alone, people coming up and talking to him on an ad hoc basis feeling somewhat out of the main stream of activities.

Tandori Birkett-Morris, who didn't know anyone, had seated herself at the end of the bar and was nursing a Desperado, alone and wondering why she had bothered to go.

Mike Morrell had sneaked in unnoticed, got himself a drink and was waiting for his chance to talk to Pauline Piffle. In the dim light no one had spotted him and even fewer of those present knew him anyway. If Piffle did see him, there would almost certainly be another altercation that night, but he hoped to avoid that if possible.

After an hour or so, it was time for the speeches, one from Piffle himself and one from his wife Pauline. Piffle went first.

'Ladies and gentlemen, boys and girls, it's my great pleasure to welcome you here tonight to celebrate the retirement of my good and close friend Anthony Jennings. Anthony has worked for me at the Diversity Action Partnership and had done, I must say, a very worthwhile job. But Anthony Jennings is more than that. He has been a loyal friend and comrade for over forty years and has done a lot for me, my family and the Gipsyville Labour Constituency Party.'

The speech droned on for another ten minutes to a muted round of applause and then it was Pauline's turn.

'I just want to say Anthony, that you mean a lot to me my dear. I've have known you since we both went to Gipsyville Secondary Modern and you have been a loyal and dear friend. I realise that your work at the office is done, but I'd like to welcome you to your new life as our gardener and chauffer at Maxwell House where you will have use of the Gatehouse to live. Everybody raise your glass to Anthony Jennings.'

'Hip hip hooray! Hip hip hooray! Hip hip hooray!'

There was a rapturous round of applause and then it was Jennings' turn. Not used to public speaking he just said a few faltering words.

'Tha-thank you P-Pauline and you Dre-Dresden. You have always been good to me and I am grateful for tonight and to ev-everyone who has come along. Ha-have a good drink on me.'

Another round of applause and the speeches were complete. The music went up a notch and people staring pouring onto the dance floor. Over the music the DJ announced the buffet would be served at 9.00.

'Hey man, this gaff is way out man, really cool,' said Lemar, lounging on the draylon sofa.

'I'm not sure about that. It's typical Piffle as far as I'm concerned, all show and no substance. Anyway, to make the fucking thing more bearable, send Tiggy to get me another bottle of champers. At least by getting pissed I can blot out the horror of it all.'

Bradley Plum was beginning to regret coming, but he did still love his mother, had been friends with Anthony and, more to the point, enjoyed humiliating his father in front of his friends, and having Lemar and Tiggy in tow certainly achieved that.

At opposite ends of the Atlee Suite two people made their move. Piffle had spotted Tandori drinking alone, and Mike Morrell had spotted Pauline Piffle going to the ladies' loos.

'Eh up love, lovely lady like you drinking alone?'

'Oh Mr Piffle you know how to impress a lady,' gushed Tandori.

'Barman get this lady whatever her poison is, and I'll have a scotch on the rocks.'

'So, what brings you to our little part of the world here in Grimewold Tandori? I'd have thought a girl like you would be working in London.'

'Well Mr Piffle, I always like a new challenge, and I believe in what you're doing, equality for women, gays, transgenders and ethnic groups. I just didn't feel right helping the Tory Party, and me being transgender myself it seemed a good place to come.'

'You certainly don't look like any man I've ever seen Tandori,' said Piffle taking in the object of beauty and sexual desire that was causing a stirring in his loins. 'You're all women as far as I can see love.'

'Oh you are kind Mr Piffle, and I hope that I can rise to the challenge and move things forward at the Diversity Action Partnership.'

'I'm sure you will my dear, and rise to the challenge in more ways than one.'

Piffles crude attempts at sexual banter had clean gone over Tandori's head, and she had no idea that the challenges he had in mind did not involve efficiency gains and staff changes at the Diversity Action Partnership, more the challenges of sexual conquest in the bedroom and elsewhere.

'Will you honour an old man with a dance Tandori?'

'Oh Mr Piffle I would love to, let me just finish my Desperados.'

Mike Morrell was waiting outside the ladies' loos when Pauline Piffle came out.

'Pauline, it's me Mike, I had to come here tonight when I knew you would be here. We have to talk about the future.'

'Mike it's not a good time, you shouldn't have come, and I hardly know you.'

'Well I know Jennings very well and I've come to pay my respects, he often used to bring me a latte in the morning. Good man. Not fair what they've done to him.'

'It's just if Dresden sees you there's bound to be fireworks, especially if he see you with me, his wife.'

'It's so bloody dark in here with those disco lights, I'd be surprised if he could spot us together or indeed anyone else. And if he does, so what? It proves nothing. I'm here to support Jennings and wish him well, and I just happened to bump in to you. It isn't a crime. Anyway, if Piffle was so interested in you, how come he isn't with you at this very moment? I bet he hasn't paid you any attention all evening has he?'

'Well Mike that is true, I haven't seen Dresden all night. He's in his element, glad-handing all his old Labour comrades, and friends going way back to Gipsyville. He never pays me any attention these days, calls me the 'Clothes Horse' and spends most of his time with that slut of a housekeeper at the villa is Spain. He thinks I don't know, but I do and I caught him in bed with two fat slags from his favourite haunt, the Black Chicken, only a couple of weeks ago. The candle of our love burnt out a long time ago,' said Pauline wistfully.

'You've said it yourself then Pauline my love. Leave the bastard and be with me. I'll look after you and treat you like a bloody queen, I will. Will you give me an honour of a dance, seeing as I've come all this way to find you?'

'Why not what harm can it do? It's just a dance. I don't know about us Mike I'll have to give it some thought. I've only ever been married to one man all these years and although it's a disaster now, I'm contented in my own way with my own routines, and I want for nothing materially speaking.'

'Well I'll give you some space, but I want you Pauline Piffle, you are the one and I can't wait forever, do you understand?'

And with that he led Pauline onto the dance floor.

Chapter 45

Piffle was engrossed in his conversation with Tandori and after a few single malts he was ready to ask Tandori for a dance, or as was his lustful way, a serious grope on the dance floor. He just couldn't take his eyes off her enormous arse, bigger in its way even than Honolulu's.

Tandori's thoughts were altogether purer and on a different plane entirely, but after four Desperados, she too was open to suggestions that otherwise would have been out of bounds.

'Come on love let's have a dance, the music is hotting up now. Just a quickie, just for old Piffle.'

'Oh Mr Piffle, I don't think I should, you're the big boss and I hardly know you and what will your wife think?'

'Bollocks to her, I call her the Clothes Horse, haven't been close for years. I'm almost single, and anyhow luv, it's only a quick dance, what harm can it do?'

'Oh alright Mr Piffle, just one quick little dance and then I should think about getting back to the Premier Inn. I've booked a taxi for 11.00

and it's 9.45 now.'

So off they went to the dance floor and joined the thong of bodies attempting to re-enact '80s disco music, despite most of them being many years past their prime.

Piffle wasted no time at all, within seconds he had clasped Tandori close and his hand moved downwards towards that luscious arse he had been eyeing all night and started groping her, a huge erection stirring in his pants.

'Oh Mr Piffle you are naughty, your hand shouldn't be going down there, and in any case I am transgender.'

Piffle had gone puce now as his blood pressure had risen in excitement like a dog on heat, but one that was struggling to keep up given his advancing years.

'Give over love, just having a friendly dance and a grope, what harm can it do?'

At that moment, he glanced across the dance floor and all thoughts of sexual conquest with Tandori came to an abrupt halt as he spotted Mike Morrell dancing closely with his Pauline, their eyes fixed on each other. The drink and jealousy combined into a huge rage that swelled up inside him and he was no longer responsible for his actions, either physically or verbally. That snake Morrell was with his bloody wife. He broke off from Tandori and launched himself across the dance floor.

'You get your bloody filthy hands off my wife. What in God's name is the meaning of this?'

With that he pushed Mike Morrell aside and glared at him.

'Calm down Piffle, I'm just having a quick dance with your wife, no harm done, and seeing as you were otherwise engaged,' sneered Mike and glancing at Tandori who had come across as well.

'Pauline go to the bar, this is man's talk,' snarled Piffle.

'I will do no such thing Sydney Dresden Piffle. How dare you barge across here and embarrass me in front of this kind gentleman? Since you have abandoned me tonight, and for that creature, I should have thought you wouldn't mind who I danced with.'

'Well I'm not bloody having it. That Morrell is bloody bad news. He's been trying to steal my business for some time now and now he's after me wife, can't you see that's what this is about? A petty vendetta because I'm successful, and anyway, he wasn't even invited here tonight. Unless, unless you invited him?'

'I did not, it was just a chance encounter.'

By this time Mike had backed off and raised both hands in a gesture of capitulation. 'Don't worry Piffle, I'm going. I just came to pay my respects to Jennings, and don't want to cause any problems for you or your marriage,' he said smirking, knowing full well he had achieved his objective tonight.

'Well get out and get out now,' shouted Piffle, determined to have the last word even though the situation had been diffused.

'I'm on my way, goodnight Dresden, goodnight Pauline and goodnight...' he looked at Tandori.

'Tandori, Tandori's the name.'

'Good night Tandori.'

And he was gone, off the dance floor and through the door of the Atlee Suite and back into the reception area. Little did he know that it was a shrewd move, he was back outside at his BMW just before 10.00 and just before the next phase of the evening was going to start.

Chapter 46

The helicopter had landed in the Auditorium over-spill car park and Phinella Phutton and the camera crew had exited swiftly and made their way to the Auditorium entrance.

By 9.30 p.m. Inspector Fleece, Constable Brahmes and the crack team of armed response officers from Humberwold Police had also assembled in the front car park ready for their raid on the Atlee Suite.

'Right team, we have reason to believe that Tandori Birkett-Morris and Anthony Jennings are both holed up in the Atlee Suite of the Auditorium and Birkett- Morris in particular has proved herself to be potentially very dangerous. We can take no chances. We have no choice but to go in armed and ready and use tear gas to stun the occupants into submission and make the arrests in the confusion that will follow. Is that understood?'

'Yes Sir,' they said in unison.

'I'm just going to brief the ITN News at Ten camera crew and the lead anchor woman Phinella Phutton. This is about to put Grimewold on the map.'

With that he strode over to the assembled camera crew and addressed Phinella directly.

'Inspector Fleece here. I'm the lead terrorist Detective on this case. We believe a highly dangerous terrorist and her accomplice are holed up in the Auditorium and my crack fire arms squad are going in in 10 minutes at 10.05 p.m. If you can be ready in the reception you can start filming and have a live feed back to London. We envisage having this all wrapped up by 10.30. Is that clear? Any questions?'

'No Inspector Fleece, my camera crew are all ready to go. We will station ourselves in the Auditorium Reception area and will broadcast live from there in 10 minutes' time. This will be going out live on News at Ten as a breaking news announcement. And Inspector Fleece, thanks for the tip-off. This is a career making event,' said Phinella.

Meanwhile the ITN helicopter had taken off again and was filming the auditorium which would be shown just prior to Phinella's piece. All in all a dramatic piece of TV history in the making.

'Right team, assemble at your positions in the reception area. At my word go in hard, with tear gas and machine guns at the ready. The element of surprise is crucial.'

Chapter 47

Inside the Atlee Suite all the guests were oblivious as to what was about to befall them.

Many were just assembled on the stage arms locked and singing the Red Flag whilst others were on the dance floor or still at the bar well pissed by now.

Piffle was on the stage with Pauline and Jennings, and Tandori was back propping up the bar. Bradley Plumb and Lemar were on the draylon sofas pissed or, in the case of Lemar, stoned on coke.

Back at Broadcasting House the lead news presenter, Alistair Stone, put on his serious face and made an announcement. 'I have to interrupt the news this evening for breaking news. We are going over live to the Auditorium at Grimewold to cover a breaking terrorist incident.' On nine million television screens an ariel shot of Grimewold Auditorium was broadcast and then the screen panned into Phinella Phutton live in the Auditorium reception area.

'Tonight I am standing in the foyer of Grimewold Auditorium. I have been tipped off that the dangerous ISIS terrorist responsible for the London flats incident and yesterday's bomb alert at Grimewold Train Station is holed up in this very building. An armed response team are standing by ready to enter through the door behind me and make an arrest.'

The camera panned round to the assembled firearms team in full attire with gas masks already on.

Inspector Fleece barked out the order, 'Go, go, go!'

The firearms team flew past the camera crew, entered the Atlee Suite and threw canisters of tear gas. The lead officer shouted, 'Everybody on the floor now! This is an armed terrorist incident. Everybody get down now and don't move!'

There was absolute pandemonium inside as everyone, except Lemar, dived for cover and all those on the stage, including Piffle, got down and stayed down. Only Lemar sat on the draylon sofa unmoved by events and turned to Bradley and said, 'Finally this gaff is getting going. Like the costumes man.' He hadn't realised it was a live terrorist incident, but presumed it was part of the night's entertainment.

With everybody cowed, Fleece strode in triumphant.

'I want Tandori Birkett-Morris and Anthony Jennings to stand up, put their hands in the air and surrender, do I make myself clear?'

Both of them did as they were asked. The lead firearms officer put them in handcuffs and they were meekly led away to the Atlee Suite door. As they reached Fleece, he looked at them both beaming. 'I am arresting both of you in connection with the terrorist incident at Grimewold Railway Station yesterday. You do not have to say anything, but anything you do say may be taken down and used in evidence against you. Brahmes lead them out to the police car.'

The two terrorist suspects were led out into the reception with the ITN cameras rolling. Fleece followed and made a statement to Phinella Phutton and the cameras. 'Today we have successfully arrested two highly dangerous suspected terrorists responsible for the Hitachi rail bomb scare yesterday and the London flats incident three weeks ago. They are being taken to a secure police station for questioning. All in all, a very successful operation and one the nation should be proud of.'

'Inspector Fleece how did you know the two terrorists would be here?' gushed Phinella.

'We in Great Britain have a highly sophisticated terrorist detection system unrivalled anywhere in the world. The public can be rest assured that all terrorists, especially dangerous Middle Eastern ISIS fanatics, will be found and arrested until this country returns to being the green and peaceful land for which it has been famous down the centuries. Thank you. If you will excuse me, I have important police work to attend to.'

'There you have it viewers, TV history in the making. The successful arrest of two highly dangerous ISIS terrorists on British soil. We will bring you more news as it comes in throughout the night on ITN

News 24. Over to you Alistair.'

And with that the ITN news at Ten resumed its normal discourse and an amazing piece of TV history was made, even though it bore absolutely no relation to the reality of the situation at all.

Back in the Atlee Suite everyone was coughing in tear gas and too shell shocked to do much but stumble round. Paramedics and psychiatric counsellors were on stand-by to assist with post-traumatic stress and asthma.

Piffle once he had got up was absolutely furious. 'What the bloody hell is the meaning of this Pauline? I've known Jennings for forty years and spent some of the evening with Tandori, and I'm telling you, never have I ever met two more unlikely terrorists, never mind bloody ISIS ones. It's a complete bloody police fabrication and cock up.'

For once Piffle was spot on and the party came to an ignominious close, the guests stumbling out to the waiting coach and taxis. Once the dust had settled the reality of the situation might become apparent, but until them Tandori Birkett-Morris and poor Anthony Jennings found themselves in prison and in Tandori's case, for the second time.

Chapter 48

Inspector Fleece was cock-a-hoop as he rode back in the BMW with Constable Brahmes at the wheel.

'I can't believe it Brahmes, it all went like bloody clockwork. Did you see Phinella Phutton give that bloody interview live on ITN News at Ten? We're famous Brahmes, bloody well famous. If this doesn't get me, I mean us, our promotion nothing will. Chief Inspector here I come. Look the Home Secretary is on the news now, I can see her on the TV screen back here on the headrest.'

'*You must be very pleased, Home Secretary, with the outcome of tonight's dramatic events in Grimewold.*'

'*Well as I've always said Alistair, it's a team effort to tackle extremist terrorism, and tonight proves that this Conservative Government takes this issue very seriously. Tonight, thanks to the wonderful work of the Metropolitan Police Service, two dangerous terrorist criminals are behind bars. The people of Great Britain can rest soundly in their beds tonight.*'

The Home Secretary had an air of smugness associated with the firm belief that her chances of becoming Prime Minister had just risen dramatically within the party and that at the very least there was going to be an electoral upswing towards the Conservatives as a result of this very fortuitous and unexpected set of events, in truth nothing to do with the manifest incompetence of the Home Office and indeed the Home Secretary herself.

'I would also like to announce, Alistair, that the Prime Minister himself has telephoned me and called an emergency meeting of COBRA for 7.00 a.m. tomorrow morning. We can't be sure there are not other ISIS terrorist cells out there planning more atrocities on British soil. The British people can be rest assured that this Conservative Government takes homeland security very, very seriously and we will do everything in our power to keep this great country safe from the scourge of terrorist activity, wherever it may be in our society. I would also like to personally thank a courageous officer by the name of Inspector Fleece for uncovering the perpetrators of this unspeakable crime, he truly is the man of the moment, a Great British hero!'

'Did you hear that Brahmes? The bloody Home Secretary has mentioned me by name. That bloody sour-faced tosser of a Chief Constable can't overlook me for promotion any longer, despite his right-on politically correct decision making of late.'

Tandori Birkett-Morris and Jennings were not in quite such high spirits, in fact it was safe to say that they were both bewildered and very fearful of this wholly unexpected turn of events. Jennings more so since his timid and reticent personality was not at all suited to the privations of arrest on serious terrorist charges. Tandori of course had been through the mill before and was more indignant at the latest dramatic change in her circumstances. They had been put in separate police cars and now found themselves in individual holding cells at Grimewold Central Police Station awaiting interrogation by Inspector Fleece an Constable Brahmes.

Inspector Fleece decided that the interrogation of the suspects could wait until the next day. He was extremely tired after the day's activities and desperately wanted a single malt scotch at the hotel bar to celebrate his success before retiring to bed. He intended to sleep soundly in preparation for tomorrow's fun and games.

Piffle was also not having the best of times. As he drove back across the Humberwold bridge in his Jag towards the family home, a number of disturbing thoughts were going through his mind. He could not get his head round the night's terrible events. Why were Birkett-Morris and, even more incredibly, his long-time friend and colleague, Anthony Jennings arrested on serious terrorism charges when all he was doing was hosting a retirement do? What was Birkett-Morris' real background and why had all this happened with ITN news present as well. It didn't make sense.

Then he was still seething about Mike Morrell turning up and chatting up his wife, and also his wayward son and his bloody entourage of southern nancy boy Tory wasters. All in all, a bloody disastrous evening.

What if that bitch, Bindle, was behind all this? Was she trying to discredit him and take over his company? He didn't know what to think. But Piffle didn't believe in coincidences and there were too many for his liking.

'Soon be home Pauline, quite a night. I hope Jennings is alright, that man just doesn't have much luck, does he?' said Piffle darkly.

'I've known Anthony since we were 14 years old and I for one am one hundred percent sure he is not a terrorist. He didn't even know Tandori until a couple of weeks ago, and I can't believe a young slip of a girl like that is a dangerous terrorist. I think that Inspector, what was him name? Inspector Fleece has got it all dreadfully wrong.'

Chapter 49

Other people were also having their own concerns that night as well. Archibald McGreggor III for one, Winton J Cuncliffe-Owen and Hazelhurst. Their plan to sabotage the Diversity Action Partnership Limited had just been holed below the water line, and Archibald in particular was incandescent with rage. He had watched the ITN News at Ten with mounting horror once he heard that Tandori Birkett-Morris had been arrested and was now in the public domain.

He was on the phone to Winton immediately, pacing around his office as best he could. 'Is that you Winton? What the hell is going on?'

Winton hadn't seen the news having been to diner in the city and had only just got back to his London flat, so had no idea what Archibald was talking about. 'What do you mean, is that you Archibald?'

'Of course it's bloody well me. Haven't you seen the ten o'clock news?'

'No I haven't, I've been at the Ivy having dinner with the Chief

Whip.'

'Well it's a bloody fucking disaster that's what it is.'

'Calm down Archibald, what is?'

'That secret bloody agent of yours, what's her name? Tandori, she's only been arrested on terrorism charges for blowing up a train carriage and bringing the whole fucking Northern Train line into meltdown. It was all over the ten o'clock ITN news, live with names mentioned and everything. The bitch has only been in Grimewold for a day and look what she's done already.'

'I am surprised.'

'Surprised, you need to be fucking surprised. Where does that leave us? She can't wreak havoc on Piffle's empire if she is banged up for God knows how long, can she? What the hell are you going to do about it?'

'Don't worry old boy, I'll speak to Hazelhurst at MI5, he'll sort it. He did it before and he can do it again.'

'He bloody well better. I want an update from you in the next two days and I want the bitch released by next week so she can do to Piffle what she can undoubtedly do to a Victorian block of flats and the entire Northern Rail network.'

Winton put the phone down. Despite his assurances this, wasn't going to be an easy sell. It was alright while Tandori was anonymous, but now half the country knew the name Tandori Birkett-Morris getting her released without good reason was going to be more challenging. Reluctantly, he dialled the direct number to get through to Hazelhurst.

'Ah Hazelhurst old man, how are you this fine evening?'

'I've seen the ITN news.'

'Well what are we going to do about it?'

'Tricky one Winton, can't really get involved now that Tandori's name has been made public. The Home Secretary would go ballistic if she was released without charge.'

'Now listen here Hazelhurst, you remember what I 've done for you in the past. Remember the poppy fields in Afghanistan we were supposed to torch? And instead you had the fucking crop harvested, put into fake coffins and brought back to Brize Norton, whilst good old Winton turned a blind eye?'

'That's just it Winton, you did turn a blind eye and who used some of the boodle to finance your election win, old boy. I bet the Daily Mail would love to hear all about that.'

'Yes, but you bought a fucking great pile in the Cotswolds with your share, so we both have a lot to lose. I suggest unless you want the proceeds of crime mob looking into your affairs, you think of a way to get that fucking walking disaster area of a girl released A S A fucking P.'

'When you put it like that, I suppose I'll have to think of something.'

'You do that, and make it snappy.'

The phone was slammed down, and Winton plodded off to bed in a foul mood.

Hazelhurst's mood was no better, but already cunning as a fox, he was thinking of a way out of another Birkett-Morris mess.

Chapter 50

'We'll tackle Jennings first Brahmes, but first get me a Nescafe. My mouth's as dry as a desert spider's arse.'

'Will do sir, what about Birkett-Morris?'

'She can wait. I think we can crack Jennings pretty quickly and then we can confront her with the evidence. Should have it wrapped up by lunch time.'

'Righty ho sir, Nescafe coming up straight away sir.'

'Oh and Brahmes, I want a one hundred percent cordon round this police station. No press, no nut jobs and especially no relatives of Birkett-Morris. In particular that fucking psychopath of a mother of hers, I don't want that lunatic within one mile of this police station, do I make myself clear?'

'Crystal clear sir.'

Inspector Fleece and Constable Brahmes sat opposite Jennings in the austere interview room, with a tape recorder ready to roll.

Jennings was shaking uncontrollably.

'Right shall we get started. Turn on the tape recorder Brahmes. Now I'm stating for the record that you Anthony Jennings are being questioned under caution. You do not have to say anything but anything you do say will be taken down and can be used in evidence against you. Do you understand?'

'Ye..s,' stammered Jennings.

'You have been offered to have a solicitor present but have declined at this stage. Is that correct?'

'I've done nothing wrong.'

'Yes or no?'

'Yes.'

'What is your connection with Tandori Birkett-Morris, how did you meet her?'

'She took my job.'

'What do you mean, she took your job?'

'Zara Bindle sacked me, and gave my job to Tandori Birkett-Morris at the Diversity Action Partnership.'

'So when did you first meet her to discuss this vile terrorist act?'

'What terrorist act? I know nothing about that. I first met her two weeks ago when I collected her from Grimewold station and took her for her job interview, to replace me. Then I collected her yesterday on her first day of work. That's the only time I have ever met her.'

'You seriously expect us to believe that Birkett-Morris planted a suspected bomb on a train, came out at speed to your car, and you sped off and you knew nothing of what she had done? Had no involvement in the detailed planning of a sophisticated terrorist act? The CCTV clearly shows you speeding off, and cleverly you parked in a way that obscured your registration number. Your mistake Jennings, was there was only seven registered Austin Maestro's in the Grimewold area, so you were easy to trace.'

The interview dragged on with Inspector Fleece getting more and more frustrated with the lack of cooperation that he perceived Jennings was giving. He tried everything to get answers, the hard-man, soft-man routine, threats and intimidation, offers of a lighter sentence for cooperation. None of it worked because none of it could work, Jennings knew absolutely nothing and was a nervous gibbering wreck by the time lunch time came round.

In the end Fleece completely lost his temper. 'Brahmes, lock this bastard up and throw away the key. We can keep him for fourteen days without any visitors or legal representation, so let's see what matey boy is like by then,' and with that he stormed off to get a Nescafe and have a fag.

By the afternoon it was the turn of Tandori to experience Fleece's particular brand of interrogation. He was not in a good mood, and after last time he was not holding out much hope of getting a coherent confession from the bitch.

He strode into the interrogation room with Constable Brahmes
in tow and sat down facing Tandori. 'Ah, we meet again Birkett-Morris,
or should I call you Tandori?'

Tandori just looked at him defiantly, saying nothing.

'We have been busy, haven't we Tandori, since we last met? Not
content with blowing up a perfectly usable grade 2 listed block of
Victorian flats, you have now moved onto blowing up railway carriages
and shutting down the whole of the Northern Line train network for at
least a week. Quite an achievement I would say.'

'I haven't blown up anything. I seem to think the British
Transport Police blew up the carriage thinking I had left a bomb on
board, which I clearly hadn't. This time I want a solicitor before I answer
any of your stupid questions.'

'Now you listen to me Birkett-Morris, and you listen good. You
might have escaped through my fingers last time, friends at court as
they say, but it won't be so easy this time. Your fucking name is all over
the tabloids this morning and they are baying for blood. The Home
Secretary has gained a lot of kudos having dangerous terrorists arrested
live on the News at bloody Ten. Comp Renda. I suggest you cooperate
pronto, and that way you might just get a long prison sentence instead
of a fucking life time behind bars.'

'I can't admit to what I haven't done. I was coming up to
Grimewold to start a new job and simply left my ruck sack on the train.

The next thing I know I was being arrested at Jennings' leaving do at the Auditorium. All that was in the ruck sack was some Miracle Grow and electric mouse traps for Daddy's mouse problem.'

Round and round they went in circles with Tandori repeating the same answers to Fleece's questions. In the end it was forensics that came to the rescue, but not until the following day.

'Sir, forensics have come back from the lab, and it doesn't look good sir' said Constable Brahmes.

'What do you mean, it doesn't look good?' said Inspector Fleece who was nursing a Nescafe at a temporary desk he had been given.

'Well basically, in a nutshell, the remains of Tandori's rucksack were retrieved and all they could find were traces of Miracle Grow and a partly destroyed electric mouse trap attributed to Wilkinson's garden department, and produced in China by a company called Xon industries of Nanjing. So it supports her claim that there was no bomb and never had been.'

'Who bloody well said there was a bomb on that train carriage then?'

'Inspector Plow from British Transport Police sir. He called in the bomb squad who blew up the train carriage because the sniffer dogs were going bananas.'

Fleece's brain was going into overdrive; he was reeling from the news. All his hopes of glory were dashed and he was staring into the abyss. He just couldn't bring himself to accept the new reality.

'Listen Brahmes, this changes nothing in the short term. That bitch Birkett-Morris is still as guilty as hell. She is a definite class 1 terrorist. Even this incident could have been orchestrated by her to look like a terrorist act and trick Inspector Plow into taking evasive action. No, I want her kept locked up under the terrorism act for the mandatory fourteen days and we'll see what else we can get out of her.'

'Whatever you say sir,' said Constable Brahmes, looking very dubious about Fleece's logic.

Tandori was led back to the police cells, to be kept under lock and key until Fleece could decide his next move.

The fate of Inspector Plow however did not take as long to adjudicate. Chief Inspector Maxwell of British Transport Police was furious. He had also had the report that there was no bomb or bomb making equipment left on the carriage by Birkett-Morris, and, that due to Plow's incompetence, not only had a train carriage been blown up needlessly, the northern train service had been severely disrupted. To cap it all off, a perfectly good, brand new BMW 5 Series Touring M5 police high-pursuit vehicle, had been written off on the notorious Cromwell Estate and he would be getting a bill from Humberwold Police fleet management department.

'Get Plow in my office now,' boomed Chief Inspector Maxwell. 'He's going to wish he had never been born!'

'Ah Inspector Plow, how good of you to join me this morning,' said Chief Inspector Maxwell, his voice brimming with acidic inference

'Let's not beat about the bush. It has come to my attention that you, that's right you, and solely you, are responsible for blowing up a perfectly good two million quid Hitachi train carriage, disrupting Northern rail services at a cost so far of four million quid. And, to cap it all off, overseeing the complete fucking destruction of a BMW 5 Series Touring estate car worth £40,000 that had just come into service two days earlier. Does that just about sum up the level of complete fucking incompetence you have presided over Plow?'

'Well I wouldn't put it like that,' bleated Plow.

'How would you put it Plow? And how do you suggest I relay the completely fucking incompetent actions of my force to the Crime Commissioner, and in particular the Home Secretary who has made a complete arse of herself on National Television blathering on about keeping the country safe from Middle Eastern terrorists?'

'It's not my fault. With the best will in the world, we had evidence on the ground of terrorist activity, and I just followed what any risk-averse Inspector would have done. The police dogs went wild when they got near Birkett-Morris's ruck sack. We acted in good faith.'

'Good faith Plow? You blew up an expensive train carriage, disrupted the entire Northern rail network, all on the basis of a couple of maniac, over-excited police dogs and a batty old women who clearly lost her marbles years ago. Someone has to take the can for this Plow and with me coming up for retirement with an unblemished Police record, it's not going to be me. No Plow, you're on your own on this one.'

'But it's just not fair sir!'

'Life's not fair Plow, you should know that by now. I'm going to put this in the hands of the Independent Police Complaints Commission and let them decide what to do about this sorry state of affairs. Now get out of my sight before I say something I might regret.'

Plow shuffled off with his tail between his legs, his dreams of promotion and glory in taters, he couldn't believe the turn of events that had conspired against him, and dreaded the potential fall out that could lead to his humiliation or at worst dismissal. Not for the first time in his life Plow reflected on his fate being out of his hands and yet here he was carrying the can for something that clearly wasn't his fault. Maybe taking logical thought through actions in a clearly illogical world was not the way to proceed in life after all. What he did know was that a lunch time drink beckoned and the afternoon off to nurse his ever growing grievances with life. Making himself scarce, very scarce seemed to be the best thing to do.

Chapter 51

Inspector Fleece was barely any happier. As far as the Fleet Street tabloids were concerned, he was a national hero, but as Fleece knew only too well, the pack of hounds can turn on you in a flash and you can go from hero to zero in no time. Once they realized a horrible mistake had been made, and Birkett-Morris and Jennings were innocent, and in fact there never was a terrorist incident just a catalogue of police incompetence, he was bound to be hung out to dry.

For now, Birkett-Morris and Jennings remained in custody. If only he could pin something on them that at least mitigated the situation and put him in a better light, he might just scrape home without being sacked, demoted or pensioned off ignominiously. A prospect that he could not begin to contemplate.

Winton J Cuncliffe-Owen was absolutely furious. Yet again, Birkett-Morris was in custody and not able to carry out the sabotage necessary to bring down Piffle. He was starting to lose patience with Hazelhurst and could envisage a nasty conversation on the phone later.

In the meantime he needed to assuage the concerns of his

friend Josiah Archibald McGreggor III, commonly known as Archibald, who was bound to have found out that Birkett-Morris had been arrested yet again. She was bloody good at being accused of being an ISIS terrorist but less good at destroying Piffle's business.

'Ah Archibald my good man, how are we today?' said Winton trying his hardest to put on an air of good-natured bonhomie.

'How are we today? I'll tell you how we fucking are today, you incompetent buffoon. Were fucking furious. that's how we are Winton.'

'Now come come, dear boy, just a little set back. We'll soon have Birkett-Morris back in the saddle, and you've got to admit, she is very good at blowing up train carriages.'

'Blowing up Hitachi train carriages and disrupting the whole of Northern rails train operation was not her fucking brief. As far as I can see, she hasn't done anything yet to disrupt that communist upstart Piffle. When am I going to see results Winton, that's what I want to know?'

'Now look here my good man,' said Winton finally losing his cool slightly.

'Birkett-Morris has only been at Piffle's company for a day, and has hardly had chance to undertake her deadly mission. Let's look on the bright side old boy, if she can instigate this much havoc in one day, admittedly not against Piffle, think what she can do in a few months of working for him. The blighter won't know what's hit him. She'll make Red Robbo or Arthur Scargill look like a pair of amateur fairies.'

'Well put like that Winton, I suppose we have got to give her ample chance to succeed, but when on God's earth do you think she will be released?'

'Look I'll speak to Hazelhurst. He got her released last time and he can do it again. I'm sure that by the weekend she will be out and as free as a bird, and then next week, let battle commence.'

With that the phone call ended with Winton feeling relieved he had escaped yet another cock-up relatively unscathed. He would call Hazelhurst later and set in motion the steps necessary to get Tandori released, so that their plan could finally be put into practise.

Chapter 52

'Hello sweetie, me bloody back is killing me.'

'Morning Mrs Neatgangs, here bright and early I see,' said Gary Wacker, not at all enthusiastic about his cooked breakfast being interrupted by the new cleaner with her crude loud-mouth outbursts.

'Always early me, Mr Wacker, you'd be surprised what I can get sorted before 7.00 a.m.'

'Not sure I'd like to speculate,' said Gary with a shudder.

'I just couldn't find a bra to fit this morning, it's a bloody curse carrying these around unsupported, you've got no idea sweetie.'

'No Mrs Neatgangs, I haven't, and I don't want to, especially when I'm having bacon and eggs.'

'What have you got that's not supported Mrs Neatgangs?' said Callum who had overheard the conversation while preparing toast with a huge quantity of Nutella chocolate spread.

Wack's 15 year old son, Callum, had a pretty good idea what

Mrs Neatgangs was talking about and he was keen to find out more. Callum was fascinated by Mrs Neatgangs crude and plain speaking and her impossibly unique figure. Being only five foot one inches tall and as big round in all directions, Mrs Neatgangs was an unlikely sex goddess for a 15 year old full of testosterone and uncontrollable yearnings, but ever since she had arrived as the Wacker's new housekeeper, she had held a sexual fascination for Callum that he could not shake off.

'Don't answer that Mrs Neatgangs,' said Wack.

'It's about time you called me Nin, Mr Wacker now that we are familiar an' all. Anyway, I best be off and get on with my duties, otherwise Mrs Wacker will be right upset.'

'Yes, off you go Mrs Neatgangs,' said Gary, clearly irritated and ignoring Mrs Neatgangs' request to call her Nin. Familiarity was not something Gary Wacker envisaged with the troublesome Mrs Neatgangs.

As Mrs Neatgangs shuffled off her huge unsupported bosoms clearly visible under her cheap white t shirt, Callum, not used to such displays, flew off back to his bedroom upstairs to try and extinguish the lustful thoughts he had towards her and the embarrassing bulge that was developing in his trousers.

At that point, Gary Wacker's mobile phone rang and he swiftly answered.

'Hey up Wack, it's me Dresden.'

'Morning mate, how's it going?'

'Could be better. The Clothes Horse is playing up again about me going back to Benidorm and she's threatening to have affair with that smooth bastard, Mike Morrell. To cap it all off, Jennings and Tandori have been arrested as potential ISIS terrorists by Humberwold Police.'

'Not going too well then Dresden. Anyway, what can I do for you?' said Gary not wanting to be drawn into the unbelievable world of Dresden Piffle.

'I'm going back to Benidorm later today to arrange with builders the start date for putting in roads, services and concrete pans at the log cabin site. I wondered if we could get together at lunch to discuss ordering the first ten log cabins from yourself?'

'Sounds good to me. How about lunch at Hungry Horse out near Morrison's?'

'Can we make it 12.00, Wack? I need to be getting the 5.00 flight from Robin Hood Airport.'

'OK see you at 12.00.'

After finishing his eggs and bacon, Wack called to his wife to tell her he was popping to the office to collect the contract for Piffle to sign for the first ten log cabins, but there was no reply from Tracy. She had obviously popped out to the hairdresser's. He left the house telling Mrs Neatgangs to lock up when she left at lunch time. He also shouted

Callum, but just got a muffled reply from upstairs.

Mrs Neatgangs decided to start upstairs with her cleaning schedule and work her way down. She took the Dyson V11 cleaner that Tracy had just bought off the shopping channel for £399 and her trusty dusters and Mr Sheen. She was getting too old for this cleaning lark being in her late 60s, but with her late husband Jack passed on after working all his life at the steel works, she had no choice, and it did get her out of the house.

When she reached the top of the stairs panting, she heard another panting noise coming from along the corridor and a half-opened bedroom door. Peering round she saw Callum furiously wanking. After seeing Mrs Neatgangs he couldn't contain himself, his sexual needs had to be satisfied.

Mrs Neatgangs, despite her boasts, hadn't had the pleasure of the opposite sex for a number of years, and certainly hadn't seen a naked 15 year old with an erect penis before.

At that moment standing in the doorway, surprised but delighted, the floorboard creaked. Callum looked up and saw Mrs Neatgangs looking at him. He immediately went bright puce and stopped wanking.

'Don't mind me sweetie,' said Mrs Neatgangs moving into the room.

'Is it these that's making you excited?' She lifted her cheap white t shirt to reveal all.

'What do you think to these Callum?' leered Mrs Neatgangs. 'I bet you haven't seen a pair as big as these sweetie?'

Callum didn't know how to respond. On the one hand. his dreams of Mrs Neatgangs had come true, but on the other he had no experience of sex or of how to deal with a 67 year old randy woman.

He didn't need to worry, Mrs Neatgangs took over the situation for him. In quick succession she pushed him forcefully down on his bed, and jumped on him.

'Oh sweetie, this is how I like it,' she said. Callum could only make squawking noises under the weight and determination of Mrs Neatgangs' activities.

One thing that Callum did know was that Mrs Neatgangs was his fantasy come true and there were going to be many more encounters if he had anything to do with it.

Gary Wacker was spared the horror of seeing the goings on at his house as he was on his way to get the contracts from his office and meet up with Dresden before the latter flew out to Alicante later that day.

'Have you got those contracts to hand Sheila? You know the ones for The Diversity Action Partnership Limited, Piffle's outfit?'

'Yes Mr Wacker, I've got them prepared here as you requested. Our lawyers have been through them and approved all the clauses.'

'That's good Sheila. I know Dresden is me friend, but you never can be too careful. Some of the best friendships have gone west over business deals going wrong, and I hate to think what my Tracy would do to me if we ended up out of pocket on this one.'

'You've nothing to worry about Mr Wacker, this contract protects us all the way down the line.'

'That's brilliant Sheila, good work. I'm heading off now to see Dresden at the Admiral Nelson pub, you know that Hungry Horse pub on the roundabout? I won't be in the rest of the day, so I'll see you tomorrow.'

With that he left the office and got into his Merc and sped off to the Admiral Nelson with a bit too much haste, but he was very excited. This was the biggest contract his firm had ever signed, and he was keen to get the deal sorted.

As it happened, Piffle was already waiting for him at a big round table near the front of the pub, as keen as Gary to get the deal signed so that things could start moving.

'Eh up Wack, bloody glad you could make it on time. Me flight is at 5.00 and I've got to get taxi back home and collect a few things and see Pauline before I go to airport.'

'Not a problem Dresden. I've got the contracts with me and once they're signed, and the first stage one payment has been made, as we agreed, my team will start working on the building of the first ten log cabins to be shipped over to Alicante.'

'That sounds champion Wack. Anyway, before we exchange contracts, do you fancy a pint and a steak and Guinness pie and chips? They're doing a special, two meals and a pint for £20. I'm keen to have some nosh because that aeroplane food doesn't feed a bloody sparrow.'

'Sounds good to me Dresden. Why not? We need to celebrate. This is going to be the making of both of us. We get our biggest order ever of log cabins, five hundred in total and you get to sell them to gullible Brits and get a huge profit, plus the ongoing ground rent.'

'I know Wack, I'm looking at making quite a few million plus an income after expenses of half a mill a year. Enough to sell Diversity Action Partnership and move to Villa with Honolulu, and finally ditch the Clothes Horse.'

Both men were cagey about their respective profits, Wack was looking at a cool £5 million and Piffle was looking at £27 million, plus the half million a year ground rent. It was no wonder they were both in a celebratory mood.

The drinks and food duly arrived, and they clicked glasses in celebration. It was only a formality signing the contracts, which laid out their respective terms. This was only for the first ten log cabins to be built and erected on site within 6 months, with Piffle paying upfront. This was not a problem since Piffle had the money in the Diversity Action Partnership savings account with HSBC.

'Right Wack, I can see me taxi has just arrived, so I'll bid you farewell. If you want to come out to Villa with Tracy you know you're always welcome, especially if you want to oversee first ten log cabins being erected by your team.'

'Thanks Dresden' said Wack, dubiously thinking that he had probably seen more than enough erections to last him a life time the last time he had been at Piffle's villa.

With that Piffle was gone in the taxi, and Gary Wacker sauntered back to his Merc with the all-important contract signed for £500,000. He would check later if the monies had landed in his company's account, then he would know for sure that stage one of his retirement plan was underway.

Chapter 53

After his meeting with Wack, Piffle arrived back at Maxwell House to collect his things and speak to the Clothes Horse before he left.

Sydney Dresden Piffle was furious with the police. Their actions last night confirmed all of his prejudices about police brutality, discrimination against the working man and their support for the establishment. He had seen it all first-hand in the miners' dispute, and now he had seen it with his own eyes. How could anyone believe that Anthony Jennings and Tandori Birkett-Morris were terrorists and needed to be arrested with brutal force?

'I'm not bloody having it Pauline, how dare those pigs arrest Jennings, and that poor slip of a girl, Tandori.'

'Well, I'd be hard pressed to describe Tandori as a slip of a girl, more like a baby elephant, but it is terrible. What are you planning to do to help Dresden?'

'First thing I'm going to do Pauline is get on blower and speak to

Trevor. That solicitor has got me out of many a scrape and I think I still get discount for being a member of Labour Party.'

'You do what needs to be done Dresden, I don't want poor Anthony in prison any longer than is necessary, he needs to be back here where he belongs. I've got his bed made up and his flat all ready for him, for when he comes to work for us.'

'Bloody fascist police, I've known Jennings since school days and I'm a pretty good judge of character, and that Tandori is no more a terrorist than I am.'

It took a while to get hold of Trevor at Twinning, Bell and Reeves Solicitors, but eventually Piffle managed to explain the situation and agree for Trevor to get down to the police station and represent Tandori and Jennings in any forthcoming police action.

'I'm glad I've sorted that Pauline, I've got to get back to villa to sort out log cabins. I need to speak to the builder and get him going with the site so it can be prepared for the first deliveries. Wack is dead keen to get started. This is the big one Pauline, we'll be sitting pretty when that log cabin site is finished.'

'I didn't think you would stay long. Off to see your fat tart are you? Don't think I'm fooled Dresden, you can do all you need by internet and speaking to Wack in person. The truth is, you never consider me Dresden, my so called husband, don't you dare pretend that this is anything about our future. The only person that shows me any respect is Mike Morrell.'

'If I hear that bloody name again, I swear—'

'Don't bother me with your hollow promises Dresden, go to the villa for all I care, you live your life and I'll live mine.'

Before long Piffle was at the airport awaiting his budget flight to Alicante airport. He was very pleased with himself that he had managed to book two adjacent seats on a budget airline for £16 each, as one would not be sufficient to accommodate his extensive girth. Because he had use of a mobility scooter at the airport and a blue badge he was also able to get help and priority boarding onto the plane, all in all a good outcome.

He beamed at the pretty stewardess as he boarded the plane and found his front two seats, 3a and 3b.

'It's a grand day lass, looking forward to your expert service luv, how long's the flight today?'

'It will be two and half hours into Alicante Airport Mr Piffle,' said the stewardess in her heavily accented English.

'Enough time for a bite to eat and a G & T then, bloody champion.'

Piffle was old enough to still get very excited about air travel and he considered it a marvel of the modern world and far removed from his life as a boy on the Gipsyville estate.

Two and a half hours later the flight touched down at Alicante Airport. Piffle was allowed off first and whisked through passport control in a wheel chair, bags collected and Paeleo was waiting with the Silver Spur to take him to the villa.

'Are there you are Paeleo, I thought you'd bloody forgotten me. Well shake a leg lad and get me bags in boot and off to Villa pronto. I've got a lot to do.'

'Ah yes Señor, I am most sorry to have not spotted you. Come, let's get you into the back seat of the Royce, and before long you can be relaxing at the Villa Almeria with your concubine, Honolulu.'

'Less of the bloody detail, Paeleo, just shake a leg and get me there pronto.'

'Of course, of course Mr Piffle. I am as always at your service,' said Paeleo bowing and scraping before getting into the driver's seat. It was soon cruising down the A1 on the way to Benidorm and the mountains beyond where the Villa Almeria waited for Piffle's arrival.

Piffle was still in a very fine mood. He could see the future very clearly and like a winning game of chess he could see all the moves falling into place, with Sydney Dresden Piffle the victor. But like all games of chess there was an opponent, but in this real-life game of chess, multiple opponents that all needed to act on a certain way for Piffle's plans to succeed. Piffle could only see the sunny uplands laid out before him. He had an assured view of his world that he, Sydney Dresden Piffle, had a right to the good things in life, just like the rich Tories he despised, and he had the skills and plan to achieve his ambitions.

The sun was shining through the window of the Silver Spur and it wasn't long before Piffle was semi dreaming. Into his mind came an even bigger villa, he and Honolulu skipping through a beautiful meadow of wild flowers, a huge yacht in shimmering turquoise blue waters off a sun kissed island with him and Honolulu sunning themselves on the deck, a race horse he owned winning the Cheltenham Gold Cup with Piffle in a top hat shouting as his horse came in

'Señor, Señor, we are here Mr Piffle, at the Villa Almeria,' shouted Paeleo.

Piffle woke with a jolt and banged his head against the glass on the door of the car. 'Christ, bloody hell Paeleo, do you have to shout so loud? You nearly scared the living daylights out of me, look what I've done now, banged me bloody head.'

'Sorry, sorry Señor. You get out and I help you to the door.'

'Eh lad it's OK, I can get there under me own steam. Honolulu can help me when I get indoors.'

Paeleo took the bags into the Villa whilst Piffle struggled out of the back of the Silver Spur.

Looking round the front garden he was immediately struck by the beauty of the white roses trailing over the front entrance, the deep red of bougainvillea, the strong lush scent of jasmine and the sound of bees. Yes, he was home in paradise and waiting for him inside would be Honolulu and the promise of a different kind of paradise.

As Piffle entered Villa Almeria, Paeleo was leaving after dropping the bags off. 'I be off now Señor. I will see you tomorrow with the Royce to take you where you want to go.'

'OK Paeleo, but what I need pronto is a meeting with that builder of yours. Can you arrange that please and pick me up 10.00 a.m. sharp?'

'Consider it done Mr Piffle, always at your service,' and with that he was in the Silver Spur and off at speed out of the drive

I'll have to keep an eye on that Paeleo, thought Piffle. There's just something about him, a bit too smooth and a bit too willing to please, not sure I trust him totally.

The thought was soon gone as before him Honolulu swept into the kitchen and into Piffle's arms.

Chapter 54

Mike Morrell was having his own version of romance back in Grimewold, along with a cunning expansion of his services at Humberwold's Speed Camera Action! Limited.

He strode into the offices of Humberwold Speed Camera Action! and told Janice to organise a strategy meeting for 10.00 a.m. sharp, but first he needed the ego enhancing therapy of a team meeting.

'Oh and Janice, nearly forgot, phone Pauline Piffle and tell her that I will meet her for lunch at Luigi's at 1.00 please. Things to discuss, and diary in a meeting with the head of the Council, thanks.'

Monday morning, the usual team meeting was taking place at 9.00 a.m. sharp. All the staff were present, standing in neat regimented rows, chanting the company's slogans.

Mike Morrell firmly believed that performance of the individual was determined by the sub-conscious mind. One of the things he valued most in his employees was absolute loyalty, which needed to manifest itself in following all the company's requests and giving 110%. Mike

Morrell's organisation was the absolute authentic example of a top down organisation, with he, Mike Morrell, making all the key decisions and expecting them to be followed to the letter. Morrell also believed that failure to abide by this doctrine would result in severe punishments, within the letter of employment law, and sackings where possible to bring the others into line.

Mike Morrell did not want free thinkers, he wanted sycophants that did as they were told and praised their leader at every opportunity. This extreme form of management control stemmed from a very insecure childhood where Mike, being one of six children, was always belittled and bullied by his over-bearing father who continually told him he was the runt of the pack.

Who was laughing now? The 'runt' had become a very successful businessman and the old man was a penniless drunken wanker still living on the Cromwell Estate in Grimewold.

'Mike is Great, Mike is Great, the greatest boss there ever was!'

'Mike is Great, Mike is Great he's the best there is!'

'Follow the leader, follow the leader, he knows best...'

'Death on the roads is due to speeding, death on the roads is due to speeding, death on the roads is due to speeding ee-i-ee-i-o.'

'One mile an hour is all it takes, all it takes, all it takes, one mile an hour is all it takes to end a kiddies life.'

'Associates, thank you again for those kind words and your

loyalty to me and Humberwold Speed Camera Action! Limited. We are undoubtedly the finest speed enforcement agency in the Country, if not Europe and the World!'

There followed enthusiastic applause to this rather dubious statement, but Mike was whipping his loyal staff into a frenzy of obedience and subservience.

'But people, we have only just started on our journey together, a journey of success and prosperity. I can announce this very day that we will be writing a new chapter in the coming months that will see Humberwold Speed Camera Action! reach new heights of success that none of us could ever have dreamed of when we started out on this journey together. Together we will succeed. God speed and let's all get back to our important duties. Thank you!'

With that Mike Morrell turned and left the staff canteen with the chants still ringing in his ears. His monumental ego had been stroked even further and now he was to launch his most audacious plan yet to take Humberwold Speed Camera Action! forward to the promised land.

Ten o'clock soon came, and Mike Morrell strode into the board room with his secretary Janice three steps behind trying to keep up and looking flustered. Ahead of him was the huge boardroom table, a modernist glass-topped affair with twelve black leather chairs around it, currently occupied by six expectant faces.

'Ladies, gentleman, thank you for attending this important

strategy meeting at such short notice, but it has come to my attention that there are legal changes that are an opportunity for us at Humberwold Speed Camera Action! Limited to fundamentally change our business model and benefit from the new macro environment that presents itself to us. Janice bring in the device and put it on the boardroom table. Quickly, quickly.'

Janice was a bit flustered, but brought in an electronic device about the size of a paperback book and put it on the table.

'Now this, ladies and gentleman, is an electronic device for measuring air quality and identifies some of the noxious fumes coming out of a motor car's exhaust,' Morrell said triumphantly. 'Now, you may be wondering what that has to do with us here at Humberwold Speed camera Action! Limited. Well, the Government has just introduced the Clean Air Act 2018, which gives councils the power to fine motorists up to £1000 for violating the emission of noxious harmful particulates and gasses from their exhaust pipes, the worst offender being NOx.'

'I don't see what that has got to do with us, given we are a speed camera operation,' said one of the younger members of the senior management team.

'Well Nigel, a good question that deserves a good answer. This is our opportunity to quadruple the size of our business at a stroke. Instead of getting 60% of a paltry £100 fine for a speeding violation, we can get 60% of £1000 each time we catch a criminal motorist emitting harmful emissions from their exhaust pipe.'

Mike Morrell pulled out a report from his leather briefcase and waved it around at the astounded strategy team. 'This, ladies and gentleman, is a report from Sweden, which clearly shows that 45% of drivers who were stopped, were producing emissions in excess of the legal statutory limits as defined by the European Union against all vehicle types and ages including nearly new vehicles. If that percentage is replicated here in Grimewold we can charge 45% of motorists a £1000 fine and keep 60% of the proceeds, providing I can persuade the leader of Grimewold Council, Ms Penelope Sykes to give us a five year contract, and I am meeting her later this week, tomorrow in fact. What do you think of that team?'

One by one they all gave their blessing to the new business opportunity their boss had presented to them. This wasn't so much as a strategy meeting as a declaration by Mike Morrell of the future direction of Humberwold Speed Camera Action ! Limited, and like all decisions in the company, it was made by him and him alone, with all the other managers falling into line with fawning acceptance.

Mike finished the meeting by ordering his team to put in place the necessary actions to make the new strategy happen. Satisfied that he had a plan in place and a timeline for achieving it, three months in this case before launch, he left the meeting with Janice in tow with the report and emissions instrument in her possession.

Chapter 55

Mike Morell's day was getting better and better. He had the delicious prospect of lunch, and maybe more, with Piffle's wife Pauline, but first he had another vital matter to attend to. The culmination of a childhood dream that he wanted to secure as a reward for all the hard work, planning and scheming that was going to make him a very rich man indeed.

When Mike Morrell was 10 or 11, he used to read the Ian Fleming book *Goldfinger* voraciously under the cover of his bed sheets long into the night. It was his form of escapism from the drab life growing up on the Cromwell Council Estate with five siblings and a father who declared him to be the runt of the pack.

His father, Reg, worked at the steel works owned by McGreggor's and his limited intellect and ambition rested there, along with his hard drinking and pathetic gambling habit that never yielded any future advancement for the family or his long suffering wife, Mike's mother, whom he adored.

Mike was fascinated and excited by Bond's glamorous life, and particularly by the car Bond drove, an Aston Martin DB3, at a time when none of Mike's friends' fathers even had a car and Reg certainly didn't. The film version had already been released and by then Bond was driving an Aston Martin DB5. But it was the rarer and earlier version from the book that Mike Morrell craved.

In his mind when he could drive the car of his childhood hero, James Bond, then he had arrived, and now with the sweet prospect of his company the Humberwold Speed Camera Action! Limited quadrupling in size and profit, now was the time to fulfil that childhood dream and own the very car that Bond drove and for which he had craved for 50 years.

The problem was, there were only a few Aston Martin DB3s in existence, but Mike had found one, and this very day it was going to be his! A car was being auctioned at Brightwell's and Morrell had put in a bid of £375,000 for a car needing a mild restoration. He would know the outcome by 12.00 when Brightwell's sent him a text stating whether he had won his online bid, and if successful he could go to lunch with Pauline Piffle, a happy man indeed. Only one hour to go.

Mike Morrell retired to his plush office and asked Janice to bring him a strong black coffee and a plate of biscuits. He lit one of his large Hamlet cigars and relaxed checking his emails. One in particular caught his eye. It was a response from the leader of Grimewold Council, Penelope Sykes, confirming their meeting later that week. Splendid, he thought, soon he would sign the contract with the Council and even more money would start rolling into The Speed Camera Action! Limited's bank account.

At exactly 12.05 Morrell's mobile phone rang.

'Morrell here can I help you?'

'It's Montague, Mr Morrell, from Brightwell's. Good news old chap you've won the telephone bid for the Aston. Very shrewd of you if I may say, you got it for £352,500, plus our standard 5% buyers commission. Congratulations old boy.'

'I can't bloody believe it, that's bloody marvellous! Well done for sorting this for me Monty. So now I've won when can I have the car transported to the restorers in Broadway? I'm keen for them to start on her straight away.'

'Well Mr Morrell, once we've checked the money has been transferred to Brightwell's account later today, our transport company should be able to take the car to the Cotswold Carriage Company later this week. That is where you said you wanted it delivering?'

'Yes, yes that will be fine. Please proceed Monty as soon as possible as far as I'm concerned.'

'Splendid, splendid old boy. You do realise that there are only a dozen of those DB3s left in the world and you have one of them? Once it's restored, if you ever want to consider selling, we will be at your service Mr Morrell.'

'Thanks Monty, but no chance of that, this one is a keeper. I'll

Piffle

have the bloody thing buried with me Monty and make no mistake. It'll only take a few weeks to restore since its in bloody excellent condition at the moment, but Cotswold Carriage are the best and money's no object to get it absolutely perfect.'

'Right you are Mr Morrell. I'll bid you farewell and if we can be of assistance in the future you know where we are.'

'Thanks again Monty.'

The phone line went dead. Mike Morrell leaned back in his buckskin leather chair with a grin from ear to ear, could his day get any better? He was about to find out.

Mike left the office and climbed into his BMW heading for Luigi's just off the ring road a mile from Grimewold centre. After encountering some traffic and the usual roadworks, he drew up into the car park at 12.45 – fifteen minutes early for his lunch date with Pauline Piffle.

'Buongiorno Signor Morrell,' said Cremonesi, the owner of Luigi's, as he entered the exclusive Italian restaurant. 'How good to see you. Your usual table?'

'Ciao Signor Cremonesi, yes my usual table. Has Signora Piffle arrived yet?'

'No Signor Morrell, she has not yet graced us with her presence.'

Cremonesi took Mike to his usual table and got him seated.

261

'Wine Signor Morrell?'

'Yes please Cremonesi. Your best white plonk, I've got a lot to celebrate today.'

'Ah here is the bella Signora Piffle arriving. She looks a picture Signor Morrell.'

'You look bloody lovely Pauline, thanks for coming. It's made my day.'

'Hello Mike, I am so glad you invited me for lunch. I'm glad to get out of the house.'

'Has that pig of a husband of yours been causing trouble for you again?'

'No, we did a have a row, but he's on his way to Benidorm to see his bit on the side, Honolulu, the so-called housekeeper. He'll be away quite some time organising his new venture, building five hundred log cabins on a huge site he's bought.'

'You're well rid of him Pauline, don't worry your pretty little head about him. I'm here now, so let's enjoy our lunch together.'

Cremonesi approached the table with the bottle of wine and poured Morrell a small measure to try.

'That is very good Cremonesi, thank you.'

With that the owner poured out two glasses and placed the bottle on the table in a stainless-steel wine cooler with copious amounts of ice to keep the wine chilled.

'Signor Morrell, are you and the lady ready to order your meal yet?'

'No Cremonesi, give us a bit longer.'

'OK, I will be back shortly.'

'Have you decided what you are going to have to eat my dear?' said Morrell in a sickly syrupy voice.

'I think I'm just going to have the Cannelloni, if that's ok?'

'No starter? OK then, well I'll order the Bruschetta to share and then I'm having the Cotoletta alla Milanase.'

'Oh Mike, you are a master of Italian dishes, aren't you? I wouldn't have a clue what I was ordering. Piffle is more a pie and chips man.'

'Why doesn't that surprise me? I bet he hasn't even tried an Italian restaurant.'

'No, he calls them all foreign muck. Even in Benidorm he tends to stick to English food, and very basic dishes at that.'

Mike clicked his fingers, 'Cremonesi, we are ready to order now.'

'Signor Morrell, I am at your service, for starters you want?'

'It's the Bruschetta to share, then Pauline will have the

Cannelloni, and I will have the Cotoletta alla Milanese please Cremonesi. Oh and a bottle of your sparkling water to go with the meal, helps my digestion it does.'

'It will be with you, as you say Signor Morrell, in a jiffy. Good day to you – the waitress will service you shortly.'

The food duly arrived, and Mike Morrell and Pauline Piffle enjoyed a very enjoyable meal together, sumptuous food, good wine and enjoyable company. Mike Morrell boasted of his business prowess and his recent coup acquiring the Aston Martin DB3 and the potential contract with Grimewold Council to implement the clean air directives.

The meal was coming to a close, but Mike hadn't finished with his attempts to seduce Piffle's wife. With a flourish, he got out from his briefcase, a small long box and handed it to Pauline.

'This is a little something for you, with my love.'

'Ooh Mike, you shouldn't have.'

Opening the box Pauline found a beautiful silver bracelet encrusted with yellow gemstones, an expensive and extravagant gift with the intention of impressing and seducing Pauline. It clearly worked.

'It is a beautiful gift Mike, no one has bought me anything like this in years, especially not Dresden.' A tear came to her eye. She leant over the table and kissed Mike Morrell who took the compliment in his stride and beamed from ear to ear. All was going exactly according to plan.

'I don't want it to end here Pauline, will you come back to mine for some drinks and I'll take the rest of the day off?'

'Of course I will, I would only be going home to an empty house in Hull.'

'If you follow me in your car, I live out at Appleton an exclusive village five miles out of Grimewold, do you know it?'

'Yes I do Mike, I could leave the car here though and you could drive me and we could pick my car up in the morning?'

Mike's grin grew even wider. This was better than he had hoped, Pauline Piffle offering to stay the night at his house.

'As long as you are sure my dear, that would be perfect.'

'Cremonesi, get me the bill please, another superb meal.'

'It is my pleasure Signor Morrell and I hope your bella lady Piffle enjoyed her meal as well?'

'Oh I did Mr Cremonesi, a wonderful meal, and wonderful company.'

With that they exited the restaurant and got into Mike's BMW before speeding off to his luxury five bedroomed house in Appleton.

They were soon at the gates to his extravagant house with two large pillars either side of electric wooden gates with two bronze eagles perched on top of the stone pillars either side with a Cotswold stone plinth out front with the name of the house in large gold letters - 'The

Eagles Nest'.

Mike pressed the electronic button on the dashboard of the BMW and the gates opened inwards. They drove onto a large circular gravel drive that took them to the house with a circular lawned area in front, with a stone fountain in the centre spraying out plumes of water like a copy of a French Chateau.

'Here we are then Pauline, home sweet home. I hope you like my humble little abode.'

'I do Mike, I can't wait to see inside.'

Chapter 56

Finally Tandori and Jennings were released without charge.
Inspector Fleece had done all he could to keep them longer, convinced
they were evil ISIS terrorists, but the laws of detention could only
stretch so far. That and some subtle pressure from MI5 in the form of
Hazelhurst swayed the Chief Constable to let them both go. The
situation wasn't helped by the Home Secretary personally ringing
Maxwell and telling him in no uncertain terms that if he or his officers
ever did anything like that again, he could kiss goodbye to his
bulletproof pension and be sacked for gross incompetence and
dereliction of duty.

Neither could quite believe that the sweet smell of freedom had
come their way so quickly, especially Tandori who was getting used to
Inspector Fleece's paranoia about her links to extreme jihadi terrorism.
Jennings was just glad to be free but completely disorientated by the
previous day's events.

'Now we are free Tandori, do you want a lift to the flat? Then I
must be on my way to the Piffle residence where they have an annexe

for me to live. It's worked out quite well you renting my flat on the Cromwell Estate, and me getting a job as handyman/chauffeur for Pauline and Dresden Piffle.'

'Well Mr Jennings, it helps me out too, having a nice flat to rent and quite close to work. I should be up here for at least 6 months, so it works for both of us.'

They reached Jennings' Austin Maestro and were soon on their way to the Cromwell Estate where Tandori was dropped off at Jennings' flat. He helped her in with her bags, showed her where the utilities were and left her to settle in. He had a good forty-minute drive to get to Piffle's house on the outskirts of Hull.

When he arrived he was surprised to see that the main house was in darkness, but he had the key to the annexe flat above the separate garage next to the house. He parked his Maestro at the side and climbed the external staircase and entered his new home. He was not surprised to find that the flat was tastefully furnished, though maybe not to his tastes, a bit too Laura Ashley and floral, but never the less immaculate, clean and stylish and befitting the women who had obviously overseen the decor and layout.

It had everything he needed. The small kitchen was open to the main sitting room with a breakfast bar overlooking the lounge, and a full array of cupboards and a cooker and sink on the back wall. The lounge had a L shaped sofa and a 55" TV over the mantle place, and high-gloss cherry laminate flooring. To the side was a large picture window with the Laura Ashley floral drapes floor to ceiling and then a door led to a double bedroom and adjacent en suite bathroom with a shower, toilet and washbasin. He could not have wished for better compared to his ex-council flat on the Cromwell Estate. He was literally a world away from Grimewold.

Despite his recent dismissal and unbelievable arrest as a suspected accomplice to an ISIS Terrorist in the unlikely guise of Tandori Birkett-Morris, he actually felt like the future for once held promise and even a degree of happiness and tranquillity he had not known for a long time.

He unpacked a few provisions which he had bought at a local convenience store on the way back from Grimewold, put a frozen pizza in the oven to cook and put the kettle on a for a cup of tea. He found the remote and put the telly on so he could watch the ten o'clock news. The newscaster that night was Tom Bradby, a man he much admired, so within a short time he was settled down on the sofa with his cup of tea, his ham and pineapple pizza on a tray and the news. Yes, he could get used to this.

When it was time to go to bed, he was surprised to find the rest of the house still in darkness. He was unaware that Dresden had gone to the Villa in Benidorm and didn't know that Pauline Piffle was having a romantic liaison not far from where he had just come from in Appleton. In the morning he would try and make contact with one or other of them, but in the meantime, he was ready for bed. The king-size bed in his bedroom looked especially inviting, even if the Laura Ashley themed floral patterns extended to the bedspread and curtains.

He didn't sleep as soundly as he might hope. In a large oak tree, across from the gravel drive, an owl decided to make itself felt by tweeting all night, a noise unfamiliar to a city dweller like Jennings. His mind was still actively going over the events of the previous few days, which made anything other than fretful sleep impossible. He had one particularly nasty dream where the owl was flying at him to attack, but instead of an owl's face the animal had that of Inspector Fleece's, leering at him as it flew in for the attack. He awoke sweating profusely and screamed out as in his dream the hideous face collided with his.

Tandoori had unpacked as well and was settling in to the flat on the Cromwell Estate. It was not as tranquil as Jennings new surroundings. She could hear youths outside, the sound of breaking glass and a near neighbour having a furious row with his girlfriend with lots of banging, expletives and threats. It was not what Tandori was used to, but it was cheap and she was hoping her job would be done within a few months, six at the very most. She quite liked Mr Piffle and felt guilty about having to undermine his business, but she had no choice in the matter. The thought of going back to prison for a crime she hadn't committed was just unthinkable, a shudder went through her body just thinking about it. No, she had to carry out Hazelhurst's instructions and that was the end of it.

Tandori had a shower, a night cap and got her business clothes ready for her return to work the next day. The sooner she could get into the Diversity Action Partnership, the sooner she could get the unpleasant job she had to do finished, and then finally she could look forward to starting a new life free from the nightmare she found herself in. She rang her mother to tell her that she was safe and sound and finally at the flat in Grimewold and assured her that she would be back for a weekend visit within the month.

She still had doubts about that nasty Inspector Fleece. Yes, he might have released her, but he was like a dog with a bone and wouldn't let go. She had not heard the last of him and that sent her into a disturbed and restless sleep.

Fleece and Constable Brahmes were still in Grimewold. The only silver lining to come out of the whole sorry episode was that Inspector Plow had taken the flack for the arrest and destruction of Network Rail and Northern Rail property. Fleece and Brahmes were bystanders to the utter incompetence of British Transport Police. That's not to say that Fleece was happy or satisfied that Birkett-Morris or Jennings were innocent, far from it.

As they drove back to the Premier Inn Fleece was still plotting his next move. 'Well Brahmes, that was a monumental cock up, but if that bitch Birkett-Morris thinks she has got away from me she has another thing coming. Once I've got a perp in my sights I won't let go.'

'No Inspector you can't be accused of letting someone off the hook,' Brahmes said dubiously, privately thinking that Fleece was possibly stark starring mad.

'No Brahmes. As far as the Chief Constable is concerned we are up here on important police business following lines of enquiry related to terrorist activity, and I intend that we don't enlighten him as to the change in circumstance. Yes Birkett-Morris has been freed, yes she may not have tried to blow up a train carriage, but I know she is as guilty as hell. I even think she's staged all this to discredit the police and make us look idiots. We're booked into the Premier Inn, and that is where we will stay Brahmes until we have caught Birkett-Morris red handed with whatever dastardly crime she has in mind to further her twisted terrorist cause, and then finally I, I mean we, will be vindicated.'

Chapter 57

Hazelhurst finally had some good news to relay to Winton J Cuncliffe-Owen, now Birkett-Morris had been released. It hadn't been his doing, but he decided it would be in his interests to take credit for it.

'Hello Winton, it's me Hazelhurst. Good news, I've had Birkett-Morris released from custody, becoming something of an occupational hazard for the girl,' he chuckled to try and ease the tension that he felt might be present.

'Ah Hazelhurst. I wondered when you'd call, finally some good news. Our secret weapon certainly knows how to get herself into some sticky situations, never known anything like it. I hope she can finally be let loose on Piffle's organisation and do the damage she was hired for in the first place.'

'Yes sir. It'll be all systems go now. She'll be reporting for work tomorrow and as they say, let battle commence.'

'Splendid, splendid Hazelhurst, you've done a good job. I'll be able to phone Archibald and give him the good news. I've found him very tiresome of late, all his ranting and raving takes it out of me. I am not as young as I used to be. I shall phone him straight away whilst the night is young.'

With that he rang off and steeled himself to ring Archibald McGreggor III, fully expecting to receive one of his tyrannical outbursts. He was not to be disappointed.

'Good evening Archibald, how are we this evening my good man?'

'Don't "good man" me Winton you useless imbecile. I've been following developments on the news since you have singularly failed to keep me informed and all I have seen is that blathering idiot of a Home Secretary crowing about suspected ISIS terrorists and mentioning that the very person you have employed to bring down Piffle is herself in custody after blowing up a fucking expensive train carriage. So I take it that we are no further forward?'

'Well Archibald, I take great exception to your tone of voice and underlying implied criticism of my handling of events.'

'There is no implied criticism you cretin, what there is, is a fucking realisation that I have employed a man that certainly lives up to his fucking surname, Cuncliffe, or near as damn it!'

Ignoring the barbed criticism, Winton decided on a humble and conciliatory response to Archibald's filthy and derogatory outbursts.

'I have some good news Archibald my dear fellow. My man on

the scene, Hazelhurst, has managed through skilful diplomacy to enact the release of Tandori Birkett-Morris. The young lady will be back to work tomorrow, immediately putting into effect our plan of action.'

That took some of the wind out of Archibald's sails, but he was only partially assuaged. 'That's as maybe, Winton, but let me tell you that every fucking day that goes by leads to another ridiculous fine coming in from that prick of a son of a fish filleter's whore who's trying to rob me blind. I want him stopped Winton, do you hear me?'

'I fully appreciate your predicament Archibald, but take heart from the fact that we are all in this together. Many, many companies in Grimewold are receiving fines from Piffle's organisation. I am sure given a small amount of time we can neuter the blighter once and for all.'

'Now you listen to me Winton and you listen good,' said Archibald working himself up again into a lather of fury. 'My fucking predicament is in no way similar to yours. You're not the one receiving a new fine every day, clocking up the £57,000 he has already fined me. Secondly, I couldn't give a flying fig what happens to other companies in Grimewold. I want Piffle stopped in his tracks, I want him to wish he had never been born, I want him decimated, I want him six foot bloody under for what he's doing to me. He'd be more useful if he was put through a mincing machine and turned into cat food! Do you understand me Winton?'

'Yes, yes, of course I do Archibald. Rest assured that from tomorrow Tandori will be doing her best to bring Piffle down. Once she's got to work on Piffle's business there will be no stopping her, just you wait and see. In my experience, she's managed to decimate everything she has ever gone near and I am sure, given just a small amount of time, she will bring Piffle's organisation to its knees.'

The conversation ended, if not on a good note, at least Winton concluded that he had bought some valuable time from the wrath of Josiah Archibald McGreggor III. He just hoped and prayed that his strategy of using Tandori Birkett-Morris was going to work, but on her past form he was 99% sure that within a few months Piffle would be in serious trouble.

Archibald was in his drawing room when he took the call from Winton. He poured himself a double scotch and sat in his favourite wing chair by a roaring fire. Apart from his desire to sort Piffle once and for all, he also was plotting the fermentation of a strike at the steel works. If he could provoke those idiots into walking out, then he could sack a good number of the blighters without compensation and close one of the three blast furnaces moving production to PING industries in India. That way he could generate another £127 million profit and quite possibly blackmail the Government into giving him a whopping great grant, estimated at £200 million to upgrade the last two remaining blast furnaces and wrap the whole thing up in positive PR that he, Archibald McGreggor, had the workers' best interests at heart and was the saviour of British Manufacturing Industry.

He just had to provoke that Union leader Barraclough and his henchman, but in past dealings Barraclough had been far too reasonable, so he had to initiate a policy so detrimental to his workers' interests that he left Barraclough no choice but to call a strike. With that happy thought, he decided it was time for bed. He rang the intercom linked to the scullery by his chair linked to summon Wilfred to get his sticks and help him to bed.

Chapter 58

It was an important day for Zara Bindle. Finally, she had got rid of that anachronism Jennings and replaced him with Tandori Birkett-Morris, the organisation's first transgender employee.

Hugo, her stay at home husband, had already made her breakfast, Flanagan's Irish porridge and granola mixed together with a dollop of Maku Japanese honey and strong black Colombian coffee.

'Now Hugo, don't forget it's bin day, it's the blue one this week.'

'I won't Zara, it's all in hand.'

'And don't forget to pick up the ironing from Mrs Gittings, I'm starting to run out of business attire.'

'No Zara, I'm popping round at 10.00 to collect the ironing.'

'And don't forget I've got my pilates class tonight so I won't be home till 7.00, so if you can have dinner ready for 7.30?'

'It's all in hand Zara.'

'Right I'm off then, have a good day, and oh, don't forget the window cleaner this afternoon.'

'No Zara,' but she was already out of the door and striding purposefully towards her black VW Golf.

By the time Tandori Birkett-Morris arrived at work it was already a hive of activity. Dressed for the part in a white blouse, pin-striped jacket and trousers, her hair short and minimal makeup, she looked quite plausibly like she was transgender, much to the delight of her new boss. As she hadn't much of a clue what she was supposed to be doing, she decided it best to report to Ms Bindle and await instructions.

'Come in Tandori, and welcome. I'll get one of the staff to make us a nice cup of tea. I thought with Jennings retired and you taking over his job so to speak. We could start by getting Jennings' assistant, Jonathan, to show you round the premises and settle you into your office. Nothing too strenuous on your first day.'

'That sounds very nice Ms Bindle, very kind as I do feel a bit out of my depth up here in Grimewold.'

'We all do, how did we end up in this God-forsaken hole of a place?' Bindle laughed.

'Oh, I'm sure it has its good points Ms Bindle, I just haven't had time to see them yet.'

Bindle's new secretary bought in a large pot of tea and a

selection of bourbons and custard creams and put them down on a separate round coffee table near to Bindle's extensive desk.

'Well Tandori, you and I are going to shake this place up. Dresden is away a lot so it's up to us to drive through the changes necessary to streamline overheads, improve cash flow, up the number of fines and realign the workforce to incorporate more women, gays, transgender and people of colour, not to mention gypsies and socially disadvantaged groups such as immigrants and Muslims. Ninety five percent of Piffle's employees are white males and together, Tandori, we are going to transform this organisation,' Bindle said with a steely glint in her eye. 'As a transgender man you are only the start, the prototype if you like, of what we are trying to achieve!'

Tandori didn't know how to respond to such an amazing outburst. All she could think of was how she was going to transform Piffle's company, but not in the way Zara Bindle was proposing.

'Well Ms Bindle, you certainly have some far reaching plans to take the Diversity Action Partnership into the 21st Century, and I as a transgender man am excited about being part of that,' said Tandori trying to be supportive when she hadn't got a clue what the crazy woman was talking about. Identity politics hadn't yet reached the simplistic world of Tandori Birkett-Morris.

'Things to do Tandori, I'll get Jonathan in to show you round and then you can get settled into your office.'

Bindle pressed the intercom, 'Get Jonathan to join us please.'

A couple of minutes passed and there was a tentative knock at the door 'Come in Jonathan, this is Tandori she has taken over from Jennings, so you will be reporting to her, I mean him.'

'Pleased to meet you Tandori,' said Jonathan shaking her hand.

'And you Jonathan.'

'Right Jonathan, if you could give Tandori a tour of our facilities such as they are, and then show her to her office she can settle in and make herself at home.'

'Will do Ms Bindle.'

Off they went for a tour of the offices of The Diversity Action Partnership Limited. First Tandori was shown the rows of school desks in the open-plan office, with the rows of clerks hand writing all of the individual client files with not a computer in sight. Then she was shown the huge metal filling cabinets at the rear of the office where the individual fines were kept, and finally the one desktop computer which spewed out the fines, which were then posted to the individual companies which had transgressed the rules pertaining to the Diversity legislation of 2010.

Tandori was then introduced to the team who went out to threaten companies who had not paid in the companies Transit vans with their high viz jackets and look of officious menace about them.

'How do you find out that a company isn't complying with the Diversity and Equality Act 2010 so that you can send out a fine?' Tandori asked innocently.

'Oh that's easy, we purchase data from HMRC about employees which includes a gender and ethnicity question. Then, to get a fuller picture, we send out a questionnaire to each company asking for further details. Under the provisions of the 2010 Equality and Diversity act any company that doesn't respond to the questionnaire is automatically assumed to be guilty and then we issue a fine. If they don't pay that, then we send the collections teams round to hand deliver an ultimatum which gives them fourteen days to pay. If they ignore that then we double the fine to £2000, and if that fails we send them a court summons, by which time further recovery costs have been added. Ninety percent of them pay up at that stage. If necessary, we go to court and we always win, or have done so far.'

'Who's the worst offender in the Humberwold region then?' asked Tandori fascinated by the elaborate process.

'Oh that's an easy one for me to answer Tandori, it's the biggest private sector company in the town, McGreggor's Steel. They owe, to date, £87,000 and have already lost a case for £57,000 at court. They're appealing and going to the High Court, and their lawyers are saying they will go to the Supreme Court if that appeal fails. It might take us another four years to squeeze the money out of them, but it's well known that Josiah Archibald McGreggor III fights dirty and will take this all the way.'

With the tour of facilities complete, Tandori was shown to her office and made another cup of coffee. With the door to her office closed it was time to reflect on what she had learned so far and how she was going to plan her next move.

From her limited knowledge of office administration, it was obvious that most of the practises she had been shown dated from a time before computers, nothing was interconnected and nearly everything was done manually. Only the fines were sent out from a computer and that was only to make them look officious, they were still posted in the normal way. There was no centralised computer system that linked clients with fines and tracked the process through to the end, so if she disrupted one part of the process then no one would be able to track the mistakes until it was too late.

As far as she could see, all she needed to do was start sending out fines to companies that either didn't require a fine or send a fine of the wrong amount. That way it would take a while for the companies to start complaining, refusing to pay or take legal action against the Diversity Action Partnership. Basically, she could cause havoc that would lead to so many mistakes and complaints that the company wouldn't be able to cope with putting things right. Eventually the Council who awarded the contract would get involved due to all the bad publicity.

She then had a light bulb moment. If she could intercept fines going out and make sure they were not sent then the revenue generated would fall and the company would be in even more difficulties. More importantly, the Council would see a drop in their share of the revenue. Another strategy might involve sending out bogus fines to companies that didn't owe any money thus generating confusion and possibly legal action.

With that splendid thought, she drank the cup of coffee Jonathan had made her and came to the conclusion this was going to be easier than she thought – providing she wasn't found out early in the process. With a bit of luck, she could be out of this dump within three months and back to Mummy and Daddy, free from the threats of Hazelhurst and Inspector Fleece.

She felt a fleeting pang of regret in so much as she was about to help ruin Sydney Dresden Piffle. He had never done her any harm, in fact she quite liked him, and he certainly seemed to like her. Oh well, in war there had to be casualties.

Chapter 59

Gordon Streake was watching a very interesting little transaction being played out in the cemetery on Lincoln road on the outskirts of Grimewold. It was the culmination of several weeks of surveillance. The two characters Streake was watching had no idea they were being observed.

He could see, looking through his binoculars from his car, that they were having some kind of altercation. Eventually money changed hands and the male handed over a packet, which obviously contained drugs.

Streake knew both the characters involved. The man was a known drug dealer, a nasty piece of work called Brett Sinclair. Or Lord Brett, which was his street name after the Roger Moore character from the old TV series, the Persuaders. Brett Sinclair was as far away from the suave character played by Roger Moore as he could possibly be. He was a shaven haired thug who had never done a day's work in his life, violent, unpleasant and with very limited intellect. He was a heavy drug user himself so could be unpredictable and violent at very short notice. He dealt in the hard stuff – crack cocaine and heroin – despite his hard man reputation he was small time, but dangerous nevertheless.

The girl on the other hand was who he was really interested in. Thirty-eight years old and a coke head, desperate for her next fix. When she wasn't getting laid for money, she was sponging off her family; went by the name of Madison, Maddy or MAD depending upon what her mood was.

Streake took some photos with a long lens so he could provide evidence to his employer of the activities Madison was involved in.

Streake spent another few minutes at the side of the road looking over into the cemetery as the two low lifes conducted their transaction and went their separate ways. He then drove to a grubby little local cafe called Mary Jane's to have a coffee and write up his file, which was nearly complete.

He was in a pensive mood that Saturday morning. That his life had come to this. A second-rate private investigator scratching around for work, mostly from matrimonial disputes where one party was trying to prove the other's unfaithfulness. At least he had his police pension, reduced though it was because he hadn't achieved his thirty years' service. His time had been cut short in the force. It was his own fault, he'd gotten greedy, taking bungs from small time criminals. Problem was, he got too cocky and started to flash the cash: a Jensen Interceptor car, gold Rolex watch and too many holidays to Florida on his salary started to pique the interest of the Police Investigations Unit.

Luckily for Streake nothing was proven, but he was told by the

Deputy Chief Constable to retire 'on health grounds' and this is what
reduced his pension. What pissed Streake off wasn't just the loss of
salary and perks, it was the fact that after twenty-five years of service,
he had to leave the force in disgrace. He could still remember the other
officers, who he was sure had stitched him up, singing their nasty little
song about him in the police canteen, *'Yes they call him the Streake,
looka dat looka dat, fastest thing on two feet, looka dat looka dat he's
always on the take, and make no mistake, that's why they call him the
Streake, don't look Ethel but it was too late she'd already been mooned.'*
They all laughed hysterically as he slunk out of police headquarters
never to return.

Yes, Streake was a man with a grudge on life itself. He always
had a scowl on his face and since his dismissal five years previously he
had let himself go. A grubby brown raincoat, stained shirt and old-
fashioned cheap nylon tie were his attire of choice, and an old Vauxhall
Vectra was a long way from the Jensen and his playboy image from ten
years ago.

He sat in the cheap cafe with a mug of coffee writing up his
report. It was nearly finished. He had found out exactly what his
employer had hoped he would. The first part of the job had been
delving into the financial situation at a small engineering firm called
SK+R Limited. It supplied engineering supplies to the steel industry,
mostly locally with McGreggor's being their biggest customer. A true
nuts and bolts outfit, buying stock in, using a work's van for deliveries
and employing one down at heel salesman called Dick Kennedy who
went round and took the orders.

It was an increasingly competitive market with purchasing departments being able to source much of the stuff online and have it delivered directly, sometimes from China, the main production centre now for most of the kit. SK+R had the overheads of a traditional salesman and still dealt with a lot of the dwindling supply of British companies trying to eke out a living producing items at much higher costs that the Chinese could supply. It was a losing battle, which SK+R were not equipped to win.

Streake had found out that in the last financial year SK+R had lost £120,000 and had needed a cash injection from the two directors to survive. This year was going to be make or break and with nothing changing, it looked like SK+R were heading for bankruptcy. A lot of the background information had come from him cosying up to two employees, Dick Kennedy (who he found out had a nickname - the Ferret), and the stores assistant, an old guy called Alistair who had been a respected accountant, but drink had got the better of him and he had been sacked ending up in a menial job at SK+R. Both were very lucid once Streake had plied them with drink on separate occasions, especially Alistair Golding, who knew a thing or two about the financial viability of the firm he worked for.

All in all, a good job, and a lucrative one. Three grand was the fee for a month's work, much better than the grand he normally received for a matrimonial job, but then the work had been that much harder to complete, but complete it he had.

Time to make the phone call so he could get paid and hand over his final report with the findings. 'Is that you Mike? It's me Streake.'

Mike Morrell was delighted to receive the phone call he had been waiting for from his old police buddy Gordon Streake, (they had been through Police training together).

'Now then Streake, what news have you got for me?'

'Not over the phone Mike, we need to meet face to face and not being funny, but I want to make sure I have my fee before I hand over anything. But I will say this much, I've got what you need and a bit more besides.'

'Well Streake, I need to be armed with the information you have for me by Monday morning, so we better meet tomorrow, if Sunday is OK for you? I've got your three grand in cash requested, so neither of us need to worry on that score. You bring the report and go through it with me and I'll hand over the cash.'

'Where do you want to meet then?'

'Best you come to my gaff in Appleton, it's called The Eagles Nest, on Main street, big electric double wooden gates, you can't miss it.'

The meeting was set for 11.00 a.m. on Sunday morning at Mike Morell's house. Streake arrived a few minutes early and pressed the intercom. The large wooden gates swung open, Streake drove in and parked up the old Vauxhall outside the front entrance.

Mike Morrell was waiting for him at the double fronted front door.

'Glad you could make it Streake, I've got fresh coffee brewing. Come in, come in!' Mike said with a beaming smile. He had cause to be happy. He was anticipating that Streake had the information that he needed to make his next move.

'I'm here Mike as you requested and as you can see I've got the finished report. Have you got my money?' Streake said scowling as he usually did.

'Yes, all in good time Streake, come and sit down, make yourself comfortable and then we can talk through your findings. Scotch?'

'Don't mind if I do, Mike.'

Morrell poured them both a generous scotch, and then placed the £3,000 on the table in a buff envelope by way of encouragement.

'Well what I've found is very interesting. Your little friend at the Council, what's her name? – Penelope Sykes – is in big financial trouble. You may wonder why when she's on £180,000 a year as leader of Grimewold Council. Well that's as maybe, but she has a daughter called Madison who has a serious class A drug problem, crack cocaine, heroin, you name it and when she's not doing a few tricks, she's sponging off mummy. We're talking a grand a week going up the bitch's nose. This has been going on years, but what's tipped little Miss Head of the Council over the fucking edge is that hubby's engineering company is on the skids and lost £120,000 last year and is set to do the same this year. And who do you think is bank rolling the majority of the losses? You guessed it, Penelope Sykes and her salary. But even she can't keep up with the losses. Is that what you want to hear Mike, am I getting close?'

A huge grin spread over Mike Morrel's face and he slapped his thigh. 'Bingo, Streake, that's bloody music to my ears. The boy done good, that information is worth every bit of three grand, here you are, take it, take it.'

'Oh, there is one more thing that might interest you Mike. I had a word with a few of Madison's friends and a word with her scumbag drug-dealer supplier, street name of Lord Brett Sinclair, and guess what I found? Well who do you think got precious Madison hooked on hard drugs twenty years ago when he was going out with her? None other than the Friday night host of Purple Haze, Sydney Dresden Piffle's wayward son!'

'Bloody hell Streake, you have been a busy boy haven't you? Good background information, well done.'

Mike Morrell wasn't going to divulge the significance of the last piece of information Gordon Streake had supplied, but it would be instrumental in Mike Morrell securing the next stage of his elaborate plan to build his business and at the same time sink the fortunes of Sydney Dresden Piffle.

Chapter 60

Piffle woke early despite not having a need to. He had a good night sleep in the arms of his beloved Honolulu, but there were things to be done, he couldn't afford to sleep in and lounge the day away however tempting that might be.

But first to the shower. He was in an exceptionally good mood and as the hot streams of water cascaded over his head and onto his substantial body, he started to sing as load as his lungs would let him

'If I was a rich man la la la la la la la la laaa. All day long I'm sitting in the Sun, la la la la la la laaa. I wouldn't have to work hard _ because I am a Tory _ la la la la la la la la la laaa. All day long I'm sitting in the sun...'

On and on the song went with Piffle's voice booming out of the bathroom. A heartfelt ditty that represented his optimism for the future and his deep-seated prejudices of the hated Tories, even as his whole life was cascading towards trying to emulate the life style of the Tories that he claimed to so despise. None of this of course occurred to Piffle. As far as he was concerned, he was working class through and through and all his actions supported his love of the Labour party and class solidarity.

Soon Honolulu was up as well and making him the full English breakfast that he loved so much.

'Dresden my love, your breakfast is ready, streaky bacon, big fat sausages, scrambled eggs, fried bread, hash brownies, baked beans, big flat mushrooms, tinned tomatoes, toast and marmalade, and PG Tips just as you like it.'

'I'll be down in a sec, just putting me dressing gown on. My, you do look after me Honolulu, I'd be lucky to get slice of cold toast off the Clothes Horse.'

'I've done you a big bowl of porridge with honey and got you a nice big iced Chelsea bun for your, what do you English say, afters.'

'Champion Honolulu, that I'll keep me going to elevenses.'

Piffle bounded down the stairs and was soon tucking into his huge extravagant breakfast whilst Honolulu busied herself with the washing up and other domestic chores in the kitchen.

'Big day for us today Honolulu, going to sign the contract with the builder that Paeleo found us. Then he can get started clearing the site and putting in the services necessary to erect the first ten log cabins. Champion.'

'This is very good Dresden, you are such a clever man, I am so lucky to have you. Now you got your jacket on and go, go and get your log cabins started. Paeleo will be here shorty with your big Rolls Royce motor car.'

'Thank you Honolulu, you just come here luv and give your Dresden a nice big hug so he can feel your big bosoms against his chest.'

'Oh you are so cheeky Dresden,' Honolulu said as she bounded into his arms like a charging baby elephant.

The embrace was far too short as within a few seconds he heard the Silver Spur on the gravel drive and Paeleo pipping his horn loudly.

'Oh bloody hell Paeleo's here, always has a habit of turning up at wrong time that lad.'

'Now I am in your arms Dresden, I don't want to let you go.'

'Well you're going to have to luv, the master is calling,' said Piffle with a touch of irony, which Honolulu didn't understand.

'Señor Paeleo is not your master, Dresden,' Honolulu said earnestly.

'Well it bloody well feels like it most of the time,' said Piffle chuckling. He extracted himself from Honolulu's embrace and made for the kitchen door.

Beep beep the car horn blared.

'I'm coming Paeleo, give me a bloody chance,' he said nearly falling down the step again.

'Last thing I need is another sprained ankle, it was bloody agony last time.'

Paeleo had jumped out the driver's door and opened the rear door of the Silver Spur, waving his hands in an extravagant gesture.

'Come come Senor Piffle, we will be late for the meeting with Senor Andretti, very important man, you must come.'

'I'm coming Paeleo, but you just remember I'm the one giving out contract. It doesn't matter how important your Andretti is or whether he has built bloody Benidorm bypass, I'm paying the piper so to speak.'

'I not understand this piper business, what you talking about?'

But Piffle was already in the back seat and Paeleo slammed the door, rushed round to the driver's door and soon they were off out of the Villa Almeria and heading down the mountain road into Benidorm town. The sun was already quite high in a cloudless blue sky and the temperature was heading towards 25 degrees.

'Put the air conditioning up a bit Paeleo, I'm bloody roasting back here. I don't want to get to meeting dripping like I've been in a shower and smelling like a brothel owner's armpit.'

'I do that for you Señor Piffle, this Silver Spur has dual air conditioning system, the power of 40 fridges, is very good, best of British eh?'

As they sped down the mountain road Piffle looked out of the rear tinted glass window of the Silver Spur and saw the beautiful orange and lemon groves at the side of the road and the pretty pink and maroon bushes against the back drop of soft cream limestone rocks contrasting with the bright flawless blue sky. Piffle couldn't help thinking that his future lay here in this beautiful landscape, not the cold, wet depressing and ugly town of Grimewold. The source of his money that was funding his life style and aspirations of wealth beyond the wildest dreams of his father Henry Herbert Piffle who had grown up on the Gipsyville estate, a 1920's vision of modest semidetached properties to house the trawlermen and their families in the city of Hull.

'Beautiful day Señor Piffle, no?'

'It is that Paeleo, be even more bloody beautiful if I sign this agreement with your mate and we get started on log cabin site.'

Soon they were at the Playa de Sol caravan site next to the giant Ikea store on the outskirts of Benidorm.

'I should of come in a taxi Paeleo, don't want your mate to get wrong idea and think I'm made of bloody money. This Rolls gives out wrong impression lad.'

'No no, you no need to worry Señor Piffle, Señor Andretti is a what you English say, a man of this world. He understand that a man like you Señor Piffle make your money by getting good deals, not by splashing the cash.'

Paeleo parked up the Rolls and Piffle lumbered across the to the old caravan at the entrance to the dilapidated caravan park and disappeared inside to wait for Miguel Andretti to arrive. He didn't have to wait long.

A battered white transit van pulled up. A short, stocky man in blue denim overalls with a balding head and shifty, beady deep-set eyes that darted around like a Golden Eagle looking for its prey stepped out. A well-trimmed beard and swarthy weather beaten complexion completed the look. Paeleo got out of the Rolls and shouted to Andretti.

' Hey Miguel, my master, Señor Piffle is in the old caravan waiting for you.'

'Hey, my friend Paeleo, it is a pleasure to see you again after all this time,' said Miguel making sure that he didn't let on that Paeleo and him were drinking buddies.

Miguel sauntered over to the old caravan and knocked on the door. He had a black leather-bound A4 folder with him so he could make detailed notes of what was required.

'Good day Señor, my name is Miguel Andretti, I am pleased to meet with you Señor Piffle.'

'Eh up lad, good to see you,' Piffle said patting Miguel on the back vigorously.

'Come in and settle yourself down.'

'So Señor Piffle, Paeleo says that you want to make big new holiday park with log cabins. Am I correct?'

'Too bloody right you are. Look here, I've me architect sketch out basic layout of site, it needs work but gives you an idea.'

'Well Señor Piffle I have much experience of big projects, such as completing the Benidorm bypass, plus some well-known hotels such as the Ambassador, maybe you know it?'

'I've heard of it, yes Mr Andretti.'

'You must call me Miguel if we are to be partners in this endeavour Señor Piffle. I will walk around the site and make some detailed notes based upon your architects sketches and drawings. Then I will get my head of works to come and spend a couple of days here to conduct a proper feasibility study and plan, and of course a detailed set of works and timescale. I suggest however, that maybe we complete one small section of the site and get say ten log cabins erected. That way we can gauge the costs and difficulties and refine our approach, and you can sell those to get some cashflow coming in.'

'Let's cut to chase Miguel. Any idea how much this is going to cost?'

'It is hard to say but for five hundred log cabins, for all the ground works and services, I would say €10 million, but if you could give me an upfront payment of €500,000 we could get some of the key services into site and put the groundworks and roads in for the first ten log cabins. Yes, I believe that would be acceptable to me.'

'Bloody hell, €10 million, that sounds a lot of money Miguel, but you get your man to properly cost it out. Tell you what I'll do. As a measure of my good faith, I'll pay you €250,000 up front and the other €250,000 on completion of the initial ground works for the ten log cabins. How does that sound?'

'I will give it some thought Señor Piffle. Now, I will need a couple of hours to walk round the site with your plans and make detailed notes regarding the requirements, then my foreman will come to the site and work up a plan of works. I assure you Señor, that we will be the cheapest as I use best quality labour from the Indian province of Kerala.'

'How long will that all take Miguel? I'm keen to get started and get this thing up and running.'

'Well it will take as long as it takes Señor, maybe a month from now. I will be in touch, and I will discuss the financial requirements once I have some detailed costings.' Miguel gave Piffle a broad smile, but it was a smile of cunning, his beady little eyes darting about and shining brightly.

'Alright then Miguel, you crack on lad, but one month max, OK? And I want detailed costings mind, old Piffle doesn't want to have his leg lifted now does he?'

The two men shook hands and Piffle was off back to the Silver Spur. He couldn't help thinking he was being taken for a mug, and he didn't trust this Miguel Andretti. There was just something about him, but then Piffle had a distrust of foreigners anyway, and Southerners. In fact, anyone really who didn't come from the East Riding of Yorkshire, and Hull in particular.

Paeleo was humming away in the driver's seat as the car sped back towards the Villa Almeria. He was happy that the meeting had gone well and his boss was going to sign a contract with Miguel, as he was going to get a small cut of a very large contract. Soon he would be a wealthy man and would not need to drive Piffle around all day in a Rolls Royce. He would own his own property and have his own luxury car and the restaurant he had always dreamed of.

Chapter 61

It was also an important day for Mike Morrell. At 10.00 on Monday morning he had a meeting arranged with the Chief Executive of Grimewold Council, Penelope Sykes, regarding the awarding of the Clean Air contract. He had decided to have the meeting well away from the council offices, and the prying eyes of his own staff, and booked a meeting room at a luxury hotel called the Oaklands Country Park and Golf Resort, not too far from his home in the village of Appleton.

Always be prepared, that was Mike's motto. He had prepared a draft contract and had a number of options if necessary, not least the valuable background information that Gordon Streake had supplied him with.

'Janice have you got the Clean Air contract ready? I'm off shortly to meet Penelope Sykes at Oaklands. Not looking forward to it to be honest, never did like the woman, but needs must. This is the big one for us Janice.'

'I've got it here Mike, two copies as you requested. What do you think our chances are of winning the contract?'

'Oh, I'm pretty sure we will be able to strike a deal Janice, remember we already have the expertise and the infrastructure in place to move quickly and start earning revenue for the council. They're under a lot of pressure with Central Government cuts to their budgets, not to mention the huge costs of social care that are coming their way. Anything that can bring in large chunks of money for them is going to be welcome, they're going to jump at the chance. We've just got to make sure it's us that gets the contract and cleans up. Right, I'm on my way Janice, wish me luck, don't know when I'll be back.'

'See you later Mike, good luck!'

With that, Morrell was out of the door and into the car park where his BMW was parked in the Managing Director's reserved slot to the left of the front entrance. Piffle's space was immediately to the right.

The BMW shot off out of the car park, rear wheels spinning and spraying loose gravel in all directions. Mike Morrell was on a quest for total victory and he wasn't going to take any prisoners, especially Penelope Sykes. Like all good chess players, he had scanned the board and was quite a few steps ahead. What he couldn't anticipate was how she would react to his generous offer of a carrot, and if necessary a stick!

It took Morrell just twenty minutes to reach the hotel and country club a couple of miles outside the village of Appleton.

The Hotel was a converted country house built in 1912 by a very rich heiress to an engineering firm based in Leeds that had supplied all the Steam Engine manufacturers like GNER sub components for the construction of their magnificent machines. After Milly St Clair had died just after the war, the house, like so many grand country piles, fell into decline and had to be sold to pay death duties. It was bought and converted into a hotel in the late 1950s, and eventually sold on in 2010 to a very wealthy Indian family who owned a string of high profile luxury hotels. They had lavished money on converting the rather shabby building into a five-star luxury hotel, spa and golf resort along the lines of an American country club. Just the sort of habitat where Morrell felt most at home and could show off his wealth and credentials, and intimidate his opponents.

Morrell parked up the BMW and strode purposefully across the car park and through the revolving doors into the marble lined lobby. On a pillar in front of him was a portrait of the Chairman staring down at him. It was the face of a smiling Indian man about 60 years old in a very expensive Saville Row suit and a gold Breitling watch. Under the hand-painted portrait there was an inscription which read *Chairman: Dr R A Mutha (RAM Group)*, with a further inscription underneath: *My Five Golden Rules to Success – Truth, Hard Work, Integrity, Character, Hope.*

Morrell studied the portrait for a moment and a wry smile crossed his face. He decided there and then that he would have a similar hand painted portrait to his power and vanity commissioned and put in the lobby of his company, but with the inscription: *My Five Golden Rules for Success – Plan, Demand, Deliver, Succeed, Reward!*

He approached the beautiful mahogany reception desk with inlaid gold and silver coloured mosaics in the Middle Eastern style and spoke to the smartly dressed receptionist.

'Excuse me, my name's Morrell, Mike Morrell Chairman of Humberwold Speed Camera Action! Limited. My secretary has booked one of your executive meetings rooms here.'

'Just a minute Mr Morrell I'll just check the reservations for today. Ah here we are, you're in the Khan Suite, named after Imran Khan the former President of Pakistan. It's down the corridor to your right, turn left at the end, you can't miss it.'

'Thank you Miss, do you know if Penelope Sykes has arrived yet?'

'No sir, she hasn't approached the desk and I haven't seen anyone who might be her.'

'OK well, when she arrives tell her I'm waiting for her in the meeting room.'

'I will do sir.'

Mike Morrell made his way to the large meeting room, opened the large mahogany double doors and went inside. Before him was a large meeting table with 12 brown leather executive chairs, a table to the side with bottles of sparkling water, cordials and biscuits, and at the far end of the room a large picture window looking out on an immaculate lawn, with beautiful English beech trees in the distance and a sturdy oak tree in the centre. A truly breath-taking setting for his make-or-break meeting with Penelope Sykes.

Morrell sat down at the head of the table facing the double doors and started to go over his notes for the meeting, even though he had rehearsed what he was going to say many times. He was sat down for less than ten minutes when there was a knock at the door. Penelope Sykes entered looking like a slightly younger Mrs Thatcher, a vision in a bright Tory blue jacket and skirt and a crisp white high-collar shirt and gold dress jewellery. Her reputation as formidable was certainly expressed in her attire and demeanour.

'Good day to you Mr Morrell, I trust I am on time for our meeting?'

'Pleased to meet you again Penelope, and yes you are on time, thank you for coming.'

'Ms Sykes please if you don't mind Mr Morrell.'

'Don't mind at all Ms Sykes.' Her haughty attitude had already riled Mike. Since he considered he had the upper hand he thought he would lay his cards on the table early on in the conversation.

'Let's cut to the chase Ms Sykes, you know why we're here because my secretary briefed you in the original email we sent. We have the contract for Humberwold speed camera fines and make your council a hell of a lot of money and we do it very well. In fact, we issue more speeding fines per head of population than any other speed enforcement agency in the country, and you get a good proportion of that money. Let me see... £15,826,000 in the last financial year according to my bean counters. We both know that the new clean air legislation is coming in the next two months and councils will have another lucrative source of income, especially if they have a partner company able to effectively test motorists cars and issue fines. The bottom line is – we are that company. No one else in Humberwold has that level of expertise, boots on the ground and ability to get the job done. In short, we have the infrastructure in place to deliver for you, just as we have delivered on the speed camera contract.'

'You certainly make a compelling case Mr Morrell, but it's not all down to me you know, and I'm not sure that I can in any way guarantee you winning a contract that's going to go out to tender. There are some big American players sniffing around who have equal resources and expertise with Government contracts, including the ones running our jails and testing of recipients of welfare, such as Welfare-Plus Inc of Connecticut who I believe we are talking to. The contract will have to go out to tender so I don't think, at this stage, there is much I can help you with. All I can do is advise you to put in a strong tender and then as chair of the Ways and Means Committee I will make sure you get a fair crack of the whip.'

Mike Morrell knew this was coming, he had dealt with these public sector morons before. In anticipation of what he was about to say a broad smile came over his face. Not a nice smile, but a sneer of contempt and knowledge that he had the upper hand. It was just that Penelope Sykes did not know what was about to hit her.

'Well Ms Sykes, I have taken the trouble to produce a report here which forecasts the revenue that my company could, and will, generate for the council if we are awarded the contract. Along with running costs, which we guarantee will be smaller than any other company bidding, because, as I have said, we have the infrastructure in place already to deliver this for you. Despite your modesty Ms Sykes, you are leader of Grimewold Municipal Council and head of the important Ways and Means Committee who determines who will win this contract.'

Mike Morrell handed her a copy of the report, which she glanced at in a rather dismissive way.

'Thank you for that Mr Morrell. I'll take this back to the Ways and Means Committee and it will provide some useful background information in our deliberations, but as I have said this is a competitive tendering process and I can't, and won't, be seen to influence the outcome. I fear you have brought me all the way out to this fancy gin palace for nothing.'

'Oh I don't know about that Ms Sykes. I'm sure we're going to have a nice buffet lunch together with some wine, but before that, let's cut the fucking bullshit lady.'

'How dare you? I've never been spoken to like that in my life.'

'Well, you prissy pain in the arse, you need to get out more often!'

'I'm not putting up with this...'

'Oh yes you fucking are lady. Number one fact that you need to understand is, I know that your useless daughter, Madison, is a grade one smack head. A crack cocaine user to be precise, who buys her gear with your money from the local drug baron Lord Brett Sinclair and I happen to have them both on video. I'm willing to put it on social media in ten minutes' time and I'm happy to contact ITN, the BBC and Sky News. Comprendo? Secondly, I know you're seriously in debt and hubby has been draining you dry with his little Engineering Company hobby. I wouldn't be surprised if you're siphoning off some council funds to keep him afloat, or giving him dodgy contracts.'

The last sentence had just occurred to Morrell and was a guess, but by the look on Penelope Sykes' face he had hit home.

'So I don't give a fuck how you do it miss prissy knickers, but you are going to make sure that the Ways and Means Committee delivers us that contract. Here is the good news for you because I'm nothing but a fair and honest man. You do that and I will make sure you personally receive twenty grand a month into a numbered Cayman Islands bank account. That way you can keep Madison in drugs, pay off your debts and save hubby's business empire. Sounds a good deal to me, in fact, the best you are ever going to get to save your crumbling reputation and make sure you stay as council leader. Let me spell out the alternative Ms Sykes. All this comes out, you have to resign, you lose your reputation and salary, hubby's business goes bust, you lose your house because you can't make the mortgage payments and you are still stuck with darling Madison on hard drugs who will become a full time crack hooker to get her daily fix. Is that what you want Ms Sykes? Your choice.'

All the arrogant composure that Penelope Sykes had displayed when she entered the meeting room was gone. Here was a woman whose whole world was crumbling down and she knew it. Mike had easily beaten her into submission, but he was shrewd enough to give her a life line. It had the added benefit of ensuring that she wouldn't go back on the deal, because if she breathed a word of this then she would be off to prison, as well as him, for a very long time. As his father used to say, carrot and stick.

'OK Mr Morrell you seem to have me beaten. I'll make sure you win your contract, but we will have to still make sure that your offer is the best – I can give you the inside track on that. I don't know how you found out about Madison, or my husband's business problems, but I'm willing to take your offer of £20,000 a month providing it cannot be traced back to me. And also on the understanding that you don't try to blackmail me further, because if you do, we will both be going to prison for a very long time. I think we've discussed what needs to be discussed, so if you don't mind, I'd rather not have lunch with you. You have forced my hand Mr Morrell, but it doesn't mean I have to like you in any way shape or form.'

With that, Penelope rose and left the room without looking back. She was not going to give Mike Morrell the pleasure of his victory over her.

For his part, Morrell ate his buffet lunch, and drank the full bottle of expensive champagne he had ordered, on his own looking out over the beautiful gardens of the hotel. He had decided to hold back on getting Piffle's contract for another day, and the fact that it was Piffle's famous son, Bradley Plumb who had got Penelope's daughter hooked on crack cocaine twenty years ago. That was for another encounter when he gauged that revenge on Piffle would enable him to win the contract from The Diversity Action Partnership, and finally put Sydney Dresden Piffle out of the game.

Feeling rather worse for wear, he went to reception and ordered a taxi to get himself back to Eagle's Nest. His work for today was well and truly done, he would pick up his BMW the following morning when he had sobered up. His mind was no longer as clear as it had been before drowning the entire bottle of Champagne but he was still able to reflect on human nature, and the fact that people were quite easy to manipulate if you knew what buttons to press, information was the key and everybody had something in the closet, luckily for him Ms Sykes had plenty of skeletons!

Chapter 62

Gordon Streake was feeling quite pleased with himself as he sat on his bed at his sister's house which he shared with her. Sitting in his dresser was the £4000 Mike Morrell had given him for his research into the financial position of the council leader, and her dark secret about her daughter's drug problem.

When he had looked in the envelope he was pleased to find a £1000 bonus that he hadn't been expecting. Mike Morrell had added it when Streake gave him the additional news that it was Piffle's son who had got Madison hooked on hard drugs in the first place. He wasn't sure how that was going to benefit Mike Morrell, but he knew that Morrell would not have given him the bonus without it being important to him. Maybe he needed to do some of his own research on Piffle's son, Bradley Plumb aka Bradley Norman Piffle? Yes, that would be his next move. Maybe there was a lot more money to squeeze out of that situation than he had originally envisaged.

He had the inconvenience of living with his sister Brenda, confined to a small second bedroom, and he wanted to get enough money together to spend his declining years somewhere warmer. Nothing fancy, the Costa Del Sol would do nicely. He just needed to find the key to unlocking the extra money he needed. Fifty grand would do, but he had to find a way of extracting that money from this fortuitous situation he had found himself in. What do they say? "Knowledge is power," and he was determined to acquire enough knowledge to gain a substantial little nest egg.

Another man who was pleased that morning was Josiah Archibald McGreggor III. Not only was Tandori Birkett-Morris now free to inflict the terrible damage he had in mind for Piffle, but he had devised a particularly cunning plan to, hopefully, engineer a major strike at McGreggor's, thus giving him the excuse to sack a quarter of the workforce, without compensation, for gross misconduct.

In the previous year's negotiations with the Trades Unions, Archibald had agreed to pay a generous bonus system amounting to an average 40% of a production line worker's take home pay, providing they hit certain achievable production targets. This limited the basic element of the workers' pay to a minimum wage far below what skilled workers would expect to achieve without the 40% bonus. However, for the production line workers to achieve the 40% bonus they had to achieve 95% of the possible production output of the three blast furnaces, which meant that McGreggor's steel mills were as efficient as they possibly could be. Everyone was a winner since McGreggor's made excellent profits running a 95% capacity and the workers got a good wage which protected their standard of living. But starting today Josiah Archibald McGreggor III was going to severely upset this beneficial arrangement.

Rarely did he go into the works now and today was no exception. He would get his Production Director, a hard-hitting American henchman by the name of Curtis Googleheimer, to come to him and take instructions for how things were now going to be.

'Get Googleheimer on the phone, I need him to come here today to discuss something important,' he barked at his long-suffering secretary, 'and whilst you're at it, get me a nice cup of strong black coffee.'

'I'll certainly try for you, but we can't guarantee that Mr Googleheimer will be available at such short notice. He's a busy man you know, Archibald. The coffee on the other hand won't be a problem.'

'Do you always have to make things difficult? Just get Googleheimer here for lunch time, he works for me, not the other way round. And so do you, so just for once in your life, do as I say.'

June had a way of winding Archibald up that was second nature to her. She scurried off to get his black coffee and telephone Mr Googleheimer. Why Archibald couldn't give her and other people a little bit of notice she couldn't imagine, but there you are, he liked to exert his authority and summon people at will.

'Here's your coffee Archibald,' said June bringing it to him in the drawing room on a silver tray: a cafetiere and a fine bone china cup and saucer, with a separate sugar bowl containing lumps of brown sugar.

'Oh and I've rung Mr Googleheimer. He's coming straight away from the steel works, so he should be here in thirty minutes. I'm off to do some paperwork.'

'For once you've done as I've told you to do. Tell me when Googleheimer arrives and send him straight through to the drawing room. It's an important day June,' said Archibald with that dreadful leer on his face that was always a precursor to some fiendish plot that he had decided upon. June knew him all too well after all these years and wondered what he had up his sleeve this time.

Before long Googleheimer arrived for his briefing in the drawing room.

'Mr Googleheimer here to see you now,' said June as promised.

'Splendid June, send him through.'

Yes, there was definitely something up thought June. Very rarely did she find Archibald in a pleasant mood, but this morning he was positively joyous.

'Ah Googleheimer, how good of you to come, and at such short notice.'

'Gee it's sure no problem for me Archibald, you're the boss.'

'Come, come my dear fellow, we both know you run the day to day operations at McGreggor's and you do it very well.'

'Anyhow Archibald, I sure am intrigued to know why you've called me in today, must be goddamned important to drag me out to your country pile.'

'Well my dear fellow, it's a year now since I employed you as Plant Director, and you came highly recommended I must say, I thought it time we had a little catch up. It is midday, and I always have a scotch, would you like to join me? I have a rather nice single malt in the drinks cabinet.'

'That sure is very kind of ya Archibald, I don't mind if I do,' said Googleheimer who was hedging his bets. He knew of the reputation of Josiah Archibold McGreggor III and didn't think for one minute he had been dragged out here to have a cosy chat and a shot of single malt, or to just exchange pleasantries. No, the old codger was up to something, but for now he would just play along and see where the conversation took them.

The very expensive single malt was duly poured and Archibald engaged in more banal banter, which was totally out of keeping with his usual personality and demeanour. After a while Googleheimer grew restless and decided to find out the real reason for his summons.

'Hey Archibald, am I right in thinkin' we ain't here to discuss the weather? So maybe you could cut to the chase and sock it to me boy. What on God's green earth do you want me here for today?'

'Well my good man, of course, how right you are. Vey perceptive old man. Yes, well the top and bottom of it is that I want you to reduce the supply of iron ore that we get from our suppliers through Hull docks by 40%, but I need you to engineer a shortage for at least a few months.'

'I don't understand Archibald, there ain't no shortage, the supplies from Poland are coming in just dandy and we need all the iron ore we can get so as to hit our production targets. There just ain't no sense to what you are saying.'

'Now you listen to me,' Archibald was struggling to contain his explosive temper. 'I mean, my dear Googleheimer, you have been employed to do my bidding, and I'm telling you to cut the import of iron ore through Hull docks by 40% by the end of the month. No ifs and no buts. Do I make myself clear?'

'Well OK Archibold, as you say, you are the boss but you do know we'll have to mothball one of the three blast furnaces if there ain't enough iron coming in? And the good old boys on the line are going to see their pay cut substantially because we won't be meeting the production targets agreed with the Union. There'll be hell to pay.'

'Don't you worry about that my dear Googleheimer, leave those little problems and the Union to me.'

'You're the boss. I just don't understand what this is all about. It's as if you want to engineer a strike.'

'You're not paid to understand Googleheimer. Just run along and sort it will you? I've got some important work to do today, if you will excuse me,' and with that Archibold swept from the room satisfied that his plan would be put into action and his strategy for making many millions of pounds would soon be within his grasp.

Googleheimer was left alone in Archibald's drawing room still with the glass of single malt scotch in his hand. The old man was up to something that was for sure. There was no way the Union was going to put up with an effective 40% pay cut because they hadn't hit their production targets through no fault of their own. Also, mothballing one of the three blast furnaces would be expensive and even more expensive to get back into working order when Archibald came to his senses, it might even need to be relined which would cost several hundred million pounds. Googleheimer had to conclude that for some reason Archibald wanted to close one of the blast furnaces permanently, but with full order books it just didn't make sense. No, Googleheimer was being set up to take the fall on this one and he didn't like the sound or the smell of it one little goddamned bit!

Chapter 63

Mike Morrell was sitting in his office when word came through via email from the Council Leader, Penelope Sykes. The council had just had their weekly Ways and Means Committee meeting and had approved the awarding of the Clean Air Contract to Humberwold Speed Camera Action! Limited after careful consideration of the options available. The contract would be for five years on the basis that Humberwold Speed camera Action! Limited would receive 40% of the income from fines, and Grimewold Council the remaining 60%, with the former absorbing the running costs of the scheme within the 40% income stream. According to Penelope, the Ways and Means Committee wanted a twelve month projection of income so it could plan increased Council spending based on the new income precept.

A huge grin came over Mike Morrell's face as he leaned back in his leather swivel chair. He'd bloody done it! Already rich from running Humberwold Speed Camera Action! for three years, he was now going to be catapulted to the next level. He could quite easily see his company making ten million quid a year, and if he could capture Piffle's company, he could make another £2 million. That way he could bungle the thing into one company and sell it to one of the big American syndicates who were breaking into so many lucrative public sector contracts these days. If he could get £50 million for the whole lot, he would be off to his own island in the Caribbean for a well-earned retirement. Not bad for a lad from the wrong side of town with a drunken abusive old man, who he was going to make sure didn't see a penny of his fortune.

'Janice, we've won that bloody clean air contract! Clear my diary I'm off to the Country Club to celebrate.'

'Will do, and well done,' came the gushing reply from his loyal secretary.

Mike Morrell picked up his mobile phone and speed dialled Pauline Piffle. 'I'll pick you up in an hour Pauline, we're off to Beverley Country Club to celebrate.'

Before he left the office, he replied to the email he had received from Penelope Sykes assuring her that the staff and resources would be put in place immediately to start the clean air monitoring process and the subsequent issuance of fines for noncompliance to the hard-pressed motorists of Humberwold County, and in particular Grimewold itself. He dubbed the project Operation: Where Eagles Dare, with a flourish of inspiration. He decided it best not to mention that he'd set up the Cayman Islands account for her to receive her monthly 'fee' but would inform her privately that the arrangements were in place. Being an ex-copper, he was well aware that paper trails were the undoing of many a good criminal enterprise.

While Mike Morrell was spending his day celebrating with Piffle's wife, Tandori Birkett-Morris was getting to work undermining Piffle's company. Because everything was handwritten and hand-processed with a file for each client, it was easy to doctor the files and generate the necessary paperwork to trigger large fines to be sent out to companies for non-payment and to make up fines for companies that had not breached the guidelines. Tandori decided the safest way to proceed was to stay back after 5.00 p.m. when the offices shut, and work on till 9.00 at night doctoring the files to her own advantage. In her first week of work she did just that.

Zara Bindle was hugely impressed with her new transgender member of staff for her hard work and obvious commitment. As the firm used a clocking on and clocking off punch card system –so Piffle could monitor employees activities and hours worked – she was able to ascertain that in her first week, Tandori had worked an impressive 58 hours and 42 minutes, well beyond the standard 40 hours Piffle's firm demanded.

Bindle was even more impressed when she received the weekly report from Jonathan showing a 22.4% increase in fines being issued. Remarkable that one young lady could make such a difference in just her first week, and Bindle noticed with pride that Tandori was using the gents' toilets thus reinforcing her transgender credentials, a clear sign she was self-identifying as a man, much to the disquiet of the male employees who mostly being ex-miners and steel workers were oblivious to the trans movement within the left wing echelons of the Labour Party.

In the eyes of Bindle, Tandori was turning out to be a truly inspirational employee. It was ironic that Bindle was championing the appointment of Tandori Birkett-Morris who was transgender when Bindle's express aim was to reduce the number of male employees, bringing them down to no more than 48% of the workforce from the current 95% that she found so unacceptable. In her mind, Bindle saw Birkett-Morris, not as a self-confessed man, but as a new breed of transgender category, neither man nor women and thus highly valued in her quest for true diversity and equality.

Tandori Birkett-Morris was further helped by the fact that Bindle was so obsessed with her mission to transform The Diversity Action Partnership into a truly multicultural, multi-faith and gender neutral organisation, that she had little time to keep an eye on the day to day running of the organisation, and therefore the unfolding disaster being implemented by her star employee. In fact, with Tandori on board, Bindle threw herself wholeheartedly into replacing as many of the white working class male ex-miners and ex-steel workers as possible, much to their disgust and anger.

It would be too mild to say they felt cheated after being given a second chance in life by Piffle, and as many of them were in their late 50s and 60s, they had little or no chance of gaining employment elsewhere. This unpleasant situation wasn't helped by the fact that many of the new employees were unsuited to office work and had a minimal grasp of the English language. Bindle certainly could not be accused of not recruiting a diverse workforce.

There was a stream of highly unusual employees ranging from a disabled Albanian gypsy mystic who Bindle had recruited when she approached her outside Barclay's Bank in Grimewold High street offering to do a reading for £60, several pensioners from the Ethiopian community who could not speak a word of English and certainly had no obvious office skills, a young female crack cocaine dealer called Dizzy-R who she recruited from the probation service as an ex-offender on license from prison, a single mother from the Cromwell Estate with nine children, four of whom she insisted on bringing with her to work, and an unemployed Irish fairground operative called Murphy. She even recruited a 97 year old lady, called Molly Mae, from a care home she had visited on the basis that she was a pacifist and a vegan, which ticked three of Bindle's diversity boxes and ensured that the organisation could not be accused of being ageist. Sadly, the old dear snuffed it before the ink on the employment contract was dry, and Bindle had to look elsewhere.

This prolific recruitment drive, and parallel redundancy programme, was accompanied by Bindle's desire to computerise and streamline the operation so that all the client files would be held on computer rather than in brown manilla cardboard folders and could be updated with ease by fewer operatives and fines issued immediately. In so much as Bindle had a plan for The Diversity Action Partnership Limited it was to cut staffing costs by 50%, whilst at the same time radically increasing diversity of employment within the company.

The problem was that Bindle did not have anyone within the company with the necessary high-end computer skills to implement such a radical reorganisation of the company as effectively as was necessary given the speed of change Bindle was pushing through. She made the bold, and some would say catastrophic, decision to promote Tandori's assistant manager, Jonathan, to the role of IT Manager simply because he had a better grasp of IT programmes than anyone else in the company. Or at least he had the nous to buy a proprietary client management system from Microsoft, not that any of the new recruits had a cat in hells chance of using it!

One of the very fortuitous side effects of all this radical change was that the displaced ex-miners and ex-steel workers were not about to go quietly. Years, in fact decades, of experience fighting capitalist bosses by way of official and unofficial wild cat strikes had prepared them for the challenge to their livelihoods they were now facing. They did what they had always done. They banded together and formed a quasi-militia group with the avowed aim of disrupting Bindle's dastardly plans to eradicate them.

This took the form of a legal challenge to their dismissal and a decidedly semi-illegal attempt to disrupt Bindle's plans. Through their extensive Trade Union contacts they managed to acquire the services of an experienced and hugely left wing London-based employment and human rights lawyer called Narah Sultana. At the other end of the scale they decided to put in place an unofficial picket line outside the front entrance of the former library and man it daily as they had done in the good old days of the 1960s and '70s, resplendent with the cut in half oil drum, flames shooting from the top, the men huddled round in their thick Aran jumpers and beanie hats. They looked like throwback characters from the days of Arthur Scargill and Red Robbo and were in many ways equally effective at disrupting the day to day operations of the Diversity Action Partnership Limited.

In that sense they were unwittingly helping Tandori Birkett-Morris in her quest to destroy the day to day running of the company, and this in itself could only speed up the demise of Piffle's empire. In short, it was being attacked from two angles. The new members of staff were told in no uncertain terms by Zara Bindle to cross the 'illegal' picket lines and clock on as usual for work, otherwise under the terms of their contracts they could, and would, be dismissed without redundancy pay for breach of contract and gross misconduct.

The wild cat strikes even started to disrupt the smooth running of The Humberwold Speed Camera Action! Limited and its new flagship division the Clean Air Directorate which had started to recruit enforcement staff and train them in the black arts of using the new hand-held air quality monitoring devices that would so effectively entrap hapless motorists with a whopping great fine.

Chapter 64

Piffle, being out at his villa in Benidorm with Honolulu, was oblivious to the goings on at his company back in England. This was despite the fact that he was still receiving his weekly briefing from Zara on a Thursday. It was just that Zara had decided quite wisely to omit all of the disastrous activities taking place and, as they say in management circles, concentrate on the 'positives'. So as far as Sydney Dresden Piffle was concerned revenue was up over 20% and fixed overheads were being reduced, meaning that The Diversity Action Partnership Limited was on course for a record quarters profits.

Piffle spent idyllic days at the Villa Almeria. The late spring sun was producing some beautiful lazy and relaxing days. He could often be found at the back of the villa on a raised deck area that was accessed by two large panoramic sliding doors leading from the lounge. The boards of the decking were painted with a soft bluey grey matt paint making it look like an old-fashioned ship. At the front of the decking were stainless steel railings with rope teasels between them, again reminiscent of a ship. The decking had a large oblong table with luxury chairs in white and blue stripped pastel colours extending to two loungers and a huge umbrella shading the table from the sun. The other half of the decked area had shaded bamboo-like matting over a wooden frame, again giving a lovely mottled shaded area interspersed with trailing honey suckle plants and tubs filled with beautiful coloured plants in orange, bright red, white and yellows.

From the decking area, stone steps led down to a large S shaped pool with a rock formation and large cascading waterfall in the centre. To the right was a small bar with a thatched roof and stools set into the base of the pool so guests could sit at the bar in the pool and have a refreshing drink. Around the pool were lush tropical gardens with a lawn border and then dense trees full of colour, including orange and lemon trees giving off aromatic scents of summer in the mountains.

Piffle's favourite endeavour was to lay on one of the loungers with a book whilst Honolulu brought him exotic cocktails until the heat of the day became too unbearable. Then he would go for a long swim with Honolulu before a light lunch. In the afternoon, he would repeat the exercise before retiring to the villa in the early evening to relax and watch television. They would sit down around 8 for a beautiful dinner and a bottle of local red wine.

In contrast, his builder Miguel Andretti was hard at work organising and planning the building works that were to take place at the Playa de Sol caravan park, soon to be a Piffle's luxury log cabin park. His works manager, Alvaro, had completed a full survey of the site and developed a project plan of the various activities, starting with clearing the front section of the site and putting in the services to support the first ten log cabins.

Meanwhile, Miguel had started to recruit the army of Indian labourers who would be flown over as migrant workers and housed on site in a large temporary double decked porta cabin. This was Miguel's unique competitive edge enabling him to undercut other contractors by using cheap non-unionised foreign labour. In fact, Miguel was only paying the migrant workers 30% of what a Spanish labourer would have cost him, which enabled him to make much more profit per job and still undercut his competitors. Because the workers had little else to do, he could also coax them into working 14-hour days without the usual Spanish siesta and get jobs done more quickly and efficiently.

Miguel picked up the phone in his office and dialled Alvaro to give him the latest update on the arrival of the Indian labourers.

'Hey Alvaro, how is it going down at the site?'

'It is good Señor, we are starting to clear the front of the site, but we need the labour urgently. How are we with that?'

'I've been speaking to my contact in India and he is sending us the first five guys over next week.'

'OK this is good, but remember Miguel, we will need 40 labourers at least to finish this job within the 12 months specified.'

'OK OK, it is not a problem Alvaro.'

'Have you contacted the electricity company and water company about providing the services to the site Miguel? It is very important as we are having to use generators at the moment and just have one tap to work off for water. It is not good, and it will hold the job up, you know how slow the municipals are at sorting things here in Benidorm.'

'Yes Alvaro, I will contact them as a matter of urgency and then we can get the power and water that we need.'

Despite all the bravado to Piffle, the harsh truth was that Miguel Andretti had never handled a construction job anywhere near as big as the one at Playa de Sol. He had exaggerated his involvement in the construction on the Benidorm bypass to Paeleo, who had then exaggerated it further to Piffle on the basis that he was going to get a huge back hander for winning the contract.

Yes, Andretti's small team had supplied labour for the bypass but only to the main contractor and he had next to no experience of handling a job as complex as the five hundred log cabin site. He was lucky that his project manager, Alvaro, was more experienced and switched on to what was required, but even so he was taking a big gamble. But as he told himself, there is no reward without risk. The problem for Piffle, as he lay on his luxury lounger in the garden of villa Almeria, was that he didn't realise how much risk was his and how much was Miguel Andretti's, but it would not be long before he found out.

Chapter 65

Madison Sykes had had a particularly drunken and drug fuelled night in one of the seedy clubs that clung to the strip in Grimewold town centre. She couldn't remember which one, and had woken in a strange bed in a dirty bedsit that she didn't in any way recognise. Sitting at the edge of the bed putting on his socks and underpants was a man she recognised even less.

'Hey baby, you was real good last night. Didn't think I'd find a bird like you at the Forgemakers. Listen, I've got to go to work now baby, so help yourself to some coffee and I'll be back at lunchtime. You make sure you stick around for old Nelson here, you understand?'

'Do I know you?' But it was too late, Nelson was gone and Madison was left alone in the grimy flat, head spinning from last night's activities. She found she was still in her clothes and after staggering out of bed she decided to head for the door. Just before she reached the front door to the flat, she spotted white powder on the table in a foil wrap. She couldn't resist going back to the table and sniffing the illegal substance getting her next high and keeping the party going. She staggered out of the flat and found herself on the London Road opposite the Grimewold central canal.

'Nelson, I love you, you are the one baby!' Madison started talking to the low wall outside the flats, and kissing it passionately. In her disorientated state she decided that the wall was a person to be loved and cherished and that's why got down on her knees and started kissing and caressing the wall. She then looked across the road and stared at the canal with the water sparkling in the bright sunlight.

'Oh baby you are by the canal, there you are.' Without any knowledge of the busy London Road she staggered across it towards the beautiful blue water she had spotted glistening in the sunlight and very nearly made it across the road safely, but it was not to be.

'I'm coming for you baby.'

It was too late, the driver of the number 18 double-decker bus coming from the bus station out towards the Cromwell Estate didn't see Madison until he was nearly upon her. The bus driver braked sharply but even his best efforts couldn't quite stop the bus in time. It hit Madison at relatively slow speed, but it was enough to catapult her into the air, she landed and rolled down the bank and ended up head first into the grimy waters of Grimewold Grand Central Canal.

It was her last view of this life as she promptly sunk to the bottom of the canal, fortunately completely unconscious by this stage. The best that could be said of Madison's untimely demise was that she didn't feel a thing and her last thoughts were happy ones, or so it was assumed.

All hell broke loose as many of the passengers on the bus had seen Madison flying through the air and into the canal. The bus driver, a recent Turkish Immigrant called Ekram Sayodi was equally traumatized, and got out of his cab, rushed down the bank to try and save the victim, but he ultimately couldn't reach her. Cars were banking up behind the bus and beeping their horns, the emergency services were called and all three turned up. The London Road was closed off for the rest of the day and specialist police divers had to be drafted in to fish the body out of the canal.

The first senior officer on the scene was Inspector Alwyn Hughes whose nick name was Taff from the days before political correctness rendered the name unusable. He had a reputation for being a particularly unpleasant load-mouthed bully with a habit of forming opinions almost immediately and then not changing his mind despite all the available evidence. He immediately ordered the arrest of the poor bus driver, and had him transported to Grimewold Central Police Station in the back of a fortified transit van, despite the poor man's protestations of innocence.

'Officers, I want that guilty man arrested and taken to Grimewold Police Headquarters for questioning,' said Inspector Hughes completely ignoring the age old concept of innocent until proven guilty.

'Who you calling guilty, cookie boy? I done nothing wrong,' shouted the bus driver as he was handcuffed and led away by two burly police officers.

'Don't you worry boyo, you're in safe hands and I will be interrogating you personally down at the station after I have finished with the crime scene.'

Inspector Alwyn Hughes immediately cordoned off the area and ordered forensics to comb the road and surrounding area. All of the bus passengers, 26 in total, were held at the scene and interviewed separately , which took a total of five hours.

Eventually the ambulance took the dead body away to the morgue for a full autopsy, given the circumstances of the death. Despite the fact that Alwyn Hughes had already determined that the death was the result of reckless and dangerous driving involving an element of excess speed, even though he had no hard evidence to back up his fully formed theory.

The grim task of informing the family fell to a seasoned police family liaison officer from Humberwold Police called Sandy Pike, who had been unlucky enough to arrive on the scene somewhat after the initial police response but seen its grisly aftermath, and it had fallen on her to visit the family of the bereaved due to her experience in such matters.

'Hello officer, can I help you?' said Gerald looking bemused and immediately wondering if he had committed an offence given some of his recent dodgy dealings with the tax authorities to reduce his tax liability.

'Hello, Mr Sykes?'

'That's right, Gerald Sykes.'

'I am Officer Pike, and I am very sorry to inform you that your daughter has been killed by a number 18 bus on the London Road, and she unfortunately drowned in the Grimewold Grand Central Canal this morning.'

'I'm sorry, but I don't understand, you mean Madison is dead?'

'I'm afraid so sir, if it's any consolation, it was almost certainly instant, she wouldn't have felt a thing.'

'How did this happen? You've said she was hit by a bus and then you said she drowned. I don't understand. Which is it?'

'Both I'm afraid, the bus clobbered her and then she was catapulted head first into the Grimewold Grand Central Canal where she sank to the bottom and drowned,' said Constable Pike, being subtle was never one of her strong points unfortunately, despite her victim support training and years of informing victims' families of their loved ones' fate.

'Oh, this is terrible news, I don't know what I am to tell Penelope, she was so close to dearest Madison.'

'I take it you mean your wife sir?'

'Yes, that's right she's the leader of Grimewold Municipal Council, she's going to be devastated.'

'I'm sure she is, is she not here? We need a relative to identify the body. It's at the morgue. There will be an autopsy due to the unusual death of the deceased,' said Constable Pike absent-mindedly.

'I'm struggling to take this in officer, what's unusual about her death?'

'Well, it's not every day that a victim is hit by a bus when she by rights shouldn't have been in the middle of the road and then was catapulted into a canal where she promptly sank to the bottom. So, we've got to ascertain was she killed by the bus, or by the drowning. There are lots of factors to consider, but you needn't worry yourself with such trivia, your daughter is dead and that's fairly final as far as you are concerned. Anyway, you'll be pleased to know that my superior officer, Inspector Hughes has arrested the bus driver. Turkish chap I believe, he's interrogating him with a view to getting a confession.'

'A confession of what Officer?'

'Oh we're thinking dangerous driving, speeding, using a mobile phone. We haven't determined the exact crime at this stage but we think, or Inspector Hughes thinks, there is bound to be one. These Turks are terrible drivers you know, don't drive to our standards at all, he's bound to be at fault according to the Inspector'

'Oh I see, well thank you officer.'

'We'll be in touch about you coming to the morgue, you know to identify the victim, and again, I'm very sorry to be the bearer of bad news but these things can't be helped.' and with that Constable Pike was off down the path and back to her panda car.

Gerald Sykes was left at his front door in complete shock and wonderment at modern policing etiquette. As it happened, he was not close to Madison being Penelope's second husband. In fact, he couldn't stand the drunken drug-addled bitch who had caused the family nothing but trouble, but he knew his wife was going to devastated at the news of losing her beloved Madison. Although in truth she had lost her many years ago to crack cocaine and heroin. He was not looking forward to his wife's return and breaking the news, but it was a date he couldn't dodge for long.

Chapter 66

Inspector Alwyn Hughes was a man on a mission. Determined to prove his theory correct, he was looking forward to the interrogation of the wholly innocent Turkish bus driver, Ekram Sayodi, who he had kept in the cells overnight and was going to interview in connection with the death of Madison Sykes. He was considering a charge of death by dangerous driving and looking forward to a potential custodial sentence of 15 years for the hapless driver. For this, he had teamed up with Constable Pike, the officer who had broken the sad and devastating news to Gerald Sykes, step-father of the deceased.

'Pike, make sure that the potential criminal is brought into the interview room. I will be handling the interrogation. Do I make myself clear?'

'Yes Inspector, right away Inspector.'

'Oh, and have the family identified the body yet so that the autopsy can start? Not that there is any doubt in my mind about cause of death.'

'I believe sir, that Mr and Mrs Sykes are attending the morgue this morning to identify the body, and the autopsy is pencilled in for this afternoon.'

'Very good, I hope to have this one wrapped up by the end of the week at the latest, if not sooner.'

The previous evening had not gone well for Gerald Sykes. He had tried to contact his wife at the council but she was not contactable and it was 7.00 p.m. before she returned to the family home and was told the devastating news that her daughter had died of a terrible accident. Penelope had not taken it well at all. Wailing and heartbreak had given way to helplessness and then anger and eventually unfairness of a life cut short by drink, drugs and stupidity and ended all too suddenly by an apparent accident with a double decker bus, her final resting place being Grimewold's Grand Central Canal. Her only child snuffed out in the blink of an eye.

The next day they had gone to the morgue together only to verify what they already knew to be true; darling Madison was gone. Deathly white and totally serene lying there on cold stainless steel. Not a mark on her body as far as they could tell. At that moment they did not care who was to blame for Madison's fate, only coming to terms with the certainty of death mattered, Penelope in particular feeling a loss than ran deep into her soul.

On the other side of town someone else was certainly very interested in who was to blame for Madison Sykes' death, and he was one hundred percent sure who that person was.

'Read him his rights Constable Pike.'

With the preliminaries completed Hughes started the interview 'Right Mr Sayodi, do you know why you are here today?' barked Inspector Hughes.

'Of course I know why I here, it is to do with accident where poor girl drowned in canal.'

'No Mr Sayodi, you are here, boyo, to help us with our enquiries into the manslaughter of Madison Sykes with that death being caused by dangerous driving , by YOU, that's what we want to talk to you about.'

'But I innocent, I just drive bus, crazy lady runs out in middle of road, I brake, boom, and she fly through air into canal, she end up dead.'

'Very convenient boyo, but that's not how it happened was it?' shouted Hughes banging the table with his fist. 'This is how it happened, isn't it? You were driving along the London Road much too fast for the conditions, you were distracted and didn't see a poor vulnerable pedestrian legitimately crossing the road. Too late, far too late, you braked but it was not enough and through your careless and dangerous driving, you hit the victim head-on, which catapulted her through the air with such force that she was already dead by the time that she hit the drink, and because she was unconscious she sank to the bottom of the canal. That's what really happened isn't it?'

'No no, that is all pack of lies, I good man, just earning honest crust doing my job.'

'Look Ekram, just make it easy for yourself,' said Hughes trying to be conciliatory. 'Just tell me what really happened. Everyone makes mistakes and if you just admit you were speeding and distracted, then we can make sure you get a fair sentence for your crimes. Admit your guilt and there doesn't need to be a long stressful criminal trial. And let's face it, a jury isn't going to believe that a Turkish man who has only been in the country a few months has the skills to drive a double decker bus safely. Everyone knows that Turks are hot-headed and drive like maniacs. Just tell Inspector Hughes the truth boyo, and I promise I will do my best to get you a reduced sentence.'

Inspector Hughes lent back in his chair and grinned a terrible grin. He felt that he was winning this game of cat and mouse quite easily, and in no time he would have a confession in the bag. 'I tell you what, Constable Pike will make you a nice cup of coffee and get you a fag and you can have an hour to think through what really happened and then I'll come back and take a statement. How does that sound?'

It didn't sound good at all to the bus driver, but he bowed his head thinking of the terrible fate that awaited him. Inspector Hughes left him in the capable hands of Constable Pike who duly made him a milky coffee and gave him a couple of fags to smoke, leaving him to consider his fate.

The rest of the investigation wasn't going too well, in that none of the evidence to date supported Inspector Hughes' theory into the demise of Madison Sykes. None of the twenty-six passengers on the number 18 bus could shed any light on the theory that the bus was speeding. In fact, none of them had found anything unusual about the journey and as none of them could directly see the driver, none could give any sort of evidence that he may have been distracted or using a mobile phone. His phone had been seized and Inspector Hughes' team were trying to ascertain if he was texting or on the phone at the time of the accident, but so far the results hadn't come back. There was also no evidence from the nearest fixed point speed camera on the London Road, which was a quarter of a mile before the accident spot, that the bus had been speeding, in fact it had been travelling at 24 miles per hour at that point.

As the morning wore on, it was looking like the only way Inspector Hughes' theory was going to gain traction was if he could get a confession, despite the evidence pointing in the other direction. But in truth the train of events which led to Madison Sykes' death had started twenty years before when she had been a dating a certain Bradley Norman Piffle, 12 years her senior. It was he who had supplied her with the cocaine and heroin which had been her downfall. Whether the Police investigation, or indeed anyone else, was going to find out the brutal truth was another matter. One thing was for sure, the truth was not going to be exposed by Inspector Alwyn Hughes of Grimewold CID.

Chapter 67

Things were moving swiftly in Benidorm as the ground works for the Playa de Sol Log Cabin site took shape.

The first ten construction workers had arrived from India and were billeted in the newly installed double height portacabins at the front of the site. The team had started to clear the site and prepare the virgin ground for the access road and the first concrete pans that the log cabins were to sit on. They were still waiting on the services for water and electricity to be installed, which was holding things up to some extent.

The main issue for Piffle was selling the log cabins off plan to British tourists visiting the town and at €150,000 each – it was going to be a tough sell. He decided to try and employ a team of ex-timeshare marketing agents of dubious scruples to bombard the tourist strip. They employed that old chestnut of a free buffet lunch providing the unwitting tourists watched a thirty minute marketing video showing what the Playa de Sol would look like when completed and the huge potential for income growth once it was established.

As usual, Paeleo was employed as the go between to go into Benidorm and recruit suitable agents with experience of ripping off British tourists. Paeleo had many contacts and it was not long before he found a Brit who met Piffles requirements exactly. Jimmy – The Fleece – Moston had been in Benidorm for twenty years and at its height had a team of 50 sales agents plying the strip and getting tourists to his marketing events to sell time share packages at twenty grand a pop.

After various scandals, the timeshare market had declined massively and with his ill-gotten gains, Moston had bought a few villas to rent out and owned a bar in the old town called *The Go-Go Bar and Grill*, which offered cheap food and booze in the day and go-go dancing at night, with a raucous happy hour between 6.00 p.m. and 8.00 p.m. It was during happy hour that Jimmy The Fleece had agreed to meet Paeleo for a meeting about marketing the Playa de Sol Log Cabin operation.

'It's like this Paeleo, me old mucker, if you want good old Jimmy The Fleece to come on board, you've got to make it worth my while. I'm a busy man what with running this place and renting the holiday villas.'

'Well Jimmy it is like this, I represent a major retail player in the Benidorm Market called SDP Luxury Scandinavian Log Cabins, and we are building beautiful unique log cabin park with five hundred units and we look for marketing partner to sell log cabins to the international buyers. We look for someone with your expertise in these matters.'

'Well me old mucker, Paeleo, you've come to the right place, but I must warn you I won't be cheap. This operation will cost mega bucks and to succeed in this town you need to have finance options in place with a low-down payment of say €15,000 and the rest on the never, never. But to extract the cash out of the mug punters you have got to appeal to their greed, their vanity and make them feel they are getting a bargain, you comprendo?'

'Yes señor, I comprendo, so what do you think plan should be Jimmy?'

'Leave it with me Paeleo, and I'll come up with a marketing proposal. But off the top of my head, you need a few log cabins finished and furnished to a very high standard, then you offer rich tourists the opportunity to upgrade to a log cabin for part of their stay to experience the quality, then you've got them. Reel them in with a low deposit and the rest on the never never and put forward a plan where they can rent the log cabins when they are not using them, so they make a profit. And get some talking-head financier to predict a big real estate boom so they get capital growth as well. That way it appeals to their greed. But for that we need pretty girls reeling the mug punters to a marketing event then, wham the offer to stay in a log cabin for free. That's the plan me old mucker, but let Jimmy work it up into a proposal for your boss, and remember if you steer Piffle my way Paeleo there is a huge bung in it for you. Never bite the hand that feeds you, that's always been Jimmy The Fleece's motto, Paeleo.'

'OK, this sounds good to me Jimmy. How long do you take to get this proposal ready and what you propose Paeleo get out of it?'

'Oh you're a sharp one Paeleo, well we'll have to see, but let's suggest 5% of everything good old Jimmy makes after costs? And I'll have a proposal in a week for your Piffle guy.'

'Make it 20% my friend and you have deal.'

'No mate, too much, 7%.'

'Not budging on less than 15%.'

'Look tell you what I do Paeleo, 10% for first €500,000 profit and 5% for anything above that? That's a bloody fair deal, and old Jimmy hears down the grapevine that you're getting back shish from the builder Andretti, so don't be greedy my friend otherwise I might have to have a word in Piffle's shell like, comprendo?'

'OK Jimmy, it seems a good deal to me. We shake on it and I make sure you get contract from Piffle,' said Paeleo backing off and realizing that he had been out manoeuvred.

The pair of them shook on the deal and finished the glass of champers that Jimmy had offered Paeleo at the Go-Go bar and the wheels were set in motion.

Chapter 68

The team of police officers sat round the large boardroom table at Grimewold Central Police Station on Thursday morning, four days after the incident that had killed Madison Sykes.

The Assistant Chief Constable chaired the meeting and to his right was the lead investigator Inspector Alwyn Hughes, and around the table seven other officers who had been involved in the investigation.

'Good morning ladies and gentleman,' said the Assistant Chief Constable.

'We are here today to review the evidence surrounding the death of Madison Sykes and to come to a conclusion whether there is enough evidence to take to the Crown Prosecution Service to charge Ekram Sayodi with dangerous driving or manslaughter. We have the results of the autopsy now, so we will start with that. Karen, can you go through the results please?'

'Yes sir. I have the results here. It is quite clear from the autopsy that Madison died from drowning, she was not dead when she hit the water, probably just unconscious from the collision with the bus. But

Piffle

here is the interesting thing, her body showed a high dose of alcohol and cocaine both of which had been consumed in the last twenty-four hours, so she would have been completely out of it with that level of illegal substances mixed with alcohol. She almost certainly didn't know what she was doing when she crossed the road.'

'Thank you Karen, now what other evidence have we got to consider with this case?'

'I have something to add,' said Alwyn Hughes.

'Yes, go on Inspector Hughes.'

'Well I have extensively interviewed the suspect sir and in my opinion he is as guilty as hell. We can't prove he was speeding but he had in his possession a mobile phone and I am sure he was distracted by it at the time of the accident, and that meant that he hit Miss Sykes, which, as we can see, led to her death.'

'Have you any evidence to back up this theory Inspector?'

'Not as such, but after twenty-six years in the force, you get a gut feeling, and I'm telling you that Turkish bus driver is as guilty as hell. You mark my words.'

'Sir, we have the phone records here for the day in question and there is no evidence of Ekram Sayodi making or receiving any calls.'

'But he could have been texting and not able to send the text due to the accident. That's what I think happened,' interjected Inspector Hughes.

346

'What about the speed camera evidence?' asked the Assistant Chief Constable, ignoring Hughes

'Again, negative,' said one of the detectives. 'The bus was travelling at 24 mph at the last fixed speed camera before the accident and none of the passengers reported anything unusual or believed the bus to be speeding.'

'It seems a pretty open and shut case to me,' said the Assistant Chief Constable.

'I tell you what I'm going to do, I'm going to go round the table and ask every one of you if you think the bus driver is guilty of dangerous driving, which led to the death of Madison Sykes. From left to right please,' which meant that Inspector Hughes would speak last.

'Not Guilty.'

'Not Guilty.'

'Not Guilty.'

'Not Guilty.'

'Not Guilty.'

'Not Guilty.'

'Guilty as hell, I'd stake my career on it,' said Inspector Hughes.

'I'm afraid, Inspector Hughes, you have been outvoted and I for one think this was a tragic accident. The obvious result of poor Madison

Sykes being high on a cocktail of drink and drugs and that meant that she collided with the number 18 bus and brought about her own demise, plain and simple. There is no way the CPS will take a case forward against the bus driver with this flimsy evidence based on conjecture.'

With that Inspector Alwyn Hughes got up and stormed out of the room obviously furious that he had been humiliated by the Assistant Chief Constable.

'So, are we agreed that we can wrap this case up, close the file and release the bus driver Ekram Sayodi?'

'Yes,' they all spoke in unison and nodded.

'Good, well Constable Pike if you can contact the deceased parents and inform them of the outcome of the autopsy and the investigation and tell them that regretfully their daughter died as a result of misadventure caused by drink and drugs, and that no one else was to blame for her tragic death.'

'Will do sir,' said Constable Pike. With that the meeting ended, the only person unhappy and bearing a grudge being Inspector Alwyn Hughes.

Chapter 69

Mike Morrell was sitting in his office when it came to his attention, in the form of a text news report from the Grimewold Gazette, that Madison Sykes had died in a bus accident due to a drugs overdose. Tragic yes, thought Mike, but here was a golden opportunity to make sure that Penelope Sykes knew exactly who was responsible for her beloved daughter's death – none other than the famous chat show host Bradley Plumb, aka Bradley Norman Piffle, only son of none other than Sydney Dresden Piffle.

He had to tread carefully as he didn't want his new lover Pauline Piffle to be aware of his duplicity, but here was his opportunity to make sure that Penelope Sykes wanted revenge for her daughter's death and Bradley Plumb, but more importantly Dresden Piffle suffered the consequences. In short, he decided that the right approach to this situation might result in Penelope Sykes making sure that Piffle's company lost the contract for implementing the Diversity and Equality Act 2010 and he ended up winning it over Piffle's firm for the next five years. Every cloud has a silver lining as they say. The funeral would be the right time to inform Penelope Sykes of those responsible for her darling daughter's untimely death. All he had to do was make sure he was in attendance supporting the grieving parents.

'Janice, come in here a sec.'

'Yes Mike, what do you want?'

'Be a pet and find out when the funeral is for Madison Sykes and which church it's being held at, unless it's the crem of course. I need to go and pay my respects.'

'Oh, that's so nice of you Mike. I'll get onto it straight away,' said Janice mildly bemused at Morrell's sudden bout of kindness, which was so out of character. She didn't suspect at all the real reason behind Mike's benevolence.

'I do try and do my best pet. Penelope Sykes is a good friend of mine and a good friend of Humberwold Speed Camera Action! Limited. It's an important week this week Janice, we go live on Friday with the Clean Air team starting on the main routes into Grimewold. That should net us a few quid.'

A few quid was an understatement; the forward planning team had estimated that fines from the Clean Air contract should net the company an additional forty thousand pounds a day split 60:40 in the council's favour, and costs of servicing the contract should only be one thousand a day.

Over in Benidorm Jimmy – The Fleece – Moston had carefully thought through the proposal Paeleo had put to him and was now in a position to make Piffle an offer he couldn't refuse. He had arranged to meet Piffle later that day at the Black Chicken to win the marketing contract to sell the five hundred log cabins that Piffle was building. Sweet, he thought, this is going to be the big one Jimmy boy. Not had cash like this on tap since 1989 at the height of the timeshare scam. Although it was fairly early, he was sitting at his bar outside in the sun drinking a cocktail, one of his favourites, sex on the beach. Nothing subtle about Jimmy The Fleece that's for sure.

At the Diversity Action Partnership things were going from bad to worse and Bindle was starting to panic. The unofficial strike was into its fourth day now and the strikers showed no signs of giving up their fight or weakening their resolve. As she sat in her office with her mug of PG tips and a plate of biscuits, all she could hear were the chants of the strikers out in the square huddled round their oil drum with flames spewing out of the top.

'Bindle is a scab, Bindle is a scab, we will not be moved, we will not be moved!'

Then they started singing *You'll Never Walk Alone* and then back to the Bindle is a scab chant.

It was very unnerving for Zara Bindle. She was the darling of the left and had received very good press in the past from the Daily Mirror and her bible, The Guardian Newspaper. She had written eloquent articles in the past explaining her views on diversity and transgender politics, and earnestly stated that it was her life's work to have landed a senior role at The Diversity Action Partnership. Now though, her views on diversity were coming into direct conflict with working class concepts of solidarity and workers' rights which she also passionately believed in.

It was so unfair, all this had come about because Piffle had employed a mono-culture as his workforce, namely white, old, working-class, male British workers instead of the rainbow culture that she had promoted, the very embodiment of left wing ideology. Now that mono-culture was fighting back and blaming her personally for their dismissal when all she was doing was putting right a wrong that had been enacted by others.

The only glimmer of good news for Bindle was that she had just had the figures in from Jonathan and the income from fines was up another 21% to a record level. Tandori's plan had started to bite and huge numbers of bogus fines had been sent out resulting in increased payments by the hard-pressed businesses of Grimewold. It would be something positive to tell Piffle during their weekly telephone conference call on Thursday.

What Bindle didn't know was that, alongside the increase in fines revenue, was an equally large number of vociferous complaints from companies refusing to pay the fines and threatening legal action. For they had been sent fines that were not valid and were asking The Diversity Action Partnership to cancel their demands with immediate effect. Without the trained staff necessary to handle the huge increase in complaints the back log was building up. In fact, over three hundred letters of complaint had been received since Tandori had started her guerrilla campaign, but so far Bindle was unaware of the dire situation unfolding.

The day was going somewhat better for Archibold McGreggor at McGreggor's Steel. Googleheimer had already put out the order to reduce shipments of iron ore coming into Hull Port, and the shortage was beginning to bite. He had the latest figures in front of him, and production was down 10% meaning that his workers were going to see reductions in their pay packets this month. It would not be long before that blithering idiot, Barraclough from the Amalgamated Iron and Steel Union, would be on to him and Googleheimer demanding urgent talks about the pay and production cuts that were being implemented. This was splendid news.

However, he did not want to see his declining steel production resulting in a reduction in income for McGreggor's so he needed to speak to the Chief Executive of PING steel in India to make sure that the shortfall through McGreggor's steel stockists and agents could be replenished by finished steel from PING, at a much improved profit margin.

He buzzed through on the intercom to June.

'Get me Mukhrejee on the phone from PING Steel, and make it sharp.' he barked at her.

'I see you're in your usual happy mood Archibald, but yes I'll try and get him on the phone.'

'I sometimes wonder what I pay you for woman!'

'And I sometimes wonder why I stay.' Their usual spat continuing as ever.

'Ah Mukhrejee, my dear fellow, how are you this fine morning?' said Archibald deciding that flattery was the best course of action.

'I am very fine thank you Mr McGreggor.'

'Oh, call me Archibald my dear fellow, and so good of you to recognise my voice, splendid, splendid.'

'I am not getting many calls from England especially this early in the morning.'

'I'm just checking how the shipments of rolled steel are going from your facility in Bangalore to our European stockists Mukhrejee, my good man? We have done as promised and reduced our own production to give you some of our market.'

'Well it is good news Archibald, the first shipment of rolled steel is on the ship as we speak and will be arriving in Amsterdam by Monday of next week and then on to your stockists. We are looking forward to a long and profitable relationship, Archibald.'

'Splendid my dear fellow, you have made my day,' and with that the telephone call ended with Archibald in a good mood for a change.

At 1.00 p.m. Piffle entered the Black Chicken after being dropped off by Paeleo in the Silver Spur. He had his usual greeting from the owner Marco.

'Ah señor Piffle, my dear friend. How good to see you again, after last time.'

'Eh up Marco, good to see you too lad. Have you got me usual table I'm meeting someone by the name of Jimmy Moston. Is he here yet?'

'No señor we have not seen your Jimmy Moston yet, but please,

please this way to your table and when he arrives I will bring him over personally. Let me get you a large glass of prosecco señor Piffle, on the house of course.'

'That's very kind of you Marco, as always a pleasure to come here lad.'

Piffle was happy to sit at his favourite table with a glass of prosecco, but he didn't have to wait long before the human whirlwind that was Jimmy – The Fleece – Moston breezed in and joined him at the table.

'Señor, I have here Jimmy Moston for you,' said Marco.

'Thanks Marco. Eh up Jimmy me lad, pleased to finally meet you. Paeleo says you're the best in the business, so I'm hoping we can do deal on marketing of log cabin development. Marco here will get you a drink and then we can get down to brass tacks.'

'Pleased to meet you Mr Piffle. Yep you're right I am the best in the business and you, my friend, have come to the right place to shift those five hundred log cabins. Make no mistake, I'm your man.'

'I'm glad to hear it lad, so what's your background then?' said Piffle eyeing Jimmy suspiciously. In Piffle's eyes he seemed too good to be true, and a bit too flash Harry for Piffle's liking.

'Well Dresden, me old mucker, you don't mind me calling you Dresden, do you? Of course you don't. I've been here on the strip for thirty-five years, got here in '85 and ran Moston International

Timeshares from then until 1998 when the bottom dropped out of the market. Had a team of fifty sales agents at the peak of the operation, selling 20,000 timeshare options a year, and a thousand villas outright. There is no one on the strip more experienced than me Dresden.'

'What have you been doing since 1998 then?' said Piffle, still probing for answers.

'After the timeshare gig went tits up, I moved into setting up the Go-Go Bar and Grill in the old town. You know, something nice and classy away from the main strip where blokes can come and enjoy themselves and have a few beers and watch some exotic dancers. The rest of the timeshare booty I put into a few nice villas that I rent out, much easier now the budget airlines fly in and we can market them through the internet. Done my own site now, and put on other people's villas for them. Business is sweet to be honest, but when me old mate Paeleo told me you were doing the log cabin development and needed a marketing push, old Jimmy thought, why not? Still got the skills and the staff to make it happen for this Piffle guy – so here I am!'

'Well lad, you've certainly convinced me that you've got the credentials to market me log cabins for me. Have you got some ideas of how you might do it so old Piffle can be convinced you can bring in the numbers? And then there's the small matter of how much money you want for doing it.'

'Well Piffle me old mucker, funny you should say that but Jimmy Moston wouldn't come here and waste your time without having a fully planned operation and costs to go with it. I think you'll find its very reasonable given the work involved and the money you are going to make out of this.'

'Well I've brought a long a proposal for us to go through. So basically, I can talk it through and see if you are interested.'

'Sounds good to me,' said Piffle, warming to Jimmy's pitch for the business.

'So what we do Dresden, is have some of my go-go girls go round the top hotels and invite punters to a free buffet with authentic Spanish tapas and drinks at my bar. Then they watch a marketing presentation for thirty minutes and are driven out, by mini bus, to see the show-house, which is a couple of log cabins decked out with all the mod cons, complete with luxury fittings and one of them Canadian outside spa baths, all set in lovely manicured grounds. Then the sales guy, on a one-to-one, hits them with the three options. One week timeshare purchase at £15,000, buy today at 25% off at £150,000 and buy on the never-never, £180,000 but interest free over five years with £20k down payment. Then you guarantee to rent the log cabin at a grand a week over 30 weeks for the first year to reel them in. That way it looks like they're making 20% on their investment instead of the measly 1% they're getting in the bank. Then, to cap it off, the ones who are wealthy but still reluctant, are offered a stay in the log cabin for a week for free to see if they like it. Works every time Piffle. If you sell 50% as timeshare for the mug punters that don't have much brass, and 50% to the rich ones, we'll have your log cabins sold in no time. What do you think? It's all here in the proposal.'

'What do you get out of it Jimmy? I need hard numbers here,' said Piffle, liking the idea but still suspicious of what this grand marketing strategy was going to cost.

'Well laying on the go-go girls and the free buffets isn't cheap, and then there are the professional sales agents and setting up the finance options with the banks and finance houses. I'll do the lot, but I want €20,000 a month to cover costs, and 10% of either the sales or the timeshare income. Can't be fairer than that.'

'Bloody hell Jimmy, that seems a lot of brass,' said Piffle genuinely shocked at the huge costs that The Fleece was laying out before his eyes. 'That's too much of a risk for me. I tell you what, I'll pay you €5,000 in advance, per month and the balance of 15,000 per month every three months providing you sell fifty log cabins a month – either as outright sales or by the timeshare option. Then on each sale you can have 5% which, let's be honest, is pure profit for you.'

'Nah, that's not enough for old Jimmy. I'm getting on and I need this to be worth my while, all the stress of it, I'd be taking too much of a risk. Tell you what, pay me €10,000 a month and the other €5,000 if I hit sales targets plus 7%. You're cutting me bleeding throat Dresden, but I like your log cabin idea and I like your guts for doing this. What do you say Dresden? Come on me old mucker, you won't get a better deal than what Jimmy is offering you and my word is my bond. I'll make a modest amount of dosh out of this and you, my friend, will be a multi-millionaire.'

'Alright lad, you've been prepared to compromise, and I like that. Send me a revised offer and let me get me lawyers to look over it, make sure its watertight and we can shake on it today.'

So, as they sat there in the Black Chicken, they shook hands as business partners to sell the log cabins and toasted with a bottle of champagne that Piffle instructed Marco to bring. It was, as they say, game on, and Piffle was looking forward to being very rich indeed.

Chapter 70

Madison Sykes' funeral was a sombre affair, especially poignant as she was only thirty-eight years old. Very much a family event and a few family friends since none of Madison's dubious associates from the world of drugs and one night stands attended the proceedings. One or two old school friends attended who remembered Madison in the days before drink and drugs got hold.

One person who was there despite not knowing Madison at all, was Mike Morrell. Waiting for his opportunity to divulge the information that would lead to the source of Madison's unhappy life and ultimate death, the person that got her hooked on hard drugs in the first place.

Mike sat at the back of the crematorium in a black suite, crisp white shirt and black silk tie. The oak casket was brought in by eight pallbearers, and Penelope and Gerald Sykes walked behind the coffin to their seats at the front , Penelope crying all the time. The oak casket was displayed at on a trestle table ready to be put through to the gas burners at the end of the service where Madison's body would be turned to ash.

The service lasted about thirty minutes with the vicar highlighting the positives of Madison's life and brushing over the years of alcohol and drug abuse, and the numerous one night stands and brushes with the law that characterised the last twenty years.

With family members, the few friends, plus Mike Morrell, there were only about fifteen people present to witness the final send off from this earth of Madison Victoria Sykes. At the end of the service, the coffin was placed on the rollers and disappeared behind a black velvet curtain to the sounds of *Cruel Summer*, a highly inappropriate choice of music as far as Mike Morrell was concerned as Madison Victoria Sykes clearly hadn't survived as the number 18 bus and the Grimewold Grand Central canal had seen to that the week before.

Mike Morrell want outside for a Cuban cigar and waited for his opportunity to say a few words to the Sykes. He knew exactly what he wanted to say.

Eventually Penelope and Gerald emerged from the crematorium and walked past the assembled mourners who all gave hushed mutterings of support. Finally, it was Mike's turn. 'I'm sorry for your loss,' he said. 'I thought I must come and pay me respects as much for the living as the dead, since I clearly didn't know Madison. Lovely service though, shame it missed out the reason why Maddison got hooked on drugs in the first place. Of course, had she not been going out with that famous Friday night TV chat show host , Bradley Plumb, whose real name is Bradley Norman Piffle, then poor Madison would never have got into crack cocaine and heroin. I thought Bradley might have been here today for old times' sake given that he supplied her with the hard drugs in the first place and destroyed her life,' said Mike Morrell as innocently as he could.

The effect was electric. Penelope went pale and her voice faltered. 'How on earth did you know all that information? How did you know who was responsible for destroying my darling daughter's life?'

'Let's just say that I had an ongoing interest in finding out as much as I could about the Piffle family and the private investigator I used is very good. It was he who uncovered the unfortunate circumstances of Madison's drug addiction all those years ago. By all accounts, Piffle's famous son is still a coke head now, effectively got away with murdering your daughter. To think that Dresden Piffle benefits every day from the council giving him the contract for the Diversity and Equality Act. That family has made millions out of others' misfortunes.'

Mike Morrell had achieved exactly what he hoped to achieve. He had dripped poison into the ear of Penelope Sykes at her most vulnerable and without a doubt, if he knew anything about the bitch, she would want revenge for the death of her beloved Madison and the Piffle's were now public enemy number one.

After the service Penelope and Gerald Sykes left for home with Penelope still sobbing. Still in much distress she turned to Gerald in the car and said, 'I don't know how Mike Morrell got all of that information about our poor Maddy, but if it is the last thing that I do on this earth, I am going to make sure that Bradley Piffle, and for that matter, his father Dresden Piffle, pays for what that family has done to us. I am going to make sure they both suffer for murdering my dearest daughter.'

Gerald had his own private thoughts about dearest Maddy and her drug and booze addictions, but he decided that he would keep his counsel. The last thing he needed was a blazing row with his distraught wife particularly just after the funeral.

'Well my dear, it is terrible to hear about those responsible for Madison's drug addiction, but it's all water under the bridge. Madison is dead and there is nothing we can do about it now, other than support each other and get our lives back on track as best as we can.'

'You might have a forgive and forget attitude,' screamed Penelope, 'but Madison was not your daughter and I'm telling you that I'm going to make sure those Piffle's pay for their crimes. You never did like Madison, Gerald and that's a fact. Well don't you worry, I'll sort out both those Piffles in my own way. You mark my words.'

Gerald knew not to say anything else. They drove home in silence with Penelope already thinking of ways that she could get her own back and avenge the death of her beloved Maddy.

Mike Morrell drove to the country club in his BMW, still humming *Cruel Summer* by Bananarama from the funeral service. Madison Sykes certainly hadn't had a good summer, but he had every intention of benefiting from Madison's demise. His main aim was to get

Penelope Sykes to cancel the contract for The Diversity Action Partnership and award it instead to Humberwold Speed Camera Action! Thus making him even richer and destroying Piffle in the process. He felt sure that his plan to get Penelope Sykes on his side was well and truly executed following his success at the funeral. Things really were going his way as he sped along the country lanes towards his beloved country club.

Chapter 71

The production cuts at McGreggor's steel were really beginning to bite. The idiot union leader, Barraclough, had asked for an urgent meeting to discuss the production and pay cuts affecting his members, which Archibald was more than happy to give. He loved his sparring matches with Barraclough and hoped this time that the man would be more of an adversary than he had been in the past. He wanted to fight a Red Robbo or Scargill-type character, not the wishy-washy, oh-so-reasonable Barraclough of old. But this time the stakes were high, and he thought that maybe Barraclough might finally start fighting back. He also thought that he would bring Googleheimer along to the meeting at add some spice to the proceedings.

Barraclough was not coming to the meeting without backup. With production cuts, he knew that if they continued then one of the three giant blast furnaces in the town of Grimewold would be shut down, and given that recommissioning costs ran into millions of pounds, the closure was likely to be permanent without his Union's intervention.

The meeting was set to take place in the boardroom at

McGreggor's works on Wednesday morning at 10.00 a.m.

Archibald wanted to get there early as he rarely travelled to the works nowadays so he had asked June, his secretary, to summon Wilfred his chauffeur to be at the house for 7.00 a.m. so that he could get to his office just before 8.00 and prepare for the fight ahead. A fight he was relishing.

He had put on a three-piece suit with waistcoat and pocket watch, and a traditional guards tie. He even thought of wearing his trilby hat to complete the 1940s look, but decided that was too much of a caricature. He did have his lop-sided grin and his steely blue eyes with a menacing twinkle to complete the effect, but these latter two features were more a by-product of his particularly nasty and vindictive personality.

Because it took him so long with his willow sticks, he had already got himself to the hallway of his substantial Victorian pile of a house where he met Wilfred.

'Ah there you are Wilfred, about bloody time. I thought I told June to have you here by 7.00 a.m. sharp and it's already six minutes past.'

'It wasn't me sir, June said 7.15 a.m. so I'm actually early.'

'Confound that bloody women, she is always disobeying my instructions. When I get hold of her later... oh never mind. Well come on man, give me a hand. We need to get a move on and get to the office.'

Out they went to the Bentley S2, Archibald struggling with his two willow sticks and finally settling into the back seat.

Wilfred took his time as well, being in his 90s, and eventually got into the driver's seat, complete with his chauffer's cap. Then they were off, travelling through the back lanes and pretty villages until they made the descent into Grimewold itself, through the town and finally to McGreggor's Steel entrance where the Bentley entered. It was a quarter of a mile along a road lined with plane trees before they reached the majestic entrance with three steps up to an imposing entrance door with two huge marble pillars either side. The foyer was equally impressive with Italian marble columns and floor tiles and a sweeping solid oak staircase to the first floor.

Archibald entered the building and immediately headed for the ancient Otis lift to the right hand side of the foyer as he could no longer climb the stairs. Once he reached the top floor, he took the moving airport style walk way along the corridor to the end where double oak doors opened into his palatial office. It was here he could get himself comfortable and prepare for the meeting with the trade union representatives in the board room next door, two hours later.

He buzzed his intercom to see if June was around yet, and to his surprise he found her at her station.

'Get me a strong black coffee June, and I mean strong, not that wishy washy piss water you usually get me, and make it sharp, I've got a lot a work to do before that idiot Barraclough turns up.'

'I'll get you a Nescafe like I always do.'

'Not a bloody Nescafe you blasted women. I mean I want a proper coffee with ground coffee beans in a cafetiere, and while we're on the subject of you disobeying me, I told you to get Wilfred to pick me up at 7.00 a.m. sharp not 7.15 a.m. So yet again you disobey me instructions.'

'I made it 7.15 a.m. because you are always late with those damned sticks and I didn't want Wilfred waiting about too long – he is 93!'

'You always have to have the last word don't you? Damn you. Well just bring the bloody coffee asap.'

It was the day after the funeral and already Penelope Sykes had taken the bait having spent a sleepless night thinking how she was going to avenge the death of her beloved daughter.

It wasn't even 8.00 a.m. when Mike Morrell's phone rang and he found himself talking to the leader of Grimewold Municipal Council.

'Morning Mike, sorry to bother you so early. I was thinking about what you said at Maddy's funeral yesterday. How did you know that Maddy's drug addiction was caused by Piffles son? I had no idea.'

'How are you feeling this morning Penelope? I've been thinking about you,' Mike lied. The only thing he had been thinking about was whether his plan was going to work – would Sykes take the bait?

'I'm fine, thank you, under the circumstances, but Gerald is not as supportive as he ought be. Now, about Bradly Plumb.'

'Ah yes, well, and I shouldn't really say this, but I employed a very good private detective to look into Dresden Piffle's affairs, and in the course of his investigation he found out about Bradley Plumb's past as a drug addict and the fact that he was dating Madison twenty years ago. It didn't take him long to discover that Bradley had been the catalyst for Madison's drug taking. Just thought you needed to know, given her unfortunate death.'

'Are you absolutely sure about this?'

'Yes, the private detective is called Streake, an ex-copper friend of mine. Very thorough, if you want his number I'll text it to you.'

'If you would be so kind Mike, I would very much like Streake's number. What's his first name?'

'Gordon, Gordon Streake. I'll text you his number right away. If I may ask, what have you got in mind?'

'Let's just say, Mike, that I want this Streake fellow to help me get some dirt on the famous Bradley Plumb, and give him a taste of his own medicine for what he did to my poor Maddy.'

'Well that's fair enough, can't fault you for that and if I can be of any more assistance don't hesitate to contact me.'

'That's very kind of you Mike, will do,' and with that the telephone call ended.

Mike Morrell was elated that his plan was coming together nicely.

Chapter 72

That same morning, Inspector Fleece and Constable Brahmes were having breakfast together at the Premier Inn on the outskirts of Grimewold. It was a large buffet style breakfast at a rather expensive £8.99, but Fleece didn't care as it was all going on expenses.

Since the release of Tandori Birkett-Morris and her accomplice Jennings, Fleece and Brahmes had been diligently following them fruitlessly, trying to ascertain if they were meeting other terrorists as part of an elaborate ISIS cell that Fleece still had lodged in his stubborn brain. The problem was, all they had learned was that Tandori had driven to the Diversity Action Partnership every day around 8.00 a.m., fought through the recently established picket line, and then worked late every night not arriving back at Jennings' old flat until 9.00 p.m. at night.

This Fleece found to be unusual. Why on earth would she be working so late every night and what fiendish plot was she hatching next? Jennings movements were even more innocuous. All he did was get up and out of the apartment above the garage at Piffle's luxury house and tend to the garden, doing totally predictable things like cutting the grass and the edges, weeding the borders, cleaning the cars and generally staying close to his new abode. Very occasionally he ventured out to the local supermarket in his beige Austin Maestro and popped into the bookies on his way back, and once a week to a local pub called The Ketch. Absolutely nothing to link them to a terrorist cell or even to each other.

'Very, very cunning those two, Constable Brahmes,' said Fleece whilst tucking into his full English breakfast. We have followed them for a week now and nothing, and I've had their mobile phones tapped as well under full surveillance through GCHQ, and nothing. They're laying low, mark my words, but they won't be wasting their time. They'll be plotting and planning their next terrorist outrage, and when they move Brahmes, we'll be there, ahead of the game this time.'

'Yes sure, I'm sure we will,' said Constable Brahmes looking decidedly unconvinced by Inspector Fleece's zeal and determination to be proved right.

'We'll just have to stay up here until the terrorists make their next move. I have a gut feeling it won't be long and then we will finally be vindicated. Now run along pet and get me a Nescafe from that vending machine over there, I'm enjoying this buffet breakfast and it'll keep us going all day.'

As 10.00 a.m. approached, Archibald made his way to the boardroom where Googleheimer joined him with his production supervisor and the director of HR, with June taking notes.

At just before 10.00 Barraclough and a small team of trade unionists were ushered into the boardroom and took their places opposite the management team looking stoney faced and determined. Archibald, despite not running day to day operations, immediately took over the proceedings.

'Good morning gentleman. I've agreed to meet you today as a courtesy, but don't be under any illusion, the path that McGreggor's is on is for the long-term good of the company. My company which my grandfather founded, and there is very little room for negotiation. Me and my team believe that what we are doing will strengthen McGreggor's and give a long-term future for this company when worldwide there is over-production of steel, and prices have been low for some time. You union barons are lucky that enlightened management like us at McGreggor's are here to keep a successful steel industry going in Great Britain. We have asked many times for government help, but you know how difficult that has been to achieve given the rules on state aid and frankly, the fact that ministers are not interested in industrial companies up north away from their constituencies.'

Archibald was quite animated giving his opening address, wagging his finger at the trade unionists for good measure and giving little hint of compromise.

'Well, thank you for putting things in perspective,' said Barraclough, 'but we have called this meeting because recent events are totally unacceptable to our members who are facing real hardship over these unjust and unwarranted production cuts. Our members are facing a real pay cut of some 40% and uncertainty about their future's with production falling. We need to know if you are planning to close one of the three blast furnaces as is the rumour in the local newspapers.'

'I think Googleheimer as production director can answer that better than me,' said Archibald.

'Now look here fellas, essentially what has happened is that the suppliers of raw iron ore that we get from Poland can no longer supply us in the quantities that we want because the Chinese and Indians are upping production and taking more of the raw materials. Truth is guys, we can't afford to pay more and are getting our allocation of iron ore cut, so in the short term we have to cut production. Now I can't give ya any guarantees over blast furnace number three, but if this carries on for anything longer than a couple of months, then we will have to consider closure with support from the government, and you know how difficult it is to get money out of a Tory Government. Those guys make getting blood out of a stone sound easy, believe me I've tried my darndest fellas. Now if you here trade unionists can get us some support through the Trades Union Congress then maybe we can keep number three blast furnace open. Truth is fellas, we are all in this together.'

Barraclough and his team were getting more agitated now, they were not liking what they heard, and compromise seemed to be a long way off, resolution even more so.

'Now look here, we on the trade union side negotiated a flexible pay package in good faith where a great proportion of the production

374

staff wages were paid on production quotas. We were promised that if we hit those targets, which we have, and productivity rose to international levels, which it has, then we would share in the rewards of good pay and stable employment for our members. We have met our side of the bargain, but now you're welching on yours. It's completely unacceptable that our members are experiencing a 40% cut in their wages. As for being in it together, no one from management is experiencing any cut in wages. So what we want to know is, what are you going to do to give our members back the 40% wages they have lost, back-payed to the beginning of the month?'

The usually mild-mannered Barraclough had gone a puce colour and was banging the table in frustration as he spoke to the management team. Archibald was secretly thoroughly enjoying himself at Barraclough's expense, who was evoking just the response he had hoped for. It was his turn to twist the knife further and goad Barraclough.

'My dear Barraclough, of course you have to try and represent your members even though many of them are quite lazy and we've been carrying them for years with generous pay and pension rights, which my father stupidly negotiated with your trade union, but we're in a different world now. Let me be one hundred percent clear. Production will not be restored until we can get fresh supplies of iron ore at reasonable prices, and your members have to be flexible. Now of course HR can help them to apply for universal credit to top up their wages whilst this crisis continues, but if, as Googleheimer says, we cannot get a grant from the government, then I see no choice but to close permanently blast furnace number three. In fact, I can announce this very day, that we will be shutting it in three months' time without government support of £200 million pounds to keep it open.'

'In that case, Mr McGreggor we, the trades union, will be calling a strike from next week, and will be balloting our members to that effect until our members' pay and conditions have been restored and the threat of closing blast furnace three has been lifted.'

'Well let me tell you Barraclough, that if your illegal and unwarranted strike goes ahead, then I will personally write to every one of your lazy, good-for-nothing communist upstart members and sack the lot of them for gross misconduct. I will make sure none of them, or their fucking useless families, ever sets foot in McGreggor's again, or indeed any other steel facility in the country. Do I make myself clear?'

Archibald was thoroughly enjoying himself. Finally, it was like the old days where he could bully his staff and the trade union representatives, and since he had completely engineered this situation for his own ends, he had no interest in a negotiated settlement. In fact, a long, drawn out strike would be perfect and also give him the opportunity to talk to the useless Minister for Trade and Industry and get the idiot to stump up some cash to keep McGreggor's going and keep open blast furnace number three which needed an upgrade anyway and if he was lucky would now be paid for by the tax payer.

'I think we all know where we stand,' said Barraclough. 'Come on lads, let's get out of here. There's no point trying to negotiate with a management that is set in the 1970s. The next you'll see from us will be on the picket line, and we'll make sure that you restore our members' rights and privileges. Good day gentlemen.'

And with that, Barraclough, and his negotiating team, stood up and stormed out of the boardroom set on a course of action which suited Archibald McGreggor III perfectly.

'Jesus H Christ Archibald, you sure know how to upset them trade union guys. Looks like we have got a major strike on our hands, I hope you're ready for trench warfare.'

'My good man, I am well aware of what has gone on here, and I, for one, am delighted,' said Archibald leaving Googleheimer mighty perplexed.

Chapter 73

Things were running much more smoothly back in Benidorm. At Playa de Sol the ground works and landscaping was almost finished for the first ten log cabins, which were due to arrive from Hull within the next two weeks.

Against Paeleo's expectations Miguel Andretti's team were doing a good job, and Indian workers had worked 14 hour shifts to complete the first phase of the project. Piffle was still enjoying his extended holiday out at the Villa Almeria with Honolulu and was receiving regular updates from Paeleo as to the progress, as well as his weekly Thursday morning update from Zara Bindle.

Over in Hull, Gary Wacker was also very happy with the progress of the log cabin contract. For the first time in years his small factory was running at 100% capacity and he had already received the money for the first ten cabins in advance. He was having to go into the office every day, six days a week, to oversee the production and make sure the delivery schedule was on track. Soon the log cabins would be winding their way across the channel for the long drive down to the south of Spain where they would be erected on site by Gary's team. The builders on site would then fit them out, and connect the electricity and water services. As a result he was leaving early and seeing very little of Tracy, but she had her own lifestyle, which consisted of shopping, meeting friends, going to the hairdresser and having her nails done. She did very little at home now that they had a housekeeper in the form of Mrs Neatgangs who was doing everything that Tracy asked of her plus a lot more besides in the form of her sexual activities with the Waker's son Callum.

This day was no different and as soon as Tracy had gone out leaving Mrs Neatgangs alone in the house with Callum, she was off up to his room for a frisky sex session. Although Callum was at sixth form college he rarely went in before lunchtime as self-study was the order of the day for modern education establishments. At nearly 17 Callum was certainly getting an education, but not the one that Gary and Tracy had in mind for their son. If they knew what was going on, they would be horrified and extremely surprised at Callum's bizarre taste in female company – namely, a 5'1", 67-year-old Mrs Neatgangs who was basically as round as she was tall.

'Are you there Callum? Grandma Neatgangs is coming to find you!' Mrs Neatgangs shouted from the stairs. For a woman of her shape and size, she was amazingly agile at bounding up the stairs. She had given up wearing her bra whilst doing the housework, much to Gary Wacker's disgust, but more recently he had been out of the house before Mrs Neatgangs arrived. She liked to parade around the house with her bosoms bouncing because she knew it drove Callum wild whilst he was having his breakfast, and it was easier then to get him in the mood for the sex sessions she craved.

'Are you there Callum sweetie? Grandma is coming so you can come too.'

'I'm in the bedroom Granny,' shouted Callum.

As she sped along the corridor to Callum's room, he opened the door just in his boxer shorts, in anticipation of Mrs Neatgangs arrival. She had already lifted her cheap t-shirt by the time that she arrived at his bedroom door for maximum effect

'Oh, Grandma Neatgangs,' gasped Callum.

'Like what you see sweetie? How is my big boy today? Oh I can see you are very excited sweetie,' she said grabbing him and making him squirm with frustration. They kissed passionately at the threshold and then dived into the bedroom and onto Callum's bed.

As the sexual gymnastics were taking place in Callum's bedroom, his younger sister returned home unexpectedly from school. Thirteen-year-old Bianca had come back feeling unwell and let herself into the house. Feeling sick, all she wanted to do was to go up to her bedroom, get out of her school uniform and go to bed as she had a headache and temperature. As she reached the base of the staircase she was distracted by strange banging and squeaking noises coming from upstairs. Thinking there might be an intruder she went to the kitchen, got her mummy's rolling pin from one of the kitchen drawers and carefully went up the stairs, making sure she didn't make any noise. As she reached the top of the stairs it became obvious that the strange noises were coming from Callum's bedroom. A rhythmic squeak and, what sounded like strangled moans, convinced Bianca that her older brother was being attacked by intruders.

She tip-toed along the corridor and raised the rolling pin to attack whoever was trying to kill her brother. She flung the door open and screeched from the top of her voice as she swung the rolling pin above her head and then, as quickly as her attack had started, she stopped in mid-air, the rolling pin above her head. The sight that greeted her was as disgusting as it was amazing. There before her, was a naked Mrs Neatgangs riding her brother like a banshee, her arse bobbing up and down, whilst Callum squealed in subservience under the considerable weight of the disgusting woman.

'What the fuck?' but the exclamation was left in mid-sentence as Callum and Mrs Neatgangs realized they had been interrupted in the act of sexual gratification.

'That's fucking gross!' shouted Bianca and ran from the scene to her bedroom where she locked herself in.

The sexual antics had very much come to an end and Callum's manhood had, by now, wilted and shrivelled back to normal size. Mrs Neatgangs tidied herself up as best as she could, putting her clothes back on and wondering what to do next.

'That was a bit unfortunate sweetie. We're in the shit now and

I'll probably lose my job, I could really do with that £60 quid a week.'

'No!' shouted Callum fiercely. 'I love you Grandma Neatgangs and I want our love to continue forever. We'll have to confront mother and father with our love for each other and commit ourselves to marriage,' said Callum not thinking through the consequences at all.

'Marriage? Look sweetie, I know you like me, but that's jumping the gun love. I'm too old for you by a long way. I do like our little arrangement sweetie, but now your sister knows I can't see how it can continue, unless you come round to my council house as I'm bound to be sacked once Bianca spills the beans.'

'I can't live without you,' said Callum earnestly, 'yes, one way or another we must continue our love affair.'

Spilling the beans was the obvious option for Bianca, but as she lay on her bed she started to think that maybe she could benefit from her brother's weird sexual preferences, and blackmail them instead. That way her brother could carry on with his disgusting sex sessions and she could get a weekly allowance from both of them. Mrs Neatgangs did plenty of cleaning, plus her old age pension, and she was convinced she could squeeze £20 a week out of the old slag to keep quiet. Yes, that would do very nicely and it would mean she could buy the expensive make-up she craved to keep up with the other trendy girls in her class and stop her getting bullied.

Mrs Neatgangs made her escape shortly afterwards, glad to be away before Mrs Wacker returned, convinced that that would be her last visit to the house and the loss of much needed money to supplement her meagre state pension.

Now that Bianca had formulated her plan for blackmailing Callum, she thought she would strike whilst the iron was hot.

'Callum, it's me,' she said banging on his bedroom door.

'Go away, you've ruined everything and when you tell mum I'll be grounded for months.'

'Listen to me you disgusting little creature. I don't know what the fuck is going through your tiny, pea-sized brain finding that old slag in any way attractive, but now we know the truth I've got a proposition for you, that's if you want me not to tell mum when she gets back?'

'What are you taking about?'

'What I'm talking about bird brain, is if you get £20 a week off Mrs Neatgangs and give it to me without fail, then I won't tell mum and dad and you can keep your disgusting sex sessions going without them finding out. Providing you go round to the old slags house and do her well away from me. What do you say bird brain?'

'I can't get £20 a week out of Mrs Neatgangs, she'll never pay up.'

'Oh yes she will, because the old slag wants to carry on earning £60 a week working for mum and dad, and she wants you whenever she can have it because, let's be honest, she isn't getting it anywhere else. Though God knows what she sees in a spotty looser like you. Twenty quid starting next week Callum, or I spill the beans. As they say, everyone's a winner.'

'I'll speak to her, I can't promise but I'll do what I can.'

'I'm sure you will. Next Tuesday Callum, £20. Just think of it as an arrangement. You and Mrs Neatgangs get your disgusting sex and I get some money for make-up. I'm sure the old slapper will find a way of making another £20, maybe she can give a few blow jobs?'

'How dare you? Mrs Neatgangs isn't like that, I love her, and she loves me and when I'm old enough I'm going to marry her, just you see.'

'I doubt that very much, but if you do, don't expect me to come to your freak-out fucking wedding. Though you could sell the rights to the *People on Sunday* if you go through with it, freak.'

Chapter 74

Now that Penelope Sykes had the mobile phone number for Gordon Streake, she had no hesitation in contacting him immediately. She wanted to put the wheels in motion to get her revenge on Bradley Plumb for ruining her daughter's life and ultimately being responsible for her death. She had seen his brand of so-called humour on his late-night Friday show, *Purple Haze*, where he interviewed other talentless so-called celebrities; told stupid, puerile jokes and got up to juvenile antics. There was a hint of a glamorous drug- and drink-filled life for him and his trendy guests at the after show party which took place every week, it was also aired on late-night TV and was called *Extra Haze*. Blatant boozing and hints of drug taking were filmed in a local celebrity night club called *Sharkey's*, promulgating a so-called glamorous lifestyle that did nothing but harm to the youth of the country as far as Penelope Sykes was concerned.

'Mr Streake?'

'Yeah, whose calling?' said Streake, immediately suspicious.

'My name is Penelope Sykes, and you have been recommended to me by my good friend Mike Morrell. I understand you used to be Police Officers together and you come highly recommended.'

'I do know Mike, yes, and good to hear that he recommends me,' said Streake warming to the conversation.

'I'll come straight to the point Mr Streake. My daughter Madison Sykes has just died by drowning in the Grimewold Grand Central Canal after apparently taking a cocktail of drink and drugs. She was only thirty-eight.'

'Sorry to hear that Mrs Sykes, I did hear about the case.'

'The point is, Mike Morrell said that he had employed you in your capacity as a Private Detective and as part of that investigation you found out that my daughter was originally introduced to the drugs scene by the well-known chat show host, Bradley Plumb, formerly known as Bradley Norman Piffle. It was him that got my poor Maddy hooked on crack cocaine and heroin.'

'OK, yes, I did find certain things out about Bradley Plumb,' said Streake, still keeping his cards close to his chest.

'Good, well I want to employ you Mr Streake to get some more dirt on Bradley Plumb. I want enough on him to sink his career and sink him, and I want you to get me the evidence to achieve that. Is that something you might be interested in? And I can tell you, I am willing to pay a very generous daily rate for you to get me the information I require.'

'I can possibly do that for you Mrs Sykes, but I don't like to discuss delicate matters like this over the phone. Never can be too careful, so I suggest we meet at lunch today and discuss this in more detail. Do you know where the Cromwell Arms is on the outskirts of the Cromwell Estate?'

'I don't, but I can find it. Shall we say 1.00 p.m.?'

'OK, I'll see you there Mrs Sykes.'

This was getting better and better thought Streake. He was planning to look into the affairs of Bradley Plumb anyway with a view to blackmailing him over his drug taking, and now this bitch was offering to pay him handsomely to do it as well. Bloody hell, for once things were going the right way for Gordon Streake. Soon he would be able to leave the cramped room at his sister's place and get his own flat, especially if he could get a big fat wad of cash out of Bradley Plumb.

Streak quickly got himself ready, put his shabby three-piece suit on and made his way to the Cromwell Arms in his equally shabby Vauxhall Vectra. He liked to meet in down-at-heel, innocuous places where people didn't know him or his clients and that way it kept things discreet, the Cromwell Arms fitted the bill perfectly. On a weekday lunch time there would just be a few drunken old timers supping pints of bitter and he could find a nice cosy corner booth and discuss what needed to be discussed with Penelope Sykes without anyone listening in or prying into their business.

The Cromwell Arms definitely wasn't the sort of place that

Penelope Sykes would frequent, but like Streake, she was glad of the anonymity the place gave her. Being leader of the Council, she had to be very careful, especially with a matter as delicate as this. For once, she had dressed down for the occasion, in a sweater and jeans she would usually reserve for gardening, but her black Audi coupe stood out like a sore thumb in the car park, but there was nothing she could do about that as she had no other car to come to the meeting in that would draw less attention.

As she entered the pub, she spotted Streake in the corner booth immediately, basically because he was the only one in a suite. She went immediately over to the booth.

'Mr Streake?'

'It is.'

'Penelope Sykes, thanks you for seeing me at such short notice.'

'My pleasure, love. Sit down why don't you? What do you want to drink?'

'I'll have a large glass of chardonnay please with ice and soda.'

Streake shouted across the small bar area to the barman behind the bar. 'Get the lady a large glass of chardonnay, Steve, will you? And bring it over here.'

Steve just nodded and went away to get the drink for Penelope Sykes which duly arrived.

'Right, let's get down to business,' said Streake.

'Before I take a job on, I need to understand what the client is looking to achieve. You know, what the outcome is to be. Maybe you can give me the run down?'

'It's very simple Mr Streake,' said Penelope. 'I want revenge. I want revenge for the death of my darling daughter Madison. From what I have already learned, Bradley Plumb is wholly responsible for getting my poor Maddy hooked on hard drugs. Heroin and crack cocaine twenty years ago when he was dating her, taking advantage of her sweet nature more like. Drug addiction ruined her life and led to her terrible death aged just 38. Meanwhile, that vile smug creature has gone from strength to strength, living the high life, getting drunk, taking drugs with impunity and living a disgusting debauched lifestyle, flaunting his homosexuality across the airwaves like a badge of honour whilst destroying the lives of others like my poor Madison. I want him exposed as a drug taker and drug pusher, and I want his career ended. That's what I want Mr Streake. Now the question is, can you help me expose Bradley Plumb for what he is?'

'Well Mrs Sykes, I am sure I can do my best. If he is taking drugs and supplying others, then I can get the evidence on him, especially photos since they go down well with the press. What you have to understand is that the TV channels are hypocrites. They want to put out a show like *Purple Haze*, hinting at a debauched life of booze, drugs and sordid sex, but they only want it hinted at in an obvious kind of way for the viewing figures. When faced with actual proof of those activities, in real life, they drop the star like a bad smell and then the tabloids are all over them accusing them of all sorts and their careers are essentially over. The media circus then moves onto the next one. That's how it works. Look at that chat show host twenty years ago, never recovered his career did he once the press got their teeth into him? That's what we're going to do with Bradley Plumb and his seedy little late-night show. Sink him like a stone.'

'That sounds perfect Mr Streake, but how are you going to accomplish that for me?'

'Well it won't be cheap. I've got to get close enough to his inner circle to get the goods on him and that will take a good month down in London. If we can get evidence of him buying drugs and then photograph him, or even better supplying one or more of his entourage, then we've got him – as long as I get the pics. If it's supply then he's looking at a stretch inside despite his fame, even though the authorities go soft of people like Plumb. But the main thing is getting hard evidence, and I promise you Mrs Sykes, I can do that for you.'

'It sounds to me, Streake, like you're my man. How much do you want for doing this for me?'

'As I said, it's at least a month and I charge £150 quid a day, plus expenses, which will run to petrol, hotel accommodation, food and out of pocket expenses. For the first month you're looking at the thick end of £9,000 and if it takes longer then you can double that. Can't do it cheaper, that's my best offer.'

'OK Streake, you've got yourself a deal,' said Penelope holding out her hand to shake on the deal.

Bloody hell, thought Streake, she didn't try and negotiate the price. He was going to be quids' in.

'Here's my email address Mrs Sykes. Send me a confirmation email and I'll send you back my sort code and account number. I'll need the first month's payment up front, £9,000, is that understood?'

'OK Mr Streake, but I want concrete results and if you don't supply them after the first month then I won't be paying you anymore. Do you understand me?'

'Loud and clear Mrs Sykes. I won't let you down, and I'll phone you every week with an update.'

Streake left the meeting in his shabby Vauxhall Vectra in an elated mood. Never had a client been so generous in the ten years he had done this job. He had chanced his arm and it had paid off.

He hadn't been entirely truthful with Penelope Sykes. What Streake had in mind to guarantee success was a sting operation where he got someone to offer hard drugs to Bradley Plumb. That way he could control the environment better and get the photos he needed. He then had to hope that Plumb would give some of the drugs to members of his entourage, which would be even more serious. He then had a choice, sell the story to the gutter press, or blackmail Bradley Plumb.

Streake being Streake thought he might just do both, that way he would get three paydays: the fee from Penelope Sykes, the bung from Bradley Plumb and then a big fat fee from one of the tabloids for exposing the debauched lifestyle and drug taking of Bradley Plumb.

He just needed someone to supply the drugs to Plumb in the first place. Anyone he could vaguely trust, and that person had to be Lord Brett Sinclair, the local drugs dealer in Grimewold. Yes, that would do nicely. He would take Brett down with him to London, with the gear, somehow get Brett close enough to him to offer him the drugs, and then whilst that was going on take the photos. He might need to get Brett wired up for that so that he had some good shots for the press and to blackmail Plumb. Streake reckoned if he was clever, he could make fifty grand out of this little number and that would be enough, together with what he had already saved, to get him off to the Costa del Sol to start his new life.

Chapter 75

Tandori arrived at work early as usual. She had realised that if she got in just before 8.00 a.m. the pickets hadn't started to gather yet. There were now more of them, not just the ex-workers that had been let go by Bindle, but a rag-bag of activists from other ultra-left wing causes such as radical vegans for justice, the fair food liberation movement, and extinction crisis, not to mention various anti-American protestors and pro-North Korean activists.

The other staff members arriving at 8.45 were not so lucky, but Tandori was not interested in them. She had a job to do, and with Hazelhurst on her back constantly she just wanted to do it and be out of there and back to the Cotswolds where she belonged. The main thing she was worried about was being caught in the act of sabotaging records and being sacked. She needed to do enough damage to the Diversity Action Partnership to cripple it before she was found out, and then hopefully Hazelhurst would keep to his word and make sure that Inspector Fleece couldn't charge her with terrorism offences *and* give her back her old job at MI5.

Today was no different, she managed to doctor 100 client files before 9.00 a.m. so that they would be sent additional fines of £2000 each. She would manage to doctor a further 200 files after work until she finished around 9.00 p.m. So far, her efforts had been in vain, because the monies received from fines had increased income since companies didn't realize that they were being fined illegally. However, some firms had started to complain and were refusing to pay, threatening legal action. Tandori was taking as many of these complaints as she could and hiding them in a file in one of the large grey filling cabinets where no one would find them. By the time that the court cases came through, it would be too late, and Piffle's empire would be seriously damaged.

Zara Bindle had mixed emotions as she sat in her office. On the one hand she had good news to report to Piffle again, that fine income was substantially up, but on the other she was becoming increasingly concerned that the strike was carrying on and getting stronger. There had even be one or two articles from left wing journalists that were highly critical of her and her handling of the workers who had been sacked. Phrases like, 'betraying the authentic working class' and 'pitching white working class heroes against minority groups' had really started to hit home.

It was the first time a Bindle had ever been seriously criticised in left wing circles, and it was a betrayal of her grandmother, Philomena's class struggles which had brought the name Bindle to prominence in the first place. It was just so unfair, all she was doing was introducing diversity into the work place which gave exploited minority groups a chance to thrive, which was just what left wing academia had been calling for. If that cast adrift a load old white middle-aged ex-miners and steel workers, who in any case could probably get enhanced Universal Credit payments due to their various disabilities, then so be it. You can't make an omelette without cracking a few eggs, but now she was being hung out to dry. Even the editor of the *Daily People*, Hugo Spires, had turned against her with a particularly nasty and vitriolic editorial with the headline

'Bindle the Beast of Grimewold!'

'Jonathan, get Tandori to come into the office and see me will you?'

'Yes Zara, I'll get her straight away.'

Jonathan immediately went to Tandori's office and called out to her, 'Bindle wants to see you.'

Oh shit, thought Tandori, has she found out what I've been up to? This could be it.

'Coming Jonathan, I'll be there in a jiffy.'

Tandori made her away to Bindle's office and knocked on the door before entering. 'Hello Zara, did you want to see me?'

'Oh, hello Tandori, come, come and sit down on one of the comfy sofas. I thought we could have a little catch up.'

Here goes, thought Tandori, I'm for it now, what the hell am I going to say?

'Hugo, my husband, thinks I was wrong to sack the white middle-aged male dinosaurs who Piffle employed and replace them with a beautiful rainbow of diversity and equality. What do you think

Tandori?'

'I don't know,' stammered Tandori, 'I guess you know best.'

'But do I? Hugo thinks that the left-wing press like The Daily People and The Guardian are going to throw me to the wolves and destroy me for standing up for diversity.'

'Well Ms Bindle, sometimes you have to stand up for what you believe in and to hell with the consequences. Visionaries are always hated or ridiculed by the establishment.'

'You're right Tandori, I was just thinking out loud really. Anyway less of me, I wanted to congratulate you.'

'What? You did?'

'I wanted to congratulate you on what you have done for us since you joined us last month.'

'Oh.'

'I've got the figures for last week and each week the fine income is getting better and better. It's up 32% on the week before, unbelievable. Piffle will be delighted when I tell him later in the week, not that he has had anything to do with it. We never see him, he's spending more and more time at his villa in Benidorm working on his latest hair-brained plan. He's building five hundred log cabins, or some such madness.'

'So fine income is up? I had no idea,' said Tandori, thinking the opposite would be true. What a disaster, she thought, and what the fuck will Hazelhurst say if he finds out? Which he will, because the bastard always does, then the threats will start again. I might even have Fleece on my back again – no it didn't bear thinking about.

'At least that side of things is going very well. What to do about the strikers and the left wing agitator's who have joined them, that's the problem. Any ideas as you seem so good at running the show?' said Bindle genuinely interested to see if Tandori had any ideas how to defeat the strikers and get the place back to normal.

'Off the top of my head, I would say that they need a carrot.'

'A carrot? What are you blabbering about?'

'You know, a carrot. You've given them plenty of stick by sacking them and taking away their only chance of a job, now they need a carrot to take the pain and anger away, and then they'll back off. I've heard Mike Morrell's outfit, The Speed Camera Action! team upstairs have just won a contract for monitoring air quality in Grimewold using hand -held devices at all the major road junctions. Why don't we ask Mike if he needs any new staff? Those ex-miners and steel workers would be ideal. They wouldn't take any nonsense from irate motorists and that would get them off your back.'

'I have to say that is an ingenious idea Tandori, but the only fly in the ointment is that Mike Morrell loathes Dresden, so I can't see him wanting to do us a favour that would help Piffle in any way. But yes, it is worth a try I suppose,' said Bindle, still wrestling with the concept of asking Mike Morrell for help.

'If I know Morrell,' said Tandori, 'he'll do something if it's in his best interests, and if recruiting reliable staff makes him more money it gives him kudos with the council. And let's be honest, it must be a pain for his staff having to cross the picket lines every day to get into this building.'

'I tell you what Tandori, since you're so full of good ideas this morning, why don't you go and see Mike Morrell and ask him? Coming from you as an outsider might be better, and then if it works we've solved one huge problem and things can get back to normal around here.'

'OK Ms Bindle, I'll go and see him this morning.'

'I keep telling you Tandori, it's Zara not Ms Bindle. You're a real asset to this organisation. I don't know what I would do without you. Now run along.'

With that the meeting ended and Tandori went off to see if she could find Mike Morrell feeling very pleased with herself. No one had ever said she was a real asset before. It felt really good!

Chapter 76

As promised Penelope Sykes had responded to Gordon Streake's email and confirmed their contract, paying the £9,000 payment up front for the investigative work he was to undertake for her, looking into the affairs of Bradley Plumb.

This morning Streake was on his way to the seedier end of the Cromwell Estate to find the person that was going to help him nail Plumb once and for all, none other than the notorious drug dealer, Lord Brett Sinclair. He wasn't difficult to find as he was at home with his live-in girlfriend, lazing about watching crap daytime TV whilst she tended to their two kids. Most of Brett's deals took place in the evening, so his days were fairly clear apart from phone calls relating to either buying or supplying gear.

Streake had come across Lord Brett on a previous investigation he had carried out for Mike Morrell, and although he didn't know Brett personally, he thought that the pictures he had taken of him supplying drugs to Madison Sykes, might be enough to persuade Lord Brett that his best interests lay in cooperating with Streake's little plan. It hadn't been too difficult to track Lord Brett's address down, he was well known on the Cromwell Estate and a few of the old timers in the Cromwell Arms has supplied him with the address after he had loosened their tongues with a few free beers.

Streake parked round the corner a few hundred yards from Lord Brett's house; number 16 Naseby Close. He didn't want Brett clocking his car or its registration number.

He strode up to the house purposefully and rapped loudly on the door.

'Get that bloody door babes!' shouted Brett. 'I'm busy.' If busy meant watching the daytime TV show *Putting Them Behind Bars* then Brett was indeed busy.

'Why don't you fucking get it? I'm busy with the kids.'

'Do I have to do everything round here bitch?'

Lord Brett went to the door and yanked it open to be confronted by a shifty looking Streake in his grubby mac and trilby hat to act as some kind of disguise.

'Brett Sinclair?' said Streake.

'Whose asking?' said Brett suspiciously.

'I'm Gordon Streake, I've got a proposition for you.'

'What do you mean? Do I know you?'

'No Brett, but I know you.'

'I ain't interested, now piss off,' said Brett who went to slam the door, but Streake beat him to it and put his boot in the door to prevent it closing.

'Not so quick sunshine,' Streake forced the door open and with surprising strength got Brett by the neck and pushed him against the hallway wall.

'What the fuck you doing?' squeaked Brett.

'What I'm offering is carrot or stick, Brett.'

'What do you mean?'

'Well, I can make you an offer that will make you a lot of money, or I can show the police evidence that you were responsible for the death of that bird that died recently, you know the one who you supplied with cocaine.'

'What are you talking about?'

'Are you willing to listen to my proposal Brett? We can talk about this in a civilized way.'

'Suppose so.'

'Good, well let's sit down in your lounge.'

They entered the lounge and sat down.

'Babes, I'm just having a meeting so don't disturb us, OK?'

'Alright,' shouted his girlfriend.

'What's all this about?'

'I am a private detective by the name of Streake and I've got a job to do concerning the famous chat show host Bradley Plumb. You know, the prick that does that Friday night chat show.'

'Yeah I know him. So where do I fit in?'

'Let's just say our Bradders likes what you supply, you know the hard stuff, and my client wants me to get the goods on him so that he gets sacked from the telly. Bit of revenge so to speak. We go down to London, get into the club he goes to after the show and offer him the gear. You get paid, which I get on hidden camera and bingo we've got him. You make plenty of dough and some new contacts, and I get enough evidence to get him sacked, which pleases my client. Should only take a week, and in return I don't shop you to Humberwold Police about the death of that bird. And in case you're wondering, here are the pics of you supplying her, so don't try and play funny buggers with me or you'll be doing a stretch for supply plus manslaughter, comprendo?'

'I dunno man, I don't like leaving my patch, never been far out of Grimewold me, like to keep me business running smoothly.'

'Listen you fucked up little wanker, I ain't giving you a choice here. Either we go to London next week or you get a knock on the door from the old bill. So what's it to be?' said Streake really turning the screws on Lord Brett now.

'OK OK, I'll do it. I'll need me expenses paying though, hotel and walk about money, and I need to get those pictures in return. If you double cross me Streake , I'll fucking well have you.'

'Then we understand each other don't we Brett? Give me your secure mobile number and I'll be in touch at the weekend. Pleasure doing business with you.'

And with that Streake left satisfied that he achieved what he wanted. Getting Lord Brett on board meant that he had a good chance of getting the goods on Bradley Plumb – famous chat show host – soon to be disgraced unemployable chat show host.

Chapter 77

Tandori went into the offices of The Speed Camera Action! Limited and went up to reception looking for Mike Morrell.

'Excuse me, my name is Tandori Birkett-Morris and I work for the Diversity Action Partnership downstairs. I'd like to see Mike Morrell please. Its urgent.'

'I can ask him Miss, but he's usually busy. Take a seat and I'll see what I can do.'

'Mike, I have a young lady in the foyer. Tandori Birkett Morris. She works downstairs for The Diversity Action Partnership and says its urgent that she speaks to you. Are you free?'

Intrigued, Mike decided to see Tandori to see what she wanted.

'Yeah, send her up to my office. I'll make time for 30 minutes then I've got other stuff to do.'

'OK Miss Birkett-Morris, Mike Morrell will see you now. His

office is up the stairs to the top floor, you can't miss it, his name's on the door.'

'Thanks very much,' said Tandori who followed the receptionists instructions and within no time found Mike's office. She knocked and entered. Mike was sitting at his expansive mahogany desk, smoking a cigar and leaning back into his deeply sprung red leather chesterfield executive swivel chair. As Tandori entered, a huge grin spread over his face.

'Come in, come in. Tandori isn't it? Take a seat and make yourself comfortable.'

'Thank you Mr Morrell.'

'Please, please, call me Mike. How nice to meet you. I understand you're in charge of Piffle's little empire.'

'Well, not in charge, but I am looking after the admin side of things. Zara Bindle's in charge.'

'Oh yes, of course she is. Well anyway, what can I do for you Tandori? It certainly is a surprise to see you given the rather strained relationship I have with Piffle and his company.'

'I've come up here because I think we can help each other out, something we could all benefit from.'

'I'm intrigued young lady, always like to do things that benefit both myself and others, what have you got in mind?'

'Well, as you can see every day, there is a picket line, a strike if you like, of ex-employees of The Diversity Action Partnership outside our offices in the square. Zara let them go because she wanted to create a more diverse workforce to the one Mr Piffle had originally employed, but Zara being Zara just sacked them and now they are awfully cross and to make matters worse all these horrible communist agitators have joined them who have nothing to do with us. It's frightful getting through the pickets each day and its upsetting morale terribly, and it must be making things difficult for your staff as well.'

'Granted it is, but I still don't see what I can do. Bindle's sacked them and upset them so it's Bindle's problem to sort it out.'

'Yes, but I was thinking, you've just won the contract from the council for monitoring pollution from road traffic, and you're going to need some new staff to do the monitoring across various points in the town and I thought, why not employ the staff that Zara has let go? They're all responsible, hard-working men who know how to handle themselves, and from what I've seen on that picket line, they would be ideal for you. No motorists are going to want to take them on and complain too loudly. If you offered them the work, then they would probably call off the strike and you could take all the credit with the Council and the press, and then all those horrible communists would go away as well. The whole situation would be resolved.'

'I can see your point Tandori, but why should I help Piffle's company get out of this situation?'

'Well if this continues much longer then the Diversity Action

Partnership might struggle to survive and you might have to move to new premises since Mr Piffle owns the lease on this building. Also, your staff would be able to get into work easier and you would look like the saviour of those poor men in the eyes of the press and the Trades Unions, not to mention the council, who I know you like to be on good terms with.'

Mike Morrell's mind was working overtime weighing up the various options and scenarios. It was all true what Tandori had said, and compelling, but why shouldn't he let Piffle's empire go tits up? Then he could sweep in with an offer to the Council to take over the contract. But that way could be messy. No, this Tandori bird was right. Slowly, slowly, catchy monkey. If he looked like the knight in shining armour, then he could take on the staff as Tandori had suggested, which would give him good quality staff and he would get all the kudos. It would also buy him time to win the contract from the Council to take over Piffle's operation with all the staff and procedures intact. Much less messy and he would come out smelling of roses in an even stronger position.

Mike lent back in his leather executive chair and grinned again.

'Well Tandori, you're certainly cleverer than you look. I like what you have had to say, and I like your style. Let me sleep on it and I'll make a decision by morning, but if I go ahead with this there might be some expenses to cover. I'm doing you a huge favour, so we would need, shall we say, £20,000 to smooth the path and make this happen. But, as I've said, let me sleep on it and I'll ring you tomorrow. But well done, good plan.'

Mike Morrell had already made up his mind and decided that the answer would be yes, but he wanted to make Tandori and Bindle stew overnight, and squeeze £20,000 out of Bindle to clean up the mess that the stupid left-wing bitch had caused for herself.

Tandori went back to her office and phoned Bindle with the news that Mike Morrell was very receptive, and she felt sure that he would take on the staff who Bindle had sacked, but she would have her answer tomorrow. She didn't tell Bindle that Morrell wanted £20,000 as a sweetener to make the deal happen, but felt sure it was a small price to pay to get Zara Bindle out of the mess she had created for herself and the company.

Tandori was feeling very pleased with herself when she left the office that night to go back to the grubby little flat. Bindle had said she was doing a great job and now Mike Morrell had complimented her as well, in a roundabout sort of way, and she was still on target to cause eventual havoc to the Diversity Action Partnership without anyone knowing.

Her good mood was soon to be altered for the worse after she got home and had her tea. Her mobile phone rang and it was a non-too happy Hazelhurst.

'Evening Tandori, its Hazelhurst here.'

'Oh evening Hazelhurst, I've just finished my tea.'

'How's it going at The Diversity Action Partnership Tandori?'

'It's going brilliantly,' gushed Tandori. 'I've been doing what you told me and doctoring the client files and sending out false invoices and the complaints and threats of court action are piling up. I'm managing to intercept them and hide them in a metal cabinet out of sight.'

'Are you sure it's going brilliantly Tandori?'

'Yes of course it is Hazelhurst, why what's the problem?'

'I'll tell you what the problem is my dear Tandori, I have it on good authority that instead of you bringing The Diversity Action Partnership to its knees, its bloody well thriving, and since you came back two weeks ago the fee income has risen by 32%. It's a fucking disaster, that's what it is. I didn't send you in there to make the bloody organisation a success, I sent you there to bring it to its knees like you usually manage to achieve.'

'That's just not fair, it's not my bloody fault that some of the clients have decided to pay up the false invoices instead of causing a stink. I'm doing my best, and in any case, how do you know that fee income is up 32% when only Zara compiles those figures and they're restricted to key members of staff. Have you got the place bugged?'

'No not yet Tandori, but I'm considering it! No, do you honestly think with your fucking disastrous track record that I was going to send you in there without back up? I had to make sure that we have another operative in there in case you screwed up. In any case, I wanted to make sure you were still doing my bidding, which I now have serious doubts over.'

'I knew you would double cross me, this just isn't fair,' moaned Tandori.

'Well life isn't fair, get over it. Now you listen to me young lady, I want this operation wrapped up so my superiors get off my back and I want Piffle's little empire brought to its knees. I'm giving you another two months to sort it, otherwise you and me are going to fall out and then I'll throw you back to the wolves and that idiot Fleece can arrest you for being an ISIS terrorist and bang you up, and you can kiss goodbye to being taken back on under my wing at MI5. Do you understand me?'

'OK, OK, I'm on it. I promise that within two months the clients will be screaming like mad and bringing court cases against the Diversity Action Partnership and Piffle's empire will collapse. These things just take time. Anyway, who is the other operative?'

'I'm not telling you that Tandori, just safe to say that I'm watching your every move and that of that nasty little communist Zara Bindle.'

The telephone call ended and despite Hazelhurt's bravado he was seriously worried that this operation was going in completely the wrong direction and if Winton J Cuncliffe-Owen found out he might well be in serious trouble as well. For now, he could keep them at bay and suggest that things were going fine. The strike was a good example of the disruption he could say Tandori was causing, even though that had nothing to do with her.

Tandori was also worried. She didn't like the thought that another operative was watching her every move and she was concerned that things were not moving quickly enough. The last thing she needed was that vile Inspector Fleece back in her life accusing of all sorts of preposterous things that she had no part in. She just hoped and prayed that soon the clients would start legal proceedings and refuse to pay fines, then her job would be done and she could get out of there – in one piece hopefully.

Chapter 78

Callum Wacker knew that his mother Tracy had a spare change tin in the kitchen where she kept money to pay for the lottery, her bingo night and the Avon lady. Usually there was about sixty quid in there. It was hidden from view, but one day he had found it whilst looking for some chocolate bars. It was well hidden behind the pasta tin in a cupboard above the toaster.

Callum decided it was too risky to steel £20 a week to pay his scheming sister her blood money, but he could risk £10 or so he thought, and get the rest from Mrs Neatgangs. It had the added advantage of giving him an excuse to go round to Mrs Neatgangs' council house on the Gipsyville Estate and hopefully indulge in one of their sex sessions where he wouldn't be disturbed by prying eyes.

So that's what he did. He carefully got the jar down and rummaged through it, finding some notes and loose change. But Callum being Callum, he got greedy and stole two tenners. One for himself to buy some sweets, and one to go towards the money for Bianca. He carefully put the jar back and went out on his push bike for the twenty-minute ride to Mrs Neatgangs house.

He was gone well before Gary or Tracy returned from their days' activities, leaving a note that he was visiting a mate and would be back about 8.00 p.m., he would get some tea then if mum could leave it in the microwave.

In no time he was outside Mrs Neatgangs house, and already he could feel himself getting excited at the anticipation of seeing her. He propped his bike against the fence that divided Mrs Neetgangs house with next door and knocked tentatively on the door. He hadn't made a specific arrangement to see her, so he was a bit apprehensive whether she would be in and what he would find.

He need not have worried. Mrs Neatgangs opened the door and as soon as she saw Callum she smiled and invited him in.

'Oh hello sweetie, come in. I wasn't expecting you to come over and see me, can't you keep away from Grandma Neatgangs?' I can see your pleased to see me,' laughed Mrs Neatgangs making a point of looking directly at the bulge in Callum's jeans.

Mrs Neatgangs was dressed as provocatively as she usually did. She had cheap black leggings that showed her panty line and a cream t-shirt with no bra as usual, as she walked through to the lounge.

'Come and sit yourself down and I'll get you a nice cup of tea.'

Callum walked into the lounge expecting that they would be

alone and they could carry on where they left off the other day, but Callum was to be massively disappointed for there in a wing chair was a much younger women, even larger and equally as plain as Mrs Neatgangs with no make-up and similar cheap clothes and obvious facial similarities.

'This is my daughter Olive. Olive meet Callum, he's the son of Mrs Wacker that I do the cleaning for. He has just popped by for a cuppa and to say hello.'

'Hello Callum, you're a big strong lad,' said Olive eyeing him up and down with a twinkle in her eye.

'You like my mum, do you?' she said making him feel as uncomfortable as possible.

'We're just friends,' stammered Callum. 'I was passing thought I'd pop in and say hello,'

'I bet you did, she's a big lady isn't she Callum? Just like me,' said Olive leaning forward in the chair.

'Olive comes over all the time,' said Mrs Neatgangs from the kitchen where she was making a drink.

'She only lives opposite and we're very close. I'm always babysitting for her, she's got six kids. The oldest is 19, but the two younger ones are only 5 and 6 years old and need looking after when she goes out to meet one of her fancy men, don't they Olive?'

'Well, you don't mind, do you mum? It means I can have a good time when I want,' Olive said suggestively.

'If you ever want to come and see me, Callum, I live over there at number 26. You're always welcome,' Olive whispered so her mum couldn't hear. 'I've got a bit more energy than mum.'

Callum didn't know what to say, but he very much doubted if Olive had any more energy than Mrs Neatgangs after what he had experienced so far.

'That's kind of you,' Callum mumbled.

'Here's the tea then,' said Mrs Neatgangs.

'Are you having a cuppa Olive?'

'No mum, I best be going. Nice to meet you Callum, and remember what I said.'

'What's that?' said Mrs Neatgangs.

'Oh, just that mum would love to see you anytime Callum, she's always up for it.'

'Stop being cheeky,' smirked Mrs Neatgangs.

'Mum's one of those women that never says no, Callum.'

'Stop it Olive, you'll embarrass the lad.'

And then Olive was gone, and he was alone with Mrs Neetgangs in her lounge drinking tea.

'Has Bianca said anything to your mum about what she saw us doing? I can see I'm going to get sacked for what we did.'

'Not necessarily,' said Callum.

'What do you mean?'

'I mean, Bianca is blackmailing us. She wants £20 a week from us to not spill the beans to mum and dad, and then we can carry on seeing each other as long as it's here, and you can keep your job. I thought if we both put in a tenner each week, it would keep Bianca sweet. Look I've already got my tenner,' said Callum showing Mrs Neatgangs one of the tenners he had stolen from the jam jar in his mother's kitchen. 'Just need another tenner from you, if that's ok?'

'Well sweetie, I suppose it is and a small price to pay to keep my job and be able to have some extras.' Mrs Neatgangs smirked suggestively.

'I'll give you the tenner before you go, then you can pay off Bianca, but seeing as you have come all this way and must be tired from cycling, maybe we could go to my bedroom after you've had your tea...?'

Never one to turn down a sex session, Mrs Neatgangs had seen an opportunity to satisfy her voracious sexual appetite and set a precedent for the future. This could be a very nice little arrangement indeed. Callum didn't need asking twice, and soon they were naked in Mrs Neatgangs bedroom.

Callum couldn't help thinking about Olive though, she definitely made a play for him to come over to her house. Maybe it was his imagination and she was just being nice, but he wasn't so sure. Olive had all the attributes of Mrs Neatgangs in a younger and larger package, and Callum being 16 was keen to explore more without thinking of the consequences of what would happen if his beloved Mrs Neatgangs found out.

Chapter 79

Just as Archibald had wanted, the idiot Barraclough had fallen into his carefully laid trap. After the acrimonious meeting, Barraclough had called an immediate ballot of his members for a strike to be called at McGreggor's steel to protect workers' pay and conditions and prevent the closure of the number three blast furnace. If approved, the strike was to start the following Monday.

On the popular *Hello Britain* news show, The Minister for Trade and Industry had called for talks and for both sides to compromise that very morning. Archibald sneered at the television screen at the stupidity and pomposity of the hapless Tory Minister. He shouted at the buffoon in frustration.

'I don't want to bloody well compromise, you useless blue communist buffoon. I want to bring Barraclough and his lazy, good for nothing members to their knees and make McGreggor's the most profitable steel producer in the whole of Europe, you fucking idiot. What's wrong with you modern Tories, no backbone, useless public-schoolboy, silver spooned runt that you are!'

Archibald was shouting at the television screen, but of course no one was listening to him, apart from his long-suffering secretary, June who was at the desk in reception outside his office.

'Are we getting worked up again Archibald? It's not good for your heart condition,' she shouted from her desk.

'I tell you what's not good for me, you imbecile, it's listening to that chinless blue communist of a Trade Secretary blathering on about talks and compromise. Great Britain wasn't forged on compromise and talks, it was forged with hard-headed resolve to defeat the enemy and a single minded pursuit of a policy of maximum profits, so companies can reinvest and be the best in the world at what they do, instead of retreat and collapse that so many industries have suffered from.'

'If you say so,' said June dubiously. 'How about I make you a nice milky hot chocolate to calm you down?'

'For Christ sake woman, what do you think I am? An incontinent vegetable? Get me a double single malt whisky with ice, and then get me Googleheimer on the phone. I want to make sure we are ready for a long drawn out strike.'

'Whatever you say Archibald.'

'Googleheimer, is that you?'

'It is Mr McGreggor.'

'Splendid, are we ready for the strike? I want to make sure that as much steel stock has been delivered from our warehouses to the stockists in case the blighters try and blockade shipments through our supply chain.'

'Sure is Archibald. I've got our haulage contractor working round the clock to move product and remember, PING steel are supplying our stockists direct. By the time the strike starts we'll have five month's supply. We can smoke those babies out if we have to.'

'Smoke them out, I like your turn of phrase Googleheimer. That's splendid news. The next part of the plan is, because of the left-wing agitators and totally unreasonable demands of the union we will be forced to close down blast furnace number three and sack 40% of the 5,000 strong workforce. And to maintain production in Grimewold at all, we will need a grant of £200 million to upgrade the remaining facilities. But that's for the future. You can announce that in a few weeks' time on *Hello Britain* to cheer the nation up. I used to like the way that Michael Edwards would threaten to close down the whole of British Leyland and sack over 100,000 workers if they didn't give into his very reasonable demands for productivity increases and pay restraint. Those were the days Googleheimer. We're going to make McGreggor's the most profitable steel maker in Europe, turnover is vanity, profit is sanity as they say!'

'Bit before my time Archibald, I'm afraid. I was a teenager on my pop's farm in Oklahoma back then, driving a big Case Combine Harvester.' said Googleheimer, wondering at the amazing turn of events. Archibald certainly was one tough cookie, and he had a cunning plan that Googleheimer was only partly aware of. He would just have to go along with things and hope to hell that Archibald knew what he was doing, as it seemed a very high risk game of craps to him, and he wasn't a gambling man.

Archibald was on a roll that morning and decided to follow up his call to Googleheimer by calling Winton J Cuncliffe-Owen to find out if there was any news about whether Sydney Dresden Piffle was on his knees yet. After three weeks surely that blasted woman they had put in there had had some effect on his business. After all, she had managed to be instrumental in blowing up a block of grade one listed prime London real estate, and destroyed a perfectly good Hitachi train carriage and disrupted the whole of Northern rail's services for weeks on end. Surely ruining Piffle was a walk in the park?

'Ah Winton my good fellow, how are things going your end?'

'Fine, fine, thank you Archibald. I saw on *Hello Britain* this morning that you have a bit of bother at the steel works. Nothing too serious I hope?'

'Never mind that Winton, I can handle a load of left wing communists hell bent of causing trouble, it's just a pity that your lily-livered Trade and Industry Secretary can't support us in our struggle for survival. They should rename the idiot the Minister for the Destruction of Industry, but I'm not here to talk about the shortcomings of the modern Conservative party. I'm here, my good fellow, to get an update on our little arrangement to destroy a certain Sydney Dresden Piffle.'

'Ah, I thought that might have been why you called,' said Winton defensively.

'Well it's good news old boy. I've spoken to Hazelhurst and he assures me that the girl is disrupting Piffle's operation significantly, and it's only a matter of time before the court cases start flooding in and the complaints to the Council, which will eventually overwhelm the blighter and finish his tawdry little operation.'

'Only a matter of time you say? Now you look here you buffoon, you get back onto your fellow Hazelhurst and tell him straight that I want results. I want that blasted Piffle dangling on the end of a meat hook begging for mercy. It's only when he is bankrupt and back in the gutter living on a park bench that I will be satisfied. No one, and I mean no one, gets the better of Archibald McGreggor III, do you understand me Winton, *old man*?' Archibald said the last two words dripping with sarcasm.

'Yes, yes, of course I understand. Feelings are running high, but you have my word that the girl is carrying out her instructions to the letter, and it won't be long now before we have ultimate success.'

'Glad to hear it, and when your Government gives me a grant to invest in my steel plant and make it state of the art, I might be a little more amenable towards you, do I make myself clear?'

'Perfectly, Archibald,'

'Good, I'm glad we understand each other. I will bid you good day,' and with that the telephone conversation ended with Archibald feeling he had pressed home his advantage and Winton feeling as ever drained

after a run in with his so called friend.

Chapter 80

Just as Archibald had wanted, the idiot Barraclough had fallen into his carefully laid trap. After the acrimonious meeting, Barraclough had called an immediate ballot of his members for a strike to be called at McGreggor's steel to protect workers' pay and conditions and prevent the closure of the number three blast furnace. If approved, the strike was to start the following Monday.

On the popular *Hello Britain* news show, The Minister for Trade and Industry had called for talks and for both sides to compromise that very morning. Archibald sneered at the television screen at the stupidity and pomposity of the hapless Tory Minister. He shouted at the buffoon in frustration.

'I don't want to bloody well compromise, you useless blue communist buffoon. I want to bring Barraclough and his lazy, good for nothing members to their knees and make McGreggor's the most profitable steel producer in the whole of Europe, you fucking idiot. What's wrong with you modern Tories, no backbone, useless public-schoolboy, silver spooned runt that you are!'

Archibald was shouting at the television screen, but of course no one was listening to him, apart from his long-suffering secretary, June who was at the desk in reception outside his office.

'Are we getting worked up again Archibald? It's not good for your heart condition,' she shouted from her desk.

'I tell you what's not good for me, you imbecile, it's listening to that chinless blue communist of a Trade Secretary blathering on about talks and compromise. Great Britain wasn't forged on compromise and talks, it was forged with hard-headed resolve to defeat the enemy and a single minded pursuit of a policy of maximum profits, so companies can reinvest and be the best in the world at what they do, instead of retreat and collapse that so many industries have suffered from.'

'If you say so,' said June dubiously. 'How about I make you a nice milky hot chocolate to calm you down?'

'For Christ sake woman, what do you think I am? An incontinent vegetable? Get me a double single malt whisky with ice, and then get me Googleheimer on the phone. I want to make sure we are ready for a long drawn out strike.'

'Whatever you say Archibald.'

'Googleheimer, is that you?'

'It is Mr McGreggor.'

'Splendid, are we ready for the strike? I want to make sure that as much steel stock has been delivered from our warehouses to the stockists in case the blighters try and blockade shipments through our supply chain.'

'Sure is Archibald. I've got our haulage contractor working round the clock to move product and remember, PING steel are supplying our stockists direct. By the time the strike starts we'll have five month's supply. We can smoke those babies out if we have to.'

'Smoke them out, I like your turn of phrase Googleheimer. That's splendid news. The next part of the plan is, because of the left-wing agitators and totally unreasonable demands of the union we will be forced to close down blast furnace number three and sack 40% of the 5,000 strong workforce. And to maintain production in Grimewold at all, we will need a grant of £200 million to upgrade the remaining facilities. But that's for the future. You can announce that in a few weeks' time on *Hello Britain* to cheer the nation up. I used to like the way that Michael Edwards would threaten to close down the whole of British Leyland and sack over 100,000 workers if they didn't give into his very reasonable demands for productivity increases and pay restraint. Those were the days Googleheimer. We're going to make McGreggor's the most profitable steel maker in Europe, turnover is vanity, profit is sanity as they say!'

'Bit before my time Archibald, I'm afraid. I was a teenager on my pop's farm in Oklahoma back then, driving a big Case Combine Harvester.' said Googleheimer, wondering at the amazing turn of events. Archibald certainly was one tough cookie, and he had a cunning plan that Googleheimer was only partly aware of. He would just have to go along with things and hope to hell that Archibald knew what he was doing, as it seemed a very high risk game of craps to him, and he wasn't a gambling man.

Archibald was on a roll that morning and decided to follow up his call to Googleheimer by calling Winton J Cuncliffe-Owen to find out if there was any news about whether Sydney Dresden Piffle was on his knees yet. After three weeks surely that blasted woman they had put in there had had some effect on his business. After all, she had managed to be instrumental in blowing up a block of grade one listed prime London real estate, and destroyed a perfectly good Hitachi train carriage and disrupted the whole of Northern rail's services for weeks on end. Surely ruining Piffle was a walk in the park?

'Ah Winton my good fellow, how are things going your end?'

'Fine, fine, thank you Archibald. I saw on *Hello Britain* this morning that you have a bit of bother at the steel works. Nothing too serious I hope?'

'Never mind that Winton, I can handle a load of left wing communists hell bent of causing trouble, it's just a pity that your lily-livered Trade and Industry Secretary can't support us in our struggle for survival. They should rename the idiot the Minister for the Destruction of Industry, but I'm not here to talk about the shortcomings of the modern Conservative party. I'm here, my good fellow, to get an update on our little arrangement to destroy a certain Sydney Dresden Piffle.'

427

'Ah, I thought that might have been why you called,' said Winton defensively.

'Well it's good news old boy. I've spoken to Hazelhurst and he assures me that the girl is disrupting Piffle's operation significantly, and it's only a matter of time before the court cases start flooding in and the complaints to the Council, which will eventually overwhelm the blighter and finish his tawdry little operation.'

'Only a matter of time you say? Now you look here you buffoon, you get back onto your fellow Hazelhurst and tell him straight that I want results. I want that blasted Piffle dangling on the end of a meat hook begging for mercy. It's only when he is bankrupt and back in the gutter living on a park bench that I will be satisfied. No one, and I mean no one, gets the better of Archibald McGreggor III, do you understand me Winton, *old man*?' Archibald said the last two words dripping with sarcasm.

'Yes, yes, of course I understand. Feelings are running high, but you have my word that the girl is carrying out her instructions to the letter, and it won't be long now before we have ultimate success.'

'Glad to hear it, and when your Government gives me a grant to invest in my steel plant and make it state of the art, I might be a little more amenable towards you, do I make myself clear?'

'Perfectly, Archibald,'

'Good, I'm glad we understand each other. I will bid you good day,' and with that the telephone conversation ended with Archibald feeling he had pressed home his advantage and Winton feeling as ever drained after a run in with his so called friend

Chapter 81

Things had also been happening in the Wacker household that morning.

'Gary have you taken £20 quid out of my bingo jar?'

'No, not touched it,' said Gary at breakfast the next day.

'That's funny, I always keep a careful note of how much is in there and it's definitely twenty quid short.'

'No, not me.'

'Well the kids don't know about it, and the only new person in this house is our new cleaner, Mrs Neatgangs.'

'Do you think it's her then?'

'Dunno love, but it's gone.'

'I'm not having that, we pay her £60 quid a week anyway and I'm not having her nicking off us as well.'

'Well, we don't know for sure that she is.'

'Yeah, but it's a bloody coincidence love, and I don't like the way she comes in with no bra. It's very distracting, those two bouncing around whilst I'm having my breakfast, right puts me off my fried eggs and bacon.'

'Can we put one of your CCTV cameras in the kitchen and see if it is her?' said Tracy.

'Yeah suppose so. I can do it today before she arrives. It'll only take me 30 minutes and I can link it up to my lap top.'

'OK. I feel bad, but we need to know for sure if she is behind the missing money.'

Gary got to work setting up the CCTV before he went off to work at the factory in Hull – Mrs Neatgangs wasn't due till 9.00 a.m. Tracy Wacker was going out to the hairdresser for 10.00 a.m., so the trap was set to see if Mrs Neatgangs was the bingo thief.

Bianca went off to school and Callum was due in college at 9.00 a.m. for a rare double teaching slot in one of the theatre rooms.

Mrs Neatgangs didn't bother to knock, but just barged in at 8.45 for her three hours of cleaning. Tracy was in the kitchen having a cup of coffee and doing her nails before she went out to the hairdresser.

'Morning sweetie, my bloody backs killing me again. Anyone would think I'd been up to it all bleeding night, but no such luck.'

'Morning Mrs Neatgangs,' said Tracy trying to ignore the crude sexual inuendo.

'I could kill a cuppa before I start, Tracy. I only drink tea, never have liked coffee, I'll pop kettle on if that's OK?'

'That's fine Mrs Neatgangs, you help yourself,' said Tracy. She noticed, as usual, that Mrs Neatgangs was wearing one of her cheap white t-shirts with no bra and the offending items were bouncing around as usual.

Since they were alone, Tracy thought she would take her chance to bring up the delicate subject of Mrs N's bra, or rather the lack of one, which was only really a problem because of the sheer size of Mrs N's bosoms and especially given her age and lack of 'support' in vital areas.

'I have something to ask you Mrs N,' said Tracy. 'A little delicate, but as we are alone, women to women...'

Here we go, thought Mrs Neatgangs, Mrs Wacker's going to bring up the sex session with Callum and I'm for the high jump and then the chop. Damn I really need this job.

'What the feck is it sweetie?' said Mrs N trying to bluff her way out.

'Well, the thing is Mrs Neatgangs... the thing is, oh this is difficult.'

'Just spit it out sweetie, we're both women of the world and we both make mistakes. I mean us women have all got needs and it just happened.'

'What are you talking about Mrs N? Well anyway, the thing is, I'm concerned, no, we are concerned, me and Gary, that is, you keep coming here with no bra on. They are very large Mrs N, and they distract Gary while he's having his fried eggs and bacon, and I don't want Callum seeing them, especially at his age. He's a delicate lad, and those bosoms bouncing around aren't doing anyone any good.'

'Ah, I see what you mean sweetie. Well, thing is Tracy, I struggle to find a bra big enough, them being a double K or larger, and if I get a bra too small the strap digs into me back whilst I'm working. I find it so much more comfortable. I didn't know Gary noticed'

'My Gary is more than happy with me Mrs Neatgangs,' said Tracy blushing, 'and the thing is, they're a distraction to all concerned, including me, so if you can wear a bra, even if the straps dig into your back, so be it. Maybe you can put some foam or padding back there to stop it hurting, or you'll just have to have a fitting and have a special size made just for you, given your unique proportions. I'm surprised you can see what you are polishing or cleaning with them in the way.'

'OK Mrs Wacker, I'll find a way of containing them if it upsets Gary,' said Mrs N relieved that it wasn't the sex sessions with Callum that had been unearthed. 'But I've got used to me cleaning Mrs Wacker, haven't seen my feet in years though,' said Mrs N laughing out loud. 'Now where's that cup of tea, I'll sit myself down.'

Mrs Neatgangs sat down a good 18 inches from the table as the space between her and the table was taken up with the offending items. If she got any closer they would be resting on the table and Mrs N decided that that would upset Tracy even further and wasn't very lady like, though seeing as she wasn't a lady it didn't matter, but it did to Tracy Wacker and she wanted to keep her job.

'Anyway Mrs Neatgangs, I'll be getting going now. I'm going to the hairdresser and it takes me thirty minutes to get into Cottingham, especially with the traffic round Castle Hill Hospital. When you're finished let yourself out. Oh, I left your weeks wages on the side there in that envelope.'

'Oh I see it, sweetie. Thank you Mrs Wacker, I'll do that and have a good day won't you?'

Tracy was gone and Mrs Neatgangs finished her cup of PG Tips relieved that the conversation only consisted of concerns about her bosoms and not the more serious subject of sex with Callum Wacker.

Mike Morrell and Pauline Piffle had settled into their journey and the first course had arrived in the buffet car. Scottish Langoustines in a light batter served with homemade mayonnaise, a pea puree, slice of lemon and some homemade crusty bread and fresh butter, with a delicious bottle of expensive Italian white wine.

'This is absolutely delicious Mike. Thank you for a beautiful day it couldn't be better.'

'Ah it is grand that's for sure. I like to treat my girlfriend, and what better way than being on the Sir Nigel Gresley, one of the most romantic steam trains in the world, with a lovely three-course Michelin-star lunch?' beamed Mike. 'And the day hasn't finished yet.'

The main course arrived in the form of top-quality marbled fillet steak with a peppercorn cream sauce, sautéd potatoes and seasonal vegetables, with a bottle of Beaujolais to accompany the dish.

Then finally to the desert: homemade millionaire's shortbread with luxurious caramel creme filling, smothered in gooey dark chocolate with creme fraiche and almonds.

They were truly stuffed after such as sumptuous meal and as the Sir Nigel Gresley coasted into Whitby Station, Mike felt on top of the world. It was a hot, sunny day and they could indulge in some retail therapy, which might include buying Pauline some local jet or pearl jewellery. Maybe they could go on one of the many boat trips and find a local pub to finish off in before getting the train back to Pickering at 5.00 p.m.

Mrs Neatgangs finished her cleaning around 12.15 and left the Wacker's house to catch the bus back to the Gipsyville Estate with her £60 wages in the envelope that Mrs Wacker had left on the side. She was grateful that Mr and Mrs Wacker hadn't found out about her antics with Callum and her cleaning job was secure.

At 1.00 Callum returned home from his morning at college and immediately went to the bingo jar got it down and stole £10. Later on that day he would go round to Mrs Neatgangs council house to retrieve the other £10, have a sexual encounter with her, and be in a position to pay his siter Bianca over the weekend so that his secret would be kept safe – or so he thought.

All in all, things were working out nicely with this new arrangement, and in the background he still had Mrs Neatgangs' daughter, Olive, on the backburner so to speak, which he was sure might lead to yet more excitement but that was for the future. For now, he was very happy with his arrangement with Grandma Neatgangs, as he called her.

Mike Morrell and Pauline Piffle had a wonderful afternoon. They strolled through the myriad of shops in the old town and Mike bought Pauline a lovely pair of jet earrings set in solid silver. They then found a very quaint seventeenth century pub, complete with leaded windows and black exposed oak beams with a full range of real ales and quality spirits and cocktails. Mike had to restrain himself as he had already polished off the best part of a bottle of wine on the train, and was driving the Aston later, so he had to refrain from alcohol much to his annoyance, but Pauline had a gin and orange with crushed ice.

The Sir Nigel Gresley left Whitby at 5.00 p.m. and this time, without a meal, they were able to enjoy the fantastic scenery of North Yorkshire, including the village of Goathland where they used to film Heartbeat, and the Yorkshire moors before arriving back at Pickering around 6.30.

A spirited drive back in the Aston with the sun slowly going down saw them back at Pauline Piffle's house around 9.00 p.m., with Pauline, by this time, a little worse for wear and very light-headed. This time the garden was empty, and Jennings had finished long ago and gone back to his cosy apartment above the garage.

It was the end of a perfect day and now, for Mike, it was going to be a perfect night as Pauline invited him in for a night cap and the promise of her bed – the very four-poster bed she used to share with Sydney Dresden Piffle. Mike parked up his prized Aston Martin DB3, and together, hand in hand, they entered Pauline's house.

Earlier in the day Tracy had returned from the hairdressers and her husband Gary Wacker had left early from work given it was a Friday. He was in good spirits as the first ten log cabins had been completed in kit form and on Monday the huge lorries were coming to transport the various sections to Spain where his team would erect them for his friend Dresden Piffle. All in all, a great end to the week.

When he got home he immediately went into his study with Tracy and together they reviewed the CCTV footage expecting to find the thief in the form of the very rotund Mrs Neatgangs. To their surprise, she didn't go anywhere near the cupboards, or the cookie jar, but later on as the film ran its course, they were horrified to see their son, Callum, go to the jar and nick £10.

'The little bugger,' said Gary. 'It's not as if he doesn't get pocket money, and he doesn't lift a finger around this house. I'm going to have serious words with him.'

'I am very upset,' said Tracy, 'he wasn't brought up like that. Hold off until tomorrow will you? There must be some explanation why he wants that money.'

'OK, but only till tomorrow,' said Gary. 'But I'm keeping a close eye on that lad, he went out for hours the other day and I'm wondering if he's doing something stupid. Got in with the wrong crowd, or buying drugs.'

'Gary! Our Callum wouldn't do that,' said Tracy.

'Well if he goes out again, I'm going to follow him and see where he goes. I'm worried he's hiding something, and you can't be too careful these days. Drugs are everywhere, even with youngsters like our Callum.'

Gary Wacker didn't have to wait long. At teatime Callum made his excuses and said he was going out for a few hours and he left on foot. Gary waited a couple of minutes, jumped into his car and followed as best he could. This time Callum didn't cycle to the Gipsyville Estate but caught the bus, and Gary found himself following the number 11 bus.

It was only a five minute walk from the bus stop to Mrs Neatgangs house, Gary abandoned the car and followed on foot. From a safe distance he observed Callum going up to the front door of a semi-detached house and knocking on the door. He was too far away to see who answered it, but from a distance it looked like a woman of some considerable width, not a friend Callum's own age, that was for sure.

After about ten minutes no one had come out, so Gary sneaked up to the house and peered through the lounge window. He received the shock of his life, because there before him was the terrible vision of his naked son in a very imaginative position, with a completely naked Mrs Neatgangs – they were having sex over her sofa. Gary could not comprehend at first what he was looking at, until the penny dropped and the horror dawned, he realised his only son was in a sexual relationship with his cleaner Mrs Neatgangs.

Chapter 82

Sydney Dresden Piffle and Honolulu were getting ready in the master bedroom of the Villa Almeria that Friday evening. Paeleo was picking them up at 7.30 to go into Benidorm for diner to celebrate the fact that the first ten log cabins were arriving from England next week. Piffle was elated that a milestone was being reached.

'Come on Honolulu, shake a leg love. Paeleo will be here in thirty minutes, you women, you take forever.'

'You want me to look my best don't you Dresden? It is not often we go out on, as you say, the tiles.'

'If you call best paella restaurant in Benidorm the tiles, then I suppose so.'

Back in England, Inspector Fleece and Constable Brahmes weren't having such a pleasant evening. They were driving back down to London for the weekend after a completely fruitless week chasing around following Tandori and Jennings, looking for signs of ISIS terrorist activity without any success whatsoever. They had decided they needed to get away from the horrendous place and get back to civilization for a few, brief days. The plan wasn't going well, they were in bumper to bumper traffic at junction 21 near Leicester Forest East due to another predictable accident and the police's insistence, these days, of shutting the entire motorway down while they investigated for health and safety reasons. Eventually they would be sent on a detour via Nuneaton, a wild goose chase which only added to Fleece's misery. It would be midnight before they got home that night, so as usual, Inspector Fleece had made the wrong call.

Gary Wacker was in a state of shock. After observing the unbelievable liaison between his son and Mrs Neatgangs he was sitting in his car with his head in his hands only a few yards away from the scene of the crime. As he sat there, an even larger and uglier women, in cheap leggings and a leopard skin top, waddled across the road and, without knocking, let herself into Mrs Neatgangs' house. God it gets worse, thought Gary, it must be Mrs Neatgangs' daughter, Olive, who the old bag keeps whittering on about when she's doing the cleaning. Saying that after six kids by six different fellas she needs to find a good man.

On the evidence of Olive's looks and size, plus the grim reality of the Gipsyville Estate, it seemed highly unlikely that Olive would have any chance of finding a decent fella. What did seem more likely, to Gary's horror, was that his son was going to take part in some sort of disgusting sordid threesome with mother and daughter. They said it's always the quiet ones you have to watch and in Callum's case that was certainly true. The lad hardly left his room, had few friends and now this. How was he going to tell Tracy what was going on? And to make matters worse, he was probably nicking the money from the Bingo jar to pay for it!

He shuddered at the thought of anyone even remotely sane paying Mrs Neatgangs and her daughter for any form of sexual or perverted activity. He drove off at that point, wanting to be as far away from the crime as possible, and needing to tell his wife the news of her son's new found 'interests'.

It was just coming up to 7.00 and Honolulu was finally ready and on time for a change.

'Bloody hell Honolulu, you look a picture, that pink dress suits you no end,' enthused Piffle.

'You look good also Dresden in your Hawaiian shirt and chinos, it takes years off you.'

Soon they were in the back of the Silver Spur with Paeleo at the wheel as usual.

'How long before we get there Paeleo? I'm famished.'

'It is 15 minutes señor to the best paella restaurant in Benidorm, the Restaurante Aitana out in the mountains. Only the locals know it, not the tourists, you will like. They make paella traditional with chicken, and rabbit, as well as lobster and mussels. It is the best, you will see. I know the owner, Mintos, he has learned paella from his grandmother, is famous around here.'

'Sounds bloody splendid Paeleo. When you drop us off we'll be a few hours, so you can bugger off in the Rolls if you like, and see a few friends. As long as you pick us up at 11.00 we'll be fine. Don't want you hanging around in car all that time lad.'

It was a beautiful evening with the rays of the sun still strong and a perfect deep blue sky. The mountains were perfect, soon they passed a deep lagoon and continued through pretty villages with orange and lemon trees and bright red bushes at the side of the road. Piffle and Honolulu were in perfect comfort stretched out in the deep leather-clad seats of the Silver Spur, the air conditioning keeping them cool and the sophisticated air suspension supressing every bump and jolt from the poorly maintained roads. Piffle couldn't be happier, so much more enjoyable than being with the Clothes Horse back in Hull and a night down the Labour Club.

Olive opened the door to her mother's lounge and found Callum and her mother at it, with Mrs Neatgangs bent over the sofa. She wasn't the least bit shocked, she knew her mother of old and had plenty of similar experiences herself. Yes, she was her mother's daughter all right.

'Gunna save some for me mam?' Olive shouted, leering at the pair who hadn't spotted her.

'Bugger off Olive, can't you see I'm busy?'

'Thought Callum might want a threesome seeing as he's so randy tonight.'

Just to emphasise the point, Olive whipped off her leopard print top exposing her bra and stood there watching.

'You always want to share my men don't you? Well come on then, I suppose you don't get any very often these days.'

It was all the encouragement Olive needed, and in no time all three of them were on Mrs Neatgangs sofa naked and carrying on with all manner of sexual antics. It wasn't the first time Mrs Neatgangs and Olive had had a mother and daughter session, the last time being in Skegness at a holiday park a couple years ago.

Gary Wacker arrived home with a new insight into his son's perversions. Bloody hell, when he was 16 he had pin ups of Marilyn Monroe and the odd fumble behind the bike sheds. Not the unbelievable activities of his Callum. He was still trying to take in what he had seen.

As he entered the house he heard his wife shout. 'Well, did you see where Callum went with that tenner? He wasn't buying drugs, was he?'

'No, he wasn't buying drugs,' said Gary. He was doing something far worse, he thought. He decided to spare his wife all the gory details and just hint at the perversions he'd encountered.

'The thing is, he went to the Gipsyville Estate and is seeing a friend.'

'Oh that's OK then, except for my tenner.'

'The problem is, his new friend is Mrs Neatgangs, and from what

I can see they are more than just friends. I saw them having a snog,' said Gary, deciding to play down the situation whilst conveying some of the horror of their son fancying Mrs Neatgangs.

'Did you say Mrs Neatgangs? You mean our Mrs Neatgangs, the cleaner?'

'Afraid so, your son has got a crush on her.'

'A crush on Mrs Neatgangs? But she's 67 years old and as wide as she is tall. And let's be honest, looks likes she chews spanners for a hobby. Just kissing you say, nothing else?'

'Well, not when I was there, but who knows?'

'Oh God, my poor little Callum has been seduced by our cleaner and it sounds like he's paying her. I think I'd rather he was gay or bi-sexual, what on earth does he see in her? Apart from the obvious and her willingness to be with him.'

Tracy shuddered at the thought of her precious son being anywhere near Mrs Neatgangs, never mind what might be happening – which was far worse than even she could envisage.

'What on earth are we going to do?'

'Well I can hardly say I had followed him and caught him. I don't know, haven't any of your friends got daughters Callum's age? If you could introduce them, then maybe he would go off Mrs Neatgangs and find a lass more suitable, you know, his own age?'

'I can think of a couple of friends of mine with nice daughters, but in the meantime?'

'Well my love, in the meantime I think we leave best leave alone. He is nearly 17 and if he likes Mrs Neatgangs, however terrible that prospect, I think we just leave him to it. Even if we sack her, he'll still sneak off round there. We can't follow him and keep tabs on him all the time. It's probably just a phase, and if you introduce him to some attractive girls his own age then maybe he'll move on and go off Mrs Neatgangs. But we'll have a word with him about stealing money from the Bingo Jar. That's got to stop.'

'I don't like it Gary, it's not natural, especially for a boy of his age. By the way, I had a word with Mrs Neatgangs for you and told her to wear a bra when she comes here as it was putting you off your fried eggs and was a bad influence on our Callum. I think that's where all this unpleasantness started.'

'That's good Tracy, let's just play it by ear and see what happens in the coming weeks. Anyway, I'm going to crack open a beer and celebrate the fact that the factory has finished the first ten log cabins for Piffle. This is going to be the making of us Tracy.'

Play it by ear, thought Tracy, not a chance. One way or another she was going to warn off Mrs Neatgangs and make sure the horrendous old bag didn't go anywhere near her darling little Callum, but she wasn't going to tell her husband that!

Chapter 83

Paeleo dropped off señor Piffle and Honolulu at the Restaurante Aitana in the mountains. With the promise to return three and a half hours later, he headed into town in the Silver Spur. Señor Piffle must be in a good mood to allow him to use the Rolls for the evening, he thought, something he rarely did.

He thought he would take the opportunity to go and see Jimmy – The Fleece – Moston at the Go-Go Bar & Grill in the old town and catch up with his old buddy. It was always one of the livelier bars in town and it gave him the chance to find out how Jimmy was getting on planning the marketing campaign for the log cabins since he had a vested interest in the success of Jimmy's plan.

He arrived near the bar at 8.00 and parked round the corner in a safe location, he didn't want the Silver Spur damaged by drunken revellers from Jimmy's bar, which was notoriously rowdy later on once the pole dancers started.

Paeleo went up to the bar, ordered a San Miguel and asked the bar tender where Jimmy was.

'I am looking for Jimmy the bar owner'

'Who's asking my friend?' said the bar tender.

'I'm an old friend of Jimmy The Fleece.'

'OK, he's out the back, I will tell him you are here, your name please?'

'Paeleo.'

Jimmy came out from the back beaming and clasped the hand of his dear friend 'My friend Paeleo, how good to see you, come, come let us get a drink together.'

The Fleece clicked his fingers at Torin the bar tender. 'Get us a bottle of Petalos Del Bierzo red wine and two brandy chasers, and bring them to the table. Thank you Torin.'

'You like red wine and brandy Paeleo? It's the best we do.'

'Oh yes señor, I like very much, but must be careful, driving Piffle's Rolls Royce tonight.'

'OK we'll be careful. Anyway, how are you my old mucker? I didn't expect to see you this evening, you're usually busy with your boss. Bloody marvellous you've come down here to the Go-Go Bar to join me. I'll order us some food in a bit, you like fillet steaks Paeleo?'

'Oh yes señor, I am liking the filet steaks very much.'

'Good and the go-go girls will be starting at 9.00 doing their pole dancing moves. You like girls Paeleo? Then you have come to the right place.'

The drinks arrived promptly, and they clincked glasses

'Oh Torin, get us two medium rare fillet steaks with French fries and a Spanish salad, plenty of crusty bread and butter, my friend here needs a good nosh up.'

Torin went off to the kitchen to tell chef to prepare the food for the boss whilst Jimmy and Paeleo talked about the future.

'How's the log cabin site going Paeleo?'

'It is good señor. The site is ready for the first ten log cabins, which will be arriving next week and then they will be erected and fitted out. Within two weeks you can start the marketing campaign and bringing the clients to stay at the show site as agreed. They will sell easily with your skills.'

'Bloody brilliant Paeleo, can't wait. Well your boss has already paid me a down-payment to get started, so tell you what I'll do Paeleo, seeing as you've come down. We'll go to the safe and I'll give you your first €1000 commission for introducing this business to good old Jimmy. How does that sound my friend?'

'Oh, señor Jimmy, it is most generous of you to pay me a little up front. It is making me very very happy that we are doing business together.'

'That's not a problem Paeleo me old mucker. You scratch my

back and I'll scratch yours, that's how old Jimmy has always worked. Everyone has to get a little tickle don't they?'

Delicious steaks arrived with the chips, salad and half a loaf of freshly made bread and salted local butter and soon the two friends were tucking in.

'Can't beat steak and chips Paeleo, that's why I set up this place. Must have been all my trips to a Bernie Inn with me dad when I was growing up in the 60's.'

'Bernie Inn? What is this?'

'It was a chain of steak houses in Blightly in the 60s and 70s, very popular, but ours is a lot better Paeleo, classy just as your friend Jimmy likes it.'

'It is very good,' said Paeleo, 'the best.'

Over at the Restaurante Aitana, Piffle and Honolulu were having an equally good meal, the very best paella you could get in Benidorm and the surrounding area. The restaurant was set in the mountains surrounded by lemon and orange groves and was a white stucco building with a large terrace at the back looking over beautiful lush tropical gardens. Dotted around there were hundreds of coloured lights giving a magical ambiance to the place.

Piffle and Honolulu had chosen a secluded table on the terrace overlooking the gardens. The paella was being cooked outside on a large purpose made industrial sized BBQ, under a thatched canopy so diners could see their food being cooked from freshly prepared local ingredients.

'This is bloody marvellous Honolulu,' said Piffle.

'Who would have thought a working -class lad from the Gipsyville Estate would be sat out here with a beautiful, exotic girlfriend eating best bloody Paella, bottle of champers, dropped off by Rolls Royce and going back to lovely villa later. Wish me dad, Henry Herbert, was here to see this. All work that lad did on railways for a few crumbs off rich man's table. Well, now I'm rich and getting me own back on posh toffs that have exploited likes of us Honolulu.'

'It is very beautiful, I am so lucky,' said Honolulu not understanding half of what Piffle was saying about his father and the posh toffs that had done him an injustice.

'Another bottle of champers over here waiter,' shouted Piffle. He was beginning to enjoy himself and he was determined to have a damn good drink to celebrate the success of the log cabin enterprise.

The food arrived and it was delicious. Piffle liked his food and it didn't take him long to polish off the paella with salad and fresh bread.

'Eh up waiter, can we have seconds over here? That Paella was bloody lovely, but I could do with another plate full, how about you Honolulu?'

'No Dresden, one portion was enough for me.'

'Well Honolulu, spoke to Wack today and he tells me that first ten log cabins are on their way from Hull first thing Monday morning, so should be on site by Thursday and doesn't take long to put them up. Within a couple of weeks that guy Jimmy will start selling them for me. We're going to be in the money Honolulu, then I can sell Diversity Action Partnership and come over here full time, ditch the Clothes Horse and be with you my love.'

'Oh, I can't wait for that day Dresden. You back and forth to Pauline and that dreary Grimewold, it breaks my heart.'

'Won't be long love, six months and I will be here all the time with you at Villa Almeria.'

'Waiter, waiter, get us pudding menu, I'm ready for next course.'

The time went all too quick at the Go-Go Bar and Grill, and Paeleo had to leave at 11.00 to get back in time to pick up Piffle and Honolulu from the Restuarante Aitana and take them home.

'Here Paeleo, before you go my friend, here is that €1000 for you, me old mucker, as down payment for all you have done for me. Now drive carefully and look after Piffle, he's our meal ticket ,so you make sure the old bugger is OK.'

'I will señor, I will, and thank you for a great time. Good food, good company, the girls and this money, it is magnificante.'

'Don't you worry Paeleo, there is plenty more where that came from, you just keep helping Jimmy and I'll keep helping you.'

With that, Paeleo got back into the Silver Spur and headed back out of Benidorm into the mountains to pick up his master. It was cooler now, and the roads were quiet. It was amazing driving this beautiful motor car and, for once, Paelleo felt that he was in the right place at the right time to benefit from the connections he had carefully made. He was what the English called a 'middle man', the man who benefitted from information and contacts to make things happen.

When he arrived at the Resturante Aitana there was no sign of Piffle or Honolulu, so he parked the Rolls outside and went into find them. They were still on the terrace and Piffle was as pissed as could be from too many bottles of champagne and a few whisky chasers.

'Eh up Paeleo, Paeleo Paeleo, oh my friend is Paeleo do da do da day!'

It took a while to get Piffle and Honolulu, who was mercifully relatively sober, into the back of the Rolls and pay the bill, by which time it was 11.40.

'Right señor, now you are comfy we will get you both home to Villa Almeria.'

'No no no,' boomed Piffle, 'want Black Chicken, dance the night away, take us to Black Chicken.'

'You think that is wise señor? Don't you think bed would be best for you my friend?'

'Friend my arse, you just don't want to stay up Paeleo, listen you drive us there we have a little dance and come back, and I give you €500 bonus for staying up, how does that sound?'

'OK OK, señor Piffle, I do as you say.' Said Paeleo, thinking that another €500 would do nicely on top of the thousand that Jimmy had just given him.

'Gun it lad, gun it. Let's see if we can get to Black Chicken in fifteen minutes, faster lad faster.'

Paeleo accelerated as fast as he dared. It wasn't that the Rolls wasn't quick, 6.75 litres of engine capacity saw to that, it was that the twisty mountain roads were not so suited to the heavy cars suspension and handling that was designed for a more sedate form of progress. The tyres squealed on the hot tarmac as they sped round corners, but Paeleo valiantly made progress and within twenty minutes they were pulling up outside the Black Chicken night club on the strip in the centre of Benidorm.

'Give us an hour Paeleo, we'll be done by 2.00 a.m. Come on Honolulu, let's have a dance.'

Soon they were inside and had found a table. A waitress took their order for more wine. The owner was nowhere to be seen at this time of night so Piffle was not going to get the special treatment that he would have got earlier in the night, not that he noticed.

He heard a tune he recognised and was up off the table. 'Come on Honolulu, I like this one.'

He dragged her onto the dance floor, and they started to dance in each other's arms.

'Ra ra Rasputin Russia's famous love machine...' the Boney M song from the 1970s blared out from the speakers where the resident DJ was choosing a selection of dance tunes from the past.

There was then a selection of songs from an era that Piffle recognised more than the modern music of today, Abba's *Dancing Queen*, Tom Jones, The Boom Town Rats, Wham!, Culture Club, Duran Duran, Bananarama – the dance music from the past went on and on and Piffle, still drinking between tunes, got more and more clumsy.

The evening didn't end well for Piffle as he kept bumping into other dancers and loudly calling them bloody idiots, or worse. His final mistake was to career into a group of rowdy Scots who had had too much to drink themselves and spill some of their beers over their clothes.

'You clumsy bastard,' said one of the bigger lads. 'Look what you've done. I want an apology sonny, and I want some compensation for spilling our drinks €50 should do it.'

'I'm not bloody paying a dickhead like you €50,' boomed Piffle. 'Do you know who I am?'

'I don't know, and I don't care, pay up old man or you will regret it.'

Piffle responded by pushing the much younger and fitter

Scotsman, and a brawl ensued fairly rapidly with Piffle being pushed and punched to the ground. Luckily, the bouncers were on hand quickly to break the fight up and Piffle was dragged away with Honolulu screeching in obvious distress.

'What have they done to my poor Dresden?' she shrieked.

'Come on you trouble makers, get out of this club, you're not welcome here,' shouted one of the bouncers.

Piffle and Honolulu were thrown out of the Black Chicken and luckily Paeleo was waiting outside in the Rolls.

'My Dresden has got into terrible fight Paeleo, get him in the car and take us home, please, please.'

'Yes yes, of course, come lets getting him into the back of the Rolls.'

'Ra ra Rasputin, Russia's famous love machine,' slurred Piffle as he staggered to the car.

It was quite an effort to get Piffle into the Rolls and his nose was bleeding from a blow that one of the Scots had landed, but as far as Piffle was concerned it was all forgotten.

'Ra ra Rasputin Russia's famous love machine,' was what Piffle continued to sing all the way home. When they reached the Villa Almeria Paeleo and Honolulu managed to manhandle Piffle into bed.

They had certainly had a night to remember, and Paeleo was

left with the feeling that he had certainly earned his extra €500, as well as his other bonus from Jimmy The Fleece that night. It was past 2.00 a.m. when Paeleo finally got home and got himself to bed. He had driven the Silver Spur back through the mountains to his apartment on the outskirts of Benidorm about 20 minutes from Piffle's villa. He put the local night-time radio station on that played music more appropriate to the time of night. He particularly liked hearing the dulcet tones of Sade as he sped along the mountain roads.

'No need to ask. He's a smooth operator, smooth operator, smooth operator. Coast to coast into to Chicago, west of Maine. Across the north and south to key largo...' Perfect music to relax him after the stress of getting Piffle back home and into bed. Yes, he, Paeleo, earned his extra euros with a demanding boss like Sydney Dresden Piffle.

Chapter 84

It was Monday morning and Gordon Streake found himself outside Lord Brett Sinclair's house on the Cromwell Estate at 5.15 a.m. They were making an early start to travel down to London and miss the traffic. As expected, Brett was late coming out as he was certainly not used to being up at this time in the morning, but they had work to do and Streake wanted to make a good start and miss some of the Monday morning traffic. It would be bad enough reaching the outskirts of the capital around rush hour, but at least they could get to their digs for the week and then go and stake out Bradly Plumb's house and start tracking his movements.

Streake was getting impatient now, where the bloody hell was he? He phoned Lord Brett's mobile again, but it just went to answer phone. Eventually, Brett staggered out of his girlfriend's house at 5.40, twenty-five minutes late and got into the car.

'Where the bloody hell have you been Brett? I told you 5.15 and

I'm not going to be screwed around by you all week, do I make myself clear?'

'Hey, cool it man. I was just saying goodbye to my woman, we've got plenty of time to get down to the big smoke and sort this Plumb guy out. I had to get the gear out as well and hide it in my bag, see I got it here man.'

'You make sure you have Brett, and no more cock ups this week, do you understand? I want this to go as smooth as a baby's arse, with no complications. And remember, do as I say and nothing more. You'll make plenty of money out of this one Brett, selling your gear to our Braders and his druggy mates, and I'll get exactly what I want for my client.'

It didn't take long for the Vauxhall Vectra to be on the motorway heading south, first on the M18 and finally joining the M1 just south of Sheffield. At this rate of progress, they should get to their digs about 10.30, allowing a stop for breakfast on route.

Gary Wacker was also up very early that Monday morning. He was at the factory for 4.30 a.m. to oversee the loading of the log cabin sections onto the five huge arctic trucks that would be taking them down to Benidorm. The crew erecting the cabins were flying out from Doncaster Robin Hood airport later that morning, but for now, he was there to make sure his team and the truckers were loading all the sections correctly.

It took a good 3 hours for that process to be completed, and at

8.00 a.m. he was glad to wave the trucks off out of his factory and off to Hull Docks to catch the ferry, which was the start of their four-day journey to Piffle's site in Benidorm.

'That's a job well done, Paul,' said Gary to his works foreman. 'I can't believe we turned all ten log cabins round in just five weeks, and now they're on their way to Benidorm. First time any of our cabins have been erected abroad and we've been paid for the job up front.'

'Well Mr Wacker, it's the first of many. Just four hundred and ninety log cabins to go over the next two years. The lads are made up that we've got full order books for the first time in a long time, and Dresden Piffle is a good man, I've known him years from him popping into the Gipsyville Labour club, he's one of us Gary.'

'He certainly is, I've known him years as well, always been a good friend to me and Tracy.'

Gordon Streake was already tiring of the juvenile pea brained arsehole that was Lord Brett Sinclair. He was fairly sure Brett was already high on coke as the moron couldn't keep still or shut up even for a few minutes.

'Stop fiddling with my bloody radio Brett, in fact turn the thing off.'

'I'm just trying to find some tunes man, not this old man shit that you've got tuned in,' said Brett, who then turned the volume right up to 28 just to annoy Streake.

'Turn that bastard down or I'll stop and make you.'

'Ooooh! Who got out of bed the wrong way? Streakey, Streakey, Steakey is a wanker! Do you want some coke? It might calm you down Streakey. Go on, be a real man, do you good getting into drugs, everybody's doing it man. I'll give you a wrap for free, get you started.'

'Shut the fuck up Brett. I don't need a prick like you going on and on all the way to London. We're here to do a job, get it done, get paid and then go our separate ways. And take your bloody feet off my dashboard, and sit up straight. It's like dealing with a bleeding six-year-old!'

Back in Grimewold, the Iron and Steel Workers' Union were starting their first strike since the major stoppages of 1981. All 5,000 of McGreggors' steel workers had come out and were manning picket lines outside of the various plant entrances demanding the reinstatement of pay and bonuses. For the first time in decades the national press and London based TV networks had come to Grimewold to report on the strike and interview strikers and management.

Archibald McGreggor hadn't felt so alive in years. He was just about to give a speech to two of the top political journalists from ITN and SKY news outside his house. He had set up a lectern in front of his double oak front door with the McGreggor logo taking up the front panel and two Union Jack flags either side of to give his 'presidential' speech and then field questions. He had purposely excluded the communists from the BBC who he had no intention of including in his PR machine. He knew they would be furious, but they hated him anyway so this was his way at getting his own back.

Archibald emerged from his front door with June by his side. He was wearing a three-piece suit which must have been 50 years old, a gold pocket watch and a top hat, which made him look like a city gent from the past. He had considered his grandfather's stovepipe hat but that would have made him look like Isambard Kingdom Brunel and even he felt it to be too theatrical for the image he wanted to convey.

He approached the lectern with a serious and stern look and started speaking.

'Good morning ladies and gentleman. Today we face a very grave situation here at McGreggor's Steel. We are facing a fight for our very survival and the survival of the largest steel rolling mill in the whole of Europe. May I remind you that this great country of Great Britain used to be the fourth largest steel producer in the world as recently as 1971, but successive incompetence by the trade union communists, and various governments over the last fifty years, have seen us come to this. We at McGreggor's have been undermined by red China dumping steel onto world markets, and countries like India using child labour with minimal health and safety legislation in place, meaning they undercut us at every turn.

My great-grandfather would be turning in his grave if he saw how this backbone of the Great British economy had been laid low by the failure of government and unions to stand up for British workers' rights and their jobs. Due to our inability to source quality iron ore at this time we have had to make drastic production cuts, and this has impacted on our workforce, who have regrettably decided to call a strike. Well, let me tell you in no uncertain terms that if Barraclough doesn't call off this strike and if the government fails to support us with a £200 million loan to re-core the blast furnaces then I, as Chairman of McGreggor's Steel will have no choice, I say it again, no choice, but to sack 75% of the workforce and cut production accordingly. We have, ladies and gentleman, limited time, but my management team and I are here working night and day to resolve this damaging strike and are open to any sensible suggestions from the union. But let's be clear, I am not prepared to give into blackmail, and if communists like Barraclough think I am, then he is very much mistaken. Thank you. Any questions?'

'When are you meeting with the trades unions and are there any signs of compromise?' asked Tom from ITN.

'Well Tom, my management team, led by our Plant Director Curtis Googleheimer, are planning talks with the trades unions later in the week, but no there are no signs of compromise at this stage. It is very difficult to deal with communists who have an ideological agenda.'

'What does the Minister for Trade and Industry think of this and are they helping?' asked Holly from Sky News.

'Well my dear,' said Archibald, using the term my dear to annoy the bitch, 'we have had no contact with any Government Ministers at this stage, and frankly on past performance we are not hopeful that this Conservative Government will be in any way constructive. But if this site closes, it will be a tragedy and this Conservative Government will have blood on its hands for helping to decimate one of our most important and strategic industries and allowing Red China to succeed. I am sorry ladies and Gentlemen, I have important work today,' and with that Archibald left the lectern and swept back into the house with June. The lop sided grin reasserting itself.

'I think that went rather well June,' said Archibald. 'Coffee and biscuits in my office please.'

'Right away Archibald.'

Finally, after six hours of interminable ear ache from Lord Brett Sinclair, they arrived at their digs for the week – two rooms in a seedy motel out towards Dagenham. Streake had considered a flat booked through Airbnb but decided that he couldn't stand a week of Brett, not for any amount of money, so this dump would have to do.

'Thought we might have been staying in a nice hotel,' moaned Brett.

'My budget doesn't stretch that far Brett, we're here to make money, not spend it.'

They went to the reception, which was no better than the rest of the motel, and an old man in a dirty threadbare maroon jumper came out and scowled at them.

'What do you two want?'

'We have two rooms booked here for the week under the name of Streake.'

'Oh yes, got them here. It's payment up front mind, £50 quid a night each for seven nights, that's seven hundred quid, prefer cash if you've got it.'

'Cash is fine,' said Streake, 'it's all here in this brown envelope, count it if you like.'

'I will sonny, can't be too careful.'

Streake would rather pay by cash, although it was remote he didn't want his stay in London traced especially with a known drugs dealer. The last thing he needed was complications.

'Come on Brett, let's get settled in, and I don't want you telling anyone where you are. Understand? Even that slapper of a girlfriend. Here, I've got a sandwich for you and a packet of crisps. We'll meet up later and go into town.'

'Where we heading?' said Brett.

'We're heading to one of Bradley Plumb's haunts. I've done my homework see, in advance, and you my friend need to make contact with the mark and befriend him. Maybe offer him a little free gear as a taster, and I'll be watching you from a safe distance, so keep to the bleeding script.'

'OK, you're the boss. I'm gonna get some kip, not used to getting up a 4.30 a.m.'

'OK, we meet up at 6.00 p.m. sharp and then head into the city.'

They went their separate ways, a plan of sorts already formulated in Streake's mind. This was it, his passport to a place in the sun and away from Grimewold for good. He just had to make sure that Lord Brett Sinclair didn't balls it up for him.

Chapter 85

Mike Morrell had had a brilliant weekend with his beloved Pauline. This was the week that his new Clean Air Champions would be starting their work at every major junction in Grimewold, including the twenty new recruits that he had taken on from Piffle's organisation.

Traffic flows would be reduced because of the major strike at McGreggor's Steel with less people travelling into work and no lorry movements in or out of the giant steel works, but that was to the good because his new staff needed to learn on the job and what better way than if the roads were quieter than usual?

To make his Clean Air Champions stand out he had given them lime green jumpsuits with the words *Saving the Planet* emblazoned on the back so that no one could miss them, or their intent. He had them working in pairs so that the inevitable altercations with irate members of the public could be handled more effectively. The fines had been set at £500 per car, van or lorry that transgressed, raising to £1000 if the fine wasn't paid by direct debit over the phone with 14 days. It was estimated that at least 40% of vehicles would fail the emissions test and be subject to a fine, thus making him, and Grimewold Council, many millions of additional revenue a year. And all for the good cause of saving the long-suffering residents of Grimewold from harmful particulate emissions.

The fact that the closure of McGreggor's steel and the three huge blast furnaces whilst the strike was on was lost on Mike Morrell. The harsh fact was, that with the steel plant running Grimewold was the most highly polluted town in the whole of the UK, regardless of vehicle movements, but saving the planet was as much about virtue signalling as it was the realities of the situation. Mike Morrell liked the idea of being virtuous, and very rich, and could see no problem with the two concepts going hand in hand.

Mike had a busy morning ahead. Firstly he had an interview with the Grimewold Gazette about the launch of the Grimewold Clean Air initiative and the recruitment of the ex-Diversity Action employees, putting himself in a good light and Piffle's organisation in a bad light. Afterwards he was going to chair the weekly management meeting with his senior management team.

'Mike, Ms Sally Beckett from the Gazette is here to see you.'

'Send her up Janice, I'm expecting her.'

'Come in Sally, pleased to meet you,' said Mike extending his hand.

'Sorry, don't do handshakes, very last century and unhygienic,' said Ms Beckett, clearly aiming to put Mike off guard.

'Whatever you say Ms Beckett. Anyway, let's get down to business,' said Mike reverting to the more formal way of addressing her.' We have a right one here thought Mike Morrell privately.

'Right then Mr Morrell, why did you decide to employ the strikers outside the Diversity Action Partnership who they had sacked only last week in, shall we say, in controversial circumstances?'

'Well, I don't want to, in any way, second guess the motives of The Diversity Action Partnership and Mr Sydney Dresden Piffle the owner of the business, but I felt that it was grossly unfair that many of his hard working staff, who had been with him from the outset, were suddenly and without warning cast adrift, with little chance of getting another well-paid job given their advancing years and experience. I wanted to do what I could and saw a fit with our organisation, what with us winning the Clean Air Contract'.

'You don't strike me as the sort of man who takes pity on people Mr Morrell, more the hard-headed businessman.'

'Looks can be deceptive Ms Beckett, and we did see a fit with the skills of those displaced workers, who Piffle so callously let go at short notice, and our needs as a growing organisation.'

'Let's move onto those needs Mr Morrell. The Speed Camera Action! Limited has grown hugely since it won the contract, and now you have won another contract for monitoring the air quality in town. You seem to be very well connected to the council, winning these lucrative contracts?'

'You're right that we have been hugely successful in reducing speed on the roads of Humberwold, and in doing so we have saved countless lives and prevented terrible injuries that would otherwise have taken place. I know for a fact that many mothers and fathers are grateful for the work that we do. I am humbled by some of the letters of support we receive here at Speed Camera Action! and we have issued more fines than any other comparable county in the country. That is down to our diligent staff, and the revolutionary pensioner teams we have introduced in many of the villages in Humberwold. Local pensioners take ownership of catching reckless speedsters in their communities. It gives them a purpose in life.'

'You've not really answered my question Mr Morrell, about being well connected within Grimewold Council?'

'That is unfair Ms Beckett, I have to say. Yes, we have just won the Clean Air Contract, against very stiff opposition I might add, but that is because of our success with the Speed Camera Contract, and remember,' said Mike wagging his finger at her, 'making this contract work for the council and us isn't a walk in the park. We have made a substantial investment in capital equipment, manpower recruitment and training that we have to get back. It is a significant risk for us, but as Managing Director, Ms Beckett, I am immensely proud of our staff and the opportunity we have to serve this community in the best way we can. I am humbled to be a servant of the people, and I look forward to the day when the people of Grimewold have fresh, clean air to breath for their children and grandchildren, and this Clean Air Contract is the start of that process.'

'Sounds like you're a saint Mr Morrell,' quipped Sally.

'I like to think that I do my bit. So yes, we are connected to the council, but only in a spirit of partnership and cooperation. Private sector management skills and expertise working in harmony with the vision and care for the community that this council undoubtedly has for the residents of this great town.'

'Well, I think that just about wraps it up Mr Morrell, I have enough to run a piece in the Gazette later this week.'

'When will the article be coming out Ms Beckett?'

'We're looking at Friday evening. Though obviously with the strike going on at McGreggor's that story takes precedent at the moment, but I hope to get you on the inside page and maybe a piece in our business section. It's a story that will be of interest to our readers and of course it affects their lives every day.'

'Thank you for coming by Ms Beckett, a pleasure to meet you.' Mike gave one of his winning grins but made sure he didn't offer his hand again. He had met feminists like Beckett before and knew how their minds worked. Let her think she had got the better of him, it was a small price to pay for good public relations and the profile he was trying to build for his company.

Inspector Fleece and Constable Brahmes were still in London and had not travelled back up to Grimewold to continue their fruitless stakeout of Tandori Birkett-Morris and Anthony Jennings. Fleece's boss, Chief Inspector Ridgeway, had put a spanner in the works and summoned Fleece to a meeting in his office.

'Ah, Inspector Fleece, thank you for making the time to see me this morning.'

'Not a problem,' said Fleece, suspicious of his boss's motives.

'Thing is Fleece, and I won't beat about the bush, I'm pulling you off the Birkett-Morris case. The fact of the matter is that there is no evidence at all linking her, or Jennings, to an ISIS terrorist cell and the set of events surrounding the railway carriage were just a coincidence. Same with the block of flats she was involved with destroying, just circumstantial evidence.'

'You're making a big mistake, I know in my bones that that bitch is as guilty as hell.'

'Now look Fleece, I have been a patient man, and so has the Commissioner, given the gravity of potential terrorist activity in this country, but the harsh reality is that there is no evidence to support your wild vendetta against Birkett-Morris. So, with police resources limited, I am calling a halt to this line of enquiry unless any new evidence comes to light. Do you understand me Fleece?'

'But—'

'No buts Fleece, you work well with Constable Brahmes, so I'm teaming you up with her. There was a stabbing over the weekend in

New Malden, so I want you and Brahmes to go and investigate that, could be gang related. We appreciate you've done your best, gone above and beyond with the Birkett-Morris case, but my hands are tied. The Commissioner wants this one buried. It's an embarrassment to the force that after building up expectations in the press and with the Home Secretary, nothing has come of it. So there we have it Fleece. Now run along and tell Brahmes the good news.'

Fleece left the Chief Inspector's office in a foul mood and immediately found Brahmes. 'We've been pulled off the Birkett-Morris case Brahmes, by that useless new Commissioner Dick of Dock Green. The terrorist conniving bitch, Birkett-Morris has got away with it. Get me a Nescafe pet, and we will discuss where we go from here. I'll see you in the staff canteen in five minutes.'

'Right you are sir, and I'm sorry,' said Brahmes, genuinely upset for her superior officer who she had grown to respect in the weeks they had worked together.

Mike Morrell swept into the board room of the Speed camera Action! Limited, with Janice his secretary and surveyed his senior management team. It was time to step up a gear now that the firm had won the Clean Air Contract from Grimewold Council.

'Morning team,' Mike boomed.

'Morning Mike,' they all said in unison.

'Coffee and buns on the way Janice?'

'Yes Mike, I ordered them in this morning, they should be here shortly.'

'Good, good. Well, let's get started team. The first thing I want to say is, well done. We have formally been awarded the Clean Air Contract by the council. The signed contract came through last week. I know it was a formality, but very well done. We were up against very stiff competition from the American's who are winning bids all over the country, but we convinced the council that we could handle a contract of this size and that we had the resources and local expertise to generate the best return for them in terms of fines and prosecutions.'

'Emily, from a finance perspective, have you done a financial analysis of the implications of this contract for us over the next 12 months? And if so, can you share that with the team please?'

'I have done a financial analysis Mike,' said Emily Sanders the Finance Manager. 'Of course it all depends if we hit our targets for the number of motorists we can fine for non-compliance, but if we can have twenty Clean Air Champions out at any one time at all the major road intersections, then we should be able to send out 200 fines a day at £500 a fine. That should generate approximately £25 million a year in fine income, of which we get 40%. So our revenue should rise by £10 million a year with estimated staff and capital costs of £900,000, meaning a gross profit to us of £9 million give or take. Which basically doubles the profits of Humberwold Speed Camera Action! Limited to £20 million a year. I've got it all in this report.' Emily handed out copies of the report to the other five people round the table.

'Great work Emily. Those figures are very encouraging providing the Clean Air Champions hit their targets. On that subject Paul, how have the Clean Air Champions performed since the back end of last week when they started?'

'Well Mike, they have got off to a good start. We've been training the new recruits from Diversity Action, so we're not up to full capacity, but we have issued 102 fines since Thursday. That equates to £51,000 of which we get £20,250 income, so I'm pleased with that.'

'OK Paul, I'm happy with that, but we need to build to 100 fines a day this month, and then next month the 200 fines a day which Emily has forecast, do you understand? And what about the Pure Profit Teams on the speeding fines side of the business? I hope you haven't let me down again,' said Mike Morrell pointedly.

'Well,' said Paul defensively, 'as I said before, it's difficult to recruit volunteers, but we are up to 74 teams now out of the 100 you wanted. It's a work in progress Mike, but those 74 are hitting their targets.'

Paul was concerned that Mike was going to explode like he did last time, but he was in a much better and more conciliatory mood.

'Very good Paul, well done, it's good to see that we are moving in the right direction. Before we wrap up, I just want to update you on the new recruits. You've probably heard that we have recruited the twenty ex-employees from Piffle's organisation who had been on strike after that Bindle woman sacked them. I thought it was a good PR coup for us and it keeps us in with the council and also helps keep the press on side. I was interviewed by someone from the Gazette this morning about the new recruits and us winning the Clean Air Contract and I'm assured a piece is coming out on Friday, which should be very positive. So just to warn you, I don't want any of you speaking to the press about this. Any questions you come to me through Janice. Do you understand?'

They all nodded in unison.

'Good, then we can wrap this meeting up until next Monday, well done team.'

They all went to file out, but Mike asked his right hand man and 'fixer,' John Harper to stay back for a private chat.

'John, have you got a minute please?'

'Yes, Mike what can I do for you?'

'Remember our conversation at the last meeting? Just seeing if you've found out anything that might influence our chances of taking the contract off the Diversity Action Partnership and incorporating it into our organisation? I really want to see if we can win that one off Piffle.'

'I've been asking around and the council are very happy with how they're performing and see no reason to change horses Mike. There are strict continuity clauses, so they would have to have compelling reasons to offer the contract to someone else, otherwise Piffle could sue them. And from my enquires they are actually ahead of target in terms of the fine income they are generating, especially since that new woman joined, Tandori Birkett-Morris, so I've had no luck in getting us any further.'

'I see. That's very disappointing, keep working on it and digging for any dirt on Piffle. There must be something, no one is squeaky clean, and I'm sure we can get something on him if we dig deep enough.'

'Will do Mike.'

'I need results John. Oh, and John, another thing, can you find the best portrait artist in the country who could do a portrait of me to go up in our reception? I want a huge oil painting of me for the staff to look up to as they come into the building. Something classy, with me in a tuxedo like James Bond with the five missions of the business, *Vision, Belief, Hard work, Delivery and Victory*, that's what I want to see in our reception. I want it up there in the next four weeks, and John, I don't want one of these new-age wankers who think a pile of bricks with a dog turd on top is art. I want a good one, like the Queen uses.'

'OK Mike, I'm on it. I'll find you someone by the end of the week. What's your budget?'

'I don't give a toss about the budget, I just want a good one that will be worth a few bob when it's finished, and I want it to make me look suave and debonair like James Bond. You know, a bit of poetic license, improve what's already there as they say. Come on Janice, lets go back to my office and see what the afternoon brings.'

Mike was up and out of the board room striding towards his office with his secretary Janice trying to keep up, a man on a mission, the Managing Director of The Speed Camera Action! Limited.

Chapter 86

Whilst Lord Brett was asleep, Gordon Streake used his time wisely. He made detailed plans for how Brett was going to make contact with Bradley Plumb and get into his inner circle for long enough to supply him with some gear, and for Streake to get the photographic evidence to satisfy himself and his client. The time passed quickly and before long it was 6.00 p.m. Streake left his dingy hotel room and walked along the corridor to Brett's room, banging the door loudly. As he suspected, Brett was still in bed and not at all ready.

'Open the bloody door Brett, we need to get going,' shouted Streake.

'Piss off, I ain't ready, arsehole.'

Streake banged the door again in frustration. 'Well get your arse in gear you useless prick, we've got work to do.'

'Alright, alright, give us ten minutes and I'll be out. It ain't that important, it's only six o'clock, take a fucking chill pill, twat.'

'I'll be down at the car, so you've got ten minutes and then one way or another I'll break this door down and drag you out myself.'

Streake went down to the Vectra in a foul mood. Whatever he earned from this little number he certainly deserved, dealing with tossers like Brett. Eventually, a dishevelled Brett appeared and got into the car.

'About bloody time Brett, have you got the gear on you?'

'Got enough to tempt Plumb, yeah. You get me in there and I'll sort the prick.'

They finally set off around 6.45 and soon hit the M25 heading into town. The traffic was fairly light as most commuters were coming out of London the other way. It took them just under an hour to reach the club Bradley Plumb frequented. It was called *Careless Whisper*, not far from Television Centre where his Friday night programme was filmed. Streake had already done his homework and gleaned the important fact that Plumb went there most nights after having dinner out with Lemar at a trendy restaurant. It was the best place for Brett to make his acquaintance and offer him some gear because it held the prospect of anonymity, relative darkness and privacy, unlike a restaurant.

Brett was well used to concealing gear, especially the small quality that he was smuggling into the club, and Streake was banking on slipping the doorman £200 to confirm his entry into the exclusive club, with the promise of more on other nights as they required. It was all coming out of expenses anyway and had to be done right. The club didn't open till 9.00 p.m. and Bradley Plumb was unlikely to get there much before 10.00 p.m., so they had an hour to kill before they approached the bouncer on the door.

Streake spotted a traditional London pub opposite called *The Mallard*. With the Vectra safely parked up the street they headed for the pub to have a drink and discuss the finer details of the plan.

'What do you want to drink Brett?' said Streake.

'I'll have a larger, Carling if they've got it, if not Fosters.'

The pub was an old-fashioned typical London pub, gloomy inside with a long dark wood bar and booths against the walls for privacy. Brett selected one of them whilst Streake got the drinks in.

'Here you are,' said Streake sitting down.

'Right the plan is as follows. I'll get you into the club around 9.30, and I'll text you when I see Plumb arrive so you can look out for him. Here, I've got a picture of him to remind you what he looks like, though I'm sure it's the sort of crap you watch on TV anyway, so you probably know what he looks like. He will almost certainly be with his black lover Lemar, and possibly his assistant, Tiggy. You won't be able to miss them, the prick likes showing off by all accounts. Try and sit near him and let him get used to you being around, and as they get pissed make your move. Start with some small talk and then ask him if he fancies some good quality gear and slip him a wrap for free. Tell him you can get him more and that you'll see him in the club later in the week. Slowly slowly, catchy monkey, as they say. The aim of tonight is just to get to know him and make him feel comfortable. Trust is everything. You got it?'

'Yeah man, I can handle that,' said Brett, 'but what if he don't want to talk to me?'

'Oh, he will once he realises you've some quality gear for him. You're just his type Brett.'

Soon it was 9.30 and time to go. They approached the exclusive *Careless Whisper* club and were immediately barred by the bouncer from entering.

'Not tonight gentleman,' said the bouncer, 'celebrities and guests only I'm afraid, and you two chancers are neither.'

'A quick word if I may,' said Streake. 'My friend here wants to sample the delights of the club, not me, just him. How about I slip you a hundred quid and you overlook your strict policy and let him in. He won't be any trouble, just wants a quiet drink.'

'No, sorry, I can't do that.'

'Well what can I do to persuade you? He's come a long way to see this club, and it would be a shame if he couldn't visit. If he likes it he'll be back again later in the week.'

'Give me three hundred quid and I can let him in, but only him, if you want to come in it'll be more.'

'I've got £250 on me that's it,' said Streake used to negotiating

,but also not wanting to seem too desperate.

'OK, £250 it is then, but any trouble and he'll be straight out and won't be allowed back in again.'

'Off you go Brett, I'll sort this gentleman out.' So as Brett entered the club, Streake pulled out a wad of notes already totalling £250 and handed it to the bouncer.

'Pleasure doing business with you, what's your name?' said Streake.

'Todd, me names Todd, and if you want to get in again ask for me. I'm on most nights except Sunday.'

'Thanks Todd, I'll make sure I deal with you.'

Streake went back across the road to the *Mallard* where he would wait for Brett to emerge later on in the evening. Stage one was accomplished, and Streake was very pleased with himself.

Now for the hard part of the operation, making contact with Bradley Plumb and gaining his confidence. He didn't like jobs where he had to rely on others, especially twats like Brett, but in this case he had no choice. He couldn't risk handling drugs himself and needed someone credible to supply the gear to Bradley. This was the only way the plan was going to work. He ordered another pint of bitter and waited. Everything was out of his hands now.

Chapter 87

As predicted, a large black Maybach limousine pulled up outside the famous gay club, *Careless Whisper*. From his vantage point in the pub, Streake saw Bradley's assistant Tiggy get out of the car, followed by his lover Lemar, and then finally Bradley Plumb himself. Plumb wore his trademark long purple velvet coat, and Tiggy dropped purple petals in front of him, which was another trademark in case there were any paparazzi around to take photos. He had dark tinted shades on as well to complete the effect. Without any questions asked, Todd, the bouncer who Streake had been talking too earlier, opened the door to the club and let the entourage through.

Lord Brett Sinclair was sat at the bar waiting for Bradley Plumb to appear, his mean little eyes darting around scanning the club for signs of his mark entering. It wasn't long before he spotted Bradley Plumb, Tiggy, his assistant, and Lemar enter the club and go to one of the large smoked glass tables near the back, well away from the dance floor. It was 10.30 right on cue.

A drinks waiter came over to them almost straight away and Plumb ordered some cocktails and champagne for them all. He was celebrating because his agent had phoned him over the weekend and said he was possibly in line for a new reality TV show called *Date in the Sun*, which worked on the principal of young women choosing a date based only on seeing twenty-five naked penises behind a screen. The twelve lucky partners would then spend a month at a resort called *The Love Shack* in Ibiza where they would be filmed live every night for an hour and undertake various stupid tasks giving them the opportunity to swap partners based upon their experiences.

As he was so popular hosting *Purple Haze* he was in the running to host this new flagship show, but he was up against a mouthy female called Poppy Minx, real name Alice Fenton-James, daughter of a multi-millionaire City Financier, Jacob Fenton-James, who had made a name for herself fronting similar reality trash shows after she had graduated with a first in Political Science from Cambridge. The yearly fee was two million quid, so Plumb was hoping he would land it. On top of the £2.5 million he got for *Purple Haze* it would make him one of the highest grossing celebrities on the circuit. Not bad for someone with zero talent, but he had the ability to 'get down with the kids' as far as the television executives were concerned, helped by his racy reputation as a gay man who liked booze, parties and drugs.

Lord Brett ordered another pint of larger. They didn't sell Carling or Fosters so he had to have some fancy German bottled premium beer at £6 a pop. Never mind, Streake was paying his bar bill tonight.

He let them settle in, then he went over and sat at the smoked glass table next to Bradley Plumb's little group. All he had to do now was bide his time and look for an opportunity to make contact. He didn't have to wait too long.

With the dance floor filling up Tiggy went for a dance, and Lemar disappeared out onto the terrace at the back of the building for a smoke, leaving Bradley Plumb alone drinking champagne. Now was his chance.

'Hey man, how you doing? Ain't I seen you on the telly, Bradley Plumb isn't it? said Brett.

'Yeah I'm Bradley Plumb, just enjoying the booze and the tunes, like to relax after the stress man.'

'Like your show, it's proper shit man, makes me piss myself.'

'Glad you like it.'

'You want a little gear? I've got some grade A shit here for us, share and share alike?'

'Supposed to go out on the terrace man, but hey it's pitch dark here, thanks I'll take a piece of the action, banging man.'

Bradley Plumb had taken the bait and Lord Brett had given him the best coke that he could get hold of in the hope of reeling him in.

'Hey, this is shit hot man. Can you get me more of this gear? I'm running a little low and my usual guy has fucked off to Marbella for a few weeks.'

'No problemo Bradley. I'll see you back here Thursday night at the same table.'

'That's cool man, really grateful, what's your name?'

'Brett, I can get you whatever you want Braders. You just ask, and I can supply.'

'Now listen Brett, I'm very careful about my privacy, but here have my card, it's got my personal mobile number on it, just so that we can keep in touch. You know, in case things change.'

With the initial contact made and Brett's sweetener, he backed off as Lemar and Tiggy soon returned and Plumb was otherwise distracted by his two companions. It was only just coming up to midnight and Lord Brett left the club and made his way across to the Mallard to make contact with Streake.

'You're back early, how did it go?' said Streake cutting to the chase straight away.

'No problem, Streakey boy. I've made contact with Plumb and even gave him a little bit of gear to whet his appetite. Turns out his usual supplier has fucked off to Marbella for a few weeks, so our

Braders is in need of a new supplier, and that new supplier is me.'

'Sounds too easy, are you sure Brett?'

'Yeah, course I'm sure. He's given me his card with his personal mobile phone number on it, and he wants to buy some gear off me on Thursday in the club. If you can get in too and get the pictures we're sorted. You get what you want and I get what I want. We're on a good little number here Streaky, might want to stay next week and do some more bizness with our Braders. The dude has plenty of dollar, could be good for both of us Streaky.'

'Well for once I've got to congratulate you Brett. Didn't think you would do it to be honest, but don't get any bloody ideas about us working together as drug dealers. I'm here for my client to nail the tosser, and if you make a tidy sum on the way selling him gear then that's your bonus, but by the end of next week I want to out of here and back in Grimewold. If you want to keep the "relationship" going with Plumb, then that's up to you, but I want no part of it and no links back to me, do you understand? And if you breathe my name to anyone, especially Plumb and his entourage, I'll make sure you never walk again, just so long as we are clear.'

Soon after that they left the Mallard and took the long drive back to the grubby motel near Dagenham. Mission accomplished.

Chapter 88

Streake and Brett had to kick their heels until Thursday. Streake spent his time leaving the grubby motel and going into London to see some sites, and get away from Brett. He particularly liked the Churchill War rooms and spent the whole day there, taking in the atmosphere of wartime Britain and revelling in the historical documents from that time in history.

Brett on the other hand spent his time in his room trying to do drugs deals for when he was back in Grimewold, talking to his girlfriend – because he was always paranoid that she was going to be unfaithful to him and his lack of control over her was doing his head in – and drinking cheap lager and taking coke. In other words, he was acting true to form and wasting away his life on mindless pursuits. Streake didn't care what the dick head got up to as long as he did what he was told, and they achieved their objectives.

Over at the Playa de Sol holiday park in Benidorm the huge arctic trucks turned up from Hull on Thursday morning with the first ten log cabins brought over in sections. The assembly team had already arrived, and they started to build the first log cabin that same day on one of the concrete pans already in place. The aim was to get all ten log cabins erected within ten days, leaving the internals to be fitted out by the onsite team supplied by Miguel.

Despite letting his builder and Paeleo get on with organising things, Piffle wanted to come down to the site and see the cabins for himself. It was a momentous day as far as Piffle was concerned, the start of his plans for a new life of leisure with Honolulu and his opportunity to finally ditch the Clothes Horse.

'Eh up Paeleo lad, it's a grand day today. I'm looking forward to seeing the first log cabins on site, can't believe it's finally happening,' said Piffle as they sped down the windy mountain road in the Silver Spur on the way to the Playa de Sol holiday park.

'It is magnificent day señor, I am so pleased for you. I cannot wait for you to see how hard Miguel has worked, you will be, what you English say, over the moon.'

'I'm certainly hoping to be over the bloody moon,' said Piffle laughing out loud in the back of the car.

By the time they arrived at the Playa de Sol holiday park, the first log cabin sections had been unloaded and the team had already started erecting the first cabin. It was the hottest part of the day, but the team were determined to get the structure of the first log cabin up and finished by the time the sun went down.

It was all hands to the pump, including the team that Miguel had assembled and Gary Wacker's experienced team. There wasn't anything for Piffle to do, other than sit in the back of the air conditioned Silver Spur and watch the progress being made.

Paeleo very thoughtfully left the huge 6.75 litre engine ticking over so the air conditioning continued to pump huge amounts of ice-cold air into the cabin and through the rear vents to Piffle. Whilst others were baking hot and sweating, with the relentless rays of the sun and back-breaking hard work, Piffle sat in serene luxury and comfort. He reflected again how lucky he was, sitting in the best car in the world, watching his dream come to life with his mistress Honolulu back at the Villa Almeria making him a homemade trifle for his tea. Had he been chosen for this life by chance or had his hard work and cunning elevated him to these new dizzy heights? Maybe he would never know the answer to that, but as he sat there he couldn't think of anything that was going to stop him becoming very wealthy and achieving the charmed life of idle luxury with the love of his life, Honolulu, that he had always craved.

Later that evening, Streake and Lord Brett Sinclair drove into London again and parked the Vectra in the same place as they had on Monday. In many ways, it was going to be a repeat of Monday's successful activities, culminating in Brett making contact with his mark, Bradley Plumb.

This time though it was going to be more tricky. They had to get photos of Brett handing Bradley Plumb the class A drugs, preferably Plumb snorting some coke, and the pics had to be good enough for the recipient to be identified as the famous TV celebrity he was, and all of this had to be achieved without Plumb or his entourage noticing. No mean feat. Streake and Brett again went over to the Mallard to fine tune their respective roles so that there wouldn't be any cock ups.

'Right Brett, you've got the small camera in your shirt button and you're wired for sound, that should get us most of what we need when you hand over the gear and take payment. We're going to need decent pics and sound to go to the gutter press. Do it right Brett, and I'll make sure you get a share of any cash the papers pay for the story, coz that's separate from what my client is paying me. You, of course, keep any profit you make selling Plumb the gear. I'll be at the bar and I'll try and get some long-range shots without Plumb or his crew noticing. I can get some close ups even from a distance as the lens is top quality. Do you understand what you're doing?'

'Yeah Streaky boy, I'll get in close and get talking to Plumb again, tell him I've got the gear and hand it over, making sure I get the cash in return. I've got five grand's worth retail to whet his appetite and make sure I identify him for the recording at the exchange. If he bites alright, we can maybe do the same next Monday to make sure we've got all the pics and audio we need,' said Brett thinking of all the extra cash he could make selling another parcel of gear to Bradley Plumb. This could be sweet for him, and even if Plumb goes down, then he might be able to carry on supplying to Lemar.

Just as before, they approached the club at 9.30, and luckily for them the same bouncer was on duty. This time, with there being two of them, it cost them £300 to gain entry. It was worth every penny since *Careless Whisper* was probably the preeminent gay club in London, and it was very hard to gain admission without celebrity status or good contacts. The fact that Brett and Streake had achieved that without being searched was a lucky bonus, and crucial to the operation succeeding.

They both went to the bar and ordered drinks at the extortionate price that the club charged and waited for Bradley Plumb to appear. It was their last chance this week as Plumb never came to the bar after his show on Friday night as he liked to drink with the guests afterwards in the green room at Television Centre, and Saturday night was a night in with Lemar boozing and taking coke.

Right on cue at 10.30 p.m., Bradley Plumb and his entourage swept into the club and went to exactly the same smoked glassed table in the corner that they had on Monday night. If nothing else, Plumb was a creature of habit.

'Get yourself over there Brett and let's get this thing done,' said Streake who had started to sweat under the stress of the it all.

They were a long way from achieving success without being found out. Although Lord Brett was cocky by nature, he too was apprehensive. A lot could go wrong and at worst he could end up in the slammer for supplying class A drugs. He had been lucky so far, but that had been on his own patch on the Cromwell Estate. Here it was a totally different ball game.

'Don't you worry Streakey boy, I'll make sure our Braders does just what he's meant to do, leave it to me,' and with that he left the bar and sauntered over to Bradley Plumbs' table.

'Hey my main man, how you doing Bradley?'

'Who the fuck's this?' said Lemar glaring at Brett 'I suggest you piss off and leave us alone. This is a private gaff.'

'No man, this is my friend Brett, he's one of the crew man. Come sit with Bradley.'

Brett did as he was told and sat the other side of Lemar who was still seething. He was obviously jealous and liked to keep Bradley all to himself.

'Have a glass of champers Brett. We've got some serious celebrating to do. My agent's just rang today and I've got a new gig going on called *Date in the Sun*. I'll be fronting it. Was up against that talentless bitch Poppy Minx, but the producers saw sense and I get to do the show. Two million quid man, time to taste some bubbles. Poppy Minx will be pissing her pants with jealousy man, but who gives a toss? Winner takes all man, that's what they say. Maybe they could bring back *Blue Peter* for her,' said Bradley roaring with laughter.

'Good news fella, maybe you want something stronger than champers to celebrate?'

'Yeah, but my man's in Marbella, unless you managed to get me some gear?'

'Got it right here Bradley, five grand's worth of grade A gear, just what you like. The pure as driven snow white stuff, but I need paying, got a little for you to try first man.'

Brett handed over a tab and Bradley unwrapped the white powder and snorted it. From the bar Streake managed to get some good long-range shots using a close-up lens, and Brett was getting the transaction on video and sound from his hidden camera.

'That's shit hot gear man, I want the rest Brett and I want it now!'

'I need the cash Bradley, five grand and it's yours man.'

'Lemar, pay Brett five grand, he's got some quality gear for us.'

'I don't like this Bradley, we don't know this guy and you've got your usual supplier nice and safe, why take the risk?'

'Because Lemar, our guy is two thousand fucking miles away and we don't know when the prick is coming back, and I, for one, want to celebrate tonight I want the fucking gear man!'

Lemar knew when not to argue with Bradley who was used to getting his own way, but when he was pissed or high he was even worse. Lemar counted out the five grand in £50 notes and gave the money to Brett discreetly in an envelope he had on him for such eventualities.

He might have been discreet, but the camera and audio caught everything, the whole transaction, which was enough to put Bradley away for a five year stretch and certainly end his career.

'Thanks man, here's the gear, now you can party, party, party all weekend man. There's plenty more where that came from. I'll come to the club Monday if you like?'

'You're a bleedin' life-saver Brett, I've been dry as a bone man. Booze is fine but you can't beat the turbocharged stuff man, takes you to another dimension. Yeah, come see me Monday night in the club and we will do some more business.'

Bradley turned away, clearly no longer interested in Brett now he had what he wanted. Brett made a discreet exit and left the club separately from Streake who drank up his single malt whisky at the bar and left five minutes later.

For very different reasons they were both elated. Brett had just made himself a cool three grand and Streake had the evidence he needed to blackmail Bradley Plumb and go to the tabloid papers with a perfect story. He should see £50k out of this, plus the fee he was getting from Penelope Sykes.

They got in the Vectra before exploding into shrieks of laughter and hugging each other. Two completely different characters, but united by a common purpose – to make money. Success smelled very sweet that night as they drove back along the M25 towards Dagenham. Next week they would finish the job, and then payday would hopefully arrive.

Chapter 89

Back in Grimewold things were going exactly according to plan for Archibald McGreggor III. The strike had been in full swing for a week now, and Barraclough thought he was achieving victory by having a wall of pickets at every entrance to the giant McGreggor's Steel Mill, which dominated the town and covered fifteen square miles of land with 6 miles of internal railway lines.

It was true that nothing was coming in and nothing was getting out. However what Barraclough failed to appreciate was that steel supplies had already been delivered to key distributors and commercial clients in the UK, and PING steel was supplying steel directly from India to the overseas clients and stockists but with McGreggor's making their usual mark-ups.

With all the staff laid off with no wages being paid, Archibald was saving a fortune. His only direct costs were keeping the three blast furnaces running with a skeleton staff. The unions had allowed this activity to continue because if the blast furnaces closed down they could not reopen without hundreds of millions being spent and years of delay because the furnaces had to be re-cored, something that would almost certainly doom the huge plant to complete closure.

He was now going to play his ace card. He was going to announce the permanent closure of blast furnace three, which he wanted anyway with PING Steel's supplies taking up the slack, and the sacking of 40% of the permanent workforce of five thousand – two thousand men in total. To preserve the rest of the plan he was going to formally ask the Conservative Government for £200 million to update the rest of the plant and move into higher value specialist steels with much higher profit margins.

He had calculated that the lily-livered blue communists who made up the majority of the modern Conservative party wouldn't be able to stomach the loss of two thousand highly paid steel jobs, five thousand contractors and the support jobs in the local economy, which relied on the giant steel mill for survival. It was estimated that at least fifteen thousand support jobs relied on the steel mill on top of the ten thousand staff. If McGreggor's closed, then the town of Grimewold, specially built by the Victorian's as a steel town, would be decimated with local unemployment at over 30%.

He was betting on the fact that no Government would be able to stand by and tolerate that in one hit. In fact, he had wagered a £1 bet with the Chairman of McGreggor's accountants, who for many years had looked after their interests, the City of London firm Montgomery and Spay, and his friend Lord Montgomery was still Chairman of the Accountancy practise created in the reign of George the Third. The £1 bet was an example of the little sporting bets they had from time to time, and it was important that he won this wager, as he had lost the last one concerning the BREXIT referendum, where he was convinced the communist creature Cameron was bound to win the vote by fair means or foul, but much to his surprise, he lost that one.

He had Googleheimer primed to make the announcement at 5.00 p.m. about the job losses, the closure of number 3 blast furnace and the need for £200 million in Government support, without which the whole plant and 25,000 jobs were in jeopardy. The timing would coincide with the 6.00 o'clock main news from BBC, ITN and Sky, and the later 10.00 o'clock news bulletins, meaning there was nothing that Government Ministers or the trades unions could do over the weekend, thus giving him maximum leverage to get what he wanted.

In short, he was attempting to bounce the government into a hasty solution involving the use of copious amounts of taxpayer's largesse. He hadn't read *Bank from the Brink* by Sir Michael Edwards for nothing, where similar tactics were employed against the trades unions and Mrs Thatcher's government to great effect. Even though in his case the financial benefits flowed directly to himself, and his restructuring would make McGreggor's the most profitable steel giant in Europe at no cost to himself. All in all, a splendid outcome.

Things were also starting to go to plan at the Diversity Action Partnership, at least as far as Tandori was concerned. Due to the false fines being sent out more and more companies were starting to withhold payment and make complaints to the council, and in some cases, start legal action. It was not yet at a point where problems had been noticed, just a series of individual complaints that the council was used to receiving anyway, so they were dutifully ignored at this stage, but the spectacular increases in fine revenue that had occurred with Tandori's arrival on the scene had started to flatten off.

In fact, Tandori was finding going into work more and more stressful as she was convinced that at any time Bindle was going to find out what she had been up to and then there would be hell to pay. She decided that this weekend she was going to go back down to the Cotswolds and stay with mummy and daddy, and get away from the stresses of work and the depressing dump that was Jennings' pokey flat and the Cromwell estate. In fact, she had decided to take Monday and Tuesday off as well and make a long weekend of it. She could take the dogs for long walks, enjoy mummy's home cooking and go into Broadway and see all the little boutique shops she loved. Yes, she had to put up with her sister Tamara, but that was a small price to pay.

Because Tandori didn't have a car she decided to treat herself to a rented one and phoned up a local firm, Grimewold Rent-a-Dream-Car, and found out they were doing a four-day special on a Range Rover Evoque for £149. On impulse she booked it straight away, and after clearing her holiday plans with Zara, she left at lunchtime to collect her gleaming steed and head south on the M1, missing the traffic and escaping the dreary reality of staying in Grimewold.

Soon she was leaving the M40 at Gaydon and cut across to the

Fosse Way, the old Roman road heading south into the Cotswolds and finishing in the beautiful town of Bath. She wasn't traveling that far and soon saw the familiar sight of Morton in the Marsh on the A429, and then took the right turn in town to Broadway, eight miles away and onto the family home. It was another world compared to Grimewold, a world of honey coloured cottages, lush green meadows, beautiful market towns unchanged for centuries, quant pubs and high-class gourmet restaurants. She parked the Evoque in her parents' drive behind mummy's full-sized Range Rover and entered the kitchen.

'Hello mummy, surprise!' she shrieked with delight. She had not told mummy and daddy she was coming and wanted to surprise them, their daughter returned after two months of frankly unbelievable adventures, if you could call it that.

'Tandori, my dear, how very lovely to see you. Nothing wrong I hope? You didn't tell your father and me that you were coming to stay. I haven't made up your bedroom with a fresh duvet or aired the room out.'

'Oh don't fuss mummy, we can do that later. It's just nice to be home and back in the Cotswolds. Is daddy back yet?'

'He should have been, but he's had another tedious meeting at the Home Office about whether transgender woman can request to be moved to a women's prison, and it's taking a frightfully long time to sort out apparently. Some of the female inmates are saying that their human rights are being breached by having to share bathroom facilities with transgender woman who still have penises. It's all very complicated and taking up a lot of your father's time. I think he gets in at 6.00 p.m. at the station from London. Maybe you would like to go and meet him and surprise him?'

'Oh that would be lovely mummy. I've hired that swanky Range Rover Evoque for a few days, so I'll go and surprise him in that. He won't be expecting me at all.'

'Anyway, let's make you a nice cup of tea, you must be tired after your long journey. It's such a long way dear from that dreadful place you are staying in, Grimewold isn't it?'

'Yes mummy, I'm glad to get away to be honest, but if you think Grimewold is bad you, should see the flat I am staying in on the Cromwell Estate. It's like something out of Syria mummy. If it was carpet bombed it couldn't be any worse.'

Tandori sat down at the large solid oak kitchen table with her cup of tea and was just beginning to relax and enjoy herself when her sister, Tamara, strolled in.

'Gosh mummy, look, Bubble Arse has returned,' said Tamara sarcastically.

'Oh look, it's Coco the Clown in a micro skirt. What have the plastic surgeons done this time? Given you a brain transplant?' retorted Tandori.

'Stop it children, can't you too just try and get on a for a change?'

'Not going to happen,' said Tamara. 'Anyway I'm off out with the girls and won't be back until much later,' and with that Tamara flounced out of the kitchen to her car and zoomed out of the drive.

Back in Grimewold, Googleheimer was giving his press conference at a specially created lectern outside the main offices of McGreggor's Steel Corp. The assembled press were already there from the world of TV: ITN, BBC, SKY, and R-Today, plus the press in the form of The Times, Financial Times, Mail, Express, Guardian and Mirror. This was big news, the first major old-fashioned strike in the private sector for years; management pitted against union barons with thousands of jobs at stake. The fact that Googleheimer was an American with a strong Midwest accent didn't help from a public relations point of view. It was 5.00 p.m. and the press conference started so that it could be broadcast as the number one item on the 6 o'clock news and then later at 10 o'clock.

'Good evening ladies and gentlemen, members of the press. My name is Curtis Googleheimer and I am the Production Director of McGreggor's Steel Corporation. As you know, this huge facility has been in lockdown for a week now due to a crippling, and totally unnecessary, strike called by the trade unions. The steel market is highly competitive and our ability to source high quality iron ore has been severely hampered by the actions of overseas competitors, resulting in a reduction in output and subsequent pay for our highly valued production line staff. The union is asking for us to reinstate former salaries despite production being down 40%. If I and our management team agreed to these wholly unrealistic demands, then McGreggor's steel would go bust within two months. As it is, because of the strike and the world situation regarding steel prices, I am announcing today the closure of blast furnace number three and the dismissal of 40% of our full-time workforce, some 2,000 men. This is now unavoidable. In addition, we are asking this day for the British Government to furnish us with an immediate grant of £200 million to overhaul this huge production facility, allowing us to produce more specialist high-value steel and safeguard the remaining 3,000 full-time jobs at the site. Without this cash injection from the British Government, regrettably this site will have to close, never to reopen with the loss locally of 25,000 jobs, a third of the total jobs in Grimewold. We will be opening negotiations with the British Government immediately and are open to constructive discussions with our trade union partners. Thank you very much.'

The audience went absolutely crazy, firing questions at Googleheimer, but he had turned his back on them and walked off the podium and behind a huge screen showing an aerial shot of the massive plant, which Archibald thought would play well with the TV audience and help bounce the government into giving them the £200 million. He had explicitly told Googleheimer not to answer any questions, thus putting maximum pressure on the government and trade unions. Let the tossers stew over the weekend was his maxim. He had watched Googleheimer's steller performance from his study.

'Excellent, excellent, he has turned out to be a good choice that

Googleheimer,' said Archibald to his secretary, June, who was watching the broadcast with him.

'That will put the fuckers in a tail-spin this weekend, make no mistake,' said Archibald thoroughly enjoying himself. Upsetting a bunch of Marxists and blue communists was great sport as far as he was concerned, especially as it was also going to profit him immensely. He knew the government wouldn't give him £200 million, but felt that he would get at least half that, plus some 'retraining grants of many millions' that he could use for other purposes. Finally, he could be rid of 2,000 overpaid, lazy morons who had accrued benefits in the 1970s and 80s when his weak and useless father had been in charge, and get the grants needed to restructure the operation and double the gross value added of the plant.

'I think it's time for a celebratory single malt June, don't you? Have one yourself if you like.'

June couldn't believe it, not in all the years of devoted service to him had Archibald been remotely civil to her, never mind offered her a drink of his finest malt whisky. He must be in a good mood, or going doolally, thought June. She couldn't work out which, but helped herself to a large shot of finest single malt whisky anyway.

Callum was on his way out of the house to see either Mrs Neatgangs or Olive, he hadn't quite decided which at that point.'

'Just popping out on me bike mam to see a mate on the

Gipsyville Estate.'

'Just a minute Callum, I want a word with you,' said Tracy Wacker.

'What? I'm in a hurry,' said Callum defensively and feeling decidedly guilty. Had his mum found out about Mrs Neatgangs somehow, maybe from Bianca?

'It's about my Bingo Jar Callum. Me and your father know you have been stealing from it, £30 in total.'

'No I ain't, it wasn't me.'

'It is you Callum because I noticed money missing and thinking it was Mrs Neatgangs, because she's new, your dad put up a camera in the kitchen and linked it to the laptop, and much to our surprise and, I must say, disappointment Callum, we found out that you were the thief. Now I know it's not a lot of money, but theft is theft Callum and as we give you pocket money, we are both very upset by this.'

'I'm sorry mum, I just wanted more sweets and didn't think it would matter.'

'Well it does, now I'm not going to say any more about it, but it stops, do you hear me?'

'Yes mum.'

'Right, well on your way then and don't be too late. I don't like you on the Gipsyville Estate late at night, and I hope you are just visiting a friend, a male, and I hope your age?' said Tracy sending a clear shot across the bows.

'Yeah, it's me mate Dean, going to play computer games.'

'OK well you take care on that bike, and me and your father will see you later. We might be popping to the Feathers around 8.00 for a drink. Your father has had a very busy week getting those log cabins shipped out.'

Callum left his house free at last but wondering if his mother knew more than she was letting on. She didn't seem convinced that he was seeing his mate. Anyway, he was free to pursue other interests of the female variety. He certainly couldn't get enough of Mrs Neatgangs, but after that tryst with her daughter as well, he had in his mind that Olive might be a better bet tonight and certainly a new experience. It was a decision that he was going to come to regret as he peddled furiously along the main road towards the Gipsyville Estate.

Callum parked his bike up against the wall of Olive's house, opposite Mrs Neatgangs', where he had been only last week and gingerly knocked the door.

Olive answered in grubby tight leggings and a low cut black lacy top.

'Oh, it's you Callum, you're in luck, me four eldest are out with their mates and me two youngest are with their dad for the weekend, so you've caught me alone. You better come in. Didn't fancy me mam tonight then?' said Olive looking him up and down.

'You look pleased to see me,' she leered.

'I am,' gasped Callum his voice hoarse with anticipation.

Olive then grabbed the lad and kissed him passionately, forcing her tongue down his throat.

'Let's go upstairs Callum and we can have some fun.'

Soon they were naked and with their clothes still in the lounge, they went upstairs and ended up lying on Olive's double bed ready for the pleasures to come. But they were not to be that night.

From her window, Mrs Neatgangs had spotted Callum's bike outside Olive's house. She had been looking out for him expecting him to turn up like he had last week, but she was absolutely furious when she saw him make a beeline for a her daughter's house. It wasn't the first time that the slut had taken one of her fellas for herself and Mrs Neatgangs when angered was not a woman to be trifled with.

She stomped across to her daughter's house and with the spare key, carefully opened the door as quietly as she could. She could hear laughter and noise upstairs, she assumed coming from Olive's bedroom and was absolutely furious. Then she saw their clothes strewn across the lounge and saw red. Quietly going up the stairs, she flung open Olive's bedroom door and found her daughter and her lover Callum naked, cuddling and kissing on the bed. She shrieked at them both and launched herself onto the cheap double bed.

It was no match for the combined weight of Mrs Neatgangs,

Olive and Callum and promptly collapsed in the middle the pine frame completely broken. With much screaming, a fist fight broke out between Mrs Neatgangs and Olive, and soon Mrs Neatgangs cheap t-shirt was torn and both mother and daughter were flying at each other. Hair was being pulled, blows were being landed and swearing of a very crude nature was emanating from the room.

Callum, fearing for his life, slipped out of the room unobserved by the main protagonists still fighting in the collapsed bed. He flew down the stairs, dressed and slipped his trainers on quickly, and was out of the door, on his bike and away.

The elderly couple next door were so convinced that a terrible domestic incident was taking place, involving extreme violence, that Humberwold Police were called. As Callum left the Gipsyville Estate cycling furiously, he could see two police cars going in the opposite direction, sirens blaring, towards Olive Neatgangs' council house.

Despite his lustful thoughts, Callum decided that visiting either Mrs Neatgangs or her daughter was a distinctly bad idea, and maybe finding a girl at school his own age might be the best course of action. It was a lesson the young lad needed to learn, and one that wouldn't leave him for a very long time.

The first police officer on the scene, PC Grimes, found the elderly couple outside their council house looking concerned.

'It's all happening in there mate,' said the elderly gentleman.

PC Grimes found the front door still open from Callum's hasty exit and gingerly entered the premises. There was clearly a terrible fight going on upstairs. Probably a fella beating the shit out of his wife, thought Grimes. That was the usual domestic he came across, especially on the notorious Gipsyville Estate.

He went up the stairs with his baton raised and entered the master bedroom. He was not in any way prepared for the sight that greeted. He looked over onto the collapsed double bed and saw a naked, elderly grandma fighting with her hugely overweight daughter, who was also stark-bollock naked. They both looked up in shock.

'Who the bloody hell are you and what are you doing in me bedroom?' shrieked Olive Neatgangs.

'Sorry to disturb you madam, we had a report of a domestic from your concerned neighbours next door, and I've come to investigate.'

'Oh those nosey tossers. They're always finding fault and looking out of their window to see if I've got a fella. Fucking curtain twitchers they are. They report me to council all the time.'

The thought of any fella visiting the creature in front of him seemed highly unlikely to PC Grimes, but then, these days anything was possible. He decided to make a tactical retreat.

'Sorry to bother you ladies, obviously nothing of police significance going on here.' He left the bedroom swiftly and got out of there as quickly as possible. He radioed in the false alarm so that he and the other police officer could be on their way to more pressing incidents.

Chapter 90

Later that night, Bradley Plumb hosted, what would turn out to be his very last appearance on *Purple Haze*, the chat show with a difference.

He arrived as usual in the black Maybach at 7.00 p.m. outside Television Centre with Tiggy and Lemar in tow, they went everywhere with him. He had on his trademark purple, velvet full-length coat and dark shades, and Tiggy dropped the purple petals on the floor as he walked up to the main entrance and then made his way to his dressing room.

The show tonight was its usual mixture of interviews with other celebrities, some well-known and some up and coming, with a mix of stupid juvenile pranks so beloved of his non-to-bright audience. Subtle it was not. There was of course, his famous opening catch phrase for each guest, 'And how long are your turds?' combined with the canned laughter carefully dubbed into the live audience laughter as well. With an audience figure of 4.2 million it was one of the most popular TV shows on a Friday night outside of the well-established soaps, and being aired after the watershed allowed for the swearing and sexual inuendo so necessary to create the shows unique character.

Tonight's show was no exception, and guests included a celebrity from Real Housewives of Newcastle, a psychic dog named Mr Tibbles who could predict disasters around the world, a washed out soap star who had been sacked for drug offences and was desperately trying to make a comeback, and an up and coming band named 'The Fish Filleters' who were to be interviewed last and who would play the show out with their latest hit single.

Plumb worked his way through the show with its normal moronic pranks, and oh so PC interviews with a hint of racy drug taking and sexual exploits thrown in for good measure. It was the last interview of the show, the lead singer of the 'Fish Filleters' Dave Strange.

'Welcome Dave, great to see you,' enthused Bradley Plumb. 'And how long are your turds?'

'Bout as long as me dick when I last looked.'

Cue: canned laughter and audience pan shot with lots of young happy people laughing and joking loudly.

'Is your real name Dave Strange?' said Plumb laughing loudly.

'Why does everyone keep asking me that? Do they ask Elton John if his real name is Elton John, or Cliff Richard, or Elvis Presley?'

'Well he's dead, Dave and his real name was Elvis Presley.

514

Moving on Dave, where did you get the inspiration to call yourselves The Fish Filleters?'

'Well Braders, we was gonna call ourselves The Fish Fuckers, but me agent, Tarquin, said that would limit our appeal to the younger audience.

'I see, but where does the name come from?'

'Me old man was a Fish Filleter in Middlesbrough, but he died.'

'What did he die of Dave?

' Lung cancer Braders, very sad really, he was only 52, all Mrs Thatcher's fault.'

'Did he smoke?'

'Yeah, he was a sixty a day man from the age of 14, died two years ago.'

'OK Dave, now about your latest hit single that's been number one in the download charts for weeks. It's called *Blue Submarine* and is a remix of the famous Beatles Song from 1966, *Yellow Submarine* and that's what you are going to be gigging for us tonight. Why Blue Submarine?'

'Well, the Tories are in again and the fucking country is sinking fast, so we figured, play on words. Tories are blue, so we'd redo a happy Beatles song from the 60s to reflect the realities of living in Middlesbrough in the new millennia. Get it? *Blue Submarine*, play on words man.'

' I see. Did you change any other lyrics Dave?'

'No, couldn't be arsed.'

'Very good Dave. And finally, Dave Strange, what is the funniest thing you've seen recently?'

'That fat bird with an arse the size of a block of flats being arrested as a Muslim terrorist blowing up a train carriage. Everybody knows Muslim terrorists come from the Middle East, have black hair, long beards and black robes, and then they blow themselves up "boom!". Don't escape with an old accomplice in a fucking Austin Maestro. When I saw the Tory Home Secretary saying it was her, I nearly pissed myself.'

'Anyway guys, that was Dave Strange lead singer of The Fish Filleters and they are going to play us out with their new hit single, Blue Submarine. They're up for a well-deserved BRIT Award, I leave you with The Fish Filleters!'

Cue: captious canned applause, pan to wildly clapping and shouting audience.

We all live in a blue submarine,

Blue submarine, blue submarine.

We all live in a blue submarine,

Blue submarine, blue submarine.

And our friends are all on board,

Many more of them live next door,

And the band begins to play.

We all live in a blue submarine,

Blue submarine, blue submarine.

We all live in a blue submarine,

Blue submarine, blue submarine...

Bradley Plumb couldn't wait to get off the set and get a shot of booze – any booze in the green room. That last interview had been a fucking disaster. Bradley Plumb was furious.

A few minutes later Dave Strange entered the green room as if nothing had happened and poured himself a shot of vodka.

Bradley Plumb approached him absolutely incandescent with rage. 'What the fuck? You useless prick, everybody knows you don't take the piss out of Muslims, Christians definitely, Jews and Hindus possibly, but never Muslims. Look what happened to that old guy years ago, Salman Rushdie. He took the piss and the fucking Ayatollah issued a fatwah against him. He was under house arrest for ten years, couldn't go out or open any supermarkets or anything. Not that it mattered to him; he was a bleedin' author and just wrote another 36 boring books to keep himself occupied, but I can't have that shit. I've just signed a deal to host *Date in the Sun* for two million quid, you selfish twat!'

'Hey, sorry Braders, I didn't think man. Just seemed something funny to say before we did the gig.'

Bradley Plumb turned on his heel, still furious. 'Come on Lemar, we're out of here. I've had enough of this shit for tonight.'

And with that the entourage left the guests drinking in the green room and headed back down to the waiting Maybach, which was ready to take Bradley back to his luxury Chelsea apartment.

Chapter 91

With the first ten log cabins due to be completed and fitted out within two weeks, Jimmy – The Fleece started to put his grand marketing plan into action over the weekend. He had assembled all the go-go girls in the games' room at the club to brief them on their role in the elaborate plan to lure in the punters and get them to sign up.

'Right girls, as you know we've got the contract to sell five hundred log cabins at the Playa de Sol holiday park. Like with all things in life, the best motto is, "try before you buy". Your role is very simple girls. You're going to be going to all the best five-star hotels in Benidorm where the higher class guests are staying – you know the ones with wonga – and I've arranged with the reps that you can give a short presentation. What you're going to be offering is simple. The punters agree to listen to a 30 minute marketing presentation – which is really 2 hours – and in return they get a free coach trip up in the mountains to the Castell de Guadalest Monastery and the Guadalest reservoir, worth €20 a punter, no more than 2 free places each. If they've got kids or relatives they are charged full price. Now, we do the marketing presentation here at the Go-Go Bar and Grill, might sell a few breakfasts and coffees before they go, and they hear the presentation before the afternoon trip. Any questions girls so far?'

'Yeah Jimmy, do they still get the free coach trip if they don't sign up?'

'Yeah, but they have to pay for afternoon tea and we make a profit out of that so that pays for most of the trip, so we should be sweet.'

'Anyway as I was saying girls, at the presentation we offer them a free two-day stay at one of the luxury log cabins and if they agree we do a credit check. We need to make sure they are good for buying either a timeshare at €15,000, or the full monty at €150,000. But the way we reel them in is, we guarantee that if they buy one, they get a 10% return on their log cabin for 2 years, i.e. €20,000 a year for all the weeks we rent it to holiday makers at a €1000 a week. So, they give us 20 weeks and they get the other 32 weeks or they can rent to friends and family. They get 10% instead of 1% in the bank, everyone's a winner. It's the real fucking deal. Who's not gonna go for that? It's the deal of the century. What do you think girls?'

'Sounds easy,' said one of the brighter go-go girls, Samantha.

'Love, it is easy. You get €50 for each punter you get along to the presentation, easy fucking peasy. And believe me, once they're sitting in their luxury log cabin with a great big hot tub on the veranda, glass of bubbly and the thought of making 10% on their money, they will sign. Yeah, the tight ones will go for a week's timeshare, but it's still a good deal for them what with the cheap flights into Alicante now. The problem's going be fighting them off with a stick once they see the deal. The guy that owns the park, Piffle, will be sitting pretty and so will we. Right girls, I've got a list here of the hotels that have agreed to take part and I've split them out, two hotels each. You contact the reps direct and agree your presentation times. I've got a presentation pack for each one of you. Read it follow the script and you'll be fine. Who doesn't want a free trip to a Monastery and reservoir in the mountains? Any further questions?'

'Yeah, when will the first log cabins be ready for them to stay in?'

'In two weeks' time the first ten will be finished and kitted out ready to roll, so if you start making your presentation dates for the week after next we'll be on course to start selling. And don't worry, Jimmy's been here before remember, and when the punters are on holiday in the sun, enjoying themselves away from some dreary job in some dump in Blighty, they're up for being signed up. What we're doing is selling them the dream, giving 'em what they want and making it look like they're shrewd. You know if you don't sign up here and now you'll miss the boat, oldest sales trick in the book.'

Chapter 92

Monday came round soon enough and Gordon Streake along with Lord Brett Sinclair found themselves driving back down to London for their rendezvous at the club that night with Bradley Plumb.

Brett was his usual annoying self, and Streake was looking forward to the end of the week when he could be rid of him.

'Did you have a nice weekend Streakey boy, get your leg over, or take some gear?'

'No, I was at home with my sister planning this week meticulously Brett, but I suspect you were not being so diligent.'

'Don't know what you're talking about man to be honest, oooh, at home with sister, that must have been nice for you. Maybe you got some "one-on-one" with your sister, you old perv.'

'Shut the fuck up Brett, you disgusting, pointless little creature.'

Ignoring Streake's riposte entirely Brett carried on. 'I got me end

522

away with me bird, and her sister when me bird went shopping, then took some gear, had a bottle of voddy and passed out. Then on Sunday I got up around one thirty, had a pot noodle for Sunday lunch then went and did a few deals on the estate. Made myself some dollar man, you should try it, thousand quid up on the start, sweet.'

'Sounds idyllic,' said Streake sarcastically, not in the least interested in Brett's chaotic and deranged life style, even though it all seemed perfectly normal to Lord Brett.

As usual, it took a gruelling five hours to get to the motel near Dagenham and check in again for a few nights; the plan was to be away by Thursday. Streake had a plan up his sleeve that he hadn't yet revealed to Lord Brett as he decided if he gave too much away the prick would screw things up for both of them. They checked into the seedy motel with the same cantankerous receptionist on duty complete with his grubby tank top and stained grey trousers. As they had arrived later, they decided to get to *Careless Whisper* around 10.00 p.m. since they knew Plumb would be getting there between 10.30 and 11.00 p.m., giving them a couple of hours to freshen up and change.

'Make sure you text Plumb when you get to your room Brett and tell him to bring the money for the drugs you're selling him tonight. It's your little sweetener for helping me out.'

'Yeah I've got ten grands worth, retail, of really good gear for him this time. That's seven grand profit for me, sweet.'

They went their separate ways to their rooms and Brett, for

once, did as he was told. He immediately texted Bradley Plumb on the number he had been given, Plumb's private and personal mobile number.

Hey Bradley, it's me Brett, I've got your shit here with me. I'll be at the club for 11.00 p.m., make sure you bring 10k in notes. Its fucking good stuff man, pure as snow.

Brett got a reply back straight away.

Got the wonga, see you at 11.00, usual table.

They arrived outside *Carless Whisper* at 10.00 p.m. and Streake bunged the bouncer, Todd, £200 and Brett was free to go in, no questions asked.

'What you doing Streakey boy?'

'I'm not coming in this time. I'll wait for you in the Mallard, when you're done come across and I'll give you the keys to the Vectra. Then you can fuck off back to the motel. I've got to wait for Plumb to come out and then I've got my bit of business to conclude, which you don't need to know about. I'll be quite some time depending on how long the dickhead takes to come out.'

'How are you getting back to the Motel?'

'Don't you worry about me Brett, I've got it all planned, best you don't know.'

Everything went exactly according to plan, like clockwork in fact.

Streake went across to the Mallard and got himself a pint, positioning himself looking out at the club. He had a brown leather holdall with him, which he needed for his plan to work. He also had a replica firearm, which was way good enough to fool anyone not used to hand guns, which he hoped would scare the shit out of Plumb, but that was for later.

Lord Brett entered the club without being searched and positioned himself at the glass smoked table next to the one Bradley Plumb always seemed to sit at. Right on cue, Plumb and his entourage appeared around 11.00 p.m. There was no point in small talk this time. The gear was discreetly handed over and the ten grand, already counted, was handed to Brett by Lemar in a brown envelope, which he put into his inside jacket pocket.

The deal was concluded in minutes and Brett left the club telling Todd he was feeling unwell. He went across to the Mallard, got the Vectra keys from Streake and was out of there, back to the Motel with ten grand burning a hole in his pocket. He was beginning to think that Streake wasn't the knobhead he had thought he was; they had worked well together and both benefitted. Shame it was going to have to end really, he thought.

Streake had other thoughts. He waited until the pub was due to shut at 12.30 p.m. after asking the barmaid and went into the gents. In one of the two cubicles he changed into a chauffeur's uniform, complete with peak cap and put his ordinary clothes in the holdall, he placed the replica gun in his inside pocket. He then went across to the waiting black Maybach and approached the real chauffeur who was having a fag standing by the bonnet. Streake believed in carrot and stick. He came up behind the Chauffeur who hadn't spotted him and jammed the replica gun in the chauffeurs back.

'Don't say a fucking word. Do you hear me?' he growled. 'Right, I've got a deal for you. In my hand here is an envelope, I've got £500 quid for you. I've got a gun here pointing at your back, but no one's gonna get hurt if you do as I say. All I want you to do is, take the £500 and fuck off for the night, no questions asked. I'll drive Bradley Plumb home. Nothing is going to happen to him, I just need a few minutes of his time, do you understand?'

'Yes,' squeaked the terrified chauffeur. 'I've got kids you know.'

'Nothing is going to happen to you providing you take the £500 and don't phone the police, or your employers, till morning, then just say the Maybach was nicked. Don't worry, Plumb won't say anything when I've spoken to him. Here's the £500, now fuck off and don't look back, you can get a taxi home. Remember not a word to the cops or I will come after you.'

Suitably terrified, the chauffeur ran away at speed leaving Streake in his chauffeur's uniform – the new driver of the Maybach.

No one had seen what happened. He had to hope that the chauffeur didn't go straight to the police or he would be fucked, but he'd put the fear of God into him. He didn't think Plumb or Lemar would notice the switch, but he got into the car anyway so they couldn't really see him when they came out. He had to wait till 1.00 a.m. for them finally to emerge.

Luckily, Tiggy had another taxi waiting to take her home, but Plumb and Lemar got straight into the back of the Maybach laughing and joking without realising that a different chauffeur had taken over the car. Streake knew exactly where Plumb lived in Chelsea, but he was going to make a little detour and put the fear of god into the fucker.

They drove for a few miles, but neither passenger noticed that they hadn't gone the direct route back to Plumb's luxury house. Streake drove into a huge empty carpark close to some swanky offices a couple of miles from Plumb's house and got out of the car.

'What the fuck's going on man?' shrieked Plumb, suddenly realising that something was wrong. He didn't have long to find out something was very wrong.

Streake yanked the door open with force and pointed the replica handgun at the two drunk passengers.

'Just a little word Mr Plumb. if I may.'

'What the fuck man? Are you going to kill us? No, please don't, it's not fair, I ain't done nothing wrong.'

Lemar said nothing, but just hid behind Plumb, presumably hoping it was him that the gunman wanted to kill or kidnap.

'It's simple Braders. What I've got here are pictures. Pictures of you buying class A drugs. Crack cocaine actually, and I've got audio backup. Need to be more careful where you buy gear, and who you deal with.'

'What the fuck do you want man?' whined Plumb.

'Simple Braders. You deposit £100k in this bank account tomorrow and I'll drop off the pictures to your house once the money has cleared. And if you don't, then these pics and audio are going to the tabloids and you will be fucked. No more *Purple Haze*, no more celebrity lifestyle.'

Streake was going to ask for £50k but had got greedy. This had been a lot to sort out and risky, and it was his one chance to fuck off from Grimewold and get a little apartment in the sun. This overpaid prick could easily afford £100k.

'I can't pay you that, that's a fucking fortune, I ain't paying.'

'Now you listen to me you fucking little piss fairy. One hundred grand is nothing to you and I know you've just won a £2 million contract to front *Love in the Sun* and you're already getting a fortune for your shit useless show. I hate parasitic little dicks like you, corrupting our youth. You're everything that's wrong with this shit useless country, so you pay up or I'll fucking blow your brains out here and now.'

'OK OK, I'll sort it,' squealed Plumb.

Lemar was so scared he actually pissed his pants in the back of the Maybach.

'But how do I know you'll give me the pictures and audio tape if

I pay up?'

'Well, you're just going to have to trust me,' said Streake leering at them. 'Unlike a snivelling little prick like you, I'm a man of my word and I can be trusted. Old school me.'

With that, he handed him the bank details in an envelope, withdrew the gun and drove them the two miles to Plumb's house in Chelsea. He dropped them off and sped off into the night leaving them crying at the side of the road.

He decided to not use the M25 in case the cops had been alerted to look for the Maybach, but nothing happened. He used the on-board satnav to get himself within a mile of the motel where he ditched the Maybach and walked the twenty-minute journey back, getting in around 4.00 a.m. Then it was simply a waiting game, and in the meantime he would get some sleep. If all went to plan, he would be a hundred grand richer this time tomorrow.

Chapter 93

The next day, Streake and Lord Brett got up late, very late, and went for breakfast up the road at a fast food restaurant, which, luckily, served what passed for breakfast until 11.00 a.m. They both had strong black coffee to try and wake themselves up.

'When can we get the fuck out of here?' whined Brett. 'I need to get back to the Cromwell Estate and do some business. I've got dollar to earn.'

'You need more patience you snivelling little prick,' said Streake who was on edge. He kept checking the overseas bank account online, but nothing.

Finally, just as they were finishing their breakfasts and coffee he checked again and bingo, Plumb had deposited the hundred grand into his overseas account. A huge grin came over his face. Bloody hell, he'd done it! He now had enough to piss off for good and have the life in the sun he had always dreamed of. Things rarely worked out for Streake, but maybe things were finally going his way.

'Right we've just got to go into London, Chelsea actually, and drop off a package and then we can be on our way back to Grimewold. Job done.'

If nothing else, Streake was a man of his word. Bradley Plumb would get a copy of the photos and the audio tape, and he wouldn't take things further. The originals were going to his client, Penelope Sykes, who could then either go to the police or sell the evidence to one of the tabloids. He didn't care, his conscious was clear. Plumb had paid him, and he had provided the pictures and audio tape as agreed.

By mid-afternoon he had dropped the package off through Bradley's door and they were on their way back up the M1 to Grimewold. Later that week he would hand over the evidence to Penelope Sykes and get paid the balance for all his hard work. In truth though, payday had already come.

Over in Benidorm things were moving apace. The first log cabins had been erected and were busily being fitted out by Miguel's on-site team; they would be ready by the weekend to accept guests.

The go-go girls were equally busy giving their presentations at the four- and five-star hotels around Benidorm, and signing plenty of punters up for the marketing presentations and free coach trips.

Samantha had got the most signed up, possibly because she had the shortest micro skirt and the lowest cut top. She was determined to win Go-Go Girl of the Month. An award that Jimmy had devised as an incentive. The best performing go-go girl won a week's cruise round the Med later in the year, and Samantha was determined to be the lucky winner.

The first marketing presentation was due to take place this coming Friday by, none other than, Jimmy – The Fleece – Moston, who was taking personal responsibility for turning the prospects into conquests, just as he used to do back in the good old days of the 1980s.

Piffle was over the moon. Everything was going his way. Fine income from the Diversity Action Partnership was at a record level, even the annoying Bindle was leaving him alone and getting on with things. His last pep talk with her seemed to do the trick, 'Don't bring me problems, bring me solutions,' was his new mantra. He'd read it in a management magazine he had seen whilst having his hair cut, and amazingly she had done exactly that.

Then there was the log cabin holiday park. The first ten log cabins were nearly finished, and everybody had performed as he hoped they would – better in many cases. He had spoken to Jimmy Moston and the first marketing presentations were to take place this coming Friday. Once the clients had experienced his luxury log cabins, he was sure that they would sell easily, especially with the timeshare option to widen the market appeal. He would be forever grateful to Paeleo for introducing him to Jimmy, that man clearly had a natural sales talent that would see all five hundred log cabins sold as planned.

Soon he would ask the Clothes Horse for a divorce and be free of her so he could marry Honolulu and stay at the Villa Almeria all the time. Then he could retire and be rid of the Diversity Action Partnership for good. Not that he had any regrets, it had been his passport to better things.

'Do us a champagne cocktail my love,' he shouted to Honolulu as he rested on one of the outside loungers by his pool reading *The Daily Mirror* on his tablet.

'I not your slave Dresden, why don't you get off your fat arse and get yourself champagne cocktail, eh?'

'Don't be like that Honolulu, I'm having a good day in the sun. It's a world away from Grimewold. That bastard McGreggor has provoked a strike with the steel workers, threatening to close site down if he doesn't get his way. You see Honolulu, as me dad used to say, you can never trust boss class or their friends in Parliament, the Tories. As my old dad used to say, there's only one good Tory and that's a dead Tory. I just hope it doesn't affect town too much, I don't want me income to go down just when we need all the money we can get to build log cabins. I've been to Banco Alicante and borrowed a €1 million to help fund the next phase of the build. They wouldn't lend me anymore because they said I was an "unknown quantity", unknown quantity my arse, it's just rich bastards trying to prevent people like us having what they've got.'

'Now listen Dresden Piffle, are you, what the English say, on your hind horse again today with all your silly politics and class warfare?

Can't we just have nice quiet day in the sun and forget about all that? I make you nice champagne cocktail for us both and then maybe we can have a little cuddle in the pool if you get your big trunks on, and I can put my sexy one piece swimming costume on, the one you like showing you my big ones. Would you like that?'

'Bloody hell Honolulu, now you're talking! You make champagne cocktails and I'll get me trunks on, I think this is going to be a bloody good day.'

Mike Morrell was sat on a dining room chair in his study with the oak panelled wall behind him as a backdrop. He was already completely bored by the whole process.

'You must just sit still Mr Morrell. I can't get you properly and I've come all this way from London to do your portrait. I need complete concentration and your cooperation, and I'm just not getting it,' said Quentin Poope in exasperation.

'I thought you were supposed to be the best? Done the Queen and everything. You can't expect me to sit here hour after hour like a lemon when I've got things to do. I'm flying up to Edinburgh tomorrow with the love of my life, Pauline Piffle, and then we're going on the Highland Steam train from Waverley station right up to Inverness, 186 miles of bloody paradise.'

'That's as maybe Mr Morrell, but I'm here to do your portrait as you requested, and it takes time. Rome wasn't built in a day.'

'Maybe not Mr Poope, but I want the bugger finished quicker than you're working. Can't we do it another way? Maybe if you take some pictures of me sitting here you can go back to your studio and do the portrait from that? In any case, can you jazz me up a bit? Make me look a little younger, a bit more like Sean Connery in Gold finger? I know I look a fair bit like him anyway so it shouldn't be too hard, should it?

'I am not a miracle worker Mr Morrell. I have my personal reputation to consider and making you look twenty years younger and completely different is not, I'm afraid, something that I am prepared to countenance. But you are the client, and you are paying me £200,000 for this portrait, so I am prepared to work from photographs in my studio, and put you in a dinner jacket with the poise and elegance of Sean Connery, but with more of, shall we say, your own features. We want your staff and visitors to recognise you, do we not?'

'Alright Mr Poope, we have a deal. Anything to stop me sitting here all day when I've got things to attend to. You take your pictures and you can be on your way. When did you say it will be finished?'

'We can't rush these things and I am a man very much in demand, but I will be able to give you the finished article in about two months' time, which I have to say, is something of a record for me.'

Quentin Poope was already deciding that the philistine wouldn't know a decent portrait if he fell over one and that he would get his understudy to knock one out so that he could get on with more worthy commissions. The two hundred grand would come in very useful this summer and allow him to redecorate his London house.

He took the necessary photos with the ghastly little client trying desperately to look like James Bond and was on his way back to his studio in London as quickly as he could. What a ghastly man, and from what he could see of Grimewold, it was not a place he had any intention of ever setting foot in again. He would get the portrait done and show it to Morrell at his Gallery in London, and then it could be shipped up to his house without Poope ever having to set foot in the Eagles Nest ever again. Poope shuddered at the horrendous things he had to do to make enough money to fund his best work. It was like comparing a Carry On film to a Shakespeare production. The former was regrettably necessary, but the latter was the prize.

After Quentin Poope had left, Mike made himself a scotch and phoned Pauline to make arrangements for their mini break to Scotland. He was finding that as his empire grew, he could allow his team of senior managers to handle things.

More and more money was coming into Humberwold Speed Camera Action! through his regular camera vans, the numerous Pure Profit Teams stationed out in the villages and staffed by old biddies as volunteers, and now the ferociously successful Clean Air Champions were up to speed and bringing in thousands of pounds a week. This had allowed him to spend more and more time with Pauline and on this romantic trip to Scotland he intended to pop the question. He wanted Pauline Piffle to be his wife and ask that loutish buffoon of a husband for a divorce.

'Pauline my love, it's me Mike. How are you today?'

'I'm fine Mike, I was just giving Jennings a list of things to do in the house and then I was off to the hairdressers to make myself look glamorous for you my love. I'm so looking forward to our five days away in Scotland. It is still on, isn't it? said Pauline sounding alarmed at the thought of a last-minute cancellation.

'Of course it is Pauline. I would move heaven and earth to be with you. I've just got rid of that boring twat, Quentin Poope. You know, the guy who is painting my portrait, done the queen and everything. I know he's the best, but Christ is he hard work. Looked down his nose at me as if I was dog shit on his shoe, you wouldn't think I was paying him two hundred grand. Anyway, I couldn't stand sitting there in the study any longer, so we decided that he could take some photos and do the portrait from them in his studio. Says it should be ready to present at his gallery in two months' time.'

'Sounds lovely Mike, but isn't it a bit expensive? Are you sure you can afford it?'

'It's just small change Pauline. You should see what the business is bringing in now that we have the Clean Air Contract, and I want staff and visitors to look up to me and see me for who I really am, a true Captain of Industry.'

'Well, if it makes you happy Mike, then I'm happy.'

'Anyway, the main reason for ringing you is to say that I've booked a limo, it's a Rolls, only the best for my Pauline, and it's to pick you up from Maxwell House and take you to Humberwold Airport. It's coming at 7.00 in the morning to take you there and I'll meet you at check in. The flight is booked for 10.00 a.m. and then we spend the day in Edinburgh, a night in the Grand Speyside Hotel and then we're getting the Highland steam train in the morning for three glorious days. The countryside is spectacular, and we're stopping at the Dunbar Whisky Distillery for a tour and a few samples. Bloody brilliant.'

'Sounds absolutely enchanting Mike. You are so good to me. I wish I had met you years ago.'

'Well you've met me now, that's the main thing. If it wasn't for me, you'd be clattering around that big bloody house with no one to see, given that Piffle is always in Benidorm with his so-called housekeeper.'

'I know, Mike and I'm so grateful. He's a pig my husband, and until you came along I was at rock bottom.'

'Well don't you worry. You stick with me kid, the only way is up.'

And with that the telephone call ended and Mike Morrell sat there in his study contemplating the wonderful week ahead with his beloved Pauline.

Chapter 94

One person who was definitely not having a pleasant week was Bradley Plumb, as well as his long-suffering lover Lemar. Despite winning the £2 million contract to host *Love in the Sun*, the new Channel 7EVEN blockbuster production starting this summer in Ibiza, Plumb was still very badly shaken by the incident on Monday night.

To be kidnapped at knife point and forced to hand over £100,000 had left him shaken and depressed. The only silver lining was that the criminal had had the decency to hand over the incriminating pictures and audio tape. He must have been watching the transaction somehow in the club and managed to take the photos. He couldn't imagine what would have happened if the tabloids had got hold of the pictures. His career on *Purple Haze* and *Love in the Sun* would be over, in fact, no one would employ him again and all his celebrity friends would shun him. It was a ghastly unthinkable outcome that was well worth paying the hundred grand to avoid. It never occurred to the dim-whited Plumb, or Lemar, that the whole thing was a set-up and that

Lord Brett, the supplier of the crack cocaine, had been in on the scam from the start.

Bradley Plumb, when faced with stress and unpleasantness in his life, did what he always did. He hid his head in the sand and used booze and drugs to supress his real feelings and anxieties. Consequently, Lemar and himself had been out of their heads since the incident on Monday night, to the point where he had nearly used up the first batch of cocaine that Brett had supplied him with last week. Not that is mattered, as long as he got himself fairly coherent for his Friday night TV show.

'I think we'll still go to *Careless Whisper* on Thursday night, Lemar.' said Bradley. 'I need to get out of this fucking house man, see a few friends and party, party, party!'

'Whatever you say Braders man, maybe we should get away somewhere soon? A cruise or stay on an island? Branson rents his one out for £50,000 a week.'

'Yeah, I like your idea man, Branson's Island. Not bad £50,000 for Branston Pickle's Island,' said Bradley slurring his words and not really taking it all in.

Gordon Streake was making plans to emigrate to Alicante for good. He would miss his sister, but not much else in his life, and especially not Grimewold, or his old sad life of seedy little jobs, mostly following losers in matrimonial disputes for a few measly grand here and there. He just had a few things to wrap up before he left.

He had already transferred the fifty grand he had saved from his building society account in the UK to his Banco Alicante account where the hundred grand was sitting from Bradley Plumb. Later today he would be meeting Penelope Sykes to hand over the incriminating evidence he had on Plumb, as per their contract, and get his final payment for delivering the goods. It looked like Plumb's career was going to be over when Penelope Sykes had finished with him. Good riddance as far as Streake was concerned. He was ultimately responsible for Penelope's daughter's death, so fuck him. Parasites like him deserved what they got. So often scum like Plumb succeeded, whereas upstanding citizens like himself where shat upon from a great height, well not this time. This time Plumb was for the high jump.

'Do you want another cup of tea?' said his sister, fussing over him as usual.

'No pet, I've got to go out shortly and meet a client, but thanks anyway. And thanks for the cooked breakfast, no one does a cooked breakfast like you. I'll miss your cooking when move to Alicante.'

'And I know you've felt a burden since they sacked you from the force, but I've loved having you here Gordon. I will miss you terribly,' said Brenda getting quite upset.

'Don't fret Brenda. Look on the bright side. Once I get settled in my apartment you're welcome to come over to Alicante whenever you like, get away from this dump of a town.'

'It's not that bad Gordon, I like it here. It's where we grew up, and I've got me friends and my bingo on a Tuesday night at Gala, and there's ASDA just up the road. No, what I'm going to miss is company every day and cooking you nice meals. You never could cook. I don't know how you're going to feed yourself Gordon. I do worry.'

'No need Brenda, and who knows, I might find a lovely Spanish señorita to look after me and feed me paella and chips every day.'

'Oh you do make me laugh Gordon. Well, let's hope you do finally find love, you deserve it. You're a good man, and the way your fellow officers stitched you up over them drugs and blamed you, just because you had a Rolex watch and a Jensen car. You always had been careful with your money, didn't mean you were bent.'

'That's water under the bridge Brenda. I've finally got the money together to do what I 've always dreamed of. Nothing too grand, just my own little piece of paradise in the sun. A small apartment near Benidorm or Alicante, that'll do me. Don't need a car as the public transport is dirt cheap, and I can get a cooked breakfast every day for €4, so I won't starve. I'm staying in the Hotel Ambassador for a month whilst I look around. I'll probably rent an apartment at first just to make sure that I am happy there. Anyway, must go, I'm meeting a client in the Cromwell Arms at 12.00 sharp, can't be late as I've got some documents for her and she owes me my final payment.'

Streake left his sister's house and got into the old Vectra. Soon he was on the Grimewold ring road and passing one of Mike Morrell's Speed Camera Action! teams with their Transit van taking photos of speeding cars. He was doing under 40 mph so fuck 'em, they were not getting a hundred quid out of him today, or any day soon.

Then he came to the traffic lights by the Gala Bingo and there was another of Morrell's money-making scams in the form of the Clean Air Champions, with their hand held air monitoring devices. As he drove past, the equipment took a reading and a photo, and then compared the reading to the official exhaust emissions specification for that vehicle. Predictably, the Vectra had failed and a £500 fine would be winding its way within seven days to his sister's house, never to be paid, as Streake would be long gone, never to return.

He parked the innocuous Vauxhall Vectra in the car park of the Cromwell Arms and went inside to wait for Penelope Sykes and give her the envelope with the pictures and the audio tape incriminating Bradley Plumb just as his client had hoped. He sat in one of the booths at the side with their gloomy lighting keeping things nice and private just as he liked.

Penelope Sykes was on time, but again totally out of place in a dive like the Cromwell Arms. All the other punters at the bar looked round at her as she walked in, spotted Streake and made her way to the booth where he sat.

'Hello Gordon, have you got me what we agreed?' she said coming straight to the point.

'Oh yes. Sit down and I will show you Penelope. I've got enough here to sink Plumb's career for good, and probably put him inside for five years if the CPS decide to press charges. Either way, his career is finished. You could even sell these to the tabloids for a good sum of money and recoup your "investment". Talking of which, my final bill is a further £11,000 and to give you this evidence, I want it in my bank account today.'

'Don't worry Streake, if you've got the goods on Plumb then I'll transfer your 11 grand whilst we sit here using my online account. The wonders of the internet eh?'

Streake showed Penelope the incriminating photos, which showed Plumb as clear as day buying the drugs and handing over the money, and the even more incriminating audio tape. Whether it was enough for the oh-so-cautious CPS he wasn't sure, but it certainly would end Plumb's lucrative TV career with Channel 7EVEN and his £4 million a year. Worse than any derisory prison sentence for Bradley Plumb.

Penelope Sykes was delighted with Streake's work and transferred the money immediately. She planned to go to the newspapers over the weekend hoping to get an exposé in the Sunday gutter press. She didn't care if they paid her or not. It wasn't about the money, it was about justice for her beloved little girl, Madison.

With the deal done they were both soon on their way, Streake in his old grey Vectra and Penelope Sykes in a sleek Audi coupe. Two different people in different worlds flung together by a common desire to see Bradley Plumb pay for his sins.

And pay he did, but not in a way that either of them could

envisage.

As planned, early the next morning, a beautiful honey gold Rolls Royce Silver Spirit glided into the drive of Pauline Piffle's house, and came to a halt outside the front door. Pauline came out with her expensive, fake zebra-skin luggage looking very glamorous in a tangerine summer dress, gloss black handbag and high heels. Her hair looked stunning, having been cut and blow dried by a top salon in Beverley the day before. Jennings was at the door to see her off.

'Now don't forget Anthony, feed the dog, and take him for a walk each day, cut the grass and get some shopping in. I've left you a list on the table, apart from that, your time's your own.'

'Will do Pauline, oh and Pauline, you look absolutely lovely, a bit different from our days at the Gipsyville Secondary Modern.'

'Thanks Tony, thanks for everything.'

Pauline got into the back of the hired executive Rolls Royce and soon she was off on a new adventure with Mike Morrell. It took about forty minutes from her house to Humberwold Airport, where Mike was waiting at check in, fretting and pacing about as usual.

'Bloody hell Pauline. I never thought you'd get here, where the heck have you been?'

'The driver in the Rolls was very slow, took his time, then we got stuck on the Humberwold Bridge for thirty minutes. It was down to one lane as usual because they had a jumper again and you know what the police are these days with Health and Safety, ultra-cautious. One of the lanes has been closed for six hours apparently.'

'Well we best get checked in. The BA flight is in an hour and I don't want us to miss it. I've got the break all planned.'

Soon they were on their way to Edinburgh airport in what passed for first class on a domestic local flight. Soon after landing and a short taxi ride later, they were dropped off at the exclusive Grand Speyside Hotel near to the famous Castle.

Mike had pulled all the stops out. He had booked the best room in the hotel with views of the castle, named 'The Presidential Suite', with a four-poster bed, separate lounge with 55" flat screen TV, walk in wardrobe, and huge jacuzzi bath.

After freshening up and changing for dinner, the golden couple went down to the exclusive restaurant and enjoyed a sumptuous four-course meal by the top Scottish three-star Michelin chef, Bernhard Phillipe McNab.

After much deliberation, Mike decided the time was right. He got out a small jewellery box and opened it, getting down on one knee he proposed to Pauline Piffle.

'I know you're still married Pauline, but I want you to be my wife and I want you to have this ring as my promise to you that as soon as you divorce your husband, you'll marry me my love and we will build a new life together.'

'Oh Mike that is so wonderful. Of course, of course I'll marry you,' said Pauline with tears in her eyes.

'Come on my love, let's go to the room and continue our enchanted night there, together in each other's arms.'

Later that night in London, as usual, the black Maybach pulled up outside the *Careless Whisper* gay night club, and Plumb and his entourage got out and followed their weekly ritual, petals and all. This time there were a few photographers lying in wait getting pictures as it had come out that Plumb was going to host the new Channel 7EVEN block buster in Ibiza called *Love in the Sun*.

'How did you beat Poppy Minx to host *Love in the Sun*?' shouted one of the so-called journalists.

'I'm more experienced man, maybe Poppy Minx can do Countdown?' he laughed putting her down with his nasty and pointless remark.

They entered the club after he allowed the photographers to get their shots of him in his dark aviator shades, long purple velvet coat and purple velvet trousers, with Tiggy furiously throwing the purple petals in front of him as he walked into the club.

They ordered their usual champagne cocktails and settled into their usual spot away from the dance floor. Bradley Plumb was soon snorting crack cocaine from the latest batch that Lord Brett Sinclair had given him on Monday night. No one would ever know if Brett got the strength wrong or whether Bradley just had too much, but soon he was completely out of his mind and decided that he was a hand-glider.

As Mike Morrell and his beautiful companion Pauline Piffle, mother of Bradley Plumb, were making love, back in the Presidential Suite, her son had other more dramatic plans for the evening.

He shot round the club with his arms outstretched pretending to be a hand-glider singing loudly. 'He flies like a bird in the sky i i, he flies like a bird and I wish that he was mine, he flies like a bird oh me oh my... Now I know I can't let Lemar go.'

For some reason he was mimicking the lyrics from the Nimble Bread advert of 1968 by the band Honey Bus, but changing the lyrics slightly to express his love for men in general and his lover Lemar in particular.

He then 'flew' out onto the balcony where people went to have a fag and launched himself over the railings with his arms outstretched still thinking he was a hand-glider.

Of course, he didn't fly at all and very quickly plunged to his death landing with a huge crash on the roof of the sleek black Mercedes Maybach, a rather fitting end really for the complete arsehole that was Bradley Norman Plumb.

Luckily for one of the photographers, a freelance guy called Jed, he was able to get the scoop of the year as he was chatting to the Maybach's chauffeur at the time of the accident and managed to get some really good shots of Plumb flying through the sky and then the bloodied shots afterwards, as Plumb lay crumpled, as dead as a dodo on the roof of the Maybach.

Jed was due a really good pay-out for that set of shots, that's for sure. So, as they say, right place, right time. Jed was lucky that he had stayed back for a fag and a chat with Bradley Plumb's chauffeur in the hope of getting a few titbits of celebrity gossip.

Chapter 95

Luckily for the tabloid press, it was just in time to change the front covers of all the main newspapers with news that one of Britain's best-loved celebrities, Bradley Plumb, host of *Purple Haze*, had plunged to his death from the top floor of the *Careless Whisper* night club, complete with some very graphic pictures of him flying through the air and then of his crumped, bloody body laid prostrate across the roof of the Maybach.

The death of Plumb was also the main headline on the breakfast morning news shows for BBC, ITV and Sky News. It was agreed that the most tactless headline went to the Daily Record with its appalling headline 'Anyone For Plumb Jam!'

The programme editor of Chanel 7EVEN had his work cut out that morning. He was straight on the phone to Poppy Minx to offer her Bradley Plumb's job of hosting *Purple Haze* that night and the contract for *Love in the Sun* was now up for grabs. The programme editor promised to put in a good word for Poppy Minx with the production company of *Love in the Sun*, Zeus Productions, but felt that as she had already been in the running it would be a straight shoe in.

'Well the show must go on sweetie, and you were second choice for both shows. As they say sweetie, it's a "plum" opportunity,' he said laughing hysterically at his own horrendous joke. As far as he was concerned, Bradley Plumb was just a commodity, and as long as that commodity could be replaced seamlessly, then it was no problem to him.

'Yeah, course I'll do it. I've wanted Braders job for a long time, do I get the same dosh as he was getting?'

'Yes of course you do sweetie, you're a hot ticket Poppy Minx, and we'll look after you, don't you worry your pretty little head about that.'

'Cool.'

Lemar was equally self-centred about the death of his lover. He spent Friday morning on the phone finding out if the life insurance was going to pay out to him and if he had been left the Chelsea pad in Plumb's last will and testament.

The only person in the world who would be truly upset by the demise of Bradley Plumb was his mother, but Pauline was on the Highland Steam Railway heading towards Dunbar, and the chance to sample the delights of single malt scotch whisky. She was blissfully unaware of her only son's fate.

It would be Sunday before she discovered the terrible truth of her son's death. Piffle, being in Benidorm, and not at all interested in news from Blighty, was also blissfully unaware of his son's fate and would not find out until Pauline rang him late Sunday night.

Because of the circumstances of Bradley Plumb's death, there would be a post-mortem which, given the back log, would put the funeral back three weeks.

One person who did learn of Bradley Plumb's untimely death was Gordon Streake who read about it in the Daily Record over breakfast on Friday morning whilst he was having his bacon and eggs.

It was a very unnerving story as far as Streake was concerned, as the death was bound to be drug related and although he hadn't supplied Plumb with anything, he had kidnapped the guy and secured a hundred thousand pounds off him two days before his death. Lord Brett Sinclair had supplied the drugs and knew of their plans, or at least enough to put Streake away for a stretch. All a bit too close for comfort. His flight to Alicante had been booked for Saturday morning, but he decided to see if he could get the evening flight out from Doncaster Robin Hood Airport and get away from the scene of the crime so to speak, and on to his new life in the sun. There were just two things he wanted to do before he went, which wouldn't take long.

'I'm just popping out for a few hours Brenda. I'll be back after lunch. I might go to Spain tonight instead of tomorrow. Something has cropped up and I need to get out there.'

Brenda knew never to ask Streake too much. He was a man of secrets, always had been and she had always left him to get on with his life, knowing in the back of her mind that often he was up to no good but trying to think the best of him.

'Oh, that's a shame Gordon, but if you have to go, you have to go. Maybe we can have a last meal together around lunch time before you have to go to the airport?'

'Yeah, that would be nice.'

With that, he left the house got into the Vectra and made his way to Grimewold Police Headquarters in the centre of town, and went straight to the staff canteen and sat there with a cup of coffee. He didn't have to wait long before the little clique of coppers who had fitted him up and put the rumours about of him taking bribes off drugs dealers came in. None of them liked him because he had had a Jensen Interceptor and a Rolex watch, and in return he loathed and detested them. They immediately spotted him sitting there, and all pointed at him, and started singing their stupid little song.

'Yes, they call him the Streake looka dat looka dat, fastest thing on two feet, looka dat looka dat. If there's an audience to be found he'll be streaking around, yes they call him the Streake... Don't look Ethel, but it was too late she had already been mooned!'

They were all laughing loudly as he approached them, singing the song and taking the piss out of him.

'You think that's funny do you? You bunch of washed out

useless knobs, still chasing petty criminals around on the Cromwell Estate. Well, I've just come to tell you bunch of corrupt two-faced piss-artist pricks that I'm retiring to a place in the sun. Made my money doing my Private Investigator work and now I'm off, villa, sun, booze and a nice señorita, so farewell fuckwits and I hope that you have many more pointless years in this festering shit hole.'

He turned on his heels and left the canteen without saying another word. They all looked at him, mouths completely lost for words. For once, Gordon Streake had got one over on them and they wouldn't have a chance to upset him ever again.

As all of this was going on in Grimewold, Jimmy The Fleece was hosting his first marketing event at the Go-Go Bar and Grill in the old town. The go-go girls had done their job and had rounded up fifty punters that morning from the four and five star hotels for Jimmy's grand presentation about the benefits and pleasures of owning a log cabin in Benidorm.

Jimmy was at the front in his Hawaiian shirt and tan chinos, tanned, relaxed and with a permanent grin, scanning the room for opportunities.

'Good morning ladies and gentleman, boys and girls. I'm Jimmy Moston and I've lived here in Benidorm for twenty-five years. Thank you for coming and I hope you've enjoyed the full English buffet breakfast and complementary teas and coffees, only Yorkshire tea mind! Was it good? Of course it was.

Well, thank you for coming here today and I suspect some of you might be suspicious. You might be thinking, "why have I been offered a free coach trip into the Mountains to see the Castell or Castle of Guadalest and the beautiful Guadalest reservoir nearby? What is the catch?" I hear you say. Well ladies and gentleman, there is no catch. This is our thank you for listening to our marketing presentation and to make you an offer you can't refuse.

Hands up please, those of you that have got a few bob in the bank? It could be thousands, it could be hundreds or it could be hundreds of thousands, if you were as lucky as Ken Dodd and had made friends with the tax man.'

Quite a few of the audience put their hands up.

'You there sir, in the front row. Do you mind telling me, and the rest of the audience, what percentage you're getting on your savings at the moment? Don't be shy.'

'Well, I'm getting about 1.2% fixed for 12 months.'

'Did you hear that ladies and gentleman? 1.2% for 12 months. That's a measly grand if you have got a hundred grand in the bank. Am I right or am I right? And I bet the banks are lending your money out at 20%, making twenty grand, when they're only giving you a grand. Greedy bastards, aren't they?

What if I was to tell you that, here in Benidorm, you could own a brand new beautiful Scandinavian log cabin, guaranteed for thirty years for only €175,000? And we would guarantee you 10% on your money for renting it out for twenty weeks a year and you could have the other thirty-two weeks for yourself, either to stay in or rent out to friends and family. You could be making ten times what the bastard banks are giving you and having a lovely five-star log cabin to stay in whenever you want, with your very own spa plunge pool, veranda and three bedrooms.

Now here is the best bit. If you sign up this week, because the development is brand new, you can borrow 70% of the money from the Banco Alicante at 0% for the first five years, and only have to pay €52,000, or around £40,000 and you get €17,500 a year guaranteed. Can't be bad. But don't worry ladies and gentleman, if that's too much, then you can buy a week's timeshare option for a special introductory price of just €10,000 in four easy instalments over 12 months, again at 0% interest.

Now, here at the Playa de Sol Holiday park we're not about to pressurise you. We are offering you a two-night stay free-of-charge in one of the beautiful log cabins for yourself whilst you're here in Benidorm. If it's not for you, it costs you nothing, but if you fall in love with the concept, as we know you will, we're here to make your dreams come true.'

The very slick marketing presentation went on for well over an hour and as the punters got more and more merry on the booze they were encouraged to buy from the bar, it became easier and easier to sign them up for the two day complementary stay in one of the log cabins. Jimmy knew that once they were in one of the log cabins and bought into the idea that they already owned one, the last push and sign up was easy. Marketing was all about giving people reasons to do what you wanted them to do so they thought that they were getting the bargain of the century and a quality product that fitted with their own aspirations. Jimmy had been here many times before and got the t-shirt, but even he had to admit that the two-story, three-bed luxury log cabins were an easy sell and a genuinely well-constructed quality product, even if they had not come from Scandinavia but from the city of Hull.

The first presentation went better than hoped and by the end, Jimmy had signed up some of the punters before letting them go on their free coach trip into the mountains.

Back in Grimewold, Streake had one more thing to do of a more benevolent nature before he left for Alicante. It was unlike him, but for once he was feeling magnanimous and if it hadn't been for the help of Lord Brett Sinclair he wouldn't be in the position he was, so he wanted, in a small way, to give him a small token of his gratitude.

He parked up outside the grubby council house on the Cromwell Estate, leaving the Vectra parked directly outside the house and banged loudly on the door.

Lord Brett's girlfriend answered the door scowling at him. 'What the fuck do you want copper?'

'I'm not a copper, get me Brett, now!'

'Brett that tosser Streake's here to see you!'

Brett came to the door, not as hostile as he had been previously. He had gained a grudging respect for Streake and in a bizarre way the feeling was mutual.

'Eh up Streakey boy, what can I do for you? No more trips to London I hope,' he said, actually laughing.

'Thing is Brett. I'm off to Spain tonight to retire, so to speak, for good. See that Vectra there, here are the keys, it's only worth a grand but it's yours now, the paperwork's in the glove box and here's a grand cash for you to have a treat with for you and the girlfriend. I owe you Brett, and thought you could use a bit of dollar mate,' he said chuckling at the use of the term that Brett used all the time for cash.

'Thanks man, no fucker's ever given me anything in me life.'

'Just let's call it a thank you for services rendered.'

And with that, Streake turned and got into a waiting taxi that he had booked earlier. He said to the driver, 'Take me to Ashlands Road, near ASDA, number 27,' and with that the taxi pulled away. It would be the last time Streake saw Lord Brett Sinclair, or the notorious Cromwell Estate for that matter.

He got back to Brenda's house and she was already in the kitchen making him his final tea. It was his favourite, rump steak and thick cut chips with a fried egg on top. They sat down at the dining table together and Streake tucked in to his favourite meal.

'I do hope you're going to be alright Gordon.' Said Brenda sniffling.

'I'll be fine Brenda. It's what I've always wanted and worked for, a little place in the sun and an early retirement. I won't have a lot of spare dosh, but who cares? I won't be working, and I'll soon make some friends. Not bothering with a car, and heating bills are cheap, so it's just me rent and food on the table, plus a few beers and wagers at the bookies. Maybe you could come over in September? I should be sorted with an apartment by then.'

'Oh that will be nice Gordon, I will miss you.'

'Don't worry love, I'll ring you every week and keep in touch by Facebook. It's only a few hours away if you do fancy a break.'

'And you will keep out of trouble Gordon?' said Brenda, a small reprimand for all the unsaid things that had gone on in Gordon's life.

'Don't you worry Brenda, it's a quiet retirement for me. Mr invisible man that's me.'

Before too long, the taxi had arrived to take him to Doncaster Robin Hood Airport. An hour later it dropped him off at Departures where he checked in for his flight and waited in the departure lounge.

As he sat there Streake grinned and laughed at his private joke. Here he was at Robin Hood Airport named after the thief that had stolen from the rich and given to the poor – just like Gordon Streake, he had stolen from Bradley Plumb and given the proceeds to a poor man —

himself. Life was full of ironies.

Chapter 96

That Friday evening Penelope Sykes was sitting at home in the conservatory thinking about the amazing turn of events. She had her precious pictures of Bradley Plumb buying crack cocaine and the audio tape of the conversation in the *Careless Whisper* nightclub. Going to the police now would raise more questions than it answered and implicate her in Bradley's death since the police would want to know how she had got the pictures and audio tape. It was the same with the tabloids, yes they would pay her for the pictures and audio tape, but could she risk being exposed as the person who gave the information to the papers? Especially as this might be classed as a murder enquiry. She didn't know if Gordon Streake had any part in Bradley Plumb's death, but she wasn't convinced he was squeaky clean. The coincidence of him being down there at the time was too great.

On reflection she had her revenge. Plumb was dead and no longer benefitting from being one of Britain's best-loved celebrities, she had got some justice for the death of her beloved Madison.

Piffle

No, she would not go to the police and she would not go to the tabloids. She decided there and then what she would do with the pictures and audio tape she had paid for.

'I'm just popping out for an hour dear,' she said to her husband. 'I've got a little errand to run to do with work.'

Penelope got into her car and travelled into town arriving at the offices of the Grimewold Gazette. She went up to the reception with dark glasses and a scarf on so no one could recognise her. She approached reception and changing her voice as much as she could said, 'Can you give this envelope to the editor please? It's very important and he will be very interested in the contents.'

'I certainly can Miss, but who should I say left the package?'

'That doesn't matter. The contents are self-explanatory and it will be a major scoop for the newspaper.'

With that she turned on her heel and left the building quickly soon arriving back at her car, which was parked well away and out of sight. That should set the cat amongst the pigeons, she thought, and it did.

Once the editor had reviewed the pictures and tape that evening with the tantalizing note saying this was Bradley Plumb buying crack cocaine on Monday night in the *Careless Whisper* nightclub, he knew he had a big story on his hands. He decided there and then that the Grimewold Gazette would get the world exclusive tomorrow and then he would sell the story and the pictures to Fleet Street for the

Sunday editions, when he didn't produce a paper. That way he would get two bites of the cherry and be paid handsomely by the Fleet Street tabloids.

He ran with the headline 'Plumb Buys Crack Cocaine Days Before Plunging To His Death'. The London tabloids were less respectful of Plumb. In death, as in life, they liked to bring a celebrity down, and the most tactless headline read 'First Cherry Coke Now Plumb Coke. Bradley Plumb, one of Britain's top comedy hosts, buys crack cocaine in seedy gay nightclub just days before his death...'

Luckily, Bradley's mother, Pauline, had no knowledge of the death of her beloved son since she was still in Scotland. She was travelling back from Inverness on the Scottish Highland Steam Train and not due to arrive in Edinburgh until Saturday night for a final stop over before the flight home to Humberwold on Sunday morning.

Some people say that for every good thing that happens in someone's life they have to pay with it by having a bad thing happen. This was certainly true for Pauline Piffle. She'd had the most amazing few days and a proposal of marriage from Mike Morrell, a man who truly loved her. She had never been happier, not even compared to the early years with Piffle.

As she boarded the BA flight with Mike he was handed a copy of the Sunday Telegraph as a complementary read on the journey home. As they got settled in first class and put their bags in the overhead lockers, Mike glanced at the headlines. He didn't put two and two together at first, forgetting that Bradley Plumb was in fact Bradley

Norman Piffle, and when the penny finally dropped that the dead chat show host was Pauline's son, he had to break the news to her on the flight.

He wasn't sure if it was the right thing to do, but keeping a secret like that from her would have been unforgivable. Pauline took the news badly. Although Piffle didn't care for his son and never had, Pauline adored her only son. She was so proud of his achievements in becoming famous hosting *Purple Haze* and his other guest appearances on trash reality TV formats. It's fair to say that Pauline was devastated and cried the rest of the way home.

That night she phoned Piffle at the Villa Almeria and told him the news that his only son had died by falling off a balcony at a top London nightclub. She explained to Piffle that because the death was unexplained there would be an autopsy and the body would not be released for burial until the Police were satisfied with the cause of death. They agreed over the phone that Piffle would not come back to England until the funeral could go ahead, which might be two or three weeks away.

Even Piffle was taken aback and quite upset by the turn of events. No, he had never approved of Bradley Plumb for all sorts of reasons, but he didn't want to see his son hurt, never mind dead. It was a tragic life cut short.

Lemar hadn't taken the death of his lover well at all. He had carried on boozing and sniffing coke all through Friday and decided that it was better to be coked out of his head all weekend rather than face reality. He had already ascertained that he was the sole beneficiary in Plumb's will, that the mortgage on the Chelsea house would be paid off and that Plumb had a substantial life insurance policy totalling £2 million, all of which was coming to Lemar – other than ten grand he had left to his long suffering assistant, Tiggy.

Never one to let the grass grow under his feet Lemar, was back at *Careless Whisper* on Saturday night trying to pick up a new lover. It didn't take him long before he had met a new man, namely Gerald Milton-Hays a senior partner in a fund management company based in Canary Wharf called Icarus Asset Management. After a booze and drug fuelled night at the club, they went back to Plumb's old house in Chelsea just two days after his untimely death.

Chapter 97

On Monday morning Tandori was still enjoying her extended weekend in the Cotswolds with mummy and daddy. After breakfast, she took their black Labrador for a walk in the woods and felt chilled for the first time in ages. If she had known of developments taking place back in Grimewold she might have been well sanguine about the immediate future.

The Grimewold Chamber of Commerce, with many members large and small, had been receiving an increasing number of complaints about the Diversity Action Partnership, including from their largest member McGreggor's Steel.

Up until recently these complaints could not be acted upon because all the companies involved were in breach of clear diversity regulations and, as such, were forced to pay the ludicrous fines imposed. But now Tandori's sabotage was starting to have an effect, it had been established by the Chamber of Commerce's legal team that many of the recent fines were in fact unlawful and had been directed at companies that were meeting the terms of the act, or firms who had already paid their fines.

As such, and with a hefty financial contribution from McGreggor's Steel, the Chamber launched a class action lawsuit for damages and compensation in the high court as all of their complaints to date had gone unanswered – primarily because Tandori had intercepted the complaints and hidden them. The class action requested that The Diversity Action Partnership repaid £262,000 in illegal fines, paid court costs and compensation for stress and anxiety for the business owners affected to the tune of a further £500,000. The total claim was for £762,000.

To make matters worse, the Chamber of Commerce were informing Grimewold Council that they were taking this action and were unhappy with the administration of the scheme through the Diversity Action Partnership Limited. It would take another week before the class action would be submitted to the court as lawyers representing the Chamber of Commerce were still drafting the final wording of the lawsuit. But, as a matter of courtesy, the council were to be informed, in writing, on Friday of the impending action. A letter was also to be sent to the council's legal team as they could be liable for some of the fallout given that they awarded the contract to Piffle's company in the first place.

Over in Benidorm Piffle was completely unaware of this impending disaster, but the morning was a mixed bag of emotions for him. On the one hand he'd had a very upbeat phone call from Jimmy The Fleece, giving him the fantastic news that after the marketing presentation and the offers of free stays in the log cabins, all ten of the first batch of finished cabins had been sold at full list price. In short, Jimmy's marketing plan was working a treat.

This very welcome news was tinged with sadness as Piffle was still coming to terms with the loss of his son. He kept wondering if he could have done anything differently. But as soon as the boy was sent to that poncy private school and decided he was gay, he was lost to Piffle. Bradley had soon gone down to London and mixed with all those shallow southern Tories and then eventually landed the role of a chat show host changing his name and embarrassing Piffle with his crude jokes and, frankly, disgusting juvenile pranks. No, it was not his fault that his son had taken the road he had taken and then got into the hard drugs which had eventually killed him.

The boy had been spoiled by Pauline and shielded from the realities of life that he, and in particular his father, had to endure on the Gipsyville Estate; not the easy run for them that Bradley Norman Piffle had experienced. No, it was his stupid mother's fault that Bradley had ended up the way he had, and his demise was nothing to do with Piffle. He would, of course, go to the funeral and pay his respects. With this chapter over he felt it even more easy to ask Pauline for a divorce, especially as the log cabin business was going so well.

'Are you feeling sad my Dresden?' said Honolulu. 'It is such big shame about your son, it is the curse of the modern world, these drugs.'

'It's one of those things Honolulu. Truth is, people make choices and my lad made a choice. If he hadn't taken cocaine he wouldn't of flown off the balcony at that club thinking he was a hand-glider. Made a terrible mess of that Maybach apparently.'

'No, it is true Dresden, you mustn't blame yourself.'

'I don't I blame me, it's that stupid mother of his the Clothes Horse, for filling his head with poncy la-di-da ideas at that public school. Turned him into a southern Tory boy and that was the end of that, poncing around with purple petals and a purple velvet coat with that black lover Lemar. Truth is Honolulu, he was a disgrace to the name of Piffle and all we stand for. I must have been a laughingstock of the Gipsyville working men's club with a son like that, all because of the bloody Clothes Horse. And I'll tell her at funeral, you mark my words.'

'Don't be too hard on her Dresden, she will be grieving. She was his mother, him her only son. A mother has, what you say, a bond with their first born, you must understand.'

'I suppose you've got a point Honolulu, but I will still be saying my piece, and no doubt that bloody Mike Morrell will be there gloating that he has got me wife.'

'Well you have me my darling,' said Honolulu.

'Yes, but it's not the same. He stole me wife from under me nose just as he intended to do. He doesn't like me that Morrell, never has, don't know why but there you are.'

Chapter 98

On Monday morning Tandori was still enjoying her extended weekend in the Cotswolds with mummy and daddy. After breakfast, she took their black Labrador for a walk in the woods and felt chilled for the first time in ages. If she had known of developments taking place back in Grimewold she might have been well sanguine about the immediate future.

The Grimewold Chamber of Commerce, with many members large and small, had been receiving an increasing number of complaints about the Diversity Action Partnership, including from their largest member McGreggor's Steel.

Up until recently these complaints could not be acted upon because all the companies involved were in breach of clear diversity regulations and, as such, were forced to pay the ludicrous fines imposed. But now Tandori's sabotage was starting to have an effect, it had been established by the Chamber of Commerce's legal team that many of the recent fines were in fact unlawful and had been directed at companies that were meeting the terms of the act, or firms who had already paid their fines.

As such, and with a hefty financial contribution from McGreggor's Steel, the Chamber launched a class action lawsuit for damages and compensation in the high court as all of their complaints to date had gone unanswered – primarily because Tandori had intercepted the complaints and hidden them. The class action requested that The Diversity Action Partnership repaid £262,000 in illegal fines, paid court costs and compensation for stress and anxiety for the business owners affected to the tune of a further £500,000. The total claim was for £762,000.

To make matters worse, the Chamber of Commerce were informing Grimewold Council that they were taking this action and were unhappy with the administration of the scheme through the Diversity Action Partnership Limited. It would take another week before the class action would be submitted to the court as lawyers representing the Chamber of Commerce were still drafting the final wording of the lawsuit. But, as a matter of courtesy, the council were to be informed, in writing, on Friday of the impending action. A letter was also to be sent to the council's legal team as they could be liable for some of the fallout given that they awarded the contract to Piffle's company in the first place.

Over in Benidorm Piffle was completely unaware of this impending disaster, but the morning was a mixed bag of emotions for him. On the one hand he'd had a very upbeat phone call from Jimmy The Fleece, giving him the fantastic news that after the marketing presentation and the offers of free stays in the log cabins, all ten of the first batch of finished cabins had been sold at full list price. In short, Jimmy's marketing plan was working a treat.

This very welcome news was tinged with sadness as Piffle was still coming to terms with the loss of his son. He kept wondering if he could have done anything differently. But as soon as the boy was sent to that poncy private school and decided he was gay, he was lost to Piffle. Bradley had soon gone down to London and mixed with all those shallow southern Tories and then eventually landed the role of a chat show host changing his name and embarrassing Piffle with his crude jokes and, frankly, disgusting juvenile pranks. No, it was not his fault that his son had taken the road he had taken and then got into the hard drugs which had eventually killed him.

The boy had been spoiled by Pauline and shielded from the realities of life that he, and in particular his father, had to endure on the Gipsyville Estate; not the easy run for them that Bradley Norman Piffle had experienced. No, it was his stupid mother's fault that Bradley had ended up the way he had, and his demise was nothing to do with Piffle. He would, of course, go to the funeral and pay his respects. With this chapter over he felt it even more easy to ask Pauline for a divorce, especially as the log cabin business was going so well.

'Are you feeling sad my Dresden?' said Honolulu. 'It is such big shame about your son, it is the curse of the modern world, these drugs.'

'It's one of those things Honolulu. Truth is, people make choices and my lad made a choice. If he hadn't taken cocaine he wouldn't of flown off the balcony at that club thinking he was a hand-glider. Made a terrible mess of that Maybach apparently.'

'No, it is true Dresden, you mustn't blame yourself.'

'I don't I blame me, it's that stupid mother of his the Clothes Horse, for filling his head with poncy la-di-da ideas at that public school. Turned him into a southern Tory boy and that was the end of that, poncing around with purple petals and a purple velvet coat with that black lover Lemar. Truth is Honolulu, he was a disgrace to the name of Piffle and all we stand for. I must have been a laughingstock of the Gipsyville working men's club with a son like that, all because of the bloody Clothes Horse. And I'll tell her at funeral, you mark my words.'

'Don't be too hard on her Dresden, she will be grieving. She was his mother, him her only son. A mother has, what you say, a bond with their first born, you must understand.'

'I suppose you've got a point Honolulu, but I will still be saying my piece, and no doubt that bloody Mike Morrell will be there gloating that he has got me wife.'

'Well you have me my darling,' said Honolulu.

'Yes, but it's not the same. He stole me wife from under me nose just as he intended to do. He doesn't like me that Morrell, never has, don't know why but there you are.'

Chapter 99

Gordon Streake had arrived safely in Alicante. He had taken a taxi from the airport to Benidorm where he was booked into the Ambassador Hotel for a month whilst he looked for an apartment to rent or buy.

He liked the Ambassador and had stayed there before with his sister, Brenda, when they had been on holiday together five years previously. The rooms were clean, but what he really liked was that he was served three square meals a day. An all you can eat buffet breakfast, lunch and an evening meal with free local beer and wine thrown in. The quality of the food was excellent, and it gave him a base from which to explore without any pressure in the short term to find an apartment.

He wanted to find his bearings and make the right choice. Now it was summer, the weather was getting really nice and after a leisurely breakfast he decided to have a walk along the front and take in the views of the beach, the sea and the bay. There were loads of bars on the front as well where he could stop off for a San Miguel, or a coffee and buy an English newspaper. He would find a nice bar, get a newspaper and sit there in the sun watching the world go by and take in the eye candy. To relax after all these years of hard work and stress was bliss, the start of his new life in Spain.

Buoyed with success, Piffle had been onto Gary Wacker and ordered the next batch of 50 log cabins, payment on completion and delivery to the site. Gary was over the moon that the first ten log cabins had sold so easily. It was all going better than expected. Piffle then phoned Miguel to make sure his team were getting on with laying the concrete pans and the roads and services for the next fifty cabins further into the site. This would take the team another six months, but Piffle felt confident that he could start selling off plan. Miguel wanted the next instalment of money up front though because he had his team to pay and materials to buy. So, with the loan from the bank sitting in his account he was able to do just that, and still have cash flow coming in from The Diversity Action Partnership.

As Piffle was sitting on the deck he received an unexpected call from Pauline, informing him that the autopsy was going ahead this week and the police had said that they could hold the funeral the following Tuesday. So he needed to fly home on Monday at the latest for his son's funeral which was to be at Highgate Cemetery in London. This was sooner than expected, so Piffle got onto one of the budget airlines and booked a flight for Monday morning from Alicante to

Piffle

London Gatwick for himself and Honolulu. He wasn't looking forward to the funeral for a number of reasons, but it had to be done and that was that.

'That was the Clothes Horse on the phone. Funeral is next Tuesday, and we're flying out Monday. I've just booked tickets with budget airline. Row of three seats, one for you and two for me.'

'Oh, this is a surprise Dresden. I thought the autopsy would take the time and it would be a few weeks, but no matter, we can go and see your son off to a better place.'

'Eh, we can at that Honolulu, end of an era. And I can ask Clothes Horse for a divorce and I am then free to marry you. If Pauline wants to be with that pratt Morrell, then so be it.'

'It is not time for rows with your wife Dresden, you just make sure you pay your respects to your son, even if in life you didn't get on.'

'I suppose you're right Honolulu. Time to let bygones be bygones, never thought lad would snuff it before me, but there you are, that's drugs for you. Takes a life too early does the hard stuff.'

On Thursday Spindles drove down to London in the Vectra with the gear hidden in the spare tyre well in the boot. This was the first shipment of Lord Brett's County Lines drug operation, and he was entering the heart of the capital, Chelsea, dominated by the Albanian drugs lords. He would have to be careful and not step on too many toes.

576

Because the drop with Lemar was already arranged and at a private house all went well. Lemar was as good as his word and had the ten grand ready to give to Spindles. All went smoothly, and Lemar assured Spindles that he could shift ten grand a week and sell plenty of gear to other celebrities and rich punters in the Chelsea area.

This was sweet as far as Spindles was concerned. Getting five hundred quid for one simple run to London, drop the gear off and come back, was his sort of thing. An easy lifestyle and easy money. Lord Brett was greedy however, and had told Spindles that once this was settled down he wanted to recruit some runners and an enforcer from the local area to handle drug sales in Kensington and Chelsea, and use kids from either disadvantaged homes or even better, from local authority care homes. That way they took all the risk and he and Spindles just handled the shipments from afar. If anyone was caught in possession, they would only have small amount of gear on them and it wouldn't come back to bite them. They just needed to find an enforcer they could trust and who wasn't going to rip them off or fuck things up. This was the next stage but for now, Spindles was happy with the current arrangement. You could say that Gordon's Streake's act of kindness, giving Lord Brett the Vectra, had helped propel him to the next level of organised and violent crime.

Monday came round quick enough, and Paeleo took Piffle and Honolulu to Alicante Airport for the flight to Gatwick, dropping them off in the Silver Spur.

'Right Paeleo, all being well we'll be back at weekend as after funeral. I want to pop to Grimewold and make sure everything is going alright at Diversity Action Partnership. Want to make sure that Bindle woman is doing her job properly.'

Little did he know just how badly his empire was being run, but he was soon to find out the terrible truth.

'This is good señor Piffle. I will wait for you to call me and I will turn up in the Rolls for you whenever your plane arrives back. I am at your service.'

'Very good Paeleo. I'll ring you when I know flight times but it will probably be Saturday or Sunday.'

With that they went into departures and booked in for the midday flight to Gatwick; Piffle with his two seats booked to accommodate his 52" waist, and Honolulu sitting next to him.

Soon they had arrived at Gatwick and Piffle organised a taxi to take them all the way into North London and to their hotel in Highgate, close to the cemetery and the church where the service would be taking place tomorrow.

It might seem strange to outsiders that Bradley Plumb's funeral would be held at St Michael's Church, Highgate and that he would be buried at Highgate Cemetery but he was a Londoner, if not by birth then by personality and place. In other words, he considered London his home and his personality had assumed that of a southerner after mixing for many years with the creative and artistic set.

Piffle was quite wrong in supposing he was a Tory just because he lived in the south. The so-called Metropolitan Elite had fashionable far left views that were totally alien to Piffle's working class values and priorities. However, Bradley Plumb like so many 'southerners' did have a huge love of money, status and ego, and realised the only way to achieve those things were to adopt a free market, selfish approach to life whist pretending to be egalitarian and 'one of the people'. In short, most of the Metropolitan Elite were total hypocrites with a 'do as I say, not as I do' philosophy. An attitude best illustrated by left wing politicians and trade union leaders sending their own children to private schools whilst trying to deny that opportunity to others on the grounds that it gave unfair advantage. Practise what you preach doesn't apply to the Metropolitan Elite.

The other reason Piffle had chosen a plot for the family at Highgate Cemetery was because his lifetime hero, Karl Marx, the accredited founder of the left and inspiration for the founding of the Labour Party, was buried there, and Piffle was determined that he and his offspring would share the same hallowed ground.

With Piffle being away it had fallen to Pauline to make the arrangement for the funeral of her beloved son and given the fairly short notice it had been a tall order. A local firm of undertakers had collected the body and an oak coffin had been chosen because Bradley Piffle was going to be buried. It was decided that the headstone would carry his stage name, Bradley Plumb, since that was the name he had chosen for himself and best expressed his persona.

Invitations had gone out to the few family likely to attend and the celebrity friends who Lemar had given Pauline details of. She, of course, would be attending with Mike Morrell and they too had travelled down on the Monday to make sure everything went to plan.

Pauline also wanted to see the body at the funeral parlour and say her private goodbyes. It was decided that the vicar would give the speech at the church and only a few words would be said at the graveside prior to the casket being covered with soil as a final act of burial. It was decided that only Pauline, Mike Morrell, Lemar and Anthony Jennings would share a funeral car, and that Piffle would be excluded on the grounds that he didn't like Bradley and had treated him badly throughout his life. Piffle was therefore relegated to observer like the rest of the attendees, something that suited him just fine. Why be a hypocrite and pretend that he got on with his son with his nancy-boy southern values.

The funeral was set for midday at St Michael's Church on Tuesday morning. For a spring day the weather was very pleasant and sunny, but still with quite a sharp wind. The Daimler hearse and following Daimler limousine pulled up outside the church and eight pall bearers man-handled the coffin and started to carry it into the church where it would rest at the front. All of the congregation for the service were already present and standing. It was a sombre affair and Pauline, Mike Morrell, Lemar and Anthony Jennings followed the coffin into the church, with Pauline wailing. Pauline had selected Bradley's favourite song from when he was a small boy, the 1976 hit by the Worzels which he used to sing all the time:

Piffle

Well, I've got a brand new combine harvester and I'll give you the key

Come on now, let's live together in perfect harmony

I've got twenty acres and you've got forty-three

Well, I've got a brand new combine harvester and I'll give you the key

I'll stick by you, I'll give you all that you need

We'll have meat for dinner seven days every week

And you know I love you, girlie, so give me your hand

But the thing I love most is all them acres of land

Well, I've got a brand new combine harvester and I'll give you the key

Come on now, let's live together in perfect harmony

I've got twenty acres and you've got forty-three

Well, I've got a brand new combine harvester and I'll give you the key...

The totally inappropriate and folksy song droned on as the hapless vicar waited for the dirge to end, at which point he started his eulogy of Bradley Plumb's life.

At the front of the church, in the front row, stood Pauline Piffle, Mike Morrell, Lemar and, very controversially, his new lover, Gerald Milton-Hays, and of course Anthony Jennings. Piffle was relegated to the back pews with Honolulu. Given his status as a famous chat show host, the Church was packed by quite a few well-known celebrities;

people from the production company Zeus and Chanel 7EVEN. Even Poppy Minx had turned up with a friend, and of course there was the inevitable members of the tabloid press and the main TV news crews from BBC, ITN and SKY.

It's hard to sum up a person's life in a few short sentences, especially one as colourful and controversial as Bradley Plumb's. His tawdry string of gay lovers, drug fuelled parties and shallow actions were all glossed over as Pauline made sure that his memory encapsulated happier and earlier times in his childhood while growing up at Maxwell House. She did make sure he was recognised for being one of Britain's top chat show hosts. The fictitious account of Plumb's life ended with the vicar saying he fell off a balcony at an exclusive London gentleman's club, a tragic accident for a man at the top of his game.

The congregation were then told they could attend the burial if they wished and in the afternoon there would be a buffet and drinks at the local Cavendish Hotel; all who knew Bradley were welcome.

The coffin was then manhandled out of the church to the hearse for its final resting place in Highgate Cemetery with the strangely inappropriate song by Gloria Gaynor, *I Will Survive*, playing where is was blatantly apparent to all concerned that Bradley Plumb hadn't survived, unless one believed in an afterlife or reincarnation.

Up until that point Piffle and Honolulu had been kept well away from proceedings, so Piffle hadn't managed to air any grievances he may have with Pauline or Mike. That was soon to change at the graveside where Bradley's coffin had been placed in the grave ready to be covered in.

Only a few of the mourners came to cemetery preferring to go to the hotel and get a drink. Close family attended, Anthony Jennings and Poppy Minx, probably to just make sure that Plumb really was dead, and a few stray photographers kept at a safe distance from proceedings.

The vicar gave his final few words culminating in, 'Ashes to ashes, dust to dust,' and threw a few clumps of earth onto the casket. Close family were encouraged to do the same, but as is usual with Piffle, an argument broke out between himself and Pauline.

'I see you've brought that prat Mike Morrell with you, to me bloody son's funeral.'

'Well, I see that you've bought that fat tart Honolulu.'

'Don't you insult me friend.'

'It's just typical of you Piffle, opening your big gob and spoiling things. It's typical of you sticking your bloody nose in where it's not wanted. You're a prize one prat, Piffle' said Mike, jabbing Piffle in the stomach.

Piffle was angry now and pushed Mike. 'Dickhead.'

'Twat,' shouted Morrell pushing Piffle harder.

'Nob,' said Piffle doing the same.

'Arse,' said Mike, and gave Piffle a final shove where he

promptly lost his footing and fell into the hole face down onto his son's casket. It just so happened that the hole was exactly 52" wide and he was completely jammed in and face down on the casket, struggling for air.

'Bloody hell, someone help me,' shouted Piffle, but it was no good.

No one could pull him out. He was too heavy and completely jammed in the hole. Luckily one of Piffle's old friends had come, a big chap who had worked on the fish docks with Piffle years ago when they had been in the union together. Bronto was almost as big as Piffle, but fortunately had come down in his old Land Rover Discovery which had a winch on the front bumper. Seeing the dilemma, he lumbered into action.

'Don't worry Dresden, I'll get me winch on the Land Rover, get the rope round you and we'll have you out in no time.'

Unfortunately, even after they had managed to get a sturdy rope round Piffle's body and attached it to the winch and started up the winch, it was no match for Piffle. Round it went trying its hardest to pull Piffle out of the hole, or at least dislodge him so he could be freed, but the winch just kept straining to no real effect.

'Right,' said Bronto, 'I'll get in the Land Rover and reverse car at speed and it'll pull him out that way. A hundred and fifty horsepower engine should do it.'

Bronto revved the engine and deciding that Piffle need a shove, reversed back at speed. The rope went taught immediately and the sudden force lifted Piffle clean into the air three feet as he shot out of the hole and landed face down on the soft earth at the side of the grave. Covered in mud, Piffle's black suit was ruined and so was his dignity.

'You bastard Morrell, I'll get you for this,' he shouted.

Pauline immediately started crying again.

'She wants a divorce,' shouted Mike rubbing it in and embarrassing Piffle in front of his friends. 'I'm going to marry Pauline and give her the life she deserves, away from a fat pig like you.'

'You're welcome to the bloody Clothes Horse,' shouted Piffle.

'I'm marrying Honolulu, she's a real woman, unlike that stick insect that I married.'

Given the state of Piffle's clothes and the unpleasant proceedings he decided not to go to the wake, but to go back to his hotel and clean himself up leaving the others to attend without him.

Yet again, the press had a field day and the Daily Record had some great pictures of the argument between Morrell and Piffle, Piffle falling into the hole and being winched out by the Land Rover.

The headline read: Plumb's Father Closer To Him In Death Than Life, and went on to discuss the family rift in depth on the front cover of Wednesday's edition. Another scoop for the Daily Record.

After all that drama, the wake at the Caledonian Hotel in Highgate went relatively smoothly, and family and friends toasted the final drama of Bradley Plumb on this earth. Even in death he was controversial, and Poppy Minx was driven off in the Maybach limousine provided by Channel 7EVEN in a state of happy euphoria knowing that he was gone and she, Poppy Minx, had got his £4 million a year salary for hosting *Purple Haze* and *Love in the Sun*. Every cloud has a silver lining, certainly as far as Poppy Minx was concerned.

Chapter 100

It was exceptionally inconvenient that Piffle didn't have Paeleo to drive him around England in the Rolls Royce Silver Spur. He managed to find a company that supplied chauffeurs and limos for the week and, after making sure that he wasn't getting a German one, ordered a limo and chauffeur for the week. It was £1500 but Piffle was used to travelling in style and as things were going well, he thought he would treat himself. The silver-grey Bentley Mulsanne duly arrived at the hotel the following morning with his chauffeur for the week, Charles.

'I'm glad to be in a British car Charles, me old dad Henry Herbert would be spinning in his grave if he thought I was in one of them German cars. He had a hard war in the Bomber Command and most of his comrades died at the hands of the bloody krauts.'

'Yes sir, you can't get more British than a Bentley,' said Charles not having the heart to tell Piffle that Bentley was owned by Volkswagen, the very car firm created by Adolf Hitler and the National Socialists as 'the people's car' and had a German built and designed engine. As long as the client is happy, thought Charles, that's the main thing.

That's the trouble with the modern world, nothing is quite what is seemed, but at 75, Piffle was in the world of the 1960s, a simple world of right and wrong, Labour and Tory, good and bad. Not this complicated hotchpotch of inconsistencies and ambiguities where nothing was as it should be.

Soon the Bentley was powering up the M1 at regal speed. Piffle and Honolulu in the back, and Charles up front with his peaked cap and chauffeur's uniform, on their way to the industrial north and the town of Grimewold.

Meanwhile, talks were being held in London at the Department of Trade and Industry between McGreggor's Steel representatives, the unions, and officials from the department to try and thrash out a solution to the damaging dispute at Europe's largest steel mill, which was now facing imminent closure and the loss of at least 25,000 local jobs without a swift resolution.

Archibald McGreggor III hadn't attended the talks himself, but had sent his trusted lieutenant, Googleheimer, to conduct negotiations. The main aim for Archibald, was to sack 40% of the workforce who were on the highest wages, keep the younger, more recent, ones on worse employment terms and get a huge grant from the Government to re-equip the works, without dipping into his own coffers.

As it happened, Googleheimer had some good news, but it wasn't from the talks in London.

'Morning Archibald, It's me Googleheimer. Howzit going old man? Difficult talks down here, them turkies don't vote for Christmas, that's for sure. But as it happens, I've just had a very interesting proposal by way of a phone call.'

'What are you talking about Googleheimer? Give it to me straight man, and stop talking in riddles.'

'Well, out of the blue, Mukhrejee, the Chairman of PING Steel in India, has called me and offered to buy McGreggor's Steel. The whole damn shooting match for 800 million English pounds, providing the British Government give a £200 million sweetener.'

Never one to look a gift horse in the mouth Archibald sat back in his chair and his cunning mind went into overdrive.

'Get Mukhrejee to up his offer to £1 billion and he has a deal. I'll sign today providing you can get those blathering idiots at the Department of Trade and Industry to agree to the £200 million sweetener.'

The talks dragged on all day, and with the prospect of the world's second largest steel maker buying McGreggor's, saving 8,000 direct jobs and many more in the supply chain, with only 2,000 redundancies, the Government reluctantly agreed to give a £200 million 'regional development grant' to support the restructuring of McGreggor's steel into a premium producer of high value added quality steel, and with two of the blast furnaces saved and only one of the three closing.

Barraclough and his team had little choice but to accept, and with the prospect of their members' salaries being restored to pre-production-cut levels, everyone in the talks could claim that they had got something out of the situation.

The deal was set to be announced on the Ten o'clock news by ITN who were given the scoop by the Trade Secretary. Who had been under strict instructions from the Prime Minister to piss the communists at the BBC off by denying them the story.

More importantly, Archibald got his billion pounds, making him one of the richest men in the country, and enabling him to finally retire and enjoy the spoils of industry – literally.

There was still the little matter of Piffle to contend with. Even with a £1 billion coming his way he wanted to finish the job he had started, and make sure that Piffle's Diversity Action Partnership was sunk without a trace. He decided to ring Winton J Cuncliffe-Owen to get the latest update, and for once, Winton found Archibald in a good mood.

'Now then Winton, how nice to talk to you, how are we today?'

'I'm very well thank you Archibald. How can I be of service?'

'I'm wondering how close we are to toppling Piffle's little empire? I've just had an offer for McGreggor's Steel for £1 billion from

PING Steel of India. I've decided to accept, but I want the loose ends tidied up of which, Piffle is the main one.'

'That's splendid news,' said Winton marvelling at the fact that Archibald could still give a fig about Piffle now that a billion quid was coming his way. 'Well, we are very close Archibald. Tandori has been working tirelessly undermining The Diversity Action Partnership and I understand that the Chamber of Commerce are about to launch a class action lawsuit against Piffle's company this week, with I understand, some financial help from Mc Greggor's Steel via your man Googleheimer. When the proverbial hits the fan there is a good chance the council will pull the contract and that will finish Piffle off for good, or that's what I am hearing.'

'So, what you're saying old chap, is that within a couple of weeks Piffle will be finished?'

'Exactly, that's exactly what I'm saying Archibald.'

'Splendid, splendid! Well done Winton, this really has made my day.'

Archibald Mc Greggor III got off the phone and, for the first time in decades, had a little jig round his study, singing 'happy days are here again,' and pouring himself a large single malt whisky to celebrate.

Over in Benidorm, Gordon Streake had eaten his huge buffet breakfast at the Ambassador Hotel and took his customary walk along the front stopping at a coffee shop and bar called Franko's; presumably named after General Franko the dictator from the 1930s. Next to Franko's a new fried chicken takeaway and eat in had opened called Funky Chicken.com, where locals and tourists could order fried chicken, French fries and sides to be delivered to their homes, hotels or caravans with an eat in option as well.

Funky Chicken.com was the brainchild of none other than Jimmy The Fleece Moston who had used the proceeds from his marketing campaign for Piffle to fund the new operation. None of this of course meant anything to Gordon Streake, but as he sat there, he overheard two of the servers talking about Jimmy and the new log cabins being built at the Playa de Sol Holiday Park.

According to the servers there were potential bargains to be had if one had ready euros. It got Streake thinking. Maybe he would have a shifty up there and have a look for himself. His very own log cabin might be just what he was looking for, especially if he could bag a bargain from this Jimmy guy who owned Funky Chicken.com, and seemed to be involved with the log cabin development somehow.

Chapter 101

Soon Piffle and Honolulu arrived in Grimewold and booked into the exclusive Hotel and Country Club near Appleton for the rest of the week. Charles, the chauffeur, was staying at the Premier Inn in Grimewold and arranged to collect Piffle the following day so he could visit the office and see how things were going at the Diversity Action Partnership. Honolulu was going to stay away and enjoy the facilities of the Hotel and Country Club , in particular the spa treatments, swimming pool and extensive grounds.

As they entered the Hotel, Piffle too was impressed by the huge oil painting of the owner of the hotel chain, the Indian businessman and Chairman, Dr R A Murtha of the RAM group of companies, who was looking down on them benevolently in his Saville Row suit with his gold Breitling watch clearly visible.

'Now there's a man with the right idea, Honolulu. Built a hotel chain with his own hands, probably came from nowt like me, and grafted all his life. Now he can sit back and look down at us in that lovely oil painting.'

It was ironic that Piffle was admiring the very same oil painting that his nemesis, Mike Morrell, had admired weeks before when he had come to the same hotel to meet Penelope Sykes, and resulted in Morrell having his own oil painting commissioned by the famous artist Quentin Poope.

'It is a wonderful thing Dresden to see a man who has succeeded from the will power of his own hands,' said Honolulu getting slightly confused with her grasp of the English language.

'It surely is Honolulu. Unlike that bastard Morrell who has cheated his way to success, stealing me wife from under me nose, and who knows what else he has got planned,' said Piffle not realising that his words foretold a future that he would neither be able to predict or understand, but was heading his way with lightning speed.

In fact, this would be the very last day that Piffle would believe that he had this unbelievably rosy future mapped out, where he would grow supremely rich from the sale of the log cabins and Honolulu and he would retire to a life of idle luxury at the Villa Almeria.

That evening Piffle decided to treat Honolulu to a sumptuous seven course meal at a renowned restaurant called Appelby Fine Cuisine around ten miles from the hotel. It was near the small village of Appleton where Morrel lived, and even though it was in the middle of nowhere, it attracted a star studied clientele. It was rumoured that both Rod Steward and Elton John had eaten there, being flown in by helicopter. Piffle used a more conventional mode of travel to get there in the form of Charles and the Bentley Mulsanne that he had hired for the week.

Honolulu wore a shimmering silver gown that hugged her vast curves. If she had been half the size, she would have resembled Shirley Bassey from the late 1960s, but as it was, she resembled something very much larger. Given that Piffle had a 52" waist and hadn't seen his shoes in years, they looked like a couple who were well suited to each other, and certainly ones that enjoyed their food. In that respect, they were both to be quite disappointed by Appelby Fine Cuisine, certainly not by the quality of the food, which was unparalleled, more by the meagre quantities of each course.

'Bloody hell Honolulu, what the bloody hell was that "stuffed pigeon" starter? It was only one bloody mouthful, where's the rest for Christ's sake?'

The next six courses were no better in terms of quantity, and after copious amounts of very expensive fine wines followed by, port, brandy and cigars in the snug afterwards, Piffle was finally presented with the bill for the thick end of 700 quid.

'I'm not buying bloody shares in the place,' said Piffle to the mâtre d', 'there must be some mistake.'

'There is no mistake Mr Piffle, if you come to one of the best restaurants in the country that is Michelin star quality, then you must expect to pay handsomely for the privilege. There is usually a six month waiting list, it is only because you are so well known locally that we have been able to squeeze you in.'

Piffle paid the bill without further protest and they went out to their waiting Bentley. As they drove off Piffle commented, 'Bloody hell Honolulu, I think we'll eat in hotel rest of week. I think that Dr Mutha who owns hotel and country club will give us nosh that's better value for money. The food was nice, but I could kill for a bag of chips or a Chinese to fill me up.'

'I could drive you into Grimewold sir and take you to a fish and chip establishment where you can get yourself a takeaway.'

'Bloody good idea Charles. You're turning into a godsend, full steam ahead.'

So they drove into Grimewold in the Bentley and parked outside Catch of the Day on the London road where Charles went in and got them a well wrapped portion of fish and chips with fish cakes and a jumbo sausage.

'That's grand, Charles. I'll take these back to room and have a good nosh up with a drink from mini bar.'

So, after spending £700 on a restaurant meal, that's exactly what they did. They went and had a £10.99 nosh up in the room with some beers from the mini bar, watching *Celebrity Big Brother* on the telly, before going to bed finally happy and contented, snuggled up in each other's arms in the huge queen-sized four poster bed.

Chapter 102

Piffle was up early that Thursday morning for his visit to The Diversity Action Partnership. He had booked Charles to take him in the Bentley to get there well before 9.00 a.m. when Zara Bindle was due to arrive. It also happened to be Tandori's first day back after her extended time off and she also had got in before 8.00 to carry on her campaign of disruption to the smooth running of the company.

Piffle entered the offices of his company and all looked normal with the office, just how he had last seen it. The huge metal filling cabinets at one end, and the rows of little wooden school desks that he had bought on the cheap when a local secondary school had closed down.

He wasn't expecting to see anyone in at this time, but immediately spotted Tandori at the far end of the office bending down at one of the metal filling cabinets, her huge arse in the air. She looked massively sexy to Piffle, even though she was in disguise as a transgender man. Hence the pink cropped hair and blue denim dungarees. He sneaked up behind her and slapped her huge arse giving her a hell of a fright.

'Oh! It's you Mr Piffle, I wasn't expecting to see you today.'

'Well I wasn't expecting to see you Tandori, but I'm bloody glad I have,' said Piffle eyeing her up and down appreciatively. 'God you look sexy, your big arse is the eighth wonder of the world.'

'Oh, you are cheeky Mr Piffle. I'm self-identifying as a man you know,' said Tandori trying her best to be nice but at the same time spurn his amorous advances.

'The bollocks you are Tandori, you're all bloody woman and make no mistake. Now come here and feel how glad I am to see you.'

He pulled her tight and grabbed her huge arse with his greedy hands thrusting his hard bulging manhood against her as he did so. 'Bloody hell, you're even bigger than my fiancé Honolulu, can you feel how horny I am for you?'

'My Piffle, control yourself, we're in the office. What if someone comes in and finds us in each other's arms? I can feel how much you like me, that's obvious, but not here and not now.'

'I need you Tandori, I can't keep me hands off you for much longer,' he said grasping her buttocks even harder.

You're not keeping your hands off me at all by the way you're grabbing my bottom, thought Tandori. She had never had a man fancy her in that department before and didn't know what to make of it.

'Well you're going to have to Mr Piffle. I am a women who has morals, so if you want to see me you will have to ask me out properly,' said Tandori stalling for time and not the least bit interested in a 75 year old sex maniac with a crude way with words not to mention other things!

Her situation was complicated enough without the amorous advances of Piffle getting in the way. All she wanted was to finish the job and hopefully, by the end of next week, be out of there, back to mummy and daddy in the Cotswolds and get her old job back at MI5 with Hazelhurst. Her plans didn't involve sex with Piffle and his fifty-two-inch waist and bulging thingamajig.

'Maybe we could meet up for a drink?' said Piffle hopefully. 'Before I go back to Benidorm, then I can get to know you properly.'

'That would be very nice,' said Tandori.

Their little tête à tête was soon interrupted by the arrival of other members of staff. However, Piffle soon began to realise, much to his horror, that all was not well. Not normal in any sense of the word that he understood. All his old mates from the steel works and docks had disappeared, to be replaced by a menagerie of strange exotic creatures who passed for human beings, all apparently employed by the lunatic Bindle. All thoughts of sex with Tandori dissipated as he looked on with horror at the new members of staff entering his offices.

First, there was the group of five Ethiopian pensioners who came in, babbling away in their own language and went past Piffle to the kitchen section to make themselves a hot drink. Then the single mother called Jodie, with nine kids came in, bringing four of them with her, and sat at her desk with the kids running riot round the office playing tag.

There was the young female crack-cocaine dealer called Dizzy-R, and finally the heavily tattooed unemployed Irish fairground operative called Murphy, who came in with a bottle of voddy in his hand, clearly not at all ready for a day's work in the office. They all ignored Piffle, apart from Murphy, who asked him if he fancied a shot of vodka, even though it was only 8.45 in the morning.

The best that could be said of the new recruits was that they were all on time. Unlike Zara Bindle, who Piffle was very keen to see about the changes she had brought in without his knowledge or agreement.

As it happened, he had to wait in her office until 9.30 a.m. because she was zapped by one of Mike Morrell's Clean Air Champions. As she was driving her nearly-new black Golf GTi, she was highly affronted at the imposition and waste of public money. She had duly stopped the car at the side of the road and entered into a heated argument with the Clean Air Champions about her human right to go about her business unimpeded and the stupidity of zapping a brand new car for emissions testing when it hadn't even had its first service yet!

The Clean Air Champions stood their ground and pointed out that in an egalitarian society everybody was responsible for their emissions from the Lord of the Manor to the humblest window cleaner, and the equipment didn't lie and if her emissions were in excess of regulations laid down by the Secretary of State for the Environment she would be receiving a fine of £1000 reduced to £500 if she paid up within seven days. It was lost on Bindle that she was only getting a taste of her own medicine. When she got into the office, much to her horror, she found Piffle sitting on her chair drumming his fingers loudly on her desk.

'And what time do you call this Zara?' said Piffle, clearly furious. 'I've been waiting here in your office for over an hour. I think we have a lot to discuss considering what I have found already.'

'I, I didn't know you were coming today. I've been delayed by an argument with those infernal Clean Air Champions that Mike Morrell employs. They zapped my VW Golf when I was coming into work and I lost my temper with them.'

'Well, you're here now and I think you've got some explaining to do. Let's start with all my staff. You know the reliable ex-miners and steel workers that used to work here? What the bloody hell has happened to them?'

'As I've told you many times Dresden, the council wants us to walk the walk, as well as talk the talk, so I had to let them go and employ a more diverse workforce.'

'Well from what I've seen of that menagerie of fucking loony tunes out there you have certainly succeeded on that one Zara. Where have my mates gone then? What did you do with them?'

'I sacked them, and there was this little dispute and then Mike

Morrell employed all of them in his company, so it was all sorted out in the end?'

'Mike fucking Morrell has employed all my talented staff? All my mates that have been with me for years, to be replaced by a bunch of bloody imbeciles who couldn't tie their own fucking shoe laces? One offered me a shot of vodka and it wasn't even 9 o' bloody clock. What the fuck have you done you cretinous loony Metropolitan fuckwhit?'

'I've done what needed to be done Dresden, and make no mistake.'

'No, I'll tell you what the mistake was lady, it was employing you Bindle. A fucking loony southern diversity-obsessed moron, where all common sense has gone out of the window to be replaced by this shit stream of lunacy. I hate to think what state my company is in. Now pack your bags and bugger off out of here, you're fired!'

'You can't do that to me. I'm Zara Bindle, granddaughter of Philomena Bindle the most famous left-wing feminist in the country, the London press will decimate you.'

'I don't give a flying fuck about your Metropolitan elite bunch of southern nancy-boy prats who have ruined this country, and ignored the concerns of real working class people like me and me mates in Hull and Grimewold, and shut all the factories, coal mines and the like and shipped production to Red China. Sold us all down the river has the likes of you Bindle, now I'll say it again get your stuff, and piss off out of my company, and take your German kraut Golf GTi with you.'

'I've never been so insulted...'

'Well, you need to get out a bit more love, try the Gipsyville working men's club in Hull.'

'You'll be hearing from my lawyers. I'll sue you Piffle for every penny...'

But already Piffle was manhandling her out of the office. He had seen red, literally, and couldn't give a toss what she was going to do. This lunacy had to end.

Bindle ran to her car, red faced and shocked. No one in her whole life had ever burst her bubble like that and humiliated her. She was a Bindle, one of the most famous celebrated left-wing families in the country and to be treated like a common criminal by an uncouth load-mouth cretin like Piffle, it was too much. She got into her car and burst into tears before zooming out of the car park and back home to tell Hugo about the ghastly day she had just had.

Piffle went back into the offices of the Diversity Action Partnership limited. Everybody was looking at him agog. No one had ever stood up to Bindle, so to see her summarily sacked and kicked out of the building was shocking.

'As you were,' said Piffle. 'Bindle has gone, I'm in charge now until further notice, any problems you come to me.'

Chapter 103

On Friday morning Gordon Streak took a taxi up to the Playa de Sol Holiday Park to see the log cabins for himself. The first ten were completed and at the front of the complex. They looked stunning in the morning sunlight. Double storey Swiss style cabins with generous verandas, a hot tub with each one, a curved road going up into the site and landscaped grounds around them with plush grass and exotic plants and shrubs.

This is way above my price range, thought Streake somewhat deflated. Never mind, he was here, he might as well make enquiries and see if he could have a look round inside on of the cabins. He spotted, what looked like, a site office and decided to go in and enquire. He entered the site office and saw a guy bending over some elaborate site plans with a yellow high-vis jacket on and a hard hat.

'Excuse me.'

The guy looked up startled slightly by the intrusion. 'Yes, can I help you señor?'

'Yes, I was passing, and I'm interested in one of your log cabins.'

'I am only the site manager, Miguel, you need to speak to the sales office.'

'Where are they then?'

'You want man called Jimmy Moston, he runs the Go-Go Bar and Grill in the old town. I have his number here on a business card.' Miguel handed Streake the card.

'Thanks, but as I've come all this way by taxi, any chance I can have a look round one of the finished cabins?'

'I am not supposed to, but cabin nine is finished and the new owners have not moved in yet. Look, I'm busy but here is the key. Have a good look round yourself and drop the key back here to me. If I'm not here just leave it on the desk, but señor I am trusting you, so don't let me down.'

'That's very kind of you,' said Streake.

'I'll only be about half an hour and I'll drop the keys back. Do you know how much they are?'

'Well señor, you will have to speak to señor Moston, but I know they should be €175,000, but there are some reductions for a quick sale.'

'I see,' said Streake looking crestfallen. If he bought one at that price it would take all his life savings, leaving him just with his reduced police pension. He could get by, but it would be tight and he would not have the lifestyle he hoped for. Anyway, he liked the look of the cabins so no harm having a look. He shuffled off out of the site office and made his way to log cabin number nine.

Streake admired the look of the cabin from the outside. Obviously made with top quality Scandinavian pine, it had two floors and a balcony in the centre coming from, what looked like, the master bedroom where you could sit and take in the view. The decking area was very spacious and went right round the cabin with an extended section at one end where the large hot tub sat.

Inside was even better. There was an open-plan kitchen/diner and generous lounge area with a L shaped leather suite and a 55" flat screen TV mounted above the mock marble fire place surround. There was a downstairs bedroom, bathroom and small study, and an open tread staircase leading to the master bedroom with en suite, and a further generous bedroom.

The kitchen was to a high standard, with genuine polished granite worktops and a trendy island dividing the kitchen from the lounge and dining table. Real wood polished flooring completed the ambiance, as did the high-quality Spanish tiles in the bathrooms and kitchen floor area. In truth, it was stunning, far better than he could hope for and set out of town in its own exclusive well-maintained grounds.

Gordon Streake wanted one, but how was he going to afford it?

He would go and see this Jimmy Moston over the weekend and maybe have a steak dinner at his bar – as it was called the Go- Go Bar and Grill, presumably it did food. Streake was as good as his word and dropped the keys back to the site office where Miguel was still working. Then he jumped in a taxi back to the Ambassador for a late lunch.

Back in Grimewold things were going from bad to worse for Piffle. The post had arrived with some very unwelcome news. He had received an official court document from a firm of solicitors representing the Grimewold Chamber of Commerce, stating that a class action lawsuit was being brought by 156 firms. The firms were suing for compensation and damages for illegal and wrongly administered fines, and that the court case was due to take place later in the year unless a sum of £412,000 was paid in respect of the claim.

Piffle wasn't exactly sure of the financial position of the Diversity Action Partnership, but he was pretty sure that he didn't have that sort of money available immediately, and he had only just borrowed €1 million and used funds from Diversity Action to help fund the log cabin development.

What had that bitch Bindle done to him and how had it got to this stage? He could kick himself; he had spent too long in Benidorm at the villa with Honolulu and taken his eye off the ball. He could hear his father now, 'Never trust anyone but yourself to get things done. No one owes you a living lad.' If only he had listened.

Piffle sat at Bindle's desk with the door closed and his head in his hands. He was thinking; thinking how to get out of this. There was nothing for it but to go to the bank his business dealt with and borrow half a million. That was it, with income being strong they would lend him the money and he could pay it back out of profits over two years.

However, things across town were conspiring against Piffle's plan for saving his company with a bank loan. Grimewold Council had also been informed of the extremely embarrassing class action by the Chamber of Commerce, detailing 156 companies claims for compensation and damages. The council was also facing legal action for not properly administering the Diversity and Equality Act 2010, and there were strong hints that 'other' companies might come out of the woodwork.

The class action appeared to be very well funded as a top London firm had been employed, as had a renowned criminal barrister who had never lost a case. The council's legal department was a hive of activity that morning and were pretty well convinced that McGreggor's Steel Corp were funding the class action – their run ins with Achibald McGreggor III had never gone well in the past. All of this unpleasant information was relayed in private to the leader of the council, Penelope Sykes, and it was decided that an emergency meeting of the Ways and Means Committee would be called for Friday afternoon to discuss the council's options and response.

It didn't take the very cautious Ways and Means Committee, egged on by Penelope Sykes, very long to decide that the best, and safest, course of action was to withdraw the contract for running the Diversity and Equality Act 2010 from The Diversity Action Partnership and suspend the scheme until a full council review could take place. The review was pencilled in and thought to take six months, and if Diversity Action Partnership were found to be negligent then the contract would be awarded to someone else and the council would claim damages from Piffle's company for the loss of earnings and other legal costs, which could run into the low millions.

In short, by close of play on Friday, The Diversity Action Partnership had no more contract and no more income, and Piffle's dream of getting a bank loan disappeared like scotch mist. With no income the company was bankrupt, and Piffle had no personal income. After the meeting broke up Penelope Sykes took great pleasure in emailing Piffle with the news that the contract was being suspended for six months pending a review and that an official letter from the council's lawyers would follow on Monday.

Piffle received the e-mail just as he was finishing work to go back to the Country Club in the Bentley; he could see Charles waiting patiently in the car park. All the other so-called staff had already left when Piffle left the building for the last time, shoulders slumped, a broken man for now.

It had all gone wrong and he couldn't understand why, when just a week before the Diversity Action Partnership was posting record results. He would have to tell Honolulu that all their plans for the future were in doubt. How was he going to fund the log cabin development now, which was going to cost many millions of euros to complete? As he sat in the back of the Bentley he thought it only fair to let Tandori know she didn't have a job to come back to on Monday.

Dear Tandori, it is with much regret that I have to tell you the council has pulled the plug on us, and the Diversity Action Partnership is going into administration. Therefore, I cannot continue to pay you as of now, so your time with us is over and you may as well go back home. Thank you for all your help and I hope that someday we can meet under better circumstances. You are a truly wonderful women and I have very much enjoyed your company. Yours forever, Dresden Piffle.

Tandori replied from Anthony Jennings' flat, she had just got in, after getting a bus from work. Her boring weekend in Grimewold was going to immediately change from being struck on the Cromwell Estate with nothing to do, to a journey back to the Cotswolds and mummy and daddy's house. Not just for a weekend break, but for good. Her time in Grimewold was over.

I can't believe it Dresden. I am so sorry for everything, I liked you too. Yours, Tandori.

Piffle didn't know what that meant, 'sorry for everything,' presumably she meant sorry they couldn't be together, or have that love tryst that he so craved?

Tandori of course didn't mean that at all, she was trying to say that she felt guilty for all that she had done to him. It wasn't Bindle who had screwed things up, it was her. Admittedly, because she was being blackmailed by Hazelhurst and didn't want that dreadful Inspector Fleece putting her in prison for a very long time for being an ISIS terrorist. She had had to look after number one, but it didn't mean she didn't feel guilty, or have feelings for Piffle. Tandori was an example of a good person driven by circumstances beyond her control.

Chapter 104

Piffle arrived back at the hotel and country club to face Honolulu and tell her about the extraordinary events of the day. It truly was a tale of hero to zero.

'I can't understand it Honolulu,' he said. 'One minute I'm getting reports that we're making record fine income and everything is going well, and the next I'm being told that there is a class action against us and the council, without warning, has pulled the rug. I'm thinking and thinking Honolulu, but I can't get me head round it at all.'

'It seems obvious to me Dresden. There has been what you English say is a mole. A person who was out to destroy you and behind your back, whilst you have been in Benidorm with me and your distractions of the log cabin park, they have struck you with a force and stabbed you in the back Dresden. And from what I can see there is only one culprit, it is obvious, it is Bindle.'

'You're probably right Honolulu but why? Why would she do

that to me when she is on a bloody good screw salary wise and had just what she wanted. Even employed all those loony tune diversity staff to work for her and make herself look good in the left-wing circles down south she likes so much. It doesn't make sense.'

'It makes sense if someone else is paying her, someone who hates you, and she has other plans to take the Judas money and do something else. Who hates you enough to try and bring you down?'

'There's only one person I can think of, Mike Morrell. He hates me, pushed me in me son's grave he did. He's nicked me wife, the Clothes Horse, and now he's taking me business too. You're right Honolulu, it's got to be Morrell. Now he can take the Diversity Contract and add it to the speed camera business and Clean Air Contract that he's just got. He's the one who gains. Got me both bloody ways. Ruined me and nicked me contract. It's him, the bastard, but it's too late, he has screwed me and that's that.'

'All you can do, Dresden, is to try and salvage the log cabin business. Maybe scale it back, or build them over a longer period of time?'

'Eh Honolulu, you're probably right. Anyway, I'll have to stick around till Monday now and sack rest of workers at Diversity before we get flight back to Benidorm. Our future is there now, whatever happens.'

As usual Piffle had got most of it wrong, but he was right about one thing – Mike Morrell was going to benefit massively from his demise on a number of fronts. Piffle went outside the hotel and found Charles waiting by the Bentley Mulsanne, having a cigar.

'Eh up Charles, thanks for waiting but we won't need you this evening. Slight change of plan, we're staying on till Monday and getting evening flight back to Alicante, so can you stay on till then and take us back Monday? We won't need you over weekend so your time's your own lad. Oh, and if you want any extra brass for staying on extra day...'

'That won't be necessary, just a small fee for paying an extra night at Premier Inn on Sunday night, but apart from that Mr Piffle, I'm at your service. If you want to go somewhere you just let me know.'

'That's very kind, there's not many blokes left like you these days, real gentleman you are. I'll make sure I put in good word for you with your boss, you know, tell him how good you've been looking after me and Honolulu.'

They stood together for a while, chatting away. Piffle telling Charles about his earlier life and Charles enjoying his cigar and telling Piffle about teaching geography at a sixth form college before retiring and taking up the chauffeur work. Charles had lost his wife of 34 years to cancer, so the chauffeur job got him out and about so he wasn't moping about at home alone. And driving a top of the range Bentley was one of the perks of life, but it was meeting fascinating people that Charles liked best. Piffle was not sure if he came into that category, but he had grown to like Charles over the week.

Zara Bindle had also had time to think after the heated exchange and sacking earlier in the day. She had gone home to Hugo in tears, tears of anger and self-pity and hadn't been able to think straight. She had told him everything over a nice cup of herbal fair-trade Nicaraguan tea and a few things had started to make sense.

'The thing is Hugo, all was going perfectly at the Diversity Action Partnership. It was a simple process. Identify the companies that were not meeting their obligations under the Diversity and Equality Act 2010, get the fines issued, and then either get paid or issue court proceedings, which usually resulted in payment. It was only very few that resisted further, like McGreggor's Steel, for ideological reasons and the fact they had very deep pockets to resist us. So, the only way things could go wrong was if fines were being handed out to companies that had either paid, or who had been wrongly accused of being in breach of the act. As most companies were in breach, then fines were being resent to companies that had already paid.'

'How could that happen?' said Hugo.

'I don't know. It might have been one of the new staff I'd taken on getting it all wrong, maybe the Ethiopians who couldn't speak English, but even then their work should have been subjected to checks, and signed off by either Tandori, or her assistant manager Jonathan. That's the only change that took place in that time, Tandori and Jonathan joining the team, and of course me getting rid of the ex-miners and steel workers and replacing them with a diverse workforce'

'So, could it have been purely a set of random events that

conspired to bring the company down?' said Hugo.

'I don't think so,' said Zara. 'I think this was orchestrated, it was meant to happen, but I can't think how, or why, or indeed, who?'

'Well my love, it's academic now. The Diversity Action Partnership is no more according to the internet, the council has had a meeting and pulled the plug ,so your chances of suing Piffle for unfair dismissal look slim. There won't be any money to pay you.'

'I don't know what we're going to do Hugo. I've never been in this position before, unemployment is a new experience for me. Luckily we have a good chunk of money from my inheritance from Grandma, it's a chance to think about a new life.'

'Yes I suppose it is,' said Hugo, 'the only real skills I've got are cooking and looking after the house, but you still have a currency in left-wing circles. Maybe you could do some writing for a newspaper, or work for a university on diversity issues?'

'I suppose so. Next week we'll have to start planning our future. One thing is for sure, I'm glad to be free of that dreadful Piffle. It was like dealing with a dinosaur from the 1970s, all clogs and coal mines and a chip on his shoulder the size of a block of flats.'

That evening, after the very unexpected email from Piffle, Tandori made her way to Grimewold Station and took a fast train to Milton Keynes. From there she could change and get a local train service to Broadway, where her father would meet her at the station around 9.00 p.m. For her the time at Grimewold was over and she had succeeded in her mission for Hazelhurst without being found out. For the first time in months she felt free: free of the subterfuge, free of the pressure from Hazelhurst and most importantly, free from that dreadful Inspector Fleece.

If she could just have some time off to recover at home with mummy and daddy she would then be ready to re-join MI5 as an operative working for Hazelhurst again. She had already sent a text to him simply saying, 'mission accomplished', and he had double-checked and then made contact with Winton J Cuncliffe-Owen who in turn had phoned Archibald McGreggor III with the good news that The Diversity Action Partnership was no more.

'I've got some good news for you Archibald,' enthused Winton.

'I've just heard from Hazelhurst at MI5, and he informs me that the mission has been a success. The council has pulled the plug on the Diversity Action Partnership and Piffle is finished, completely bankrupt, just as you wanted Archibald.'

'That's splendid news my dear fellow. You see, life eventually works out, karma old boy. I get a billion pounds for selling McGreggor's Steel, and Piffle gets nothing, not even the shirt on his back. Maybe he'll be a tramp on the sea front in Benidorm, begging for a few crumbs off the tourists. That's how I imagine it will turn out for that communist creature, just as the good Lord intended.'

'Well, let's hope so,' said Winton, thinking Archibald was being a bit harsh on his fellow man. 'Anyway Archibald, enjoy your retirement and enjoy the spoils of success. We have done our bit anyway and if you need me in the future you only have to give me a call.'

'I will Winton, and thank you, thank you for everything.' It was an uncharacteristic of show of gratitude from Archibald, but he had had a number of things go his way which changed his outlook on life. Finally, Piffle was no more, and he Archibald McGreggor III ruled supreme. Very rich and very idle – everything Piffle despised.

Chapter 105

Not wanting the grass to grow under his feet, Gordon Streake was up early on Saturday morning and walked into the old town to find Jimmy Moston's Go-Go Bar and Grill. He got there just in time to have a full English breakfast despite already having a breakfast at the Ambassador earlier in the morning. After he ate the breakfast and drunk a big mug of Yorkshire tea, he asked the waitress if Jimmy Moston was around.

'Who shall I say is asking?' said the waitress.

'He doesn't know me, my name is Streake, Gordon Streake and I'm interested in buying one of the log cabins he's marketing. I've been up and had a look at them.'

'OK Mr Streake, I'll go and see if Jimmy's available.'

In due course Jimmy Moston came and sat at Streake's table.

'Hello there, I'm Jimmy, Jimmy Moston. I understand you're interested in buying one of the log cabins?'

'Yeah, I've been up there and had a look. I've just moved here from England and I'm looking to buy somewhere to live, and I quite liked the look of the cabins,' said Streake trying to be non-comital so he could strike a better deal price wise.

'They're bloody brilliant, best opportunity in town, great opportunity and investment. What are you looking to spend?' said Jimmy smelling a sale.

'I've got £100,000, about €120,000.'

'Nah, I can't do it for that me old china. Best I can do, strictly limited offer this, is €160,000, about £130,000, but that's all in, fitted out with a hot tub and everything, just like the ones you've seen. I've got to tell you, they're selling fast.'

'I'll have to think about it.'

'Don't take too long, the price I've offered is for one week only. I need an answer from you by this time next week. The only other thing you can do is borrow the €30,000 from the Banco Alicante who we have a deal with. That protects some of your savings and we can rent out your log cabin for a month a year to pay for the repayments. Think about it. If you had a relation back in Blighty you could visit for a month, that way you'd get the log cabin for essentially the price you wanted with just a little bit of inconvenience.'

Jimmy was never one to let the opportunity for a sale slip by, and had given Streake another option that might just work for him.

'I'll give it some thought. That second option might just work for me.'

On Monday morning Piffle had the unenviable task of going into the Diversity Action Partnership and giving the menagerie of strange staff, who Bindle had employed, their marching orders. Luckily for Piffle he wasn't having to sack his mates from the old days, and because all the newcomers had only been there for a couple of months at most, he didn't feel too bad, although *any* sackings went against his socialist principles.

That done, he left the office and got Charles to take him back to the hotel to collect Honolulu, pay the bill, check out and be on their way to Gatwick for the flight back to Alicante International. After a long and tiring day, Piffle was back home at the Villa Almeria, he drank a shot of single malt before bed and then slept soundly till morning.

However, his happiness at being back in Benidorm and at the villa didn't last long. News had spread of the collapse of the Diversity Action Partnership and money that should have been transferred to Banco Alicante to help fund the log cabin business had been stopped. Fearing for their investment of €1 million as a secured loan, the bank called in the loan with immediate effect, and finding that Piffle didn't have enough money to cover the loan, they foreclosed on the Playa de Sol Holiday Park. By close of play on Wednesday the holiday park was now in the possession of the bank, who were keen to off load it to get their €1 million back.

Panic had ensued with all the people who were relying on Piffle to pay their way. Miguel suspended building works on site and laid off the Indians who found themselves marooned with no way of getting home. Jimmy The Fleece was still owed his commissions for selling the first ten log cabins and the fees agreed with Piffle, and Piffle's friend Wack was happily building fifty log cabins on site in Hull for which he hadn't been paid. The whole house of financial cards was beginning to collapse around Piffle. A pyramid scheme with all roads leading to Piffle himself.

The first threat of violence came from Jimmy The Fleece who heard of Piffle's financial difficulties through his contacts in the Benidorm business community. He had used his own money to finance the marketing plan and employed his go-go girls as agents. He was thousands of euros out of pocket and on the back of expected income had borrowed heavily to establish FunkyChicken.com on the front at Benidorm.

'It's me Piffle. Your bloody cheque has bounced for all the bloody work I've done for you. What the fuck are you going to do about it? I've kept my side of the bargain, now it's your turn Piffle.'

'Don't worry lad, I'm working on it. Once the funds have cleared for the first ten cabins we've sold I'll be able to pay you. It's just a little hiccup Jimmy. Nowt to worry about. You know your old mate Piffle is good for the money.'

'Now you listen here Piffle. I've come across your sort many times before, all bastard promises and no action, over-extend yourself and then fuck over others while you ride off into the sunset. Well not this bloody time, matey boy. If you don't pay me my money within a week, one week, I'll come over to Villa Almeria and burn the bastard down with you and your mistress in it. It will be roast fucking pork for tea, you mark my words.'

'I'll get you the money Jimmy, don't worry, no need to resort to violence. It's just a little delay, that's all, cashflow problem. I've got assets and money in England, don't you worry.'

Piffle came off the phone genuinely shaken. He didn't tell Honolulu what was going on as he didn't want to frighten her, or admit that they were in serious financial difficulty and that he had lost their holiday park to the clutches of the bank.

Chapter 106

Mike Morrell moved with lightning speed. He had foreseen that Piffle would lose the Playa de Sol Holiday Park once Diversity Action Partnership had gone bust. Penelope Sykes had rang him over the weekend and told him the good news, and that Speed Camera Action! Limited would be in line to win the Diversity contract once things had settled down and the council had completed a review into the circumstances leading to the collapse of Piffle's company, and the class action by the Chamber of Commerce.

Morrell found out that Piffle had debts through the Banco Alicante and once they had foreclosed on the loan on Wednesday and taken control of the site, Mike contacted them and offered to buy the site for half of what Piffle had paid, but importantly, giving just enough to pay off Piffle's debts to the bank, Gary Wacker and Jimmy – The Fleece – Moston.

By close of play on Friday the deal was done and signed, and the ownership of the Playa de Sol transferred again from the Banco Alicante to Mike Morrell, who set up a new holding company to hold the assets. He didn't really want a holiday park in Benidorm, but at the price he had paid was a bargain, and with the revenue from his UK company he had the resources to finish the five hundred log cabins and make all the profits Piffle had been planning.

He rang Jimmy and immediately transferred his outstanding monies to him, then contacted Miguel and did the same. He then contacted Gary Wacker, who had no idea his friend was in difficulties, and told him that he was the new owner and things would continue just as before, but they would have a meeting next week to discuss things. Piffle knew he had lost his holiday park to the bank but not that his arch enemy, Mike Morrell, had acquired it from under him and really did own everything dear to Piffle's heart.

On Saturday Mike Morrell went into Hull to the 'Build a Bear' shop. Customers can record a message to be placed into the bear, so when it arrives the recipient presses a button, which then plays the message . Mike recorded a message specifically aimed at Piffle which said, 'I've won your wife and now I've got your business, Piffle.'

He then put a note in with the bear saying, 'If you want to know why I've done this to you, meet me next Friday lunchtime, twelve o'clock sharp, at the Black Chicken in Benidorm and all will be revealed.'

He then put the bear and note in a big box and posted it to the Villa Almeria, confident that the package would arrive in time and Piffle would attend the Black Chicken for the final showdown, just him, Mike Morrell, and Sydney Dresden Piffle.

Piffle received the large package on Tuesday the following week. The bear gave him the intriguing message in Morrell's voice, speaking to him as if from the grave with a strange electronic tone, clearly Morrell's but somehow different and detached. The note was also intriguing, and although Piffle hated Mike Morrell, and clearly didn't want to ever see him again, he felt compelled to have one last meeting to find out what on earth Mike Morrell was talking about. The final showdown. Mike Morrell had clearly gone to a lot of trouble if he was specially coming over to Benidorm to see Piffle.

Mike hadn't told Pauline the real reason he was to be away for two days. He said he had some business to attend to down south to do with speed camera equipment at the suppliers. A white lie, but a necessary one.

Very early on Friday morning Mike parked his BMW at Doncaster Robin Hood Airport and took the shuttle bus to the departures terminal with just hand luggage as he was only staying one night. He caught the 8.00 a.m. flight and got into Alicante airport and was through customs by 11.00 a.m. Plenty of time to get a taxi from the airport for the thirty-minute drive to Benidorm and the Black Chicken bar where he was to meet Piffle at 12.00.

Piffle likewise didn't tell Honolulu where he was going, just that Paeleo was taking him to the log cabin holiday park to assess progress.

He still hadn't had the heart to tell Honolulu that the log cabin park was lost to the bank due to repossession.

Paeleo turned up at 11.00 a.m. in the Silver Spur and together they drove down the mountain road to the Black Chicken as they had done many times. Paeleo had the local radio station playing, Benidorm FM, and they were playing *Cruel Summer* by Bananarama, the 1983 hit song that Piffle decided was very fitting for the plight he found himself in. A cruel set of circumstances destroying his hopes and dreams.

'How long do you need Dresden before I come back?' said Paeleo.

'Oh, I don't know Paeleo. Come back in an hour. I can't think we'll be more than that, go and get yourself a spot of lunch lad and I'll see you back here at 1.00.'

'OK señor Piffle, I will do that, always at your service.'

Piffle went into the Black Chicken and found a table. He ordered a bottle of wine, waiting patiently for Morrell to arrive. The owner was nowhere to be seen and the Black Chicken was pretty much deserted.

Exactly on time, Mike Morrell entered the bar and spotted Piffle. He strode over in his dark pin-stripped suit, rather out of character for the Black Chicken bar and the hot weather outside. They did not shake hands.

'I suppose you're wondering why I have invited you here today Piffle. We didn't exactly hit it off at your son's funeral. Sorry about that,

Piffle

I didn't mean for you to fall onto the casket, but I'm not sorry for anything else.'

'I'm wondering why the elaborate message and the bear with your voice coming at me?'

'Yes, Piffle just my little joke. I had to come up with something, something intriguing that would get you here'

'Well, here I am Mike, tell me finally, what is this all about lad?'

'I had a girlfriend once, a long time ago Piffle. Beautiful Welsh girl, younger than me, and you know what she said Piffle? She said that everything always has a reason. That always stuck with me.'

'And what's your bloody point Morrell? Yes, everything does have a reason I suppose.'

'I must just tell you that, yes I'm going to marry your wife, Pauline. I love her mind, more than you ever have, but what you don't know is that I'm the new owner of the Playa de Sol Holiday Park. Bought it from the bank on Friday, so now I own that as well, and the council are going to give me your Diversity Contract when things settle down. Then I'll have it all Piffle, your wife, your business and your money – all of it – leaving you with nothing. I doubt that Honolulu will be in any way interested in you when she finds you've got nothing to give her.'

'You don't surprise me,' said Piffle resigned to the situation.

'You clearly hate me Morrell and have planned all this. But why? That's what I'm here to find out.'

628

'You've done a lot of it yourself Piffle, brought your house of cards down, but yes, I hate you and I've played a huge part in your downfall. Helped by Archibald McGreggor III, even though I've never met him.'

'Where the bloody hell does he fit in?'

'It doesn't matter Piffle, but ask around and you will find out why the Diversity Action Partnership suddenly collapsed, and it wasn't anything to do with Zara Bindle. She was set up, as you were. No, what matters is why I hate you and wanted to bring you down.'

'Go on then, bloody well tell me Morrell.'

'Do you remember when you were running the union at the fish docks back in the late 70s and early 80's before you became a Labour Councillor? And then you became wealthy through your contacts?'

'Of course I remember those times.'

'Do you remember a young lad on the docks called Sheamus Mallone, shy lad, worked with your crew?'

'Vaguely, yes, I remember him, why?'

'Well you bastards, you and the *lads* in the union bullied young Sheamus mercilessly, every day for months. You stuck his head down the bog, stole his sandwiches every day, made him buy you rounds of drinks till he had no money so he would be more popular. Well, one day in the summer of 1981, it all became too much you see. Young Sheamus Mallone was the first person to throw himself off the new Humberwold

Bridge, where he fell to his death. Only 28 years old, but he didn't land in the sea, no he landed on the bloody car park, splat, dead, a one hundred and fifty foot drop. Horrible, cruel way to die.'

'So? You're still not explaining yourself.'

'No Piffle, maybe I'm not. Well, young Sheamus Mallone was my baby brother. Back then I was called Mike Mallone, but later in life I changed it to Mike Morrell. I wanted to reinvent myself after all that happened. I was working on the docks too, and I saw how you Hull bastards treated outsiders. You've all got chips on your shoulders the size of blocks of flats and my baby brother being Irish was easy pickings. I tried to protect him, but that summer I got the chance to join Humberwold Police as a new recruit. I took it, knowing that the docks were going bust and I wanted a future for myself, you know, better myself, and I did. But young Sheamus had no one then to look after him and you and the *lads* drove him to commit suicide. We had always been close because that bastard of a father of ours was always beating us with a belt, especially when he got drunk, which was most of the time. I was always there for my baby brother, and as soon as we could leave Grimewold and get away from our father we did, we went to Hull and got jobs on the docks.'

'I'm sorry to hear that, but it wasn't my fault that your brother committed suicide.'

'Oh but it was Piffle. You and your bully boy union friends on the docks. Ever since that day I vowed I would get my revenge on you Piffle. I worked my way up the police force, changed my name and disowned my drunken father. The drunken prick still lives on the Cromwell Estate, god knows how he's still alive, but he is, hanging on with nothing but memories. He won't get a penny out of me. Anyway, then I got the chance of the Speed Camera Action! Contract and the chance to rent an office from you. You thought you were being so clever offsetting the rent of the old library building onto me. Another one of your scams, but I didn't care. I wanted to be in that building, nice and close, looking for every opportunity to bring you down, without you even knowing who I was.'

'But you didn't specifically bring me down, did you? That bitch Bindle did.'

'You're wrong there Piffle, wrong again. I was helped in my quest by two people. I had a private investigator called Streake find out that your lad Bradley Plumb had gone out with Penelope Sykes daughter twenty years ago and got her hooked on heroin, name of Madison Sykes. She died recently and when I told the head of the council who was responsible, she wanted you sorted. I know she wanted evidence on your son Plumb to discredit him and ruin his career, so she employed Streake as well. He got the evidence, but something went wrong and your lad took too much cocaine and fell to his death. When it came to taking the contact off you last week, it certainly didn't help your case that Penelope Sykes had it in for you big time.

Then there was Archibald McGreggor III. He wanted you ruined because the Diversity Action Partnership had sent McGeggor's fines for £57,000 and Archibald wanted you sunk and destroyed. I don't know how he managed it, but he got someone into your organisation to fuck up the invoices and the fines being issued which led to the class action, which was funded, incidentally, by Archibald McGreggor himself. That person wasn't Bindle. She hadn't a clue what was going on, too interested in recruiting a bunch of idiots to create her dream of a diverse work force. It all helped me in the end. Together, between us all, we brought you down Piffle, and now I've got the lot, your wife, your business, your money and your future, and you my friend, have got nothing.'

Piffle didn't know what to say. For once he was speechless. Eventually he looked at Mike Morrell and said, 'So you did all this, all this elaborate planning to bring me down, to get back at me for the death of your baby brother, Sheamus Mallone all those years ago in 1981?'

'Yes I did, and it feels good to finally be able to tell you. You're finished Piffle, and make no mistake.'

With that, Mike Morrell got up from the table and left the Black Chicken and got into a waiting taxi to take him back to his hotel. He had done what he came here to do. He would visit his new holiday park, and see Miguel and Jimmy The Fleece whilst he was over here, but essentially it was Piffle he wanted, and he had got him, big time.

Piffle just sat there with his glass of white wine, unable to take in what had been said and what had been done to him, but despite what Mike Morrell thought, all was not lost. He had one more ace up his sleeve which Morrell wasn't aware of. He smiled for the first time in days. Down, yes, but not totally defeated.

Piffle would rise again, and with that thought he walked out of the Black Chicken into the waiting Rolls Royce Silver Spur, his Rolls Royce, and drove off back to the Villa Almeria with his trusty employee, and now his only employee, Paeleo in the driver's seat.

Epilogue:

ONE YEAR LATER

Sidney Dresden Piffle

Piffle had lost most of his fortune. But one thing he had learned from his father, Henry Herbert Piffle, was always have your fallback position. Piffle had taken two crucial steps in that fatal period leading up to the collapse of his empire. He had made sure that the Villa Almeria had been transferred into Honolulu's name, which he had done many months before once he had determined that he was going to marry her. He had also put away a substantial quantity of euros in cash in his safe in the basement of Villa Almeria. €500,000 to be precise, enough to live a comfortable life in retirement and keep Paeleo on as his part-time chauffeur, still driving the Rolls Royce Silver Spur, which he had also transferred into Honolulu's name.

That night a year ago, after he got back to the Villa Almeria, had had explained to Honolulu all that had happened, and the loss of his business in England and the Playa de Sol Holiday Park, but the good news that they had retained the villa, the car and a substantial amount of money in cash. As he said to Honolulu that night, 'The thing is Honolulu, as my old dad Henry Herbert always used to say, you've always got to have your 'drop dead' money, son, as there is always some Tory bastard trying to take it away, and I've always followed that advice. It's saved our bacon, that's for sure.'

In the year since the confrontation with Mike Morrell, Piffle had got divorced from the Clothes Horse and married Honolulu. They enjoyed their life together at the Villa Almeria and still went to the various restaurants in the mountains and to the Black Chicken for a night out. At 75 years of age Piffle still had a choice, retire into obscurity or plan his revenge against his foe, Mike Morrell, the choice was his, and his alone.

Mike Morrell

Two months after the collapse of Piffle's business empire, Quentin Poope, the artist, invited him to his London studio to show him the huge finished oil painting, which he had produced in record time for £200,000. Mike was delighted that the oil painting captured him in a James Bond like pose with a black dinner jacket and a look that enhanced his own looks substantially, whilst still retaining his likeness. He had the oil painting transported to the foyer at the old library building where it was hung up, pride of place, for all to see. The inscription below read:

Mike Morrell, Chairman, and Chief Executive of SCA Group of

Companies Limited

Which was his new name for the company that covered its various activities, and the mission statement:

Plan, Demand, Deliver, Success, Reward!

A year on, following Pauline's divorce, Mike married her during a lavish wedding held at the huge local stately home, Appleton Hall, home of Lord Appleton of Humberwold. They drove off in the Aston Martin DB3 with Mike trying to look like his suave hero James Bond, and honeymooned on a tropical Caribbean island.

Within six months of the demise of the Diversity Action Partnership, Penelope Sykes made sure that Mike Morrell was awarded the Diversity Contract to add to his Speed Camera and Clean Air Contracts. With huge amounts of money rolling in he found no difficulty in financing the Playa de Sol Holiday Park. One year on, two hundred and fifty log cabins had been completed and sold with the help of Jimmy The Fleece's cunning marketing plan.

His new wife, Pauline Morrell, moved into Eagle's Nest after the honeymoon and sold Maxwell House to her good friends Tracy and Gary Wacker, who had always admired the family home, and now that Gary's firm was doing so well they could finally afford their dream property.

Every month, as he had done for the last 38 years, Mike Morrell visited the grave of his little brother, Shemus Mallone at the Hesslewood Cemetary and laid flowers. His drunken, useless father still lived on the Cromwell Estate in Grimewold. Mike didn't invite him to the wedding and didn't give him a penny of his substantial fortune.

Mike finally had what he craved, a successful business, respect as a pillar of the community, and a glamorous wife by his side. More importantly, he had avenged the death of his baby brother, finally after years of planning and plotting and now he could move on with his life, putting the past behind him and onto a golden future, with Pauline by his side

Archibald McGreggor III

Archibald had enjoyed orchestrating the strike, beating Barraclough and bringing Piffle down. It made him feel alive again, and important. Now, a year on, he had his billion pounds for the sale of McGreggor's, renamed PING-MAG (Europe) Corporation and headed up by Curtis Googleheimer, who was promoted for brokering the end of the strike and securing the £200 million grant from the Government.

Despite having achieved what he wanted and having more money than he could ever spend, Archibald felt deflated. He had kept June on as his PA, even though there was little for her to do. After 35 years of shouting at her and bullying her, he was too set in his ways to stop now and it was worth paying her a salary just to be able to continue as he had always done.

Wilfred still drove him around in the Bentley S2, even though he was now 94. Archibald had embarked on a world cruise, but nothing compared to the cut and thrust of business and outwitting opponents.

He still saw Winton J Cuncliffe-Owen from time to time, who was thinking of retiring from the Conservative party at the next election and his role as deputy chairman of the 1922 committee. They met, as they always had, at the Hotel and Country Club, often for a game of golf and reminisced about the good old days.

The Trade and Industry Secretary resigned one month after the strike was over at McGreggor's and after he handed £200 million of taxpayer's cash to the company for restructuring. The Tory press were up in arms that he had subsidized a 'lame duck' company as they saw it, and called him a Blue Communist, no better than the days when British Leyland and British Steel were handed billions of pounds to keep going. The PM, frightened of the backlash, forced him to resign to 'spend more time with his family', but after six months he was appointed Chairman of PING-MAG (Europe) Corporation on £6.2 million a year, compared to his salary of £120,000 when he was the Secretary for Trade and Industry. The renumeration committee at the company put in a formal complaint, but the big shareholders dominated by the pension funds nodded it through and the unbelievable salary was retained, probably for services rendered. The former Trade and Industry Secretary knew nothing about the Steel Industry, but Googleheimer's reforms, together with substantial investment, ensured that PING-MAG (Europe) Corporation became the most profitable steel producer in Europe, producing high grade steel, railway tracks for HS2, and stainless steel and armoured steel for the defence industry and nuclear submarines.

Zara Bindle

Bindle and her husband Hugo decided on a career change after Bindle's dismissal from the Diversity Action Partnership. It deftly combined their twin passions of cooking and cleaning, in the case of Hugo, and diversity and transgender politics in the case of Bindle.

They decided to set up a luxury B&B retreat aimed at the transgender market, the first transgender B&B in the country. They found that the Old Vicarage in Appleton was for sale with twelve bedrooms, and managed to buy it with the money Philomena Bindle had left Zara in trust, together with a £250,000 start-up loan and a £50,000 grant from the Steel Recovery Fund. A fund established by the Department for Trade and Industry to help the displaced steel workers set up their own businesses in Grimewold and the surrounding area following the 2,000 redundancies by McGreggor's steel.

By advertising on transgender social media sites, they soon had a thriving business with Hugo doing the breakfasts – full English using locally sourced organic meat and eggs – or the popular vegan option. Zara gave counselling and support sessions to those making the move to a new sexual identity.

At £150 a night it was not cheap, but soon they were fully booked all year round. They were thrilled to receive their first guest twelve months after Bindle's dismissal, a forty-eight year old man who had self-identified as a ten year old girl, complete with a pretty pink dress and a blonde wig with pig tails, even though he was 6'3" tall and weighed 16 stone. He came with his wife of 24 years and their 14-year-old daughter called Catalina, who loudly proclaimed that her father was a complete freak and it was so unfair, why couldn't he be like other dads?

Bindle and Hugo had finally found their vocation and Bindle was able to write academic papers on transgender politics and even give guest lectures at various progressive universities around the country. She missed seeing Tandori, and even to this day, had no idea that it was her who had undermined the Diversity Action Partnership and despite looks to the contrary, was not a transgender man at all. Luckily, Zara never found out how she had been betrayed and completely deceived by Tandori. Sometimes ignorance is bliss, but without the amazing set of events twelve months previously, Bindle and Hugo would not be where they are today, so maybe some good did come out of the situation after all. Bindle was certainly very happy with her new life and that's what mattered.

Inspector Fleece

Fleece went back to the Metropolitan Police a laughingstock. He still believed Tandori and Jennings were dangerous terrorists until, out of the blue six months later, he received a text message from Hazelhurst of MI5 asking to meet him for a coffee and 'a little chat about things'.

Intrigued, Fleece met Hazelhurst in an upmarket coffee shop in Camden Town where Hazelhurst told Fleece the terrible truth that Tandori was in fact an MI5 operative that had been on a secret mission in Grimewold of upmost importance to national security, and that Jennings was just an innocent bystander. Fleece could scarcely believe what he was hearing but it was true, Hazelhurst had brought along enough evidence to convince Fleece that he had been chasing ghosts, and Tandori was not and never had been an ISIS Terrorist.

However, Hazelhurst had a very unexpected offer for Inspector Fleece. He and his boss had been impressed with Fleece's dogged tenacity in pursuing Tandori to the ends of the country, going way beyond the call of duty and they were offering him the chance to leave the force and join MI5 as an operative in the field. It had all been cleared with the Metropolitan Commissioner, Richard Maitless, or Dick of Dock Green as was his nickname. Maitless was more than glad to be rid of Fleece as he had become an embarrassment and laughingstock within the force. Hazelhurst said that MI5 needed people with special skills as exhibited by Fleece, despite him getting everything wrong about Tandori. He assured Fleece that he wouldn't ever have to work with her, and Fleece found himself agreeing to join MI5 on one condition, that his side kick and partner in crime, Constable Brahmes, could join him and the team. It was all agreed over a cup of Costa coffee and Inspector Fleece had a new lease of life more suited to his tenacious and suspicious personality.

Tandori Birkett-Morris

It all worked out in the end for Tandori Birkett-Morris. She had fled the Diversity Action Partnership just in the nick of time before it went bust and before anyone suspected that it was her who was the cuckoo in the nest, the person most responsible for its demise.

She moved back with mummy and daddy near Broadway in the Cotswolds and got her old room back. Numerous fights, verbal and physical, with her sister Tamara resulted in Tamara leaving the family home in a fit of rage one weekend and moving in with her boyfriend.

Hazelhurst was as good as his word and after things had settled down, he recruited her back into MI5 as an operative, all her past failings brushed under the carpet. She loved her life, getting the train from Broadway into London most days and then being given any exciting and hush-hush assignment taking her far and wide. As she was the least likely secret agent, she was able to get things done which others would have found impossible.

At the weekend she would walk the dogs in the beautiful Cotswold countryside and spend her time with mummy and daddy. The only thing missing from her life was a love interest, but she was sure that eventually a nice boy would find her as alluring as Piffle clearly had. She would just have to be patient and take life as it comes.

The main thing she was glad about was that that dreadful man, Inspector Fleece, was no longer pursuing her as an ISIS terrorist and she heard, amazingly, he had been recruited by MI5 as well. Although Hazelhurst assured her that their paths would never cross. It was a promise that she dearly hoped Hazelhurst would keep

Gordon Streake

As the Playa de Sol Holiday Park was snatched from under Piffle's nose by the Banco Alicante, things were looking dire financially and Jimmy The fleece contacted Streake and cut a deal with him allowing him to buy log cabin number eleven for £100,000, just as Streake had hoped for. It was money that was desperately needed just before Mike Morrell stepped in and bought the park from the bank for a knock-down price.

Now, one year on, Streake was a very happy man. He loved his log cabin, the large veranda and the hot tub in the corner, where he sat out in the evenings with a bottle of wine. He had kitted out the cabin just to his tastes with a beautiful tan L shaped sofa, exotic Moroccan gold ornaments and highly polished yew furniture, giving his home unique and luxurious feel.

He had become friends with Jimmy The Fleece and paid regular visits to the Go-Go Bar and Grill in the old town to have steak and chips, a few drinks with Jimmy and to watch the go-go exotic dancers.

His sister, Brenda, had been over twice for extended holidays and he had even managed to find himself a love interest after years of being alone. Like so many things in life, it had happened by chance, he had met one of the local Spanish cleaners on the holiday park called Veronica. Twenty years younger than Streake, she had jet black luxurious hair and beautiful hazel eyes and a calm loving smile with a personality to match. Soon after them meeting and dating she had moved into the log cabin with him, his happiness complete.

For all the bad things that had happened to Streake finally, in retirement, he had found happiness and the loving partner he had always wished for. Thoughts of Grimewold and his old job as a Private Investigator were but distant memories as he looked forward to his retirement in the sun with the woman of his dreams. A woman he had every intention of marrying in the future.

Gary and Tracy Wacker

After the complete shock of Piffle going bankrupt with such speed and finality, it was of huge relief when Mike Morrell contacted him and agreed to continue paying him for the log cabins contract. He had done an excellent quality job and his whole workforce and future depended upon the contract being honoured. One year on, two hundred and fifty log cabins had been ordered and delivered on site, and as a result Gary Wacker was now quite a wealthy businessman.

With their friend Pauline Piffle marrying Mike Morrell, it seemed logical, and very fortuitous, that Pauline wanted to sell Maxwell House, the Piffle's family home on the edge of Beverley, quickly and at a reduced price. Gary and Tracy had always admired Maxwell House, and with Gary's business on the up, they snapped it up and moved in six months after the demise of Piffle's empire. They still needed a gardener and handyman and it was agreed that Jennings would stay on in that capacity, still living in the flat above the garage, carrying on very much as before. Jennings was very sorry to see Pauline, his first love from school days leave for her new life, but was grateful for the chance of a job and flat well away from the Cromwell Estate.

Gary treated himself to a new Range-Rover Sport and Tracy was a given, for her birthday, a car she had always loved since being a teenager but could never afford, an MGB GT coupe in RAF blue with a black leather interior. She immediately christened the car Bluebell and used it to go to the hairdressers and to get her nails done, and visit friends for coffees at their houses. It truly was her pride and joy.

Mrs Neatgangs kept her job as house cleaner, but because the house was so much larger she came on the bus from the Gipsyville Estate four days a week, and her wages went up accordingly, to £80 a week.

After Tracy's 'little talk' she managed to find bras big enough to cover her bosoms, which pleased Gary greatly while he was having his bacon and double eggs in the morning for breakfast.

Callum had started at Beverley Sixth Form College and had moved on from Mrs Neatgangs to girls his own age; it had just been a phase, his lusts for Mrs Neatgangs and her incredible figure. On the other hand, Mrs Neatgangs slowly got to know Anthony Jennings. Although when he was young and handsome he had had designs on Pauline Piffle, he now realized that in his early 60s 'beggars can't be choosers' and he started to take Mrs Neatgangs out in his Austin Maestro for trips to Bridlington and the odd fish and chip supper. Soon they were an item, and Mrs Neatgangs took to staying over at the flat.

Back on the Gipsyville Estate, with six kids by six different fathers, Olive Neatgangs struggled to have the same success as her mother. She was still looking for her knight in shining armour, however unlikely that was on the stony ground of the Gipsyville Estate. Maybe one day someone would come along for her, as she said, 'If it can happen to you mum, it can happen to anyone!'

Lord Brett Sinclair

It's funny how one small act of kindness can change the world and the future for an individual. Such was the case for Lord Brett Sinclair. Gordon Streake's decision to give Lord Brett his old Vauxhall Vectra when he went to Benidorm to live.

That small act of kindness enabled Brett to deliver the gear to Lemar in Chelsea each week and grow his business by establishing his County Lines drug operation. This, in turn, enabled him to make enough money to take on the lease of the Oliver Cromwell pub, which became his headquarters.

On the first and second floors he put in place a crack cocaine operation, where some of his lads would cut the ingredients and split the gear into parcels to sell to the punters on the estate and beyond. He also put his own office up there, where he could be found sat behind his huge mahogany desk running his ever expanding criminal empire. He also had a bedroom next door to the office where he could get away from his girlfriend and entertain which ever slag took his fancy when he had got himself high on coke, which was quite frequently.

However, the Oliver Cromwell enabled him to expand in other ways. As a front for being a legitimate businessman he put Murphy in charge of the pub, and Murphy got the food side of the business going and the pub gained quite a good reputation for a Sunday Carvery and traditional pub grub throughout the week. They did curry night, pie night, fish and chip night and steak night, as well as expanding the number of regular drinkers with a quiz night on a Thursday, and upgrading the pool tables and dart boards in the games room.

The real money came from the activities in the basement, however. Lord Brett converted the basement area into six self-contained bedsits and by nefarious means, recruited six Bulgarian ladies who he forced into prostitution on the basis that they 'owed' him £40,000 each for bringing them over with the promise of a legitimate job in a meat packing factory. He kept the six ladies under lock and key, and then had one of his minders take them across to the knocking shop that he used to ply his prostitution trade on the estate. The knocking shop was in fact his girlfriend's sister's house which she rented from a private landlord. He forced her out and made her move in with his girlfriend on the council house. It was a bit cramped the two sisters, five kids and himself, but soon the confined space and his lack of morals or scruples resulted in his getting both his girlfriend, Chenisse, and her sister, Chantelle, pregnant within a month of the new arrangements being enacted.

Another one of Lord Brett's plans involved renting some land from a struggling dairy farmer out at Appleton and erecting a large number of poly tunnels where he grew huge numbers of cannabis plants for his expanding drug operation. That way he could undercut other suppliers of weed on the estate and put them out of business, whilst getting more youngsters hooked on drugs so he could persuade them to progress onto the more profitable class A drugs of heroin and crack cocaine.

One benefit of the arrangement with Farmer Rawlings was the opportunity to store his prized 'guards red' Porsche 911 Turbo in one of the barns, well out of the way of the thieving toe rags of the Cromwell Estate. He took it out for a spin at very high speed from time to time, either alone or with one his latest conquests with a view to impressing her with his flash car and gold jewellery. A year on, as he sat at his mahogany desk, Lord Brett reflected on how far he had come in just a year, all because of Gordon Streake. One day he would have to thank his old mate Streakey and give him a nice big wad for that act of kindness twelve months ago.

Jimmy – The Fleece – Moston

Jimmy had got a new lease of life selling the log cabins, first for Piffle and finally for Mike Morrell. He was making plenty of wonga again and the Go-Go Bar and Grill was going great guns as well. This time however, Jimmy wasn't going to blow all his new-found money on fast cars and even faster women. He had done that in the 1980s and look where that had got him. No, this time good old Jimmy had made some shrewd investments.

He already owned two villas which he rented out, and decided to buy two of Mike Morrell's log cabins to rent out as well. This led him to develop an online website to rent villas in the Benidorm and Alicante area taking 5% for each booking secured online. This became big business for Jimmy.

His other business venture involved expanding FunkyChicken.com, and over the year it grew from one site on the front at Benidorm, to ten sites across the town and beyond. Twelve months on Jimmy The Fleece was making more money than he had in years, and there was still a further two hundred and fifty log cabins to sell.

He was still friends with Paeleo and had made friends with Gordon Streake. Life was sweet, and Jimmy could see a time soon when he would sell it all up and retire to a life of sun, sea and sangria, all because of his introduction to Sydney Dresden Piffle and the Playa de Sol Holiday Park.

Piffle

Printed in Great Britain
by Amazon